THIRD EDITION

WINE

From Grape to Glass

Jacket front:	The proper glass for heavy red wines *(see also page 223)*.
Jacket back:	A vineyard in the hills near Montecarotto, in the Marches of Italy, home of verdicchio and of the red wines made of montepulciano grapes *(see also page 154)*.
Photography:	Michel Guillard/Scope, Mick Rock/StockFood, Hendrik Holler, Christian Schulz, Studio Eising *(see also Picture Credits, page 256)*.
Computer Graphics/Drawings:	Klaus Rummel, Spectre (Markus Weissenhorn, Christian Heine, Georg Feigl, Roland Schunk), Enno Kleinert, Beate Brömse
Aerial Photography:	Luftbilderverlag Bertram/Gorkenant, Munich; Kartographie Huber, Munich; Herb Lingl Photography, San Francisco
Satellite Photography:	Deutsches Fernerkundungsdatenzentrum der DLR, Oberpfaffenhofen; Planetary Visions Limited
Design:	Georg Feigl

ENGLISH-LANGUAGE EDITION

Editors:	Miranda Ottewell, Russell Stockman
Jacket Designer:	Paula Winicur
Production Director:	Louise Kurtz

First published in the United States of America in 2006 by Abbeville Press,
137 Varick Street, New York, NY 10013.
First published in Germany in 2005 by Verlag Zabert Sandmann GmbH, Munich.

ISBN 978-0-7892-0917-7

Third edition
10 9 8 7 6 5 4 3

Library of Congress Cataloging-in-Publication Data for first edition:

Priewe, Jens.
    [Wein. English]
    Wine : from grape to glass / Jens Priewe.
    p. cm.
  Includes bibliographical references and index.
  ISBN 0-7892-0608-0
  1. Wine and winemaking. I. Title.
  TP548.P739513 1999
  641.2'2–dc21
                                    99-41865
                                    CIP

For bulk and premium sales and for text adoption procedures, write to Customer Service Manager, Abbeville Press, 137 Varick Street, New York, NY 10013, or call 1-800-ARTBOOK.

Visit Abbeville Press online at www.abbeville.com

THIRD EDITION

WINE

From Grape to Glass

Jens Priewe

ABBEVILLE PRESS PUBLISHERS
New York   London

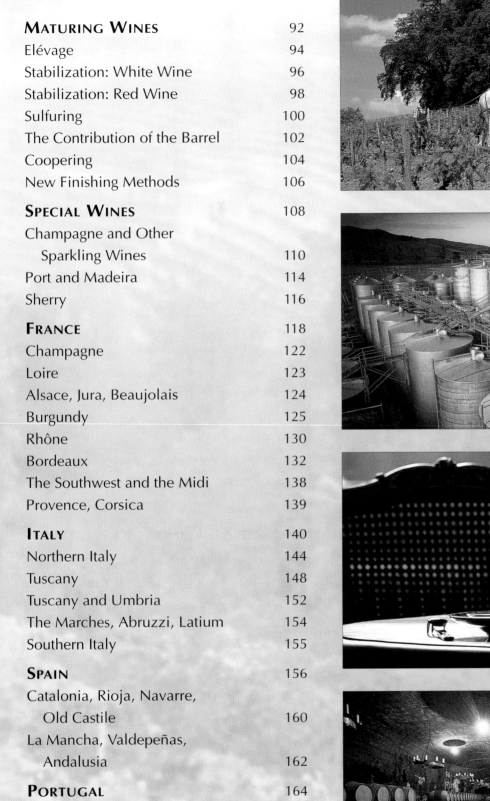

Contents

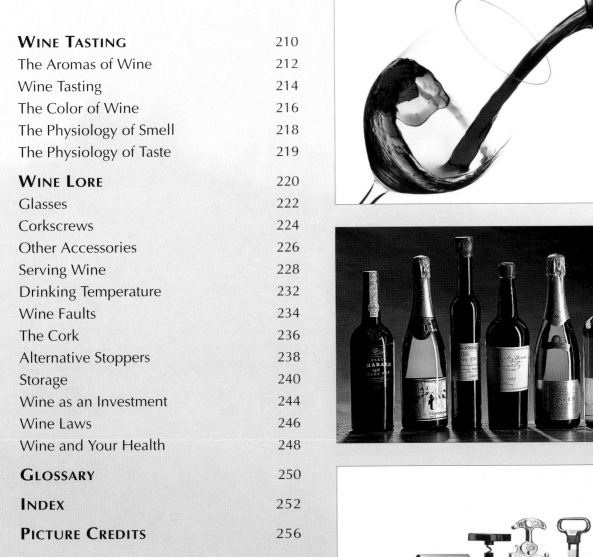

Wine and the Thirst for Knowledge

If a hundred years from now someone happens to be writing the history of wine in our times, he will have no choice but to call the end of the twentieth century the golden age of wine. What characterizes the last two decades is an astonishing improvement in quality, unfaltering ambition among producers, and a seemingly infinite demand for fine wines in the marketplace. We are encountering an undreamed-of enthusiasm in many parts of the world for the drink that—except for water and milk—is the oldest in the world. Grape growing has expanded into new regions, and winemaking has undergone significant innovations, quickly absorbing and applying the discoveries of modern oenology. All these new developments need to be absorbed into our thinking as well. We need a new, comprehensive reference work to understand what it is we are drinking and to appreciate the work that goes into offering our senses pleasures they never enjoyed before. *Wine: From Grape to Glass* was written to quench the exquisite thirst for knowledge that lovers of wine feel arising within whenever they uncork a bottle of fine wine.

Fabled Vintages and Other Good Libations

Wine: From Grape to Glass was written not for those who exclusively love French, German, or Italian wines, or for that matter, any other particular wines. It is for those who will drink this today and that tomorrow, but are always reaching for the best. And what is best? That depends on each eclectic wine lover's mood. Yesterday it was a simple country wine brought back from a vacation. Today you go through the ceremony of opening one of the grand, awe-inspiring vintages. Tomorrow it might be a completely unknown wine, maybe from a country only recently added to the world's wine atlas. All of these wines have their own personalities. On the wine merchant's shelf, they stand side by side. What differentiates them is their prices. This book helps to explain why one wine may cost a hundred dollars, another only ten. It tries to provide a key to the complex language of wine, and to illuminate the science of winemaking while honoring the art that creates great wines.

Take Part in the Wine Revolution

Drinking wine is an experience. For this reason, a wine book should not be dry reading. *Wine: From Grape to Glass* is a book that presents the reader with the visual experience of the nature of wine, of the way it grows, of how it is made out of grapes. You will learn about whole-bunch pressing and find out what is meant by *bâtonnage*. Your eyes will see where great taste comes from and where the famous vineyard of Romanée-Conti is located. You will be shown why wines age faster in small barrels than in large ones and why it is sometimes a good idea to decant even a young wine. The book goes into its subject deeply enough to ensure that while you taste the characteristic flavors of great wines, you become conscious of exactly what you are experiencing. All the information is important: it makes clear what separates a good wine from a great one. Only when wine connoisseurs appreciate what winemakers do can they grow with the revolutionary changes now taking place in the world of wine.

Triumph of a Climber

Wild vines that bore grapelike fruit existed long before man appeared on the stage of history. Fossilized grape seeds have been found to date back 60 million years. Grapevines grew in the endless forests that then covered the temperate zones of the earth. To reach the light, the plants had to fight their way up. They developed tendrils and were able to clamber up the huge trees. *Vitis silvestris,* the "forest vine," is what botanists have called this plant that learned to scale the trees. Originally, the habitat of the grapevine included a much larger area than that now cultivated for wine. Grapevines grew in Afghanistan, Egypt, along the river Amur, in the American Middle West, in the Caribbean, and in Mexico. Granted, the climate was warmer then. With each ice age, the grapevine withdrew into the temperate zones— the region around the Mediterranean, and Asia Minor. As soon as the earth warmed up again, it began spreading north.

In contrast to our cultivated grapevine varieties, the forest vine was dioecious; that is, there were plants with only male flowers and others with only female ones. The wind was responsible for spreading the plant's seeds, and of course, berry-eating animals and birds did their part.

From Intoxicant to Epicurean Delight

When man first cultivated grapevines and where he first made wine out of grapes is a matter of conjecture. It is certain that wild grapes proliferated in many regions of the world, but wine was not made out of grapes everywhere they grew.

The earliest indication of the existence of wine was unearthed in the Republic of Georgia, on the east shore of the Black Sea. Shards of clay pitchers found there, dating from about 6000 B.C., are decorated with a relief of grapes. Other evidence that man knew how to make wine in Neolithic times was found in the region between the Euphrates and the Tigris, in the southern Caucasus, along the Nile, and somewhat later in Palestine. We may assume that early wine was not a tasty drink. Why else would it have been sweetened with honey and spiced with herbs such as wormwood? It is likely that man revered wine purely for the inebriation its alcohol content bestowed.

The Enigma of North America
Strangely, in North America, where plants of the genus *Vitis* were well represented, there is no historical evidence of any form of wine. One explanation for this remarkable difference from the Old World is that the North American species of grapes are not well suited to wine production. Some do not produce enough sugar, while others are too acidic or not tart enough. It may also be that the airborne yeasts needed to transform sugar into alcohol were not present. It is also possible that wine did exist, but was simply unpalatable. At any rate, wine appears very late in the history of the American continent. Even today, wines produced from the American species of the genus *Vitis* are characterized by an extremely strong taste, which experts refer to as "foxy."

Vitis vinifera
The discovery of wine is probably due to fortunate chance. The people of Asia Minor tended to store the juice of grapes in pitchers or in tubes made of goat or camel skins. In the hot climate of the region, the juice would naturally tend to ferment. Whether the juice would ferment completely, remain sweet, or oxidize and turn to vinegar is of course a matter of conjecture. The very existence of wine in this region attests to the fact that the grapes themselves were very sweet, and their juice fermented into a potable, intoxicating liquid. For this reason, later botanists be-

Wine as a symbol and stimulant: Jean-Marc Nattier, The Lovers.

stowed the name *Vitis vinifera*—the grapevine that bears wine grapes—on the grape indigenous to Europe and Asia Minor.

Wine in Ancient Greece
With the rise of Greek civilization after about 1600 B.C., grapes were cultivated systematically around the Mediterranean. Mycenae and Sparta appear to have been the main centers of wine production, as witnessed by numerous motifs on vases from those areas. Wine was used as a ritual drink—to celebrate victories, to honor the gods, to enhance festivities. Methods of wine production were amazingly well developed, though salty seawater was often added to the wine during the process of fermentation, supposedly to make it smoother. Greek colonists brought wine and grapes to Syria, Egypt, Cadiz, and Marseilles around 600 B.C. and, a hundred years later, to Sicily as well. The Greeks, however, saw their god of wine, Dionysus, not simply as a benefactor who taught their farmers the art of winemaking but also as the dangerous god who could befuddle men's reason and even make them mad.

Dissemination of the Grapevine by the Romans
After the decline of Greek power, the cult of wine spread rapidly through the Roman Empire. Wine became a status symbol, a medium of exchange, a form of medicine, and a ritual offering. It was used, for example, to seal contractual agreements. The white Falernian was the most famous wine of the period. Its vine grew north of Naples, where it was trained up the trunks of elms and mulberry trees. According to Pliny, the wine could be acid or sweet but was always high in alcoholic strength. At that time winemakers were already experimenting with different ways of making and storing wine, and the many grape varieties were being distinguished. Virgil writes that there were as many grape varieties as there are grains of sand on the beach.

From Rome, wine lore reached southern France, the regions of the Mosel and the Rhine, and certain parts of Spain. The French and the Spanish are sure, however, that some of their indigenous tribes grew grapes and made wines long before the Romans arrived.

The intoxicating beverage must also have been known in Italy in pre-Roman times, at least in central Italy, the territory of the Etruscans. To them wine was a symbol of affluence and of a voluptuous lifestyle as early as the third century B.C. Whether the Etruscans used cultivated or wild grapes in the preparation of their wines is unknown, though we do know that they traded in wines.

From the Middle Ages into Our Times

In the Christian era winegrowing and wine-making spread though Europe like wildfire. During the Middle Ages, monks served as pioneer wine producers. The Benedictines, who liked to enjoy themselves, brought the cultivation of the vine and the skilled manu-facture of wine to a very high level. Later their split-off order, the ascetic Cistercians, also made significant contributions. It was from their monasteries at Cluny and Citeau that viticulture moved into Burgundy, turning it into the wine region it now is.

During the Renaissance, the further ex-pansion of grape cultivation shifted into the hands of enlightened rulers and rich burgh-ers; leading the movement were undoubtedly two Italian families, the Antinori and the Fres-cobaldi. Grape growing in Europe reached its widest extension in the sixteenth century. The total area planted in grapes was almost four times what it is today, and average wine con-sumption must have reached about 45 gallons (200 liters) per person per year. This golden age of wine soon came to an end, as wars, the plague, and a general cooling down of the climate reduced the vineyard areas of Europe to roughly those core regions we know today.

Mildew and the Phylloxera Louse: Major Catastrophes

The greatest setback in the history of viticul-ture was without doubt caused by powdery mildew and the plant louse phylloxera, which arrived in Europe on seedlings brought from America. Powdery mildew appeared first in France in 1847, destroying entire vintages. A black year for winegrowers was 1854, when the French grape harvest amounted to less than one-tenth of its normal yield. Even more destructive was the ravenous phylloxera. Starting in 1863 in France, this insect ate its way though the vineyards of Europe, halting production in entire regions for decades. When by 1910 winegrowers finally found a remedy, untold species of grapes, among them no doubt some valuable ones, had forever disap-peared. The assortment of grape varieties we have today pales beside the diversity available before the blight.

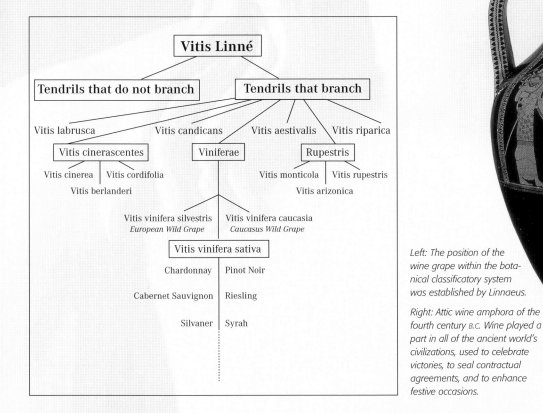

Vitis Linné

Tendrils that do not branch — Tendrils that branch

Vitis labrusca — Vitis candicans — Vitis aestivalis — Vitis riparica

Vitis cinerascentes — Viniferae — Rupestris

Vitis cinerea | Vitis cordifolia — Vitis monticola | Vitis rupestris

Vitis berlanderi — Vitis arizonica

Vitis vinifera silvestris — Vitis vinifera caucasia
European Wild Grape — *Caucasus Wild Grape*

Vitis vinifera sativa

Chardonnay | Pinot Noir

Cabernet Sauvignon | Riesling

Silvaner | Syrah

Left: The position of the wine grape within the bota-nical classificatory system was established by Linnaeus.

Right: Attic wine amphora of the fourth century B.C. Wine played a part in all of the ancient world's civilizations, used to celebrate victories, to seal contractual agreements, and to enhance festive occasions.

Wine Likes It Cool; Heat Means Trouble

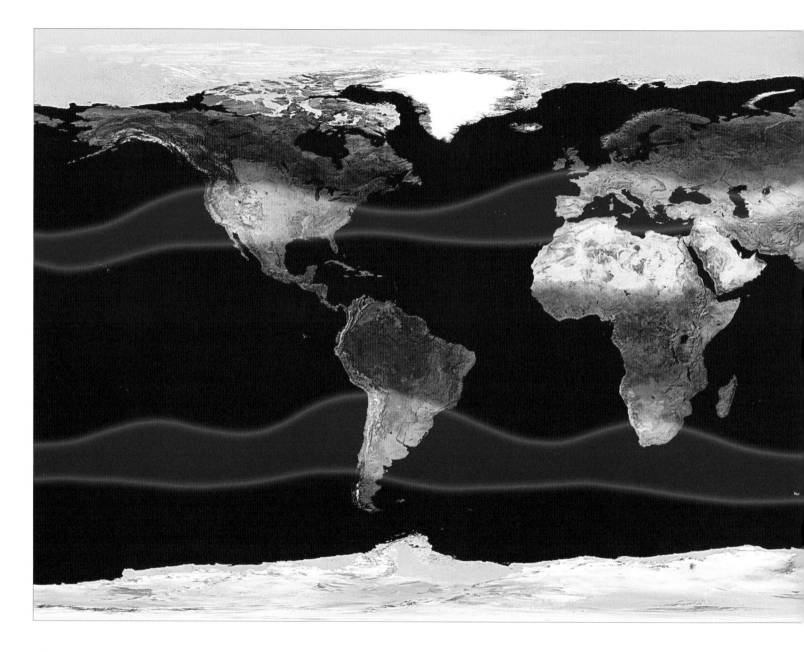

Winegrowing is essentially confined to the temperate regions of the world. In Europe these are located between the 40th and 50th parallels; in the Americas and in the Southern Hemisphere, between the 30th and 40th parallels.

In order to ripen, grapes do need warmth, but fine wines require low temperatures. By slowing down the development of sugar in the grapes, cool weather prevents the wine from becoming excessively alcoholic and heavy. Moreover, it ensures that during the process of ripening, acidity is not excessively reduced. A trace of acidity is one of the elements that add a certain elegance to both white and red wines.

Sun, Warmth, and Precipitation

German scientists assume that for the cultivation of the grapevine, a minimum of 1,600 hours of sunshine per year is required. American scientists stress that grapes need a minimum temperature of at least 50°F (10°C) for at least 2,500 hours a year. These limits, however, are not invariably applicable. Steep slopes, for example, will increase the effect of sunshine significantly. Alternately, in warm climates the critical factor is not heat but the amount of precipitation. An annual mean rainfall of at least 23 inches (600 mm) is needed to make wine. And even this limiting criterion does not universally hold: grapes can thrive on as little as 12 inches (300 mm) of precipitation if they get it partly during the spring, the period of maximum growth, and partly in the summer, when rains serve to break up dry spells, which in some areas can last from three to four months.

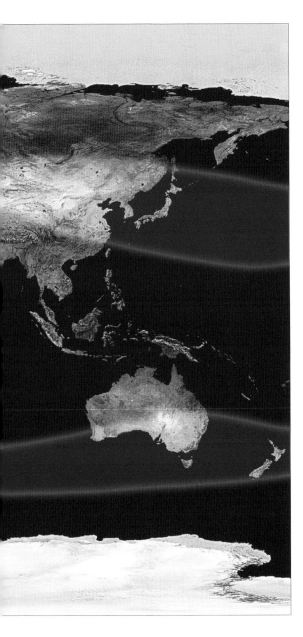

Grapes are grown in both the Northern and the Southern Hemispheres. Two narrow bands of moderately warm climate constitute virtually the globe's entire acreage (hectarage) under grapes.

Vineyards in Cold and Hot Marginal Areas

Grapes are cultivated well to the north of the global vineyard belt. Parts of the Mosel and Rhine regions are at 51° north latitude, as are the vineyards of southern England, in Cornwall. Similarly, to the south, the vineyards of southern Europe and North Africa are clearly outside of the grapevine belt, namely around 36° north latitude. These regions produce mainly wines that are heavy and rich in alcohol: sherry, marsala, Sámos Doux, Cyprus sherry, and red wines used for blending; wines that resemble port and fortified wines are produced in parts of South Africa and Australia.

A Shift into Cooler Regions

During the last twenty-five years, there has been a worldwide expansion of grape cultivation into cooler climatic zones. This trend is especially clear in Australia, South Africa, and Chile, and it is also noticeable in Greece. In California and Oregon, this development is now well established. A deliberate movement into the cool countryside within the Pacific climate zone is in process, specifically to increase the production of white wines.

Most Commonly Grown Vine Varieties
(Distribution of *Vitis vinifera* as a percentage of the total world acreage [hectarage] under grape cultivation)

1.	France	19.26 %
2.	Italy	19.16 %
3.	Spain	14.02 %
4.	USA	7.78 %
5.	Argentina	5.67 %
6.	Australia	4.78 %
7.	China	4.29 %
8.	Germany	3.75 %
9.	South Africa	3.03 %
10.	Portugal	2.72 %
11.	Chile	2.26 %
12.	Romania	2.09 %
13.	Hungary	1.69 %
14.	Russia	1.53 %
15.	Greece	1.41 %
16.	Brazil	1.19 %
17.	Bulgaria	1.07 %
18.	Austria	0.99 %
19.	Moldavia	0.92 %
20.	Ukraine	0.84 %
21.	Croatia	0.74 %
22.	Serbia	0.69 %
23.	Mexico	0.54 %
24.	Switzerland	0.45 %
25.	Japan	0.44 %
26.	Georgia	0.43 %
27.	New Zealand	0.33 %
28.	Uruguay	0.33 %
29.	Macedonia	0.31 %
30.	Slovenia	0.21 %
31.	Algeria	0.21 %
32.	Cyprus	0.20 %
33.	Czech Republic	0.19 %
34.	Canada	0.19 %
35.	Slovakia	0.18 %
36.	Uzbekistan	0.16 %
37.	Tunisia	0.13 %
38.	Morocco	0.12 %
39.	Turkmenistan	0.11 %
40.	Turkey	0.11 %
41.	Albania	0.07 %
42.	Lebanon	0.07 %
43.	Luxembourg	0.06 %
44.	Kazakhstan	0.06 %
45.	Peru	0.05 %
46.	Madagascar	0.04 %
47.	Belarus	0.03 %
48.	Malta	0.02 %
49.	Israel	0.01 %
50.	Bolivia	0.01 %

Distribution of world wine production by continent

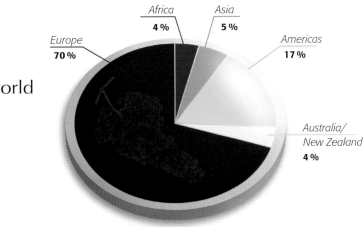

Africa 4 %

Asia 5 %

Europe 70 %

Americas 17 %

Australia/ New Zealand 4 %

A Powerful Producer of Sugar

The grapevine has the capacity to produce immense amounts of sugar, which it stores in its berries. There, the sugar is split into glucose and fructose. Fifteen to 25 percent of the grape berry consists of these two forms of sugar. By comparison, apples and pears contain only 12 percent sugar.

Of all the fruit-bearing plants in the world, the grapevine is the best at accumulating sugar. Between 15 and 25 percent of grape juice consists of sugar that is available for fermentation. For this reason, the grape is better suited to wine production than any other fruit.

The grapevine is one of the toughest, most undemanding, and most adaptable plants in the world. It grows as willingly in poor soil, lacking in nutrients, as under extreme temperatures. In cold northern areas such as Champagne or parts of the Mosel and Rhine valleys, grapes have become resistant to frost. The wood of the vine is able to withstand winter temperatures as low as minus 4°F (minus 20°C). In the torrid vineyards of central Spain, by contrast, the plant can weather dry periods of ninety days or more.

The Secret of the Grape's Adaptability

Grapevines tend to build a strong root system. Their roots not only anchor them firmly in the soil but also serve to store nutrients. In dry regions, such as the Ribera del Duero in Spain, the principal roots will penetrate six meters deep to reach moisture. Thanks to its roots, the grapevine bears fruit even in climates that other cultivated plants could not withstand.

Canopy and Light

Grapevines carry a lot of leaves. Much of the energy they need to grow they can obtain through this canopy. The process is called photosynthesis, and it oc-

curs not only in grapevines but in all plants. The green pigment in the leaves (chlorophyll) combines carbon dioxide from the air with water to form sugar. The one thing indispensable to photosynthesis is light. In order to reach the light, the grapevine uses its tendrils to climb upward toward the sun. Nor is it an accident that so many vine regions are located along rivers and lakes, where the water surface reflects and thereby magnifies the light. For wine production, ideal conditions for photosynthesis consist of temperatures between 77 and 82°F (25 and 28°C) and light levels of 20,000 lux, conditions that maximize sugar production. Even under otherwise ideal circumstances, the creation of sugar in the fruit can be reduced by stress due to a shortage of water. With excessive dryness, the leaf of the grape will close its pores to prevent the further evaporation of moisture, thus closing off its breathing organ. The result is that sugar formation ceases. The grapevine, however, is resistant to moderate drought.

Weaknesses of the Vine

The most serious weakness of the plant is its susceptibility to diseases and pests. This is at least true of the noble vine, the European *Vitis vinifera;* the original American strains of *Vitis* were much more robust. Downy and powdery mildew, black rot, mites, and nematodes can all damage it profoundly. The vulnerability of grapevines also increases significantly with strong fertilization and increased yield.

1 *Bud or node* (oeil, bourgeon): *Out of this either a leaf or a fruit-bearing shoot will develop.*

2 *Inflorescence: The flowers of the grapevine develop out of tendrils. They cluster on a specialized shoot that will later bear the berries. The flowers of the grapevine are perfect or hermaphroditic; that is, they contain both male and female parts: functional stamens and an ovary within a pistil.*

3 *Fruit set* (nouaison): *The first stage in the development of the berries after flowering.*

4 *Green grapes: Still full of chlorophyll, these tiny balls are an in-between stage in the development of the fruit.*

5 *Véraison or coloring: This is the transition from green to color in the fruit. It usually takes place in July, after a certain level of sugar has accumulated within the fruit.*

6 *Ripe grape: The final stage in the ripening process of the fruit.*

7 *Water shoots or lateral shoots: These unwanted suckers develop on the wood of the vine and will occasionally bear small fruit. Such grapes remain puny and may not be harvested. As a rule, water shoots are pruned out during the summer.*

8 *Tendrils: These are the climbing organs of the grapevine. Tendrils coil around and grasp anything they touch. After the harvest, they become woody and harden.*

9 *Leaf: The breathing organ of the grapevine, which also serves to nourish it. Its shape, the size of the lobes, and the dentation change with each variety.*

10 *Trunk or vine: Also called old wood, the vine's major stem is the weakest part of the plant. It is balanced by the root system.*

11 *Arm: Also called two-year-old wood, this is where the fruit-bearing shoots develop.*

12 *Shoot: Also called one-year-old wood, the shoot carries the nodes from which the leaves and clusters of grapes will grow. When shoots harden, they are called canes.*

13 *Shallow roots: This root system, close to the soil surface, catches surface precipitation. It is destroyed when the vineyard is plowed, but it quickly grows back.*

14 *Subterranean roots: These anchor the vine securely in the soil.*

15 *Principal roots: The vine uses these long roots to search for water and nutrients. They store large amounts of carbohydrates before the plant's winter rest.*

What Makes the Taste

A grape is 90 percent water. What can turn it into a noble wine is the other 10 percent.

The bunch or cluster of grapes is the fruit of the grapevine. About the bunch there is little to tell. In the autumn, its stem bears from 80 to 150 berries. The size of the cluster varies with the grape variety. Riesling and pinot noir have a very small, compact cluster. The picolit variety, which grows in Italy's Friuli region and produces expensive dessert wines, will carry only about 50 berries per bunch. What is more, these bunches tend to be loose and irregularly shaped; this variety is affected by wet spring weather, and generally only a small percentage of its flowers are ever fertilized. White ugni blanc, by contrast, is of very copious habit: it bears up to 150 berries. The wine made of this variety is used in the production of cognac.

Winemaking without Stems
Winegrowers harvest clusters of grapes, but they only need the berries. As soon as red grapes reach the winery, they are destemmed; that is, the berries are removed from their stalks. With a few exceptions, stems and stalks are not used in the making of wine. The stems contain tannin, which tastes harsh and unripe. Although white grapes are usually pressed with their stems, the must is fermented without them.

White Wine from Red Grapes
The type and the quality of the wine depends on the characteristics of the grapes used. Their flesh holds the sugar-rich juice or must, which is fermented into wine. The color of the must is always grayish green, no matter whether it is pressed out of red or white grapes.

A wine turns red only when the skins are fermented along with the must, for the pigments that give color to wine are in the skins. Fermenting the juice without the skins produces a white wine. The only exceptions to this rule are the grape varieties bred for red-colored flesh, such as the teinturier.

One example of a white wine made from red grapes is Champagne; two of the commonly used varieties in making this sparkling wine are pinot noir and pinot meunier, both of which have red grapes.

The juice of white grapes makes white must, as does the juice of red grapes. Thus white wines can be made from red grapes. Red wine only results when the skins of red grapes are fermented along with the must.

Brush: This part of the pulp near the stalk forms the link between the stalk and the flesh of the fruit. On destemming, most grapes will leave behind this portion of their flesh; it continues to be called the brush.

Tissue around the seeds: This holds 30 percent of the sugar and 52 percent of the acidity.

Inner pulp: This contains 37 percent of the sugar and 31 percent of the acidity.

Stem: Contains 22 percent of all the polyphenols.

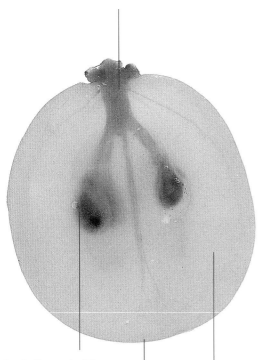

Seeds: The seeds of the grape are firmly held within tissue that is relatively devoid of juice.

Flesh or pulp: The bulk of the fruit, the pulp is richest in juice.

Skin: Contains 13 percent of all the polyphenols.

Seeds: Contain 65 percent of all the polyphenols.

Skin: A waxy layer encases the skin; it is called bloom.

Outer pulp: Holds 33 percent of the sugar, and 17 percent of the acidity.

Quality Is in the Skin

More important than the size of the bunch is the size of the berry. Grapes that are grown for the table have fat, round fruit that can weigh up to half an ounce (15 g). This pleases those who eat them. Some grapes grown for wine also have relatively fat berries; when pressed, their must yield is commensurately generous. This pleases mostly the makers of mass-produced wines. By contrast, all the valuable grape varieties have small fruit that weigh less than a tenth of an ounce (1–2 g). Though the yield in must is modest, it is very concentrated. Many of these varieties also have thick skins. This is important because the skins contain most of the substances that determine the quality of the wine. Apart from the all-important sugar, this means the phenols.

Everything Hinges on the Phenols

The skins contain the greatest portion of phenols. Since these include the pigments, the tannins, and some of the substances that contribute to taste, they are referred to collectively as the polyphenols or polyphenolics. The polyphenols are molecules of oxygen and hydrogen that polymerize, undergoing ever new combinations. The juice of a grape berry contains untold phenol combinations.

As a rule, red grapes contain more phenols than white varieties. Breeders of red grapes are always trying to produce grapes with a higher phenol content in order to obtain wines intense in color and taste and rich in tannins. The best phenols for red wines are contained in the skin. The largest percentage of the available phenols is in the grape seeds, but these phenols are not desirable.

Anthocyanins

The blue or purple pigments of the berry are called anthocyanins. Located almost exclusively in the skin, they are easily soluble in alcohol, somewhat less easily in water. To produce the light red color of a rosé wine, it is therefore sufficient to accord the must a few hours of contact with the skins before fermentation; that is, before the sugar in the must has been turned into alcohol.

Instead of anthocyanins, the skins of white grapes contain flavones, which contain yellow pigments. Accordingly, white must that has been given some hours of exposure to its skins will make a wine that shows a lemony or golden coloring.

Tannins

Tannins are odorless phenol combinations with a slightly bitter, astringent taste. They pucker the tongue. Grape tannins are held in the skin, the seeds, and also in the stems.

In white wines, tannins are considered undesirable and tend to be present only in trace amounts. Red wines need tannins, which give complexity to their taste. Tannins also help the red wines age well. By combining with the trace amounts of oxygen that gradually seep into corked bottles, they slow down the process of spoilage.

The Components of Taste

The substances that lend taste to wine can be volatile or not. The volatile chemicals supply the aroma, bouquet, or fragrance. Among them we find methoxypyrazin, which gives cabernet sauvignon its characteristic grassy aroma; nerol, which is responsible for the flowery, muscatlike bouquet of Riesling; and megastigmatrienone, which accounts for the leathery tobacco smell of Brunello di Montalcino. The nonvolatile tannins give wine its taste. Some of these are bound to sugar molecules and do not develop fully until the wine is of considerable age.

Warm Days, Cool Nights

The French have a saying: Great wines grow along great rivers. In truth, great wines need more than water nearby: they need warm slopes, dry soil, and a lot of light.

To grow, the grapevine needs above all heat and light. Light is necessary for photosynthesis; heat accelerates the entire growth cycle and thereby hastens ripening. The ideal growing temperature for grapevines is between 77 and 82°F (25 and 28°C), according to scientists at the Geissenheim Research Institute. Most vineyards offer these optimal conditions only during a few weeks of the year. This is the reason why great wines are very rare, produced only in narrow, favored strips of land or in tiny ecological niches. Often it is the topography of the land that determines how far ideal growing conditions can be realized. Seemingly insignificant factors can make the difference between a good wine and an outstanding one.

Altitude

The altitude of a vineyard will influence the temperature that prevails in it. Temperatures tend to fall with rising altitudes. To be precise, temperature drops 1.1°F (0.6°C) with every 110-yard (100 m) rise in elevation. Therefore, in hot areas of cultivation, such as the Bekaa Valley in Lebanon, grapevines are planted at 3,280 feet (1,000 m). The highest vineyards of the Spanish Ribera del Duero reach an altitude of 2,600 feet (800 m). Some of the best wines of Sicily grow at 1,970 feet (600 m). Similarly, in Australia, South Africa, Chile, and California, grape growing is shifting more and more into higher, cooler regions. By contrast, in many European wine regions, with their cool continental climates, it is a

Topoclimate of a Typical Grape-Growing Landscape
Yellow: The sun hits the steep slope at an angle of almost 90 degrees; this maximizes the heat reception.
Blue: From the high plateau cold air drifts down into the river valley, where it is carried away by the moving water.
Red: Water cools off more gradually than the air. In autumn the grapevines profit from the retained and reflected heat of the river.

matter of making use of every available degree of heat. Here the vineyards are planted between 160 and 1,500 feet (50 and 450 m) above sea level.

Hillside Siting

The ideal site for a vineyard is a slope. On hillsides, soil tends to be shallow and poor. The sun falls on slopes at an advantageous angle. In addition, the topoclimate of a slope guarantees a continuous supply of heat. Cold air currents drain away overnight into the valley, where they are rewarmed during the following day. As the air begins to warm up in the morning, it climbs the slope. This cyclical movement of air is especially important for white wines. The Riesling that thrives in Alsace, along the Mosel, along the Rhine, and in the Danube Valley needs the constant change between warmer days and cooler nights to retain as much acidity as possible.

In cool winegrowing regions, however, the flow of air can also represent a danger. Not only in Germany, Austria, and Alsace but also in Champagne and in parts of Burgundy, the crowns of the hills are deliberately forested in order to curb the flow of prevailing cold airstreams. This measure has to be taken to retain more warmth and to ensure that the grapes develop enough sugar and that the must weight not fall below acceptable standards.

Solar Radiation

Siting a vineyard on a hillside has other advantages, at least in temperate zones: a slope receives significantly more sun than a flat area, and in the case of a vineyard, every extra calorie of warmth can be of importance. The sun's radiation is most efficiently used when its rays reach the soil at a 90-degree angle. This ideal condition is reached only in a few steep locations, but the closer the slope of the hill is to this ideal angle, the more sun the vineyard will receive. The sun warms the soil, and the heat of the soil is reflected onto the vines—at least, where the ground is stony.

The Proximity of Water

Being close to rivers, lakes, or the ocean is important for grapevines, primarily because the water surfaces reflect light. Light is immensely important for photosynthesis in the leaves. Light exerts its maximum impact on photosynthesis at 20,000 lux, a level avail-

able even under a thin cloud cover. When a heavy cloud cover is present, the level of light will be reduced by varying amounts.

In wine regions with a cool Atlantic or continental climate, the ability of water surfaces to collect and reflect light becomes important. This is true even when the grapes are planted a mile or so from the body of water. When the vineyard is right next to the shore, the water bestows an additional benefit by storing heat, at least in the warm months of the year. This means that during the evening and at night, when the air cools off, the water radiates heat directly into the vineyard. A disadvantage of being next to the water, however, is the danger of frost in winter when the temperature of the water is lower than that of the air.

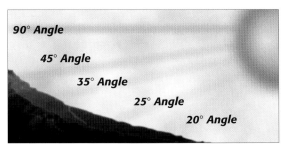

90° Angle
45° Angle
35° Angle
25° Angle
20° Angle

The steeper the hillside, the more efficient the use of the sun's rays.

The Morphology of Vineyards

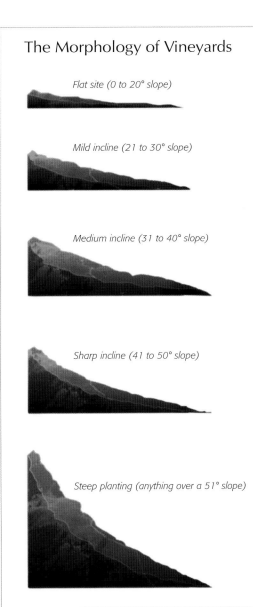

Flat site (0 to 20° slope)

Mild incline (21 to 30° slope)

Medium incline (31 to 40° slope)

Sharp incline (41 to 50° slope)

Steep planting (anything over a 51° slope)

Climate Types

Northern Climate

This is the climate that prevails in northern European grape regions: generally cool, with Atlantic influences. In many years there are as few as 1,300 hours of sunlight. Summers are short and warm; winters are cold, and in some regions, such as Champagne and Germany, they extend well into spring.

Continental Climate

The climate of central Europe's land-locked areas, where the difference between the highest and lowest temperatures of the year is very dramatic.

Maritime Climate

This climate is characterized by minimal fluctuations in temperature between summer and winter. It is found in wine regions near the ocean as well as many of the vineyards of the Southern Hemisphere.

Dry Climate

A very warm climate with little precipitation. Without watering, grape growing is impossible in such conditions, which are typical of parts of southern Australia and of South Africa, of Chile, and of California's Central Valley.

Average number of hours of sunshine between April and September

Jerez (Spain)	1,930
Alicante (Spain)	1,847
Oran (Algeria)	1,784
Patras (Greece)	1,778
Montpellier (France)	1,771
Florence (Italy)	1,697
Mendoza (Argentina)	1,688
Palermo (Italy)	1,619
Perpignan (France)	1,619
Adelaide (Australia)	1,544
Dijon (France)	1,433
Bordeaux (France)	1,252
Reims (France)	1,226

The Foundation for Excellence

Gravel Soil of the Médoc
The ground in the Médoc, comprised of alkaline river gravel, drains very quickly. It offers few nutrients, so grapevines must put down deep roots to find nourishment and water. Beneath the gravel lies a thin layer of marl, which rests on a thick bed of lime. The roots have to penetrate this far down to reach nutrients.

The Chalk of Champagne
Lime is considered an ideal subsoil for pinot noir and chardonnay. In Champagne, the layer of lime begins half a meter under the humus-rich topsoil. Its composition is partly loose, well-drained chalk and partly solid limestone. The roots of the vines reach deep into this bed of lime, which is 65 million years old, and in places 65 feet (20 m) thick.

"The soil determines the quality of the wine," say the French. Yet no scientist has ever discovered which soil will make the best wine.

The ground in which a grapevine grows is of paramount importance for the type and the quality of the wine produced from its grapes. What exactly constitutes suitable soil is a matter on which scientists and practitioners disagree. The French and the Germans, on the one hand, start with the assumption that the composition of the soil, specifically its mineral composition, gives the wine its style and char-acter, which will vary, depending whether it grew in loess or granite, in sandstone or in limestone. Americans and Australians, on the other hand, tend to the view that the texture and structure of the ground, more than its mineral and organic composition, shape the character and quality of the wine.

Does the Soil Determine the Taste of the Wine?
The European assumption is supported by many arguments. The best pinot noir grapes in the world thrive on the limestone of the Côte d'Or in Burgundy. The wines of Pouilly owe their particular character to the lime-stone mixed with flint (silex) on the slopes of the Loire Valley. Some Alsatian *grands crus* receive their characteristic mineral bouquets from the weathered gneissic soils found only at the foot of the Vosges mountains. Some people even claim that you can taste the slate in those German Rieslings that grow in the central Mosel Valley, where blue Devonian slate predominates.

Quality Grows in Many Soils
Still, we have to grant that the winegrowers of the New World have a point: Riesling, sauvignon blanc, and pinot noir grow there in very different soils, and they yield good to very good

The Slate Soil on the Mosel
The best vineyards on the slopes of
the central Mosel Valley grow on
slate. This slate was formed in the
Paleozoic era and has weathered
down in the course of millions of
years. Slate warms up quickly and
radiates this heat. The top-quality
Riesling wines that grow in this soil
show clear mineral tendencies in
their bouquet; local growers call
their special character "slate notes."

Terra Rossa in Coonawarra
Coonawarra is considered one
of Australia's best, if not its
very best, region for cabernet
sauvignon and for shiraz. The area
consists of a strip, about 10 miles
(15 km) wide, of henna-red earth.
Beneath it lies a layer of water-
retaining lime. Coonawarra
produces dark red wines with a
sweet, soft tannin and a whiff
of mint in the nose.

wines of strong character. This is even more
obvious of cabernet sauvignon and chardonnay: California wines made from these varieties have frequently bested their French
counterparts—or been mistaken for them—in
blind tastings. This is true even though the
soils of the Napa Valley, being acid, are completely different from those of the Médoc or
the Côte de Beaune, which are alkaline.

There Are Many Good Soils and Some Are Simply Better

In the end, both views must be taken into account. In order to be able to grow quality wines
at all, certain conditions must be met: Light,
warmth, dry soil with just the right amount of
organic material to maintain healthy vegetative growth, but not too much or too little. Beyond that, a certain type of soil, with a certain
type of mineral composition, can be particularly congenial to a specific variety of grape,
that is to say, it can determine the superior-
ity of a specific wine. Examples are the flint
on the Loire, the Tertiary sediments of the
Danube Valley, the slate on the Mosel.

Terroir Means More than Soil

The European philosophy of wine quality was
developed by the French; they describe it as
terroir. Terroir is much more than just soil.

Bruno Prats, owner of Château Cos d'Estournel in Saint-Estèphe, once expressed this concept of quality as follows: "An infinite number
of factors influence wine: temperatures, both
day and night, the distribution of rain over the
year, number of hours of sunshine, the deep
structure of the ground, its pH value, its ability to retain water, its mineral composition,
the shape of the terrain, the direction of the
sun, to name only a few. The effect of the
interaction of all these factors is what we in
France call *terroir.*"

Tending the Vineyard

The vineyard is where quality starts. While in the 1970s and 1980s many winegrowers invested in glitzy cellars and in modern winery technology, many of them are now returning to the root of quality: cultivation of the vineyard. It is the art of cultivation—and not cellar work—that ultimately determines whether the full potential for excellence offered by the ground is realized or not. The care of the soil, the training of the vines, the harvest, and prevention of damage by pests and diseases—these things are critical for turning an average wine into a good one, a good wine into a very good one, and a very good wine into a great one. The vintage then becomes the culmination of the wine year; it reveals whether the quality that we diligently created with what nature had given us can successfully be delivered into the safety of the cellar. The better the wine, the harder it is to mechanize vineyard work. The sweat on the forehead of the grape picker who carries the filled pannier and the steaming body of the horse that pulls the plow, these are the things that make up the price of the wine. (Here: Château Magdelaine, Saint-Emilion.)

The Triumph of Intensive Cultivation

In a modern vineyard, method reigns. The furrows are unwaveringly straight, the number of leaves is exactly calculated. However, not all that looks modern necessarily improves the wine; a vineyard must be laid out in such a way that it can be worked efficiently. Otherwise, the price of the wine will be exorbitant.

Nowadays, vineyards all over the world are planted as monocultures. Grapevine grows beside grapevine, and other plant life is not admitted. Such intensive viticulture is not without its problems. This type of planting is extremely vulnerable to pests and diseases and requires extensive protection for the vines.

Nor has this type of vineyard always been de rigueur. In the Médoc, fields of cereals traditionally grew beside the vines. Along the Rhône, the Rhine, and the Etsch, fruit trees grew among the rows of grapes. In the Steiermark and the Friuli, chickens and goats used to run about under the vines. In central Italy, especially in Tuscany, mixed viticulture predominated as recently as the 1960s: between the rows of grapes, oats or wheat were sown, and after every fifth grapevine an olive tree was planted. In some regions the grapevines climbed up the trunks of mulberry trees and elms.

The Modern Vineyard

Since labor has become scarce and expensive, mixed plantings have disappeared from viticulture. New vineyards are laid out according to the needs of machines; the distance between rows corresponds to the width of the tractor. The rows themselves usually run vertical to the hill, so that heat can rise unhindered, or they may be planted at right angles to the prevailing wind, to prevent the wind from blowing away the accumulated heat. The number of wires stretched between posts for the vines to cling to is set by the planned height of the foliage. Since the size of the canopy is closely related to the number of clusters produced, this allows growers to calculate and control the optimum yield.

How close to the ground the grapes will ultimately hang is also calculated in advance: deep enough so that the foliage cannot throw shade on them, high enough to prevent mold from ground moisture. Similarly, the system of training, fertilization, the selection of the clones of the chosen variety— all are calculated with mathematical accuracy to meet the standards of the desired quantity and quality.

Density of Planting

Perhaps the most important question for quality-oriented grape growing is how many grapevines to plant per hectare. Scientists agree that the quality of the wine depends primarily not on a low yield per hectare but on a low yield per vine. In the *grand cru* areas of Bordeaux, Burgundy, and Champagne, the vines carry barely more than a pound of fruit—a single, small cluster. This minimal yield per vine is compensated for by a correspondingly large number of vines. In those regions, there might be 10,000 grapevines per hectare, often even more.

Working such a vineyard is not cost-efficient: for

1,100 Vines per Hectare

Many Spanish vineyards, as here, in Zamora, are still planted with the traditional distance between rows. The distance between vines in a row is 8 feet (2.5 m), while the rows are 11 feet 6 inches (3.5 m) apart. This means few vines per hectare of land, but each vine carries many clusters. That may be fine for table grapes and for rustic wines; this planting system will not produce outstanding wines.

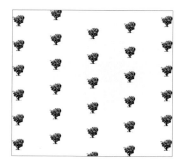

3,500 Grapevines per Hectare

Vineyards in many grape-growing areas of the world where quality wines are made are laid out in such a way that they can be worked with available standard machinery, as shown here in the Alexander Valley, California. The number of vines varies between 2,300 and 3,500. This means that the vines are 5 feet (1.5 m) apart and that the space between rows measures a little over 6 feet (1.9 m). These vineyards produce good to very good wines.

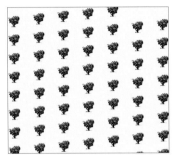

standard tractors the space between rows is too narrow, and much of the work must be done by hand. The higher production costs are of course offset by higher quality and higher prices.

Not in France alone, but in certain high-quality wine regions in other countries, new vineyards are being planted more densely than in the recent past. In the warmer zones of the Mediterranean growers now aim for 4,500 to 6,000 vines per hectare so as to get grapes of higher quality. Some old vineyards of the Mosel and the Saar, established before mechanization, are planted with 8,000 or 12,000 grapevines per hectare, for dense planting also has a long tradition. In the last century, when vineyards were worked with horses and mules, 20,000 vines per hectare was not uncommon. In ancient times, the Romans planted as many as 35,000 vines in an area of similar size, according to wine historians.

10,000 Vines per Hectare

Here, a typical example of a dense planting in Champagne. The distance between vines is no more than 3 feet 3 inches (1 m), and the rows are the same distance apart. This causes intense root competition, which in turn forces each vine to put down very deep roots and keep its clusters close to its trunk. The plant thus saves energy by keeping the supply channels for nutrients as short as possible. For the cultivation of such densely planted vineyard, the French have developed a special, high-sided tractor called an enjambeur, *which can straddle a row of vines as it plows beside it.*

Limits to Growth

Goblet system: The oldest training system, it is widely used only in grape regions where quality wines are made.

Guyot system: This classical wire frame method curtails the growth of the vine.

The grapevine is a climber. To grow, it needs something its tendrils can cling to—stakes, a trellis, or stretched wires. The way these aids to climbing are arranged determines whether the vine will produce many clusters or only a few.

There are dozens of grapevine training systems. Which is used depends on climatic conditions, on the structure and composition of the soil, and on whether the vineyard is worked by hand or by machine. Each wine region also tends to have its prevailing vine-training traditions. Ultimately, most training systems are variations on one of three basic training types.

Goblet System

The goblet system is the oldest training style still in use. Probably invented by the ancient Greeks, it was taken over by the Romans, and it is still employed around the Mediterranean. It is found all over southern France, along the Rhône, and into the Beaujolais, as well as in Spain and in parts of southern Italy, in Apulia, and in Sicily. The trunk is kept very short, only 12 to 25 inches (30 to 65 cm), and the vine is pruned so that at its head only three upward-growing arms remain. In the autumn, these arms are bent under the weight of the grapes that grow on their shoots, much like the ribs of an open umbrella.

Other names: Gobelet; alberello; en vaso; bush vines.
Support: Single posts, or none.
Method of pruning: The shoots are kept short so only one or two buds remain.
Analysis: The yield is low, so it is not suitable to mass production. It is being used more and more in the production of quality wines in hotter wine regions.

Guyot System

This is the training system most commonly used by quality European winemakers. We find it in Bordeaux as well as in large parts of Burgundy, in the Côte Rôtie, the Loire, and Alsace—also in the most significant wine regions of Italy (Tuscany, Piedmont), of Spain, and in parts of Germany and Austria. In this system, the vines clasp taut wires, which are arranged as follows: one shoot (the second nearest to the trunk) is left long at the winter pruning, so that it carries from six to fifteen nodes. This shoot is bent down and tied to the lowest wire. It will carry the grapes. The spur closest to the trunk is reduced to two nodes. It will not bear fruit till the following year. The trunk itself can be kept as low as 12 or as high as 30 inches (30 to 80 cm).

Support: Wire trellis.
Method of pruning: From six to fifteen buds.
Analysis: Depending on the severity of pruning, yields can be small or moderate. If two shoots are left to bear fruit, the harvest can be generous.

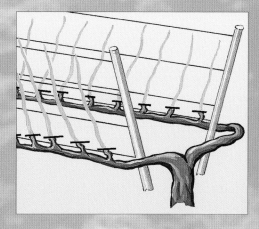

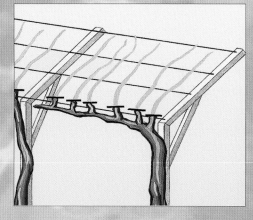

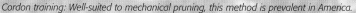
Cordon training: Well-suited to mechanical pruning, this method is prevalent in America.

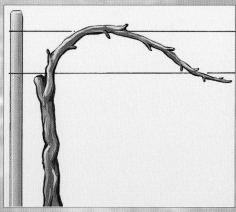

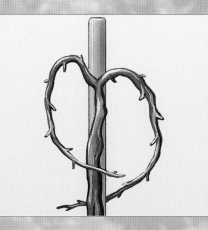

Cordon Training

The cordon training system is the one most widely used around the world. It has the advantage that pruning and tying the vine is relatively easy, requiring little experience or skill. The worldwide shortage of experienced vineyard workers makes this a very important consideration. What is more, the cordon system makes possible the mechanical pruning of the vines, and later allows the harvest to be accomplished by machines as well. The cordon system entails leaving one or two arms permanently on the vine and attached to a wire. This training system is widely used throughout North and South America, South Africa, Australia, and New Zealand. Even in Europe, especially in a few Burgundy villages—for example Chassagne-Montrachet—the vines are trained according to the cordon system.

Support: Wire trellis.
Method of pruning: The shoots are pruned to two to five buds, according to the desired yield.
Analysis: This system is practicable in the mass production of wine.

Other Vine-Training Systems

Lyre: A successful new method developed in Bordeaux, which takes the form of a Y.
   Advantages: The canopy is split to form two walls, giving the grapes more sun.

Pergola: An old, overhead training system, whereby the vines are supported by a wooden, arborlike trellis. It is used mostly in a few alpine valleys, in the Alto Adige, the Trentino, and in Valpolicella.
   Disadvantage: Promotes too many clusters per vine.

Arched-cane system: Especially common in Germany, it can take the form of a flat curve, a half circle, or a double curve.
   Advantage: Easy to take care of, though the wood is apt to break when it is bent.

Full-curve system: This is the traditional stake-training method along the Mosel, the Saar, and the Ruwer. It is still widely used in these areas.
   Advantages: The bunches hang close to the ground and receive ample warmth and light.

The High-Performance Vineyard

Grafting Grapevines

Nowadays, new vineyards are planted with grafted vines— rootstocks to which the scions of noble grapevines have been attached. The scion bears the genetic inheritance of the desired grapevine variety; the rootstock contributes the qualities needed to form an appropriate root system. Although the variety of the rootstock is not critical, its genetic makeup must be suitable to the soils into which it is to be set; above all, it must be genetically resistant to the phylloxera louse. It also has to be free of viruses. Grafting is usually done by machines that stamp out complementary shapes in the rootstock and the scion, so that the two can be joined seamlessly. Nurseries specializing in viticulture tend to assume the delicate work of grafting. To protect the wound, they cover it with a thin layer of paraffin. When the grafted vine begins to

grow in the spring, the new leaf breaks through the paraffin.

To preserve their own grape varieties, some winemakers will graft them onto selected rootstocks, as was done with the vine at Romanée-Conti, below. In California grafting is used to replace

cabernet sauvignon vines with merlot; in the Chianti area, white vines are grafted with the red sangiovese variety. The first grapes are harvested three years after regrafting.

A bordeaux mixture has been used for a century to improve the resistance of the leaves and flowers to disease.

The modern vineyard requires intensive cultivation. Without outside intervention, its biological and ecological systems cannot maintain a state of equilibrium.

The most significant area of intervention is the soil. In the spring or summer, the ground between the rows is plowed. The soil is aired and the weeds are mulched under. This is important because in dry seasons the grass between the vines, by absorbing surface precipitation, poses serious competition for available water. Mulching is done by grubber or plowshare. In the past, these implements were pulled by horses, mules, or oxen; today these have been replaced by tractors. Very steep sites are an exception: the slopes are worked by plows pulled by cable installations, and in some steep spots, the spade is still used to lift the ground.

Mulching

During mulching, the shallow root system of the vine is destroyed. The plant, however, suffers no damage; the process merely promotes growth in the principal root. Another advantage is that, should the autumn turn out wet, the vine will not be able to take up too much moisture. This is good, since at the final ripening stage too much water would swell and dilute the berries. Mulching is at the same time a form of green fertilization and encourages the formation of humus. Vineyards used for mass-produced wine do not mulch: the growers use chemical means to destroy the weeds, i.e., herbicides.

Fertilization for a Sustainable Vineyard

Like any other plant, the grapevine takes up nutrients from the soil, which must be returned to the earth. Thus at times, some form of fertilization is called for. Some growers spread manure, green fertilizers, grapevine chips, or straw; the choice and the frequency of fertilization (annually to every three years) depends upon the composition of the soil. Some growers use compost made of recycled garbage from urban areas. Mineral fertilizers are not considered appropriate for quality winemaking, though in some instances they may become necessary to replenish the soil's nitrogen, potassium, and phosphates.

Problems Caused by Overfertilization

In making wines of quality, fertilization always serves the purpose of promoting the healthy growth of the vines, never of increasing the yield of grapes. For this reason it is called balanced fertilization. Overfertilizing the soil was the fashion during the 1960s and 1970s, when mass production held sway. It still is practiced in some regions.

Ample fertilization does increase the grape yield, but subsequently it leads to ever graver problems. Must weights decrease as grape yields increase. The grapes ripen late or incompletely. Acidity values can fall. Above all, the vines become more vulnerable to diseases. In addition there is the serious ecological problem of groundwater becoming contaminated by fertilizers.

Erosion

Since grapes are often grown on hillsides, the vineyard's surface is constantly being carried into the valley. The traditional solution to this erosion problem in Burgundy was to carry the soil back up the hill in baskets. Similarly, even today, in steep plantings on the Mosel, along the Rhine near Nierstein, and on the Côte Rôtie, after heavy rains the eroded soil is collected and returned to the vineyard.

In an effort to prevent erosion, the ground of vineyards is often deliberately given a cover crop. This keeps the hill in place. The grasses and other plants that are chosen must have shallow roots, so that they do not rob the vines of too much moisture. Mustard is sown among the vines in California's Napa Valley as a cover crop. Oilseed rape *(Brassica napus)* and clover are typical erosion stoppers. Winter rye can serve to curb wind erosion.

Fighting Pests

Vines grown in intensive monoculture are vulnerable to fungal diseases and insect attack. Both calamities can lead to serious losses, even the forfeit of the harvest. No question, insecticides and fungicides take care of the problems. This way of protecting the vintage is expensive, however, especially if prophylactic spraying is done, not to mention the fact that it has frequently been observed that both vines and insects quickly become resistant to certain poison sprays. When this happens, the following year tends to bring an explosive spread of the blight.

Finally, more and more people have come to feel that for a luxury item like wine, nature ought not to be damaged. For this reason, many winegrowers are switching to near-organic cultivation methods, such as interrupting the pattern of monoculture. Many practitioners of integrated viticulture, moreover, aim to refrain from prophylactic spraying by attempting to control the flight patterns of insects and using weather forecasts to predict possible attack. Organic viticulture means spraying with less dangerous chemicals, such as a solution of copper sulfate called bordeaux mixture, which increases the resistance of leaves and flowers.

Irrigation

In areas where rain falls only in winter, grapevines have to be watered artificially. The common method is drip-irrigation: from a hose permanently installed in the row of vines, drops of water are released into the soil at intervals of ten or twenty seconds. This type of slow irrigation may be indispensable, particularly in the dry months. Its purpose is not to increase yield, but to ensure the survival of the crop. New plantings, not yet old enough to bear fruit, also may need drip irrigation. These uses of irrigation are quite unlike large-scale sprinkler installations, which spray whole rows of grapevines liberally with water to support harvests of 200 quintals per hectare, or even more. Such liberal irrigation takes place in California's Central Valley, the Australian Riverland, northern Chile, and South Africa's Robertson Valley.

Upper left: Fighting pests with synthetic, chemical poison sprays is simple, but it hurts the environment, is expensive, and in the long run is not very effective.

Upper right: Vineyard soils have to be aired; in steep plantings along the Mosel, this is accomplished with plows pulled up the hill by heavy steel cables.

Lower left: High grape yields per hectare are possible only if mineral fertilizers are used. In quality wine areas, organic fertilizers are used merely to replenish the soil.

Lower right: Shallow plowing loosens only the top layer of soil, leaving the deep principal roots undisturbed.

Quality Versus Quantity

How Maximum Production Limits per Hectare Are Stated

Production limits in France, the pioneer in modern quality wine production, are usually given in terms of hectoliters of must per hectare. (Italian wine laws, by contrast, speak about quintals [a quintal is 100 kilograms] of grapes per hectare, but in the table below, all limits are given as hectoliters of must per hectare.) The average must yield of grapes, by the way, is around 70 percent.

Maximum Yields per Hectare

France*

Bordeaux sec	65 hl
Pauillac	45 hl
Margaux/Saint-Julien/ Saint-Estèphe	45 hl
Saint-Emilion	45 hl
Saint-Emilion *grand cru*	40 hl
Pomerol	40 hl
Chambertin *grand cru*	35 hl
Pommard *1er cru*	40 hl
Montrachet *1er cru*	40 hl
Meursault	45 hl
Beaujolais	65 hl
Coteaux du Languedoc	50 hl
Côte du Rhône	50 hl
Champagne	60 hl
Alsace	80 hl
Alsace *grand cru*	55 hl

Italy

Chianti	65 hl
Chianti Classico	55 hl
Brunello di Montalcino	55 hl
Barolo/Barbaresco	55 hl
Collio (Friuli)	80 hl
Soave	100 hl
Teroldego (Trentino)	120 hl

Spain

Ribera del Duero	60 hl
Rioja	60 hl

Germany

Rheingau	100 hl
Mosel-Saar-Ruwer	125 hl

Austria

All regions	70 hl

Switzerland

Lake Geneva (or Lac Leman)	90 hl
Wallis	80 hl

California, Australia, South Africa

No production limits.

*The given base limit may be exceeded by 20 percent, in cases where an application is made and granted.

Summer pruning: In July or August if the fruit is too abundant, the grape grower may remove some of the still-green clusters to improve the quality of the wine.

The rule of quality or quantity states that the quality of the wine improves when the vine carries fewer clusters. Where nature does not limit the quantity, man must intervene and do so.

Quality winemaking all over the world is based on more or less strict curtailing of the production of fruit. In other words, the vines may not bear more than whatever the vineyard's grapes-per-hectare ratio will permit. Unless a quality grower meets these strict yield limits, his wines could lose their classification as quality wines and be degraded to ordinary table wines. Setting maximum limits for production is the task of governmental wine control agencies. Maximum production limits vary from region to region. They range from 35 hectoliters (of must; about 2 tons) in the *grand cru* appellations of Burgundy to 200 hectoliters (over 11 tons) in California's and Australia's irrigation areas, which do not produce quality wines in the European sense of the term.

While it is of course permissible to reduce yields to *below* the set limits, at a certain point this is no longer a guarantee of higher quality.

Low Yields

The quantity/quality rule is based on a biological fact: a plant can bring only a limited amount of fruit to a state of ripeness. The more clusters that hang on a vine, the more slowly they will ripen. In cool regions there is always the danger that by harvest time the grapes will not have fully ripened.

Although in warmer climates grapes are sure to build up sufficient sugar, under these hot conditions they may not develop many other desirable components. Flavor compounds, for example, may be low, making the must watery and insipid. Thus a high grape yield brings with it a loss of quality, concentration, and density. Of course, high yields also mean higher income through greater volume, and accordingly many growers are willing to accept some loss of quality.

Targeted Reduction of Yield

Most plants, including the grapevine, tend to produce abundance, climate and soil permitting. It is therefore

An abundant producer: Carignan vine in the south of France.

Winter pruning: The most important way of limiting yield.

the remaining buds (six to twenty), and the smaller the fruit set.

Summer Pruning

If the fruit is too ample after all, the grape grower can go through his vineyard in July or August and remove some of the still-green clusters. If the fruit production has been curtailed naturally by disease, hail, frost, or damage to the flowers, the grower will obviously skip this task.

Natural Limits to Yield

The level of a plant's yield, its vigor, depends in no small part on natural factors. In dry, stony ground—"warm soil"—grapevines cannot deliver massive harvests. In moist, nitrogen-rich "cold soil," they will bear very generously. Climate also plays an important role. In a cold, wet spring, it may happen that not all the flowers are fertilized: the clusters will thin out. Late frosts in May can literally destroy the inflorescence. Another serious danger looms in the form of vine diseases, which can decimate the vintage. In summer, hail is a threat to the ripening clusters. The suitability of a region for quality wine production is therefore dependent on prevailing natural conditions.

Two famous wines from old vines: Didier Dagueneau's Pouilly Fumé "Silex," from the Loire, and Willi Bründlmayer's Riesling "Alte Reben," from the Kamp Valley in Austria.

the grower's task to limit the grapevine's natural productivity; that is, to reduce its vigor. This can be achieved in several ways.

Choosing the Right Training System

The training system has a profound influence on the vigor or productivity of a vine. Training to a single, arched cane limits fruit set more drastically than training to two canes. In general, pergola training offers the vine a more ample growth potential than a wire frame does.

Density of Planting

How densely the vineyard is planted also influences the vigor of the plants and their yield. When more vines are planted within a specified area, each vine will bear less fruit. This reduction in vigor is brought about by the intense competition for nutrients among the plants (see page 30).

Choosing the Right Vine Clone

Grapevine nurseries breed numerous clones of each variety, and these differ in clearly specified features. Thus, for example, clones of a certain variety may be bred for ample fruit set, which means many clusters with many grapes. Other clones of the same variety will show a loose fruit set, with few grapes.

Winter Pruning

Vines are pruned during their dormant period in the winter. At that time, most of the old wood is removed. The fewer shoots left (one or two), the fewer

The Age of a Vine

How old a vine is also influences its vigor, or productivity. The plant gives its best harvests between the ages of twelve and twenty-five. After that, performance declines steadily. Most wine growers dig up their vines after twenty-five years and replace them with new ones. Château Margaux, however, in the production of its *grand vin* relies solely on vines that are at least forty years old; for its second wine, Pavillon Rouge, it uses grapes from vines at least twenty-five years old. The more age has reduced the vigor of a vine, the higher the quality of its grapes. Other famous wines of France, and of other countries, sometimes show the words *vieilles vignes*—"old vines"—on their labels. This description is not regulated, however.

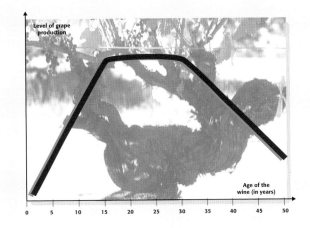

Productivity of the grapevine: After fifteen years, a grapevine reaches full vigor, its level of maximum yield. After twenty-five years, performance slowly declines. Quality, however, improves.

Level of grape production

Age of the wine (in years)

0   5   10   15   20   25   30   35   40   45   50

The Long Road to Ripeness

Budbreak

Budbreak or budburst *(bourgeonnement)* refers to the opening of the buds that remained after winter pruning. When the buds burst, small green leaves emerge, quickly unfolding. This happens when daytime temperatures begin to average about 46 to 50°F (8 to 10°C). Some varieties break their buds somewhat earlier, as for example, chardonnay; others open later, like cabernet sauvignon.

Until now, the grapevine has obtained its nourishment from the stores of carbohydrates it laid down in the fall. Once the leaves have developed, the vine begins to nourish itself through photosynthesis.

The winegrower can detect the signs of oncoming budburst some days before it begins. The cuts that resulted from the winter pruning begin to show little drops of sap, a sign that dormancy is over and the juices of the plant are beginning to flow. Soon, the nodes swell up. They are ready to burst.

Inflorescence

Flowering *(floraison)* occurs forty-five to ninety days after budbreak, or between the middle of May and the end of June (in the Southern Hemisphere, from November to mid-December). During this interval, new shoots have grown and put out the peduncles on which the blossoms will sit. Because of its small scale, flowering is almost imperceptible to the eye.

The blossoms are covered with a brown cap of fused petals, the kalyptra, that will pop up and disclose the stigma and the stamens. Almost all *Vitis vinifera* vines are hermaphroditic; that is, they can fertilize themselves. Fertilization is the process of the male pollen adhering to the sticky surface of the female stigma. Rain or strong winds at the time of inflorescence can prevent the pollination of all the flowers. If that happens, the harvest will be reduced more or less drastically come autumn. Grape growers call this shatter or *coulure.*

A Year in the Life of the Vine

The difference between a good year and a mediocre one is not simply a matter of autumn weather. Spring and summer hold risks as well—especially with respect to yield. Like every other plant, the vine has its own vegetative cycle, a growth phase followed by a ripening phase followed by a dormant phase. This last begins after harvest in the fall, when the vine has an adequate store of carbohydrates in its trunk and roots. At that point the leaves yellow and fall off. Only in March—in September in the Southern Hemisphere—do rising temperatures bring budding and the start of a new cycle.

Fruit Set

The pollinated pistils immediately begin their transformation into berries, while unfertilized blossoms wither and fall. In their place, the cluster will show a gap. At the beginning the fruit is very small, green, and hard, but the grapes increase in size rather quickly.

During this phase, the grapes are most vulnerable to attack by larvae or caterpillars and by powdery and downy mildew. In moist, warm climates, fungal blights can also spread rapidly and must be controlled. Under certain climatic conditions, the leaf roller deposits its eggs in parts of the plant. In August, ripening begins (in the Southern Hemisphere, in January). Only then do the grapes begin to turn color.

Véraison

With the start of véraison, or "coloring," the vine enters its ripening phase. White wine berries slowly acquire a yellowish tinge; red berries gradually turn reddish blue. What probably triggers this process is that a certain level of sugar has been reached within the juice of the berry. Not all grapes take on color at the same time. Those that have received the most sunlight and heat color first, while grapes growing on the shady side still remain green.

The French word véraison has become internationally accepted as the technical term for coloring. In warm summers, véraison begins earlier, in cold summers later. Vines that bear an ample load of fruit ripen later than those that bear little. With coloring, the last phase in the growth cycle of the grapevine begins, and the most critical one for the quality of the vintage.

Leaf Roller: This moth lays its eggs inside the flower caps. When the larvae emerge, they proceed to devour the efflorescence. Toward the end of June, the larvae of another species enter the young berries and hollow them out from within. Invasions by these dangerous insects are detected by setting traps for them; they have to be fought with chemical sprays.

Leaf Roll Virus: This leaf disease is relatively new to Europe, but has achieved epidemic proportions in France, Germany, and Italy. The leaves roll inward and fall off.

Other Damage to Grapevines

Poor fruit set: *Coulure* ("shatter") and *millerandage* are terms for conditions that lead to fewer berries on the bunches at harvest time. In wet, cold springs, the weather adversely affects pollination and fruit set. The gaps in the bunches can cost the grower very dearly.

Chlorosis: When soil is missing nutrients, leaves cannot produce chlorophyll. They turn yellow, and the plant's main source of nutrition—photosynthesis—stops. Usually caused by a shortage of nitrogen, magnesium, or other minerals, chlorosis is more likely to occur in calcareous soils.

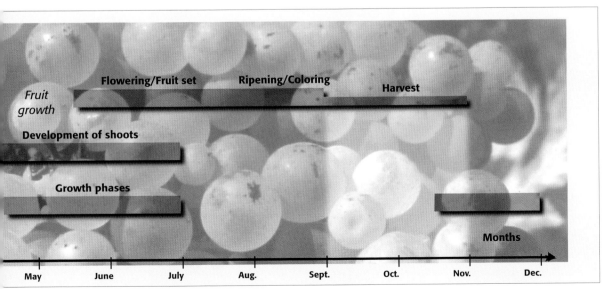

Fruit growth

Flowering/Fruit set — Ripening/Coloring — Harvest

Development of shoots

Growth phases

Months

May — June — July — Aug. — Sept. — Oct. — Nov. — Dec.

Cleaning Up the Old Wood

After the old canes are cut, they have to be removed. After the harvest, the green shoots lignify; that is, they turn woody. Having been cut, they are most easily disposed of by burning. A fire is usually lit right in the vineyard. Over great grape-growing regions you can see columns of smoke all winter long. In California, at that time of year, the yellow mustard is also blooming between the vines.

Some outstanding vineyards save their old wood and turn it into chips. Then they compost it, so that at a later time they can return it to the soil. This practice helps preserve the bacterial cultures of a vineyard.

Tying the Canes

After most of the old wood has been pruned out, the remaining canes need to be tied up. Pallissage is what French growers call this work. The canes are attached vertically or horizontally to the wires with elastic willow wands. From these canes, in the spring, the new shoots will grow.

Though tying up requires skill, it takes no strength; many vignerons like to do this outdoor job personally. On large estates, however, this work is increasingly done by migrant grape workers, who tend to be hired to do the winter pruning as well.

Winter Pruning

In winter the vines are dormant, but much work is done in the vineyards nevertheless. Teams of migrant workers range through the vineyards, cutting off 90 percent of the old fruit canes to control the coming summer's yield. Around their waists they wear a work belt in which they keep their pruning shears, or secateurs. Today, secateurs are commonly powered by portable compressors; pneumatic secateurs are faster and easier on the hands. Some large vineyards begin winter pruning as early as November, when the canes are still green; many wait till January or February, when they have turned woody.

Grape Harvest

With the harvest, the winegrower's year reaches its zenith. For the last time, everyone's energy is mobilized to pick and gather into the cellar the ripe and healthy crop. After the vintage is in, the grower's year ends abruptly, and the growth cycle of the grapevine also comes to an end. The leaves stop making chlorophyll, change color, and fall. The green fruit-bearing shoots lignify and turn brown. Most of the carbohydrates that were stored in them are transported into the trunk and roots. Winter's rest begins. But it will not last very long.

Summer Pruning

After the grapes have begun to color, or even before, the owner of the vineyard sends his workers out among the grapevines to do the summer pruning. Also called trimming, this operation involves crop thinning; still-green bunches are cut or broken out to lower yield. Makers of quality wines routinely prune out up to 50 percent of the young clusters in order to ensure timely ripening and good must concentration for the rest. Only when late frost or damaged florescence reduce fruit set is it customary to forego summer pruning.

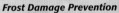

Frost Damage Prevention

Some of the more northerly grape growing regions, such as Chablis and Champagne, may be threatened by late-spring frosts. When temperatures are predicted to fall below 32°F (0°C), winegrowers spend the night in the vineyard, tending oil heaters or even burning tires in an effort to heat up the air around the vines. In California, wind machines are set in motion to circulate the cold air and drive it away from low-lying grapes. In Germany, large-scale irrigation is used to form a thin layer of ice around the grapes: the release of latent heat as the water freezes around the vines protects their tissue from injury. The most feared of all frosts are those that come late, in the month of May.

As Harvest Approaches

Early harvest in Australia: In hot grape-growing regions, the harvest of white grapes is usually moved up.

Must weight is the amount of sugar held in solution in the juice, or must. It is an important indicator of quality, but by no means the most critical one, as some winemakers would like to believe.

The ripening phase—the most important in the vegetative cycle of the grape—begins with the coloring of the berries in August and ends with the wine harvest. Sugar is produced in the leaves and then stored in the fruit. The more light and heat the leaves receive, the more sugar they will collect; the more sugar stored in the grapes, the higher the alcohol content of the wine that is made out of them. It takes about half an ounce (16 g) of sugar to create 1 percent alcohol in a liter of wine.

The Point of Ripeness

During ripening, the grapes double in size. Their color intensifies. The skin becomes thinner, and the grapes themselves soften. How long this will take depends on the weather—especially the weather in July, August, and September. Besides building up stores of sugar, the grape is also reducing its high levels of acid, which make unripe grapes inedibly tart.

When sugar and the remaining acids are nicely balanced, the grape is considered ripe—but the moment of ripeness and the time for picking the grapes are not necessarily identical. Some grapes are picked *before* they are ripe; others, at the point of optimum ripeness; still others, when they are overripe.

Early Grape Harvests in the Hot South

In warm regions, grape picking will start earlier, in cold areas later. On Cyprus, it starts in July; on Sardinia and in parts of Sicily, by mid-August. In these regions, it is so hot that the desired sugar content—and with it the desired must weight—is reached without any difficulty. The early grape harvest is aimed at retaining some of the acidity.

How Sugar Content of Grapes Is Measured

Most wines have an alcohol content of about 11 to 13 percent by volume. To reach this level, it is possible for the grower to calculate what sugar content his grapes will have to reach by harvest time. The sugar level is reflected in the must weight, which is measured with a refractometer or an hydrometer.

There are several scales for measuring must weight. In France and in Australia, must weight is measured in degrees of Baumé; in the Americas, in degrees of Brix or Balling; in Italy in degrees of Babo; in Germany, in degrees of Oechsle. Austrians use their own scale (KMW), devised at Klosterneuburg.

All these scales are based on the fact that grape must is heavier than water. One milliliter of water weighs 1 gram. The excess weight of 1 ml of juice is the weight of the substances dissolved in it. Since 90 percent of the solutes in grape juice are sugars, this is regarded as a pretty accurate means of determining the sugar level of must.

The simplest measure of must weight is the Baumé scale. It gives the potential alcohol content of the wine, assuming that all of the sugar is changed to alcohol by fermentation. A must with 12° Baumé would therefore yield a wine with 12 percent alcohol by volume.

Must Weight Is Not the Whole Story

Must weight is unquestionably a significant factor in setting the time for the wine harvest. In Germany and Austria, where the cool climate makes ripeness by harvest time a matter of some uncertainty, must weight has become the chief criterion in the official designation of quality. A Riesling Spätlese from the Mosel has to show a must weight of at least 76° Oechsle, and an Auslese should show 85° Oechsle.

This classification of Germany and Austria's finest wines by their must weight makes little sense in warmer climates. Any simple French country wine has the must weight of an Auslese, and an Italian Amarone from Valpolicella shows the must-weight equivalent of a Beerenauslese. Yet Auslese and Beerenauslese are both highly distinguished German wine categories. Thus, in Mediterranean and other warm climates, must weight, though still a measure of ripeness, is not a significant measure of quality.

In warm areas, what is important at harvest time is acidity or pH value, or what is now called physiological ripeness (see below). Even in Germany and Austria it is now generally admitted that must weight is only one among many factors that need to be considered in determining ripeness.

Sugar and Acidity

No simple formula exists for setting the time for the grape harvest. Most growers analyze the grape juice. During the period of ripening, after *véraison*, the sugar content of the juice steadily increases, with a simultaneous decrease in acidity. While in cooler regions growers concentrate on accumulating enough sugar, in warm regions they try to retain enough of the acids. In most wines the acidity should lie between 7 and 10 grams per liter. Some areas express the acidity in terms of pH—the ideal range is between 2.7 and 3.7.

Definitions of Ripeness

Ripeness is necessarily a standard set by each grower. In Germany, "perfect ripeness" is that state when the amount of sugar deposited in the berry during the day from photosynthesis is smaller than the amount decomposed at night. This means that in a fully ripe grape, there is a net decrease of sugar.

In cold countries, this stage of perfect ripeness is reached so late in the year that only grapes picked after the general grape harvest is over can be called fully ripe. In Germany these late-picked grapes are called "Spätlese," as is the wine made from them. The bulk of a northern grape harvest brings in grapes that are ripe, but according to some short of "perfect ripeness." Commonly, growers compare the increase in grape sugar to the decrease in tartness, and when sugar production is slower than the decrease in acidity, it is time to pick the grapes. For most dry wines, if too much acidity is lost, the wine will lack freshness. In each country, different rules apply for determining the perfect relationship of sweetness to acidity. In areas where wines are mass-produced, grapes are picked when their composition ensures the prescribed alcohol content and acidity level in the finished wine.

Refractometer

This instrument measures must weight by means of a calibrated prism. When held against the light, a drop of juice on the glass causes light to be refracted in proportion to the concentration of sugar in the must.

Table of Comparative Must Weights

Degrees Oechsle	Klosterneuburg Must Weight Scale (KMW)	Baumé	Brix/Balling	Potential alcohol content in % per volume
60	12	8.1	14.7	8.1
65	13	8.8	15.9	8.8
70	14	9.4	17.1	9.4
75	15	10.1	18.2	10.1
80	16	10.7	19.2	10.7
85	17	11.3	20.3	11.3
90	18	11.9	21.4	11.9
95	19	12.5	22.4	12.5
100	20	13.1	23.6	13.1
105	21	13.7	24.7	13.7
110	22	14.3	25.7	14.3
115	23	14.9	26.8	14.9
120	24	15.5	27.8	15.5
125	25	16.9	28.9	16.9

Physiological Ripeness

The concept of physiological ripeness was introduced in the United States and represents a departure from the traditional European definitions of ripeness based on sugar concentration and acidity. This way of thinking places emphasis on the degree of coloring of the skin (in both red and white grapes), on the elasticity of the pulp, on the ripeness of the seeds, and, last but not least, on the taste of the grape.

European growers like to talk about physiological ripeness as well, and this is not surprising at all: experienced winemakers and oenologists have always pinpointed the ripeness of grapes by tasting them. How sweet are they? How thick is their skin? The owners of châteaus in Bordeaux, the proprietors of domaines in Burgundy, and all other dedicated growers have always gone out to taste their grapes practically every day as they ripen.

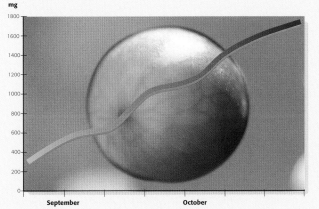

Color pigments (anthocyanins) in the grape as it ripens.

Acid Versus Must Weight

In warm growing regions vintners are less concerned about high must weight than about maintaining acidity. It gives wines freshness and elegance—especially white wines.

Acidity is increasingly seen as a valuable component of wine, especially in warm growing regions, and especially for white wines. In such areas, the time for the grape harvest is set not by must weight but by acidity values.

During the ripening phase, in addition to accumulating sugar, the grape also loses acidity. If this did not happen, all wine would be far too sour to drink. Some acidity has to be retained, however; an important constituent of wine, it lends freshness and a welcome "lift." This is particularly true of white wines. Thus in regions with a Mediterranean climate or with even warmer weather, great care is taken to prevent too much acidity being lost.

If acid levels stand between 7 and 9 grams per liter of must at harvest, the acidity of the resulting wine will be between 5 and 7 grams per liter. Although it is not allowed in most parts of Europe, in other parts of the world, such as America, acidity can be added to the wine.

Maintaining Acidity

The accumulation of sugar and the decomposition of acids are parallel processes. The warmer the days, the higher sugar values will mount. With more heat, more acids are lost through respiration. While simultaneous, the two processes do not necessarily go on at the same pace.

Cool nights slow the reduction of acids, a retardation that is especially welcome in hot growing regions, such as the Alto Adige and Friuli in Italy, the Mâconnais in France, and Penedès in Spain. In California, white wine production is steadily shifting from the hot Napa Valley into Carneros, the Russian River, and the Alexander Valley, which are situated within the cooler Pacific climate.

Tartaric Acids and Malic Acids

Most of the acids found in wine are of two types: tartaric acids and malic acids. Together, they account for 90 percent of the total acid content. Tartaric acid has an agreeable, soft taste and is welcomed by winemakers; grapes are the only fruit in which it occurs.

The taste of malic acid, on the other hand, is harsh. Too much of it, and the wine will taste sharp and hard. Makers of white wines tend to allow a limited amount of it to remain; it lends young, fruity wines freshness and bite. Thus Riesling, Grüner Veltliner, Sancerre, or the white wines of northern Italy contain varying amounts of malic acid, as does chardonnay when it is fermented in stainless-steel tanks rather than barrels.

In red wines, malic acid has no place. It must be removed, or more precisely, turned into softer lactic acid. To achieve this change, red wines undergo, after the alcoholic fermentation, a second one, called malolactic fermentation (see page 76).

The actual amount of malic acid present depends on several factors. Some grape varieties, such as

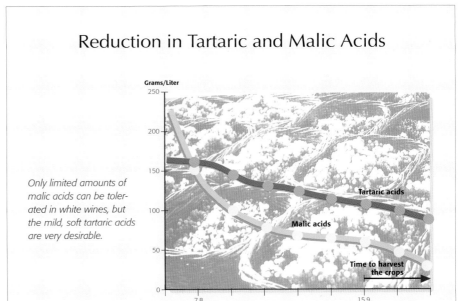

Reduction in Tartaric and Malic Acids

Only limited amounts of malic acids can be tolerated in white wines, but the mild, soft tartaric acids are very desirable.

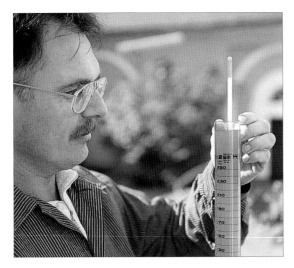

Measuring the must weight with an Ardometer. The level shown on the measuring tube corresponds with the density of the must.

pinot noir and malbec, have a generally high level of malic acid in the first place. Furthermore, natural levels will go up in cool summers and drop in sunny ones. Heat causes malic acid to decompose faster than the more pleasant tartaric acids. The quality of a vintage depends on its malic acid content.

Total Acid Content Versus pH Value
The indicator for the level of acidity of a liquid is its pH value. In a laboratory, this is measured by counting the free hydrogen ions. A high pH value indicates low acidity; a low pH value, high acidity. Nonetheless, there is a difference between pH value and total acidity. The reason is that some acids are volatile, while others are fixed. Total acidity includes the volatile acids, while pH values show only those acids that can be tasted. For this reason, pH is a better indicator of must quality.

What Is Extract?
The sum of all the nonvolatile components of a wine is called its extract. Included are sugar, acids, and glycerin as well as the substances that are present in trace amounts, namely, phenols, pectin, protein, and minerals. If the wine were boiled until it evaporated, what would remain behind is its extract.

Extract is an indicator of quality. The fewer grapes a vine bears and the fewer water molecules the fruit contains, the higher the concentration of other components; in other words, the higher the proportion of extract. Wine made from grapes picked very late in the season can have as much as 30 grams of extract per liter; by contrast, wines that were picked early seldom reach even 19 grams per liter.

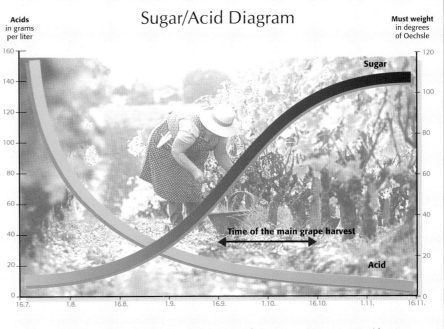

The process of ripening: While the grape stores more and more sugar, its tartness or acid content steadily declines. Too little acid makes for a flat wine, too much sugar gives wine excessive alcohol.

The Boon of a Late Harvest

Restsüsse ("residual sugar") Spätlese from the Mosel: A light wine with 9 percent alcohol, but its extract is high.

Rare, elegantly sweet Spätlese from Italy: In hot climates, picking grapes with noble rot is a rare achievement.

Smaragd ("Emerald") from the Wachau, in Austria: A highly priced, dry white wine from somewhat dried grapes partly affected by noble rot.

Vendange Tardive from Alsace: Literally translated, this means "picked late," but in fact it is a high-quality selection of the best grapes with noble rot: usually elegantly sweet, sometimes dry.

Trockenspätlese from the Rheingau: A wine with an acidic tone, made of healthy, perfectly ripe berries.

Grapes do not necessarily have to be picked as soon as they are ripe. As long as the autumn sun is shining, they can go on ripening until they are "perfectly ripe" or even "overripe." With warm fall weather, they can be made into fine Spätlese and elegantly sweet Auslese wines.

Late picking makes for fuller, stronger wines; sugars increase, while acids diminish. This is true both of white and red grapes. In cold continental climates, growers try to put off harvesting some grapes to achieve higher must weights and more full-bodied wines. Often this happens as a matter of pure necessity, for in those regions grapes ripen slowly and late. In parts of Germany, Austria, and France, it takes four weeks longer than in warm regions for the grapes to achieve a comparable must weight, yet in good years the cold climate permits a length of ripening impossible in hot areas.

Late Picking: Perfectly Ripe Grapes

If day temperatures continue to be warm during the autumn, even after the grapes are ripe, the vine will continue the process of assimilation and the accumulation of sugar in the fruit. Must weight increases. The grapes reach perfect ripeness. This is how Spätlese wine is produced. Wines from grapes that are picked late are incomparably rich in composition, with complex aromas. Of course, the nights at that time of year are rather chilly. Some of the sugar that is built up is lost by night, which means that the net gain in sugar begins to decrease with each day. At a certain point, what is lost at night equals what is gained by day. This point of equilibrium may be reached quite early, say, at the beginning of October, though in some years it does not come till the end of the month. At the end of October at the latest, the grower will send his workers into the vineyard to cut the remaining grapes.

Wine Picked Late Is Rich in Extract

Left on the vine late, grapes generate more extract substances, more polyphenols, and in the case of red grapes, more anthocyanins. This creates full-bodied, concentrated wines and, because the grapes had more time to build sugar, higher alcoholic strength. By itself, alcohol is not a criterion of good quality. However, given a fine wine rich in extract, an alcohol content that is commensurate with its complexity and aroma is needed to balance and harmonize it. And the extract, which contains—apart from sugar—glycerin, acids, minerals, and phenols, keeps increasing as the grapes ripen further.

The First Stage of Ripeness
According to German wine law, healthy, ripe grapes with a must weight of at least 70° to 80° Oechsle (at least 17° KMW) qualify for the designation "Kabinett." The berries are ripe, the skin is taut and still green. Sugar content has not yet reached its maximum potential.

The Second Stage of Ripeness
Perfectly ripe, usually still healthy grapes with a must weight of more than 80° Oechsle (at least 19° KMW) qualify for the designation "Spätlese" ("picked late"). The grapes are very soft, sometimes showing some wrinkles. Their color is changing into yellow-green. The sugar gained during the day equals the amount lost at night.

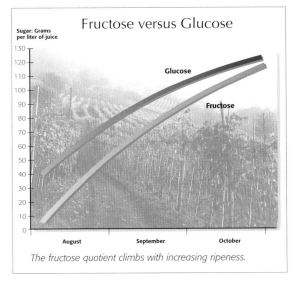

Fructose versus Glucose

Sugar: Grams
per liter of juice

Glucose

Fructose

130
120
110
100
90
80
70
60
50
40
30
20
10
0

August   September   October

The fructose quotient climbs with increasing ripeness.

Wine Made of Overripe Grapes

In certain cooler wine regions, some growers leave a portion of the crop, though ripe, on the vines. These grapes will reach the stage of overripeness, when more sugar is lost at night than is built up during the day. Despite this negative sugar equilibrium, the grape juice gets sweeter: in overripe berries, water is evaporating as well, and as the grapes

slowly change into raisins, sugar concentration increases steadily. Must weight goes up, and when it finally undergoes vinification, the wine is called *Edelsüss* or "noble-sweet." "Noble" distinguishes these refined and expensive wines from cheap ones that are sweet but lack body and character. In noble-sweet wines, the must has acquired so much sugar that some of it is not transformed into alcohol during fermentation but remains in the wine. What is more, to produce just the right degree of this sophisticated sweetness, the winemaker may deliberately halt the fermentation process, preserving as much of the sugar as he wants.

Glucose and Fructose

The sweetness of wines made of the overripe grape crop is due to their high fructose content. Fructose is a sugar with sweetening abilities much higher than those of glucose, the second major sugar formed in the grape. While glucose constitutes over 80 percent of the sugars in unripe grapes, with greater ripeness fructose increases more and more. In ripe grapes the two sugars are about equally balanced; in overripe ones, fructose predominates. The beneficent mold *Botrytis cinerea*, which invades practically all overripe wine grapes, feeds on glucose more than on fructose.

The Modern Tradition of Late Harvesting

The potential of a late grape harvest had been discovered in Roman times, but it was not systematically exploited until 1775. The winemaker of Schloss Johannisberg in the Rheingau—a monk—had to obtain written permission from his abbot before beginning the annual grape harvest. The required document was always delivered by a messenger on horseback. This autumnal courier arrived late that year and, when he finally came, some of the grapes had begun to rot. The monks vinified the rotten grapes anyway, but separately. One of them later reported to the abbot that these "rotten" grapes had yielded "such a wine as has never before passed my lips." Today, a statue of the mounted messenger stands in the courtyard of the castle.

Actually, wine was being made from overripe grapes at Tokaj, in Hungary, over a hundred years earlier. The monk winemaker at that castle is said to have been forced to put off the grape harvest because of an impending attack by the Turks. When the danger had passed, noble rot had spread. According to legend, that is how the first noble-sweet wine was made out of botrytized grapes.

In France, the value of noble rot was fully understood in 1847, at Château d'Yquem. The owner, marquis Bertrand de Lur-Saluces, returned late from a trip to Russia; the grapes in his vineyard had acquired noble rot. Nonetheless, they were picked, and 1847 turned out to be the greatest vintage of the nineteenth century.

The Third Stage of Ripeness

The majority of the grapes in the bunch are affected by noble rot. The must weight is between 125 and 159° Oechsle (at least 25° KMW). The botrytized grapes in the bunch may have to be harvested with scissors. They furnish little must, but their extract is extremely potent and high in fructose.

The Fourth Stage of Ripeness

The bunch is completely withered by noble rot, with an Oechsle reading of over 160° (at least 30 KMW). The grapes have practically shrunk down to raisins and contain a minimum of juice. The must is all the richer in sugar and acids. Often botrytized grapes are picked one at a time with fingers or even tweezers.

The Climax of the Vintner's Year

Grape picking at Château Haut-Brion in Bordeaux: The shorter the distance from vineyard to cellar, the faster the grapes are brought to safety.

The harvest is the culmination of the wine year, but also its most critical point. Only through carefully planned picking is it possible to bring the grapes into the cellar without losing some of the perfection the vineyard produced.

On the surface, picking grapes is a simple process. The bunches are cut from the vine with a pair of scissors and placed in a small plastic basket or box, which is periodically emptied into a wooden vat or tub. The grapes are finally poured into a larger container, often called a gondola in the United States, or into a trailer, and pulled by tractor into the winery, where they are processed. In rough outline, this process is the same no matter where grapes are grown. Whether very good grapes will yield a very good wine, however, depends on many, many details, not least of which is the cleanliness and design of the pickers' tubs. Tubs, baskets, and vats cannot be too large or be filled too fully, or the grapes on the bottom will be crushed by the weight of the ones on top. The skin of ripe grapes is thin and fragile.

The Danger of Oxidation

It is crucial that the grapes reach the winery quickly and without injury. Spilled grape juice oxidizes quickly when it is exposed to air; this is true especially of the juice of white grapes. To prevent oxidation, grapes have to be treated with sulfur dioxide, the first of several necessary operations that can diminish the perfect quality of the crop.

Another danger arises from the fact that spilled grape juice quickly starts fermenting, particularly in the warm temperatures that generally prevail at harvest time. Such uncontrolled or wild fermentation can give the must a vinegary sharpness, and there is a possibility—undesirable in both white and red grapes—of phenols being leached out of the stems by the juice of injured grapes.

Speeding the Process of Harvesting

The closer the vineyards are to the cellar, the fewer difficulties will arise. The world's top winemakers, such as Domaine de la Romanée-Conti or Château Mouton-Rothschild, get their picked grapes into their cellars in no more than two hours time. Cooperatives and large wineries are happy if their grapes are in the winery

the same day they were picked—and with fixed working hours and strict laws governing labor conditions, that is no mean feat.

Lessening the Differences Between Vintages

In wet autumns, rains may cause the ripe grapes to take in lots of extra water, seriously diluting the must. Some of the Bordeaux châteaus use completely new techniques to minimize the effects of rain. To prevent the fruit from absorbing the sudden floods of water, some owners cover the ground with plastic sheeting, which keeps the water from soaking into the soil. Other châteaus try to use hydrolysis (artificial removal of water) after the grapes are crushed, to reconcentrate their diluted must. This is also called reverse osmosis. Still other winemakers send their grapes though a heat tunnel before crushing them, which at least dries their skins. The owners of Château Pétrus have been known to keep a helicopter hovering low over the vineyards after a rain to dry the grapes before picking them. Not all of these measures are completely successful. Some are merely expensive. One thing is certain: the damage done

1

2

3

4

5

6

It is important to get the grapes into the winery quickly and without damage. The smaller the collecting bins, the better the chances that no grapes will be crushed prematurely.

1 *Lidded collecting bin of plastic.*
2 *Cane baskets let air circulate through them.*
3 *Small, perforated collecting box.*
4 *Traditional wooden tub.*
5 *Stackable, medium-sized collecting tubs.*
6 *Old-fashioned wooden trug.*

by bad weather at harvest time can nowadays be curtailed considerably.

Grape Harvest by Night

Many wineries in hot regions of Australia, where daytime temperatures reach between 35° and 45°C, have begun to pick grapes after dark. This can mitigate the danger of oxidation and wild fermentation. Since the nights are cooler, the otherwise unavoidable application of sulfur dioxide can also be skipped. Night harvesting is only possible when it is done by machines; mechanical harvesters are equipped with halogen lamps that beam their strong light onto the vines.

Handpicking or Mechanical Harvesting?

Machines are found in more and more grape regions of the world: the grapes are picked not by hand but by so-called integrated machine harvesters. Nor are they used only in areas where wine is mass produced. Grape harvesters are sent out in some of the well-known domaines of Burgundy and *grand cru classé* châteaus of Bordeaux. They roll above the rows on high wheels and literally knock off the grapes with a complicated shaking or striking mechanism, which separates the bunches from the shoots.

The greatest advantage of mechanical harvesters is their speed. One machine can harvest in one hour what it would take thirty grape workers to pick in the same time. With machines it is possible to bring in the entire harvest at the optimum moment. In wet years, the harvesters have proven especially useful: in the short intervals between bouts of precipitation, they can harvest considerable portions of the remaining crop.

In wet years, when gray mold is a possibility, the wet-picked grapes have to be checked by hand—machines cannot select for quality. Harvesters also have disadvantages: they can injure the canopy of the vines and tend to damage more of the fruit than handpicking would.

The Sweet Sweat of Angels

The work of picking out the good berries: In the vineyard of the Ruwer estate Maximin Grünhäuser, grapes affected by noble rot are set apart for valuable Auslesen and Beerenauslesen.

Sauternes combine sweetness with high alcoholic strength (14–15 percent by volume). German Beeren-auslesen and rockenbeerenauslese combine sweetness with high acidity, yet their alcohol content is very low (about 7 percent by volume).

The last grapes to be picked are those destined for late sweet wines; they may have to wait until November. At that point, they do not look very good: brown, shriveled, and rotten. Picking them is meticulous work. For sauternes or Trockenbeerenauslese, the grapes sometimes have to be picked off the bunch with the fingers or with a pair of pincers.

When grapes are allowed to hang on the vines after they are fully ripe, they begin to lose their juices. In this manner, sugar and acids become concentrated. This is the natural process on which the production of the elegantly sweet wines rests.

Two factors make the process possible: on the one hand, the skin of the fruit becomes thinner and thinner, until it allows water to pass through. On the other, there is the appearance of the grape mold *Botrytis cinerea,* whose spores grow through the skins and leave behind microscopic holes. The first produces raisinlike, shriveled fruit; the second covers the shriveled fruit with a mold. These two factors have the same effect: they cause the water within the berries—which is originally 90 percent of its bulk—to evaporate through the now-porous skin. The outcome is that the relative concentration of the other components of grape juice, the extract, increases.

The best-known wines made from such grapes are the French sauternes, the Hungarian Tokays, and the German and Austrian Beerenauslese and Trockenbeerenauslese. These supersweet, intensely flavored wines are counted among the world's rarest, most expensive, and most sought-after wines. They are nectar, say the connoisseurs—or "sweet angel sweat."

Special Climatic Conditions

We find the beneficent mold *Botrytis cinerea* only in temperate regions, and there only under certain special circumstances. Where moist morning fog is regularly dissolved by the sun of warm autumn days, the grapes get wet, but have a chance to dry completely by evening. Such conditions are rare.

In sauternes, the moisture is supplied by the river Ciron, and the daytime heat by the sun of Bordeaux. In Germany the early morning mists rise above the Rhine, the Mosel, the Saar, and the Ruwer, and high temperatures result from the intensity of the sun in autumn and from the angle of the vine slopes, which receive reflected heat from the waters and from the stony ground. The unique wines of Austria are due to a combination of the proximity of the Neusiedlersee and the hot autumns of Pannonia. As for the Hungarian Tokay, it is moistened by the fog off the Tisza and Bodrog Rivers and dried by the heat trapped within the region by the Carpathian Mountains.

With or Without Botrytis

Noble rot does not appear every year. In 1985 and 1990, for example, very few sauternes were affected by *Botrytis cinerea.* Thus, the concentration and sweetness of the wines resulted from the normal evaporation of water from the grapes alone. Wines made in such years are somewhat less sweet and have a slightly higher acid content than those made from in-

Grapes for the Vin Santo of Tuscany: Picked early, then spread on straw mats to dry.

Wine That Comes In from the Cold

One of the rarities in the sweet category is ice wine. This wine gets its special quality by being harvested and crushed while frozen. Obviously, for this to happen freezing weather is indispensable.

Since the water content of the berries has largely turned to ice, what little juice can be pressed out contains a very high proportion of sugars, acids, and other extract components. In other words, the lower the temperature and the more solidly frozen the grapes, the more concentrated the must. The grapes have to be at least at 19.4°F (minus 7°C) when they arrive at the presses. Often such low temperatures are not sustained until Christmas or even into the new year.

Ice wines are produced in quantity only in Germany, Austria, and Canada. They have a higher acid content than wines made from botrytis-infected grapes. Occasional pressings of frozen grapes did occur in the nineteenth century, but the first official ice wines appeared in 1949, on the Saar. In 1961

Ice wine grapes: Pure extract.

they were introduced with great publicity everywhere in Germany. Attempts to produce artificial ice wine by freezing fully ripe grapes after picking have not yielded satisfactory results, and to do this is now illegal.

fected grapes. Whether these variants are preferred to botrytized wines is simply a matter of taste.

Greater Complexity

The complexity of taste that differentiates botrytis-infected wines from other sweet wines comes from their higher levels of oily-sweet glycerin and volatile acetic acid and several enzymes all their own. The noble rot also reduces total acidity more than sugars. For this reason, wines from affected grapes are sweeter than those made from normally shriveled ones, in which sugar and acids are reduced at about the same rate.

Undesirable Gray Mold

Hot and humid climates exist in many grape-growing regions. If moisture does not dry rapidly, and particularly during prolonged rains, the *Botrytis* fungus will spread through the vineyards. This feared variant of *Botrytis cinerea*, called gray rot or bunch rot, causes the skin of the berry to burst and the pulp to be washed away—the grapes rot on the vine. Because the risk of gray rot is especially great in hot Mediterranean climates, in these regions dessert wines are not achieved through late grape harvests. Instead, the grapes are harvested early, laid out on straw mats to shrivel, and gathered into the cellar only after about two months of drying. The must is correspondingly rich in sugar.

Picking ice wine in Rheinhessen: Grapes for ice wine must be pressed at 19.4°F (minus 7°C). The more solidly frozen they are, the higher their sugar concentration and, therefore, their must weight.

Survival of the Fittest

The research of ampelographers, or grapevine specialists, has turned up about 10,000 different varieties of the species *Vitis vinifera,* but relatively few of these have any commercial significance. Ninety-five percent of the world's wines are made from the fifty most commonly planted grape varieties, which originated in Europe or in Asia Minor.

In prehistoric times, an infinitely larger number of grape species must have existed. Diseases, droughts, and cold weather have caused the extinction of most of them. Only those vines that could adapt to local climatic and soil conditions survived. This adaptation went so far as to change the color of the berries of some species to dark blue or deep red, to give them protection against the strong sunlight in hot regions. Untold mutations have also developed over the millennia. In addition, new strains have come into being through accidental crossbreeding of wild vines, which are dioecious; that is, they produce different plants for bearing male and female flowers.

Over time, growers have selected those grapes best suited to winemaking, cultivating and propagating them through cuttings. Today's selection of varieties is the result of this complex process.

Cabernet Sauvignon

Cabernet sauvignon, an old grape variety that is planted around the world, is valued for its low yield and its high tannin content, which makes for very noble, dark red, long-lived wines with a scent reminiscent of black currants, cedar wood, or black pepper. What matters in cabernet sauvignon wines is their fine and complex bouquet, which develops with age. Wines made from fully ripe grapes are many-layered and tannin-rich. The variety ripens relatively late, so it can only be planted in warm regions or the wine will taste grassy or like green peppers. The cluster of the cabernet sauvignon grape is medium in size and densely set with dark blue, thick-skinned fruit.

For a long time, the provenance of this variety was a mystery. Then researchers at the University of Bordeaux determined that it is the scion of a spontaneous cross between cabernet franc and sauvignon blanc.

It was only toward the end of the eighteenth century that cabernet sauvignon was planted over large areas of Bordeaux. Since it was called *bidure*, ampelographers consider it likely that it is identical with the Biturica grape described by Pliny in his first-century treatise *Historia naturalis.* The name derives from the Bituriges, a tribe that had, in Pliny's time, established itself around the northern perimeter of the Pyrenees.

Today Bordeaux, and in particular the Médoc, with its pebbly, well-drained soils, is considered the homeland of cabernet sauvignon. In recent years the variety has also been planted in more southern regions of France, and it has become fashionable in Italy and Spain. The largest plantings of cabernet sauvignon outside France are in California, Chile, South Africa, Australia, and New Zealand. As a rule, cabernet sauvignon is combined with other varieties.

Aglianico
Counted among southern Italy's best black-skinned grapes, aglianico originated in Greece. Today it predominates in Campania and in the Basilicata, where it yields dark-colored, intense yet velvety wines, rich in tannins and very durable. The best-known Aglianico wine is Taurasi.

Alicante-bouschet
This teinturier, or red-fleshed grape is planted mostly in southern France. It is the result of a cross (petit bouschet x grenache). Its chief use today is to add color to blends of pale red wines.

Aramon
The oceans of pale red, flat wine mass-produced from aramon grapes are without any redeeming value. The variety is planted mostly in the Languedoc, Roussillon, and Hérault.

Blauer Portugieser
This vine furnishes mild reds with little tannin that are faintly reminiscent of burgundies. They are manufactured for mass consumption. Whether or not the vine really comes from Portugal or not is not clear, but its presence in Austria in the eighteenth century is well documented; from there it spread to Hungary, Yugoslavia, and Germany.

Blauer Wildbacher
This ancient variety is indigenous to western Styria, in Austria, and even today it is preserved almost exclusively in that region. Traditionally it is fermented into a local wine the color of onionskins, characterized by high acidity, known as Schilcher.

Blaufränkisch
Dark berries and an aromatic raciness are the hallmark of Austria's most significant red variety. Cultivated mostly in the Burgenland and in some vineyards in the Carnuntum region, along the Danube, the variety produces distinctive, richly faceted wines. They have recently been blended in noble *cuvées* with cabernet sauvignon and other wines.

In Germany the variety is known as Limberger or Lemberger. It is grown in Württemberg, where it yields wines that in some years turn out to be superior to those made of pinot noir grapes. In Hungary, the variety is called Kékfrankos.

Brachetto
Now rare, brachetto stems from Piedmont. Originally it yielded dry reds, but it is now used mostly for a sweet, *frizzante* (semisparkling) red wine and for sweet dessert wines. In France it is known as Braquet.

Syrah

One of the noblest of black grape varieties, Syrah grows above all on the Rhône. More or less pure Syrah wines include the majestic Hermitage, the elegant Côte Rôtie, the lighter Saint-Joseph and Cornas, and the red Crozes-Hermitage. Syrah is also blended into Châteauneuf-du-Pape and other wines of the southern Rhône region. All of them are deeply colored, rich in tannins, and can boast of a bittersweet, spicy (berry) aroma.

No one knows whether the vine is native to the Rhône Valley or whether it was indeed brought there by traders from the ancient Persian city of Shiraz. It is called Shiraz in Australia, where, aside from cabernet sauvignon, it is the most widely planted vine variety.

Cabernet Franc

Presumed to be a mutation of cabernet sauvignon, cabernet franc cannot come anywhere near sauvignon's noble quality. Cabernet franc is used mostly in assemblage with cabernet sauvignon and merlot. Five to 15 percent cabernet franc serves to lend a Bordeaux its sparkling aroma of spice. Valuable cabernet franc varietal wines are only made in Saint-Emilion; good ones, along the lower Loire (Bourgueil, Chinon, Anjou-Villages, Champigny).

The variety is widely planted in the Alto Adige, the Veneto, and Friuli, where it is fermented into relatively simple, grassy single-grape wines. In the grape regions of the New World, it is grown exclusively for blending.

Gamay

A traditional red Beaujolais variety, gamay is usually made into light, hearty wines with the aroma of fresh fruit, though a few more substantial wines are also fermented from it. These are made in the Beaujolais *cru* vineyards, such as Brouilly, Morgon, Chiroubles, Fleurie, or Moulin-à-Vent. This latter group of wines can be aged for a few years, while the light reds, too poor in tannins and acids for durability, must be enjoyed young. Gamay is also planted along the Loire, where it is used for simple table wines. Switzerland also has some extensive gamay plantings. The variety has not taken hold in California.

Garnacha (Grenache)

The black-berried vine most widely established in Spain, both in the north (Navarre, Riocha) and in the south (La Mancha), garnacha is usually allowed to produce too heavily. Nonetheless, given poor soils, it can yield fine, even superior wines. The best ones are fermented in the isolated Priorato, where garnacha was once the most widely cultivated grape, only to be supplanted by cariñena.

The garnacha vine probably originated in Aragon, in northern Spain. From there it found its way to southern France, where, called grenache, it has been extensively planted. It is made into Lirac and Tavel, both rosé wines, and also yields the base wine for Châteauneuf-du-Pape. In Sardinia it is grown under the name cannonau.

Brunello

This grape is the source of Brunello di Montalcino, a wine of southern Tuscany. Brunello is a name used in Montalcino and refers to this local variant of the sangiovese grosso grapevine.

Canaiolo

A native of central Italy, canaiolo is a generous bearer and yields a somewhat rustic wine. It has traditionally been the second most important variety in Chianti, but it is more extensively established in Torgiano, in Umbria.

Corvina

From the deeply colored clusters of the corvina, the basic wines for both Valpollicella and Amarone are made. Although it was traditionally blended with rondinella and molinara, nowadays it is also made into a pure varietal table wine.

Cot or Côt

Another name for malbec, it is found in southwestern France, mostly in Cahors, and is now rarely planted.

Counoise

A good-quality, late-ripening grape that contributes in small amounts to many Châteauneuf-du-Pape wines.

Dolcetto

Indigenous to the Piedmont, this variety is made into purplish, fleshy, dry wines. They serve as popular everyday wines in Monferrato and in the Langhe.

Dornfelder

This German hybrid (Helfensteiner x Heroldrebe) has in the last few years been established in the Palatinate and in Württemberg. In those regions, its wines tend to be dark red, with aroma and fruit, and are often more successful than the late-ripening Spätburgunder (pinot noir) wines.

Durif

An alternative name for petite sirah, a grape grown in California.

Feteasca Negra

While quantitatively this is the most significant grapevine of Romania, in terms of quality it is not important. It is better known as black maiden's grape.

Freisa

This old native of Monferrato in the Piedmont, light red in color, is now less commonly planted. Mostly, it is made into sweet, sparkling red wines, but it is also capable of yielding strong, dry reds.

Merlot

The merlot grape's range of uses offers a varied picture. On the one hand, since it is an immensely productive vine, unless its vigor is curtailed by the grower it will make simple peasant wines. On the other hand, some of the greatest red wines in the world are created from merlot grapes. The best are those from Saint-Emilion, especially those from the Pomerol region, first among them the legendary châteaus Pétrus and Le Pin. The gravel soils of this part of the Bordeaux region are interleaved with clay, and on these, merlot yields ruby-red, full-bodied wines of enormous distinction. Although these wines have fewer tannins, less acidity, and a correspondingly lower durability than wines made of cabernet sauvignon, they have higher alcoholic strength. Their aroma, when young, resembles that of young cabernet sauvignon wines, but instead of the rough, aristocratic strength, they present a rich fruity and malty nose.

The oldest records seem to indicate that the Saint-Emilion and Pomerol regions are the merlot's native habitat. It is certain at least that at the beginning of the eighteenth century the merlot vine was very well established in that area. From there it reached the Médoc, where is has become, after cabernet sauvignon, the second most planted variety.

Today merlot has spread around the globe, and the acreage under this variety is growing faster than that planted with cabernet sauvignon. There are at least four reasons for this relatively faster expansion. First of all, merlot ripens a week or ten days earlier than cabernet sauvignon, presenting less of a risk of failure to reach ripeness before cold weather sets in. Second, merlot blends comfortably with other wines. Third, merlot does not require quite so favorably exposed sites and will thrive in cooler microclimates. Fourth, it is naturally more prolific than cabernet sauvignon. In Italy, in eastern Europe, and in Australia it is being established in many vineyards. In California it became a fashionable variety in the 1990s. In the Ticino, in southern Switzerland, merlot has been cultivated for decades.

Frühburgunder
This early-ripening, thick-skinned black variety is considered a mutation of the pinot noir grape, known as Spätburgunder in Germany, where it is planted in limited amounts. Although its color is weak, it can be made into outstanding quality wines.

Gaglioppo
Calabria's best red variety, gaglioppo delivers robust, aromatic, tannin-rich wines. Originally a Greek grape, it was imported to Italy more than 2,000 years ago. The best-known gaglioppo wine is Cirò.

Jurançon Noir
A rather simple black variety nowadays used only for blending, in grape regions like Gaillac or Cahors. The grape can also be encountered in the Jurançon region itself, where it is *not* used to make white Jurançon wine, however.

Lambrusco
This grape is found throughout the length of Italy, from Venice to Sicily. The beverage industry bottles it as a sweet and *frizzante,* or frothing, drink, but the true lambrusco is a still, dry, and thoroughly satisfying everyday wine.

Marzemino
Marzemino grows in the small district of Trentino. It is made into a simple, tasty red with a cherry aroma.

Montepulciano
Rooted in the Marches and the Abruzzi, this grape has spread all through central Italy. It produces a somewhat rough, often alcohol-heavy wine. At its best, it is delicate and full of character. Often combined with sangiovese or Uva di Troia, it adds power to such well-known wines as Rosso Conero and Rosso Piceno. It is not planted in the city of Montepulciano.

Morellino
Only found in southern Tuscany, near Scansano, this is a regional variant of the sangiovese grosso variety.

Mourvèdre
Today this originally Spanish variety is experiencing a renaissance in Provence, especially in Bandol. With its small, thick-skinned grapes it is able to yield dark, tannin-rich wines of gamy fruitiness. They are ideal for blending. In Spain, the variety is called monastrell. It dominates the regions of Alicante, Valencia, Jumilla, and Almansa.

Cinsaut

Cinsaut has been known for centuries in the Languedoc; some quality winemakers in the *départements* of Aude and Hérault rediscovered this strain during the last few decades, and the cinsaut grape has since had a revival throughout southern France. With good *terroir* and severe pruning, the variety is well suited for blending with mourvèdre, grenache, and even cabernet sauvignon. With its dark color and fruitiness, cinsaut adds aroma to these grand varieties. It is hardly ever fermented by itself. The variety is also widespread in Algeria, Morocco, and Lebanon. Sometimes it is spelled cinsault.

Carignan

Known as carignane in the United States, this prolific new producer is widely planted now in southern France; European wine surpluses are significantly augmented by it every year. The grape is called Cariñena in Spain, where it is widely planted in the northeast. Because of its high productivity, the vine is popular also in southern California, in Mexico, and in Latin America, where it is used for mass-produced wines.

Despite this general misuse, winemakers in Languedoc and Roussillon, and in parts of Spain such as the Priorato, have shown that, properly pruned, carignan can be made into fine wines that are full of character.

Barbera

A Piedmont variety, Barbera is usually fermented by itself into wines such as the well-known Barbera d'Asti and Barbera d'Alba. The vine is mentioned for the first time in 1799 as *Vitis vinifera Monferratensis.* Today it is cultivated all over Italy, in places such as Oltrepò Pavese, Franciacorta, Valpolicella, the Trentino, Emilia-Romana, and southern Italy, as well as in California. Barbera grapes are characterized by low tannins and high acidity. Unless severely curtailed, the variety tends to overproduce; it is therefore used in the manufacture of simple and super-simple wines.

Nebbiolo

Nebbiolo is a demanding grape, late to ripen, relatively light in color, but rich in tannins and consequently able to yield wines of great longevity. The vine has been documented in northern Italy since the year 1303, but it is certain to be much, much older. The most famous nebbiolo wines are Barolo and Barbaresco. Both of them are fermented as pure varieties. Gattinara and Ghemme are nebbiolo wines that may be assembled with small additions of other varieties. Roero and Nebbiolo d'Alba are also made solely of Nebbiolo grapes.

Petit Verdot

Petit verdot is a valuable variety planted chiefly in the Bordeaux region, where it has been established longer than cabernet sauvignon. Wines made from it are almost a black red, tannin-rich, strongly acidic, and with a fine nose. Not planted very much today, petit verdot is present in all Margaux wines to the level of 5 percent.

Petite Sirah

This grape variety of middling quality does not have a clear pedigree. In California it is called durif. One thing is certain: it has nothing to do with the true Syrah grape. Planted in the hot San Joaquin Valley as well as in the cooler Monterey area, it has proved useful in blends with zinfandel and pinot noir.

Picpoul or Piquepoul Noir

Picpoul is an ancient native grape of the Languedoc, growing in the sandy, coastal vineyards of the Mediterranean. It is one of the thirteen varieties permitted in Châteauneuf-du-Pape.

Pinotage

In 1925 pinot noir and cinsaut were crossed to produce this hybrid vine. It is particularly suitable to the conditions prevalent in South Africa, where it is widely planted with good result. Pinotage wines are relatively dark in color, and in youth they have a earthy, spicy aroma. This soon develops into a beautiful, expressive fruitiness. South Africa also manufactures many low-quality wines out of pinotage grapes.

Pinot Meunier

Because it is so resistant to frost, meunier is the most frequently planted variety in the Champagne; it is also one of the three grape varieties traditionally assembled into Champagne, albeit only to a small extent. Although pinot meunier is regarded as rustic and overly fruity, according to the traditional view it has to be part of every good Champagne precisely to lend the recipe some of its fruit. The variety descends from pinot noir. It is also planted in Württemberg, where it is called Schwarzriesling or Müllerrebe. The leaves of the vine are downy and look as if they had been dusted with flour. This explains the reference to millers *(meunier, Müller)* in its names.

Plavac Mali

The best red variety in Slovenia and Croatia, plavac mali yields dense, full-bodied wines of extraordinary longevity.

Pinot Noir

One of the world's oldest vine varieties, pinot noir can yield wines of elegance and grandeur as well as plump and modest ones. Its color is a medium cardinal red, its aroma conveys mellow fruitiness. The clusters are remarkably small, closely set with numerous thin-skinned grapes. When vinified, they yield a wine correspondingly low in tannins. Many winemakers press pinot noir grapes with their stalks to augment the tannins.

Burgundy is without question the home of pinot noir. It is well documented there; records mentioning the variety date back to the fourteenth century, but it is assumed that it grew there at least a thousand years earlier. Today, pinot noir completely dominates the vineyards of the Côte d'Or, having supplanted gamay. Chambertin, Musigny, Pommard, and Volnay are some of the great names the region is known for. The most famous wine estate is Domaine de la Romanée-Conti.

The pinot noir grape has spread well beyond the borders of Burgundy, however. It is raised in Alsace and in Champagne; vinified into a white wine there, it constitutes the basis of champagne. In Germany, where it is known as Spätburgunder or Blauer Burgunder, it is found in the southern Pfalz, in Baden, in Assmannshausen on the Rhine, on the Ahr, and on the central Main, around Klingenberg. In Austria there are some plantings in the Burgenland, and in Italy, in Alto Adige. The grape grows as far south as Tuscany, though it does not vinify well in warm climates.

Because of its predilection for cool weather, in the United States pinot noir is planted more in the cooler state of Oregon than in California. Only occasional plantings are found in Australia and South Africa. Pinot noir is one of the few grapes that is almost always made into pure varietal wines.

Prugnolo Gentile
In the Tuscan region of Montepulciano, Prugnolo Gentile is a local variant of the Sangiovese variety.

Sagrantino
A very valuable red variety of Umbria, most dominant in the area around Montefalco. It yields strong, dark red wines with palpable spice and a light sweetness in the bouquet. In the absence of any markets for great sagrantino wines beyond the region's borders, for decades the grape was used for sweet dessert wines. Today it is once more made into high-caliber dry red wines of great complexity.

Saint Laurent
Although the probable provenance of this grape variety is Alsace, nowadays it is only encountered in Austria. This vine makes few demands on the soil, guarantees good yields, and—under the best circumstances—produces a velvety, aromatic red wine. In many years, however, its wines turn out flat, lacking all expressiveness.

Samtrot
From this mutation of the Müllerrebe, which has recently been established in Württemberg, quite solid, even fine varietal wines are now made.

Schiava
Italian for Vernatsch, a grape of the Alto Adige or South Tyrol.

Schwarzriesling
One name for pinot meunier grapes in Württemberg; also Müllerrebe.

Shiraz
In Australia the syrah grape is called Shiraz, after the ancient Persian city of that name.

Tannat
Native to the southwest of France, tannat makes high demands on the grower. Its wines are deep red and tannin-rich. The grape is seldom used for varietal wines, and is usually blended with other varieties. It is chiefly found near the Pyrenees, for example, in Madiran, in Irouléguy, in Tursan, in Béarn, and even in Cahors.

Teinturier
French name for all grape varieties with colored flesh, designed to mask or enhance the paleness of other red wines. Most teinturier grapevines are based on the dark-colored Teinturier de Cher, which was crossed with the pale aramon to yield the petit bouschet variety. Petit bouschet, still widely planted in France, was then used in many experimental hybrids, until the teinturier (red-fleshed) grape was developed.

Sangiovese

Tuscany is the most significant wine region dominated by the sangiovese vine, Italy's most important variety. There it constitutes the basis for Chianti, for Vino Nobile di Montepulciano, and for Brunello di Montalcino. Other areas, notably, Emilia-Romana, Umbria, Latium, and the Marches, also have substantial plantings of sangiovese. The variety has numerous local variants, the most important of which are sangiovese grosso and sangiovese piccolo. The grape ripens relatively late and brings forth wines that are fruity, with the toughness of tannins and the liveliness of acids, and require proper aging.

The sangiovese vine is mentioned for the first time in Tuscany in 1722. There also is some evidence to suggest that it goes back another 2,000 years to the Etruscans—to the very first attempts at winemaking in Italy.

Tempranillo

Tempranillo is Spain's most significant vine. The wines of the Ribera del Duero and to a large extent those of the Rioja are made from this variety. Locally it is also known as tinto fino or tinto del país, as for example, in the Ribera del Duero. Wines made of tempranillo are dark, full of tannins, strongly acidic: clearly predestined for a long life.

It is uncertain whether the tempranillo vine is of Spanish provenance or whether it was imported to Spain from France during the Middle Ages. What is certain is that in our time it is no longer found in France.

Malbec

Malbec used to be a very popular variety, but because of its tendency to shatter *(coulure)*, it is now in decline. Its wines are dark in color and strong in tannins. The most famous malbec wine is Cahors, from the southwest of France. The variety is there called cot or côt, and it is blended with others to make the "black wine of Cahors." While the variety used to be widely established in Bordeaux, it is now only used in a few wines and to a very small extent, for example, in some wines from the Graves region.

Zinfandel

Wines of very different character are made out of this red variety: reds, rosés, and, when the must is fermented without the skins, whites. Nonetheless, the typical and distinctive zinfandel wine is red.

It is almost exclusively in California that zinfandel is widely planted. Californian winemakers ferment zinfandel grapes into some top-quality wines, but it is also used in the mass-production of cheap jug wines. White Zinfandel is a sweet wine.

Zinfandel is assumed to descend from an Italian variety, the primitivo grapevine, which covers much acreage in Apulia. There it is made both into modest and simple table wines and into sweet fortified wines.

Teroldego

An ancient variety that thrives on the pebbly soils of the Trentino around Mezzocorona. Since the variety is forced to bear heavily, most wines made from it tend to be one-dimensional, with no tannins or acids. At its very best, however, teroldego yields wines with a lively character and great depth of aroma. Vine experts suspect that the Teroldego grape belongs to the syrah family.

Touriga

Touriga Nacional is a valuable Portuguese variety that forms the basis of all good vintage port. This small-fruited vine produces very sparingly, and for this reason is planted less frequently nowadays. Its wine also constitutes the main ingredient of all good Dão wines.

Trollinger

Although established in Württemberg, the Trollinger grape is really from the Alto Adige (South Tyrol), where it is known as Vernatsch. The grape is fermented into modest pale red wines that can rise to great heights of delicacy under certain circumstances. The wines tend to be retained in the Württemberg area.

Tsimlyansky Cherny

This is the most significant sparkling-wine variety of the Commonwealth of Independent States (CIS), especially along the Don River. In the Crimea it is used to produce a red champagne. High in alcohol and low in acidity, its wine has to be blended.

Vernatsch

In the Alto Adige or South Tyrol (as this German-speaking part of Italy is still called), this is the most common vine. In better versions, it offers a light, velvety wine with a delicate fruit and almond aroma. Most frequently, however, it is made into an unassuming red without much expression. The best-known Vernatsch wines are Saint Magdelener and Kalterer See. The variety has at least a half-dozen local strains. In Italian it is called schiava.

Xynomavro

The best of the Greek red vines, xynomavro is an ingredient in the well-known Macedonian wines Naoussa and Amynteon.

Zweigelt

This grape is an Austrian hybrid (Blaufränkisch x Saint Laurent). Its wines are noted for their fruit bouquet, their velvety body, and their taste of cherries. Zweigelt is encountered in practically all Austrian wine regions.

Chardonnay

Chardonnay is a noble grape variety. With great certainty its provenance can be traced back to Burgundy, where there even is a village named Chardonnay. Today the variety has spread all over the globe, producing wines that range from outstanding to ordinary, depending on clone selection, location, and cultivation. Of all white varieties, chardonnay has experienced the fastest growth rate in the last twenty-five years.

The very best chardonnay wines grow on the calcareous soils of Puligny-Montrachet, Meursault, Corton-Charlemagne, and Chablis. In these locations, pure varietal chardonnay wines are made. They have a nutty aroma that acquires a tinge of petroleum with age. In the recipe for champagne, Chardonnay represents 50 to 70 percent; in the *blanc de blancs*, this proportion becomes 100 percent.

Other large plantings of the variety are found in Mâconnais and on the Côte Chalonnaise. In Italy, one encounters chardonnay grapes mostly in the Trentino, in Alto Adige, in Franciacorta, and in Friuli. Recently, the variety has also taken root in Austria, where it is called Morillon in the south of Styria, and Feinburgunder in the Danube Valley. Outside of Europe, the chardonnay grape is extensively planted in California, mostly in Carneros and Sonoma Counties; in Maipo, Chile; and to some extent in South Africa, in New Zealand, and in Australia. In Australia chardonnay is usually fermented in small, new oak barrels that lend the wine a slight caramel taste.

The success of the chardonnay grape rests on its ability to produce wines of attractive quality on practically any type of soil. Chardonnay buds early, and the grape harvest cannot be left late, or valuable acids will be lost. It is now recognized to be a variety in its own right and not a mutation of the white burgundy grape, although many books still claim that it is.

Airén
Airén is the most common vine in Spain. Because of its good resistance to drought, it is planted above all in the torrid La Mancha area, where in the past it was made into heavy wines with high alcoholic strength. Today it is usually fermented into light, neutral, fruity ones.

Albana
Albana is an indigenous Italian vine especially widely distributed in Emilia-Romana. In that region it is made into a light, moderately fruity, rather short-lived wine named after the variety.

Albariño
An interesting, slightly fragrant variety, albariño yields dry, white wines full of character. It is chiefly planted in the Rias Baixas region of Galicia, in Spain. In Portugal, it is known as alvarinho and constitutes a part of white *vinho verde*.

Aligoté
Another Burgundy native, aligoté is made into pure varietals and makes powerful, full-bodied white wines with a character all of their own, which should be enjoyed when still young. The best of them come from the village of Bouzeron. Much aligoté has now been replaced by chardonnay, but outside France, in Bulgaria, Romania, and other eastern European countries, the variety is frequently encountered.

Assyrtico
The island of Santorini is the home of this top-quality Greek vine. It delivers both robust dry, white wines and the famous Liastos, sweet, liqueurlike, wines produced from semidried grapes.

Auxerrois
Auxerrois is a term used for a number of varieties but is also a variety in its own right. It had spread through France all the way to Germany, but today it is found only in Alsace and in the Palatinate. The variety is in no way related to either chardonnay or pinot blanc. In the southwestern part of France, the Cahors, they call the malbec grape auxerrois.

Bacchus
A hybrid (Silvaner x Riesling) was crossed with Müller-Thurgau to make this grape, which is planted in many regions of Germany. It produces a simple wine, lacking in acids, often with residual sweetness. Its powerful flavors make it a popular jug wine.

Chasselas

A classic Swiss variety, chasselas is documented as growing in Vaud canton 400 years ago; it is also known there as dorin. Today, almost half of all of Switzerland's vineyard acreage is planted with chasselas vines. Most of the wines made from them are light, simple, and often lacking in acids and expressiveness. Better chasselas wines do exist, however; among them are Fendant, Yvorne, Aigle, Saint-Saphorin, and Dézaley.

In Germany the variety is called Gutedel, and at the beginning of the century it was the country's most widely planted vine. Nowadays you have to go to the south of Baden to find vineyards of any size planted with this vine.

Chenin Blanc

Chenin blanc is a French grape, popular as a heavy producer. This variety is to be found in Anjou and in Touraine, on the lower Loire, where it is made into simple whites, such as Vouvray and Saumur. These wines are often finished sparkling, with residual sugar.

In the best locations, by contrast, chenin blanc will yield powerful, long-lived white wines that offer a definite acidity, as for example is the case with Coulée de Serrant. Outside of France, the most significant plantings of chenin blanc are in South Africa, where it is known also as Steen.

Gewürztraminer

Gewürztraminer is a valuable white grape variety with slightly reddish fruit. Because of its low and uncertain productivity, it is not planted frequently today. It is assumed to be a variant of the Traminer grape, which has yellow berries and is less aromatic. The Traminer is said to be from Alto Adige, an area still known among German speakers as the South Tyrol. When picked late, Gewürztraminer grapes can yield great qualities: golden yellow, strong, "masculine" wines, often with an alcohol content of well over 13 percent. Despite low acidity, they have a long life. Great Gewürztraminer, with the typical nose of lychee and roses, can be found in Alsace and in Germany.

Pinot Gris

A number of wines are produced from this popular white grape, many of them simple, others more complex, and a few that are exquisite. Its territory includes France, especially Alsace, (where they also call it Tokay), Germany (where it is known as Grauer Burgunder), Austria (where it is sometimes called Ruländer), and northern Italy, i.e., Alto Adige, and Friuli (where it is called Pinot Grigio). In the Veneto and the Trentino, the grape is used to make wines that are atypical but commercially very successful. The fruit may show a reddish blue shimmer, which attests to their descent from the pinot noir grape.

Bouvier

This Austrian hybrid is planted mostly in Styria and the Burgenland. It is regarded as a mass-producer and, as such, grown as a table grape. Its alternate reputation, as a "sugar collector," qualifies it for the production of distinguished wines.

Clairette

This variety from the south of France used to be the preferred grape for making vermouth, but is now used mostly in blending simple table wines.

Cortese

A simple, prolific grape variety from the Piedmont, cortese is best known for Gavi, a varietal wine made entirely from this grape.

Feteasca or Fetiaska

The most widely planted white variety of Romania, Feteasca yields fragrant and, at their best, full-bodied and long-lived wines. This vine is also planted in Bulgaria, in Hungary, and in Russia.

Folle Blanche

Folle Blanche is used for making cognac and is cultivated solely for this purpose around Nantes and Cognac, but in the past, it used to cover much land in the rest of France.

Furmint

Widely distributed throughout eastern Europe, but especially in Hungary, the furmint grape is made into fiery, alcohol-rich wines, which may be dry or sweet. The best known of them is the noble, sweet Tokay, one of the best and most long-lived dessert wines in the world.

Grechetto

Grechetto is one of the ancient grapes of Umbria; it is a traditional component of Orvieto and of the white wines of Torgiano.

Greco di Tufo

Originally from Greece, the Greco di Tufo vine is cultivated in southern Italy. The wines made from its grapes are full-bodied and occasionally fine, like the Greco di Tufo from Campania, the Cirò Bianco from Calabria, and the sweet wine Greco di Bianco.

Gutedel

This is the German name for the chasselas grape. In Germany, it is found in quantity only in the Margräflerland, in southern Baden.

Riesling

Riesling, or White Riesling, is a late-ripening variety that delivers outstanding wines in cool growing regions. The major domains of Riesling are Alsace and Germany. The grape is also raised in Austria, in Russia, and, to a small extent, in Australia and in California. It is difficult to determine whether it is indigenous to the Rhine, the Mosel, or the Palatinate. We know that in the fifteenth century it was widely planted along the Rhine, and in the sixteenth, also along the Mosel. There is a possibility that as far back as about 800 A.D. Riesling grapes were planted on the Rhine on the order of the German king Ludwig. Another theory is that in that region the variety had developed spontaneously out of wild *Vitis vinifera* grapes.

Whatever its provenance, the Riesling grape is demanding. In Germany, Alsace, and Austria, it will only yield significant wines if planted on steep, sunny slopes. All Riesling wines, even if picked late, retain a definite acidity. They are also rich in extracts and are extremely durable.

Because of its thick skin, the Riesling grape is fairly resistant to rot, which makes it unsuitable for the creation of sweet Beerenauslese wines, for which noble rot is a necessary condition.

In comparison to other varieties, Riesling loses less of its quality when it is made to produce somewhat heavily, but the result of the extensive mass-production now being practiced is a long list of moderate wines, many of them out of Germany, where the variety is a permitted ingredient of Liebfraumilch. In the United States, Riesling is variously known as Johannisberger Riesling, White Riesling, or Rhine Riesling.

Kerner
The Kerner grape is a hybrid (Trollinger x Riesling) that is mostly planted in Germany. It is a hardy variety that can make very good, light wines, somewhat emphatic in bouquet and acidity.

Macabeo, Maccabéo, or Macabeu
A traditional white variety, Macabeo is found in Rioja, Navarre, and other wine regions of northern Spain. It is also grown for cava production, i.e., blending into the Spanish sparkling wine that is made using the traditional Champagne method.

Malvasia
This name covers about a dozen strains of a white vine that, as a rule, produces wines of high alcoholic strength. It is widespread in Italy (Friuli, Piedmont, Tuscany, Latium, Sicily, Sardinia), but it can also be found in Portugal, where it is a component of port and Madeira.

Manseng
The manseng grape is a native of the French Basque country. It has a very valuable strain called petit manseng, which has been rediscovered and more widely planted in the last few years. This latter variety yields the base for the famous Jurançon wines made around the city of Pau in southwestern France, namely, the Jurançon Sec and its sweet version, for which the grapes are first dried before pressing. This variety is also much appreciated in Béarn and in Gascony, especially for making Pacherenc du Vic-Bilh. The less refined manseng gros serves mostly as a blending wine.

Marsanne
Found mostly in the northern Rhône valley, marsanne is a vigorous producer. Its wines are heavy, short-lived, and rather flabby. It is the basic component in Crozes-Hermitage.

Melon
This relatively undemanding, neutral-tasting variety grows almost exclusively around the mouth of the Loire. White muscadet wines are there made from melon grapes, e.g., muscadet de Sêvre-et-Maine. Since the variety can be traced back to the south of Burgundy, it is also known as melon de Bourgogne.

Morio-Muskat
Now in decline, this hybrid (Silvaner x Weissburgunder) was once a widely planted vine, especially in Germany. It produces white wines of excessive grapiness. It is unrelated to any muscat.

Grüner Veltliner

Grüner (green) Veltliner is a popular and generous vine. One-third of Austria's grape acreage is planted with it. Its highest concentration is found in the Weinviertel. The vine, which buds early and is harvested relatively late, there produces light, slightly effervescent wines that have a peppery spiciness. They are drunk when young, often with a shot of water ("G'spritzer").

In the best locations, Grüner Veltliner can be made into wines with plentiful extract and a high alcohol content. These *Spätlese* wines are made in the valleys of the Krems, the Kamp, and especially the Danube. There, the grape has been grown for only 100 years, but at its peak, bottled as Smaragd ("Emerald"), Grüner Veltliner yields highest-quality wines, longer-lived than Rieslings.

Müller-Thurgau

This is Germany's most frequently planted grapevine. It was known as a hybrid of Riesling and Silvaner, but is now recognized as the product of Riesling x Chasselas. It was bred in 1882 at the viticulture station in Geiseheim by a vine specialist named Hermann Müller, who came from the Thurgau canton in Switzerland.

Müller-Thurgau wines are usually simple, flat, and fragrant, with a slight muscat tone. They are the base wine for Liebfraumilch. Under the name Rivaner, the grape is fermented into smooth, elegant table wines. Finally, since the grape ripens early and collects sugar quickly, it is used also for Auslese and Beerenauslese wines. In Hungary, the variety is known as Rizlingszilváni (Riesling x Silvaner).

Muscat Blanc à Petits Grains

This very old, aromatic variety was probably known to the ancient Greeks *(anathelicon moschaton)* and Romans *(uva apiana)*. Today muscat grapes grow around the world, and there are many strains of the variety. The most valuable strain has many French names: muscat blanc and, because of its small, round fruit, also muscat blanc de petits grains or muscat de petits grains ronds, as well as muscat de Frontignan. It is known in Germany as Gelber Muskateller, "the yellow muscat." Some of the wines made from this fragrant variety include the Alsatian Muscat, the Muscato d'Asti from Piedmont, the dry Styrian Muskateller, and the Spanish Moscadel del Grano Menudo.

Scheurebe

This hybrid (Sylvaner x Riesling) was created in 1916 by Dr. Georg Scheu, then head of a vine research station situated near Worms, in Hessen. It turned out to be one of the very few new varieties to thrive and spread in Germany. Planted in good locations, the Scheurebe generates delicate wines that impress with a cassis-scented bouquet. Unfortunately, good locations are generally reserved for Riesling grapes, so it is rare to find a great Scheurebe wine. Mostly the variety is made into flowery wines with too much bouquet, and not infrequently, with residual sweetness as well.

Mtsvane

This valuable variety is grown in Georgia and the Crimean. It produces stylish, fruity-fresh whites of good quality.

Muscadelle

Contained in small amounts in most of the bordeaux whites, muscadelle bears generously and ripens early. Its coarse fruitiness and rusticity are not in demand today, and it is now rarely planted. It has nothing to do with the muscat grape.

Muscat d'Alexandrie

A minor variant of the muscat vine, this is used for making sweet fortified wines and brandies in Spain, Portugal, Sicily (where it is called Zibibbo), South Africa, and Chile. Otherwise, it is a table grape that is also used for making raisins.

Muscat Hamburg

This variety is hardly used for winemaking any more; it is a table grape. Its pigmentation tends to turn it a dark blue. It is, however, a member of the muscat family.

Muscat-Ottonel

Probably the product of a cross between muscat de Saumur and chasselas, this variant of the muscat vine is less valuable than the muscat blanc.

It is still widely established in Austria and Hungary, but it is now in decline there, as is also the case in Germany.

Neuburger

Austria's Burgenland and Thermenregion are the places where Neuburger plantings can be found. The origins of the grape are unknown. The wines made from it are strong, with a neutral fruit and a delicate nutty aroma.

Pedro Ximénez or Pedro Jiménez

Pedro Ximénez vineyards used to cover large areas of Jerez, where the grape was used in the production of sherry. The variety has declined sharply in Spain; the largest plantings of it are now in Australia. It is made into fortified wines and brandies.

Picolit, Piccolit, or Piccolito

This white grape variety from the Friuli is made into a simple, sweet, and extremely expensive dessert wine. The picolit grape has a tendency to shatter *(coulure)*, so its yields are very limited and uncertain.

Sauvignon

Sauvignon, or sauvignon blanc, is a high-class vine variety that has spread all over the globe, and is still expanding rapidly. Although the vine's budbreak is fairly late in the spring, the grapes can be picked relatively early in the fall. It is very likely that the variety's native habitat was Bordeaux, where it is still the most-planted white grape.

Together with sémillon—and in some cases with muscat—sauvignon forms a reliable component in such wines as Graves, Pessac-Léognan, Entre-Deaux-Mers, as well as in white bordeaux and nobly sweet sauternes. Yet today, the most significant wine region with respect to sauvignon is without a doubt the central Loire, the areas around Sancerre and Pouilly-Fumé. The flinty limestone soils of that region seem to bring out most clearly the characteristic aroma of sauvignon, reminiscent of gooseberries, nettles, or green fruit. Other important European sauvignon regions are Styria and the Burgenland in Austria—where the old and misleading name Muskat-Sylvaner is still in use—as well as Slovenia and the Italian Friuli.

Outside of Europe, the sauvignon grape has given rise to fashions such as the Californian Fumé Blanc, fermented in wooden casks. It is also planted in Chile, Australia, and to a great extent in South Africa. Sauvignon wines from New Zealand surprise with their intensive perfume.

Most sauvignon wines are heavy: their alcohol content is usually over 13 percent, especially those made in the New World. In contrast to the high-class chardonnays, sauvignon wines show their finesse while they are still young and do not age well.

Plavac
Out of this, the most important grape of Slovenia, simple, neutral-fruit wines are made. They quite often have a full-bodied palate.

Prosecco
Native to the Veneto, this grape ripens relatively late and produces wines with relatively high acidity. It is suspected that the original vines came from Istria. The grape is known mainly for prosecco frizzante or prosecco spumante, less for the still wines made from it.

Ribolla
A variety used for light, racy, rustic wines in Friuli.

Rkatsiteli
By a wide margin, this is the most frequently planted grapevine in the Commonwealth of Independent States, also one of the most commonly grown white grapes of Europe. It can be made into powerful, full-bodied, and acid-rich wines; sweet, fortified wines; or sherry-like aperitif wines.

Rotgipfler
This is a traditional grape from Gumpoldskirchen in Austria. It yields full-bodied, durable white wines with a distinctly spicy character.

Roussanne
Roussanne is a demanding vine that grows along the Rhône. It is usually fermented together with marsanne.

Ruländer
This synonym for pinot gris is often employed in Germany to refer to full-bodied wines made of that grape, but finished with some residual sweetness.

Savagnin
The French Jura is the home of this noble grape. It is made into the famous, sherry-like *vin jaune*. One also encounters it in the Arbois district.

Savatiano
Used more than any other white grape in Greece, Savatiano yields the base wine for the alcoholic, resinated retsina.

Steen
Steen is the traditional name for chenin blanc in South Africa.

Tocai or Tocai Friulano
An aboriginal grape variety of Friuli, Tocai grows in the majority of the vineyards of that region. Most tocais are fresh, fruity everyday wines. The best can have personality.

Sémillon

Sémillon, a Bordeaux variety, is regarded as a noble grape because many valuable sweet wines are made from it, as its thin-skinned fruit makes it particularly vulnerable to noble rot. The most famous of these sweet wines is Château d'Yquem, which consists of 80 percent sémillon.

Fermented normally, the grape will yield full-bodied, "fat" wines; when young, they taste rather neutral. For this reason, sémillon is usually blended with sauvignon and other varieties.

Unless well pruned, the variety tends to produce too generously. It is planted mostly in the Bordeaux region, but is also found in the Dordogne, in Chile (Maipo), and in Australia (the Hunter and Barossa valleys).

Silvaner or Sylvaner

This old vine is indigenous to Germany, where it is still counted among the most-planted varieties. Since it is generally allowed to produce abundantly, the wines made of its grapes are modest and without expression. When its fruitfulness is curtailed, however, it can yield full wines with a tender fruit. These are found most frequently in Franconia, in Alsace, and in Austria, where the name is spelled Sylvaner. In the Rhine-Hesse region, the simple wines made of Silvaner grapes are aimed at the mass market. In Switzerland, where the variety is called Johannisberg or Gros Rhin, it produces some notable wines.

Viognier

Viognier is an old variety, low in yield, that thrives and gives best results in the dry, warm climate of the Rhône Valley. Its best-known wines are white Condrieu and the rare Château Grillet, both heavy, long-lived white wines with relatively high alcohol content and heady aroma. Viognier is permitted in the red wines of the Côte Rôtie, up to a level of 20 percent. In Languedoc and Roussillon, viognier is often fermented with other white varieties, but since the 1980s, pure varietal whites are also being made of viognier grapes in those areas, a trend that has now taken root also in Italy and California.

White Burgundy or Weisser Burgunder

Very good wines with strong personality can be made from this old grape variety. It covers much territory in Baden and the Palatinate, in Germany, where it is also called Weissburgunder and Clener. It enjoys equal success in Austria, in the Italian Alto Adige and Friuli, in Hungary, in Slovenia, and in Croatia. The French name for it is pinot blanc. Inside France, it is only grown in Alsace, where it is used with good results. For decades the variety was called pinot chardonnay, but now it has been established to be a descendant of pinot noir, a connection borne out by the wine's tender-spicy bouquet and its racy acidity.

Traminer

This white vine, also known as red traminer, is the mother-vine of Gewürztraminer. Slightly aromatic wines of good quality are made of traminer grapes, but very seldom outstanding ones.

Trebbiano

This is the Italian name for the ugni blanc variety, which can be counted among the world's most popular white vines. It is an undemanding and unexpressive variety that occurs in Italy in numerous guises, as Frascati, Soave, Lugana, Procanico, and Bianco di Val di Chiana. It is also a brandy grape.

Verdejo

Verdejo is an old and noble Spanish grapevine. It supports all the white wines that grow in Spain's premier white wine region, the Rueda.

Verdicchio

This grape has been known in the Italian Marches since the fourteenth century. It is still cultivated there. It is usually made into neutral, fruity white wines.

Vermentino

A white grape with personality, vermentino is now found in quantity only on Corsica, on Sardinia, in small vineyards in Liguria, and in the northern part of Tuscany.

Vernaccia

Although an old variety, it is not particularly valuable. It grows in the hills around the little Tuscan city of San Gimignano and yields a delicate, dry white wine. This vernaccia is not related to the Sardinian vernaccia di Oristano.

Welschriesling or Wälschriesling

Austria's second most popular variety, Welschriesling grows on the shores of the Neusiedlersee, in Styria, and in the Weinviertel. It can yield light or strong white wines, the best sprightly, with a fine spiciness, the worst lifeless and neutral. The variety has nothing in common with the Riesling grape. It is called Olasz Rizling in Hungary, and Riesling Italico in Italy.

Zierfandler

Zierfandler is a good-quality white variety. Its wines have body and definite acidity. In Austria's Gumpoldskirchen wine region, it is the most important vine.

The Human Factor

Wine is a natural product, not a scientific one. The ancient Greeks understood this, calling wine "the gift of the gods." Nature still makes the vines grow and causes the grapes to ripen. Even the fermentation of their juice happens without human intervention. And when all the sugar in the must has been turned into alcohol, fermentation will cease of its own accord. Very little has changed in all this. Therefore, in theory the winemaker—not to mention his complicated technology—is superfluous.

In practice, many factors influence the growth of the vine as well as the process of fermentation. To control the latter is the job of the winemaker. Not that he really is a maker of wine; he cannot *make* the wine. What he can do is create the necessary conditions for the development of the best possible wines. For example, he can ensure that the must is cooled during fermentation. This may cause contemporary wineries to resemble oil refineries, but in hot climates, such as prevail in New Zealand's Marlborough region, the production of fine wines is quite impossible without such high-tech measures.

Turning Grapes into Wine

Grapes being delivered to a winery on the Russian River in California. Preserving the quality of the grapes and bringing them into the winery undamaged are top priorities of all wine estates.

Treading the grapes—one of the gentlest ways of crushing them, but very labor-intensive—was traditional in the making of port wine until the very recent past. Today, even on the Douro, it is largely history.

No wine can be better than the grapes from which it came. Yet again and again it can happen that winemakers take good grapes and manage to make bad wine out of them.

Vinification, the transformation of grapes into wine, begins with the delivery of the grapes into the winery and ends when the fermented wine is racked off its lees (mostly dead yeast cells). The process takes between less than a week and three months, depending on the wine and the fermentation methods employed. Most wines ferment for ten to fifteen days. Many a simple red wine has completed its fermentation after only four days, but white wines can take three to five weeks, and nobly sweet wines up to three months.

The rate of fermentation depends on the temperature in the cellar. This is usually set by the winemaker. The higher the temperature, the faster the process of fermentation. The cooler it is, the slower fermentation will be.

Alcohol and Carbon Dioxide

Alcoholic fermentation is a complicated chemical process that goes through several stages and involves not only alcohol but numerous byproducts, some very desirable, others unwanted. The most important byproduct is carbon dioxide (CO_2), an odorless gas that escapes from the fermenting wine in the form of bubbles.

Crushing station in Montalicino: Freshly delivered grapes are advanced toward the grape crusher by an Archimedes' screw.

Products and Byproducts of Alcoholic Fermentation

Ethyl alcohol	47–48%
Carbon dioxide	46–47%
Glycerin	2.5–3%
Succinic acid	0.2–0.5%
Butylenglycol	0.05–0.1%
Acetic acid	0–0.25%
Lactic acid	0–0.2%
Acetaldehyde	0–0.01%
Methanol	0.05–0.3%

The chemical formula for the transformation of sugar into alcohol and carbon dioxide is as follows:

$$C_6H_{12}O_6 \text{ (sugar)} \rightarrow$$
$$2C_2H_5OH \text{ (alcohol)} + 2CO_2$$
$$\text{(carbon dioxide)}$$

Carbon dioxide may also be present in the form of carbolic acid (H_2CO_3). The byproducts total about 4 to 5 percent of the wine. Only a few of them are truly undesirable: acetaldehyde, which will oxidize the wine; fusel oil, which is a higher alcohol, disagreeable in its taste and/or in its effect, and methanol, a poisonous substance that is unavoidably generated during any alcoholic fermentation. More than 25 grams of methanol per liter would turn any liquid into a deadly beverage. Fortunately, its presence in wine tends to be limited to tiny trace amounts, never more than .3 grams per liter. Another byproduct that the winemaker tries to minimize is acetic acid: this volatile acid has adverse effects on the wine's aroma.

To let CO_2 escape freely, most fermentation vessels are open on top. When bubbles rise to the surface of the wine, the winemaker knows that fermentation is in progress.

Differences Between Red and White Wines

Fundamentally, there is no difference in the preparation of white and red wines. In practice, the most important difference is that red wines are fermented with their skins, while for white wines only the juice is fermented. This means that white grapes are pressed as soon as they reach the winery; their juice is caught and fermented. Red grapes, instead of being pressed, are only crushed—that is, gently squeezed, so that their skins burst open. The juice, the pulp, the skins, and the seeds are then fermented together. Only after fermentation is the sediment (then called the pomace) pressed.

The wine that runs off without pressure being applied, the free run, is the most valuable. Wine that actually has to be pressed out (press wine) is of secondary quality; it contains many harsh tannins, which is the reason it is not usually added to the main wine. Only in weaker years is a small amount of the press wine sometimes added to the free-run wine—a common practice in the Bordeaux region.

What Happens to the Pomace

In the past, the pressed skins of red grapes were dried, shaped into briquettes, and sold as fuel. During the winter they lent their warmth to many a rural home. Argol, crude potassium hydrogen tartrate, is also obtained from the pomace; it is an important raw material for the pharmaceutical industry (in Rochelle salt, or sodium potassium tartrate, a mild purgative) and for the food industry (in cream of tartar, the base for baking powder). Nowadays, potassium hydrogen tartrate is made synthetically, so this source of income for winemakers has dried up. The pomace is now usually composted and spread through the vineyard as organic fertilizer. Some wineries also sell the pomace to distillers; it is then turned into pomace brandy, which is called grappa in Italy and marc in France.

The skins of white grapes, which still contain sugar, are diluted (mixed) with must and fermented into wine, which is then distilled to make brandy.

Today, practically everywhere in the world, red grapes are separated from their stems before being crushed and fermented. In the past, only wealthy châteaus could afford destemming.

Fermentation—Risky Business

All wine needs yeast to ferment. Without yeast, it will remain grape juice. There are many strains of yeast, each with its own characteristics, not all of them positive. The quality of the final product depends in part on the yeasts that helped to ferment it.

The changing of sugar into alcohol is accomplished by yeasts. Yeasts are fungi, and like bacteria, they are single-celled, thus counting among the simplest of microorganisms. They multiply by division, the energy for this process being supplied by the sugars that are present in grape must, dissolved glucose and fructose. The sugar forms, so to speak, the nourishment of the yeast, while the resulting alcohol is the byproduct of the yeast's proliferation.

Complete Fermentation of the Wine

At most temperatures above about 59°F (15°C), yeast will go on multiplying continuously until the last trace of sugar is used up and the wine is as dry as dust. At that point, the yeasts die off and fall to the bottom of the vessel. This sediment of dead yeast cells is termed the lees. Unless the winemaker intervenes, almost all wines will ferment completely. The only exceptions are musts with an extremely high sugar content, which will sometimes retain some unfermented sugar even after the process of fermentation has come to a spontaneous halt. The reason for this is that alcohol is inimical to yeast: yeast is killed off as alcohol levels rise, and when they reach about 15 percent by volume, fermentation stops. This happens regularly

Different Strains of Yeast

The botanical name for wine yeast is *Saccharomyces ellipsoideus* (sometimes called *Saccharomyces cerevisiae*). Similar yeasts are used in making beer and in baking bread. Each species of yeast includes many strains, however, and wine yeast is no exception. Each strain of yeast reacts differently with the chemical components of the grape must it ferments, and the different compounds created give to the finished wine a slightly different character, very much as the soil and the microclimate of the vineyard do. Thus some yeasts are particularly sensitive to alcohol, remaining active only up to an alcohol level of about 5 percent by volume. After that, different yeasts take over. Other yeasts are sensitive to heat, and yet others produce a

Red wine under fermentation. The yeasts ensure that the grape sugars are transformed into alcohol.

The activity of the yeast is limited by certain conditions. At high temperatures, yeast multiplies quickly, causing a stormy fermentation. Low temperatures make yeast lazy and slow down fermentation. Below 54°F (12°C), most yeast will cease all activity. Fermentation stops–the nightmare of all winemakers.

with nobly sweet wines, but sometimes it also occurs with high-grade musts that should ideally ferment through. The most spectacular example of this disaster is the 1992 Montrachet of the famous Domaine de la Romanée-Conti, which never reached the market because it did not ferment completely, retaining some unwanted residual sweetness.

lot of hydrogen sulfate, which can damage the wine's aroma. Certain yeasts lend aroma to young wines, and one strain, selected especially for working in sauvignon blanc, sometimes gives the wine now a soft aroma, sometimes a more aggressive one. Champagne yeasts are known for forming large flakes as they die off.

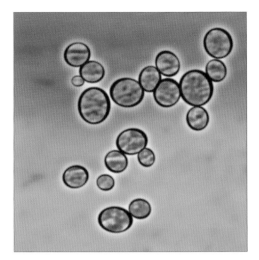

Saccharomyces chevalieri: *Elliptical yeast cells, used mostly for the fermentation of red wines.*

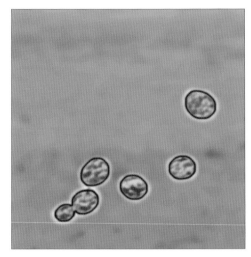

Saccharomyces oviformis: *Egg-shaped yeast cells, resistant to a higher alcohol content.*

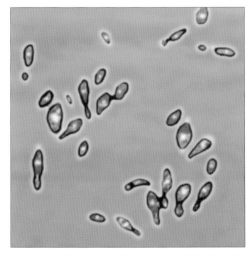

Torulopsis stellata: *Small, elongated yeast cells, adapted to the fermentation of grape must affected by botrytis.*

The Sources of Yeast

Wine yeasts can come from nature, as natural or wild yeasts, or out of the laboratory, as pure cultured strains. Since yeasts occur wherever grapes grow, each strip of land, and sometimes every vineyard on it, has its own natural "ambient" yeast cultures. These usually come into the winery with the grapes, or are already there, provided the wine is made in an area where grapes already grow. Intense spraying with fungicides and insecticides can also curtail the growth of natural yeasts; the spores of yeasts are spread not just by the wind but also by insects, particularly by the fruit fly. In rainy, cool summers, not much yeast will build up. Thus some European winemakers use their own, ambient yeasts, but in cold years resort to the use of cultured yeasts.

Two Different Approaches to Yeasts

Today most winemakers use pure, cultured yeast strains—natural yeasts, selected and fed under laboratory conditions, that reach the market in dried form and are then used to "inoculate" the must—to begin the fermentation process. Pure yeast strains are more reliable, as they minimize the risk that the must will not ferment at all or that fermentation will produce undesirable aromas in the wine. Outside of Europe, pure yeast cultures are used practically without exception. No other choice exists in some grape regions of California, Australia, and South Africa, since the hot climate does not allow the development of natural yeasts. Many winemakers in Europe—and not only of large producers or cooperatives—are equally committed to the use of cultured strains, usually because of painful experiences with their ambient yeasts.

The downside of this safe policy is that all the wines from a certain grape-growing region can acquire a similar taste. Natural yeasts add to the characteristic differences between grape varieties and soils, unlike cultured yeasts. Even if growers and winemakers take a lot of trouble to achieve their own wine styles, if all the winemakers of a region use the same cultured yeast strains, the sameness in their wines can become pronounced.

Preserving Natural Yeasts

This monotonous predictability could never happen in a region where natural yeasts are used, or so winemakers of Bordeaux, Burgundy, and many parts of Germany assure us. They are able to make individual, complex wines because the native yeasts of each area are not pure strains but comprised of several strains, each of which will leave its special mark on the wine. While oenologists from Australia and the United States smile at such old wives' tales, many top-quality European winemakers passionately maintain their local yeast strains. They do this by composting chips of grapevine wood, pomace, and the lees and returning them to the soil of their vineyards. The compost, a natural fertilizer, also perpetuates the wild, local yeast strains.

Louis Pasteur (1822–1895)

The Man Who Discovered Wine Yeasts

The first person to describe alcoholic fermentation fully and precisely was the French chemist Louis Pasteur. Wines had been fermenting long before his time, of course, and for a very long time it had been known that the sugar in the must is transformed into alcohol. Yet no one knew that it was the activity of yeasts that brought about this mysterious transformation. The discovery of the role played by yeast in bringing about fermentation was dependent on a new invention, the microscope.

The Explosive Growth of Yeast

Yeast is invisible to the naked eye. When enlarged 600 times under a microscope, it can be clearly identified. During fermentation, yeast multiplies with amazing rapidity. If you took a cubic centimeter of fermenting must and counted the yeast cells in it you would find 80 to 120 million of them. Before fermentation begins, the same amount of must would contain only 260,000 yeast cells, and the count would be only 120,000 in grape juice in the vineyard.

Minding the Pot

There are few rules but many procedures for the fermentation of red wine and these have to be readjusted with every vintage. French oenologist Emile Peynaud has summarized the difficulties involved with red wine as follows: "A mediocre vintage is produced very differently from a great vintage."

One of the rules is that red grapes are destemmed and crushed. The crushed grapes and their must are then fermented in a stainless steel tank or open wooden cask. When all the sugar has been used up, the wine is drawn off the pomace, and the pomace is pressed; this ends the vinification. In practice, fermentation of red wines is more complicated because it involves much more than the creation of alcohol. During fermentation, color and phenols from the grape skins are transferred to the fermenting wine, a process called extraction. Winemakers did not worry much about extraction in the past, since it happens along with fermentation. No special technical knowledge or procedures were required for color and tannins to be transferred to the wine.

Today, however, the mechanism of extraction is subject to close observation, and its progress is precisely controlled. For example, in cold years, when the skins have had little chance to develop their color and tannins, it is important that the wine not rest too long on the skins or it will take on some of their harsh, unripe flavor.

Open Fermentation on the Skins

Red wines will, as a rule, ferment much faster than white ones. After only a few hours, the first bubbles appear on the surface of the must; within twelve hours, the liquid has begun to "cook"; and by the next day it is in full fermentation. The pace of fermentation is sped up because the must has contact with oxygen, and in the presence of oxygen, yeasts can grow much faster. Fermentation vessels are kept open so that carbon dioxide, a gas produced during fermentation, can escape.

In their rush to the top of the liquid, carbon dioxide bubbles pull the floating skins along. Quickly they accumulate on the surface, filling the upper part of the fermentation vessel.

Making red wine: The grapes are destemmed and crushed. Two intermeshed counter-rotating rubber rollers break their skins, so that the juices escape. The must, skins, and grape seeds are pumped into stainless steel tanks (or open, wooden casks), there to undergo fermentation.

This layer of skins, the "cap" *(chapeau)*, has to be broken up and submerged again and again to give the young wine more contact with it. This used to be done by hand: workers would perch on the rim of the vats, break up the cap with poles or paddles, and push it under the surface of the must—sometimes with their feet. In Burgundy, this form of punching down, or *pigeage,* is still practiced. The modern way, however, is to draw the wine from the bottom of the fermentation vessel and pump it over the cap. This mechanized process—*remontage*—is found in most up-to-date wineries, where the stainless steel tanks are equipped with pipes and pumps to ensure a continuous circulation of the fermenting wine.

Duration of Maceration

The higher the temperature of the fermenting wine, the faster the process will be. Conversely, the rate of fermentation can be slowed down by cooling the fermenting wine, which has a natural tendency to heat up as it ferments. Since nearly all fermentation is now temperature-controlled, winemakers are able to direct the process. If fermentation takes place in stainless steel tanks, it is very easy to keep it cool. The large, traditional wooden casks *(cuvés)* still in use in many Bordeaux châteaus, for example, are now also equipped with cooling coils attached to their inside walls. Sometimes simple measures, such as hanging a cooling plate or lowering a plastic bag filled with ice into the vessel, are also effective in keeping the fermentation temperature down. Simple red wines, like Valpolicella or Beaujolais, ferment in about four days. Reds with more content, such as

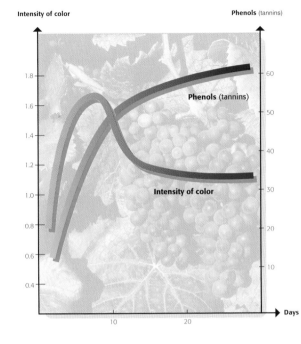

Intensity of color — Phenols (tannins)

Phenols (tannins)

Intensity of color

Days

Color Development and Tannin Content

The leaching of color and phenols from the grape skins is called extraction. The pigments are extracted in a short time; the tannins take longer.

Alsatian pinot noir, Spätburgunder from the German Baden, or Austrian Blaufränkisch from the Burgenland, require about eight days of contact with their skins. Heavy red wines undergo about two weeks of maceration. Traditional Barolos and cabernet sauvignons are left on their skins for four weeks.

Stopping Fermentation and Maceration

Most of the pigment is extracted from the skins within the first few days: the wine has become dark red, while the skins have been leached down to a pale purple. The solvent that extracts the color is the alcohol that is being generated from the sugar. This process of extraction is facilitated by warmth.

It takes somewhat longer to leach out the phenols (see graph, above). Whenever the winemaker decides that the wine has acquired enough "structure," he draws it off its lees.

As fermentation slows with increasing levels of alcohol, the skins begin to sink to the bottom of the vessel, since no carbon dioxide bubbles are produced to keep them afloat. The winemaker can now open a tap in the fermentation vessel and let the wine flow off. Skins, dead yeast cells, and pieces of pulp that have accumulated on the bottom of the vessel are pumped into a press and squeezed dry. Should any sugar still remain in the new wine, it will continue to ferment without the skins. Otherwise, fermentation is over.

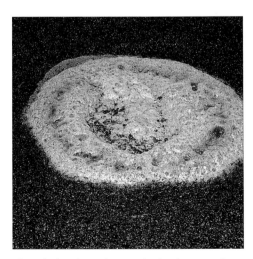

After only three hours, fermentation has begun—carbon dioxide forms a cap of foam on the surface of the must.

After five hours, the yeasts have multiplied—a storm rages within the mass of must, skins, pulp, and grape seeds.

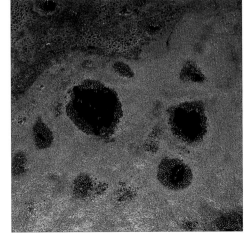

On the second day, fermentation is in full swing. The temperature within the liquid is rapidly rising.

The Soul of Red Wine

Carbonic Fermentation

Louis Pasteur discovered in 1872 that uncrushed, intact grape berries will undergo fermentation without the presence of yeast if they are kept in an oxygen-free environment. This information was soon put to good use by French wine producers; many of them began fermenting at least a portion of the red grape vintage by this method. The experts call it carbonic fermentation, or *macération carbonique,* and it results in a very aromatic and fruity wine.

Carbonic fermentation is usually carried out in a closed stainless steel tank into which carbon dioxide is pumped, so that the oxygen is completely displaced. The fermentation that occurs changes some of the sugar in the juice within the cells of the grapes into alcohol. Since only approximately 2 percent alcohol by volume can be achieved in this way, the grapes will still have to be crushed and fermented in the normal manner.

Beaujolais and Other Wines

Carbonic fermentation is typically associated with Beaujolais, where the bulk of the vintage is made into Beaujolais Nouveau. This wine is marketed a few weeks after the grape harvest, without malolactic fermentation. Other areas of France and also of Italy have taken up the production of *nouveau,* or, as it is called in Italy, *novello* wines. Many winemakers add a small amount of uncrushed grapes to the macerating must in order to emphasize the grape aroma of their wine.

What makes a great red wine is the superior quality of its tannins. They are, as the late Baron Philippe de Rothschild once put it, "the soul of the wine." How to capture only the best tannins for a red wine is a question that preoccupies oenologists.

Tannins are found in three different components of the fermenting wine: in the grape skins, in the small quantity of stem fragments that has found its way into the vat after destemming and crushing, and in the grape seeds. Of these, the skins constitute the softest, least woody tissue. The tannins lodged in the skins are particularly fine, especially if the grapes have had a chance to reach full ripeness. The tannins in the green pieces of stem are coarser, and those contained in the woody seeds are the harshest. Winemakers therefore tend to spurn the tannins from the stems and always reject those contained in the seeds. In other words, they concentrate on extracting the noble tannins from the skins. These account for 20 to 30 percent of all the available phenols.

Maceration and Circulation

Maceration, the process of soaking the color and phenols out of the grape solids, proceeds more or less simultaneously with fermentation. The skin tannins are relatively easy to leach out, and even small amounts of alcohol in the must serve to speed this extraction, so it begins soon after fermentation starts. For this process to proceed smoothly, the skins must have as much contact with the fermenting wine as possible. Returning the skins into the liquid again and again as they rise is therefore one of the most important operations during vinification. Referred to as punching down *(pigeage),* this stirring of the fermenting mass involves breaking up and submerging the "cap." The cap is a thick layer of skins and other grape solids that forms in the upper portion of the vessel. During the first few days of fermentation, the cap has to be punched down or submerged by pumping the liquid over it *(remontage)* several times a day; it is in this phase that both the color and the phenols from the skins are transferred to the wine. At later stages, submerging it once a day is sufficient.

Once the tannins in the skins have been leached out, circulation has to stop; at that point, it would serve only to increase the release of tannins from stems and seeds, which is to be avoided. It takes much experience and a good deal of art to know how to control the extraction of just the right phenols. In rainy years, when the skins contain little phenolic material, circulation is reduced, but for great vintages, it is increased. The turning frequency also varies from one variety to the next. Intensely colored varieties like syrah or cabernet sauvignon, for example, have to be turned more often than relatively pale varieties like the schiava grape in the Alto Adige.

Traditional stirring of fermenting mass: Already red, new wine is drawn off the bottom of the tank to be pumped over the top.

A modern Rototank: The stainless steel tanks turn periodically, agitating the macerating wine.

Old wooden cuvés at Château Margaux: Many top winemakers in Bordeaux still ferment their wines in open wooden casks.

Stirring the wine with poles assures that the rising grape solids do not form a dense cap on the young wine's surface.

Pigeage on the Rhône: Winery workers at the Chapoutier estate press the risen solids back down into the liquid with their feet.

Modern red wine fermentation: In the Chilean Santa Rosa winery, automated tanks turn over their contents during maceration.

Short but Intensive Maceration

The duration of fermentation affects the tannin content of wine only indirectly—more important is the temperature. Many contemporary oenologists advise a short fermentation for wines that are high in tannins: maybe only a few days, in extreme cases, only thirty-six hours. Fermentation for such short periods has to be correspondingly intensive—it takes place at 86°, even 95°F (30 or 35°C). In this short time span, only the softest, most easily dissolved tannins are extracted. After that, the partially fermented wine can be drawn off its lees and finish fermenting slowly in another vessel. Many burgundy wines are fermented in this manner, as are some of the newer Barolo wines. Their tannins are soft and sweet, and in many cases they are more intense than they might have been with normal, low-temperature maceration. Thus it is clear that the duration of maceration alone does not determine the tannin content of a wine.

Rotation Tanks

To optimize extraction, engineers and oenologists are always exploring new ideas for tank construction. In Australia, fermentation on the skins takes place in horizontal stainless steel tanks that turn at periodic intervals, stirring up the new wine. These rototanks eliminate the need for submerging the cap manually.

In Germany, rototanks are made with a set of internal paddles that stir up the liquids within. The seeds fall into a groove on the bottom of the vat and are not moved about with the other grape solids. This tank was developed to supply more "structure" to German red wines, known for their low tannin content and pale color. In Italy, a tank is used with two pistonlike plungers that take turns pressing the rising grape solids back under the surface. All of these devices are just variations on the old practice of submerging the "cap" with paddles and wooden punches.

Fermentation with the Stems

Before the development of destemming machines, most red wines were fermented with their stems. Châteaus that demanded a high price for their wines could afford to destem the grapes manually. Some vineyards still retain this old way of fermenting the grapes, but not because they cannot be bothered to destem them—for their particular wines, the tannin in the stems is necessary. This is particularly true of pinot noir wines, which by nature are poor in tannins.

In Burgundy it is held that when grapes are ripe, the tannins in the stems have reached ripeness as well, so a part of the vintage is fermented with the green stems. Having the stems in the vat creates small channels within the otherwise dense cap of grape solids that forms on top of the vessel. The channels allow the new wine that is periodically pumped back over the cap to penetrate into it, thus softening the cake of skins and seeds more efficiently.

Thermovinification

In Germany and Switzerland it is customary to use heat to extract more pigments from pale varieties, such as Blaufränkish, Trollinger, Spätburgunder (pinot noir), and gamay. Thermovinification is the term used for this procedure. It can involve temperatures as high as 185°F (80°C) for short periods of time. Wines treated in this way achieve dark color, but have no more tannins than normal. They can be very attractive in the first two years, but they lose quality faster than normally macerated wines.

Rosé or Blush Wines

True rosé wines are made of red grapes. They obtain their light red color through exposure to their skins before fermentation for anywhere from four to twelve hours. Then they are pressed, and the must is fermented. The international wine industry long ago accepted the practice of making rosé wines by mixing red and white ones, however. In some countries, such as Germany, this method is outlawed, Württemberg's Schillerwein being the only wine to be exempted from this national rule.

The Composition of Red Wine

70–85%	Water
11–13%	Alcohol
17–19%	Other components

Other Components
(grams per liter)

10–12	Glycerin
3–3.5	Ashes (potassium nitrate, potassium, calcium, iron, etc.)
2–3.5	Tannins
2–2.5	Wine acids
2–2.5	Lactic acid
1–1.8	Anthocyanins
.5–1	Unfermented residual sugar
.5–1	Succinic acid
.4–1	Volatile acids
.6–.8	Butylenglycol
.4–.5	Nitrogen compounds
.2–.3	Carbon dioxide in solution
.1–.3	Citric acid
.005–.03	Free sulfuric acid

Attack of the Bacteria

All red wines undergo a second fermentation after the alcoholic fermentation is completed. It is called malolactic after the Latin word *malum,* "apple." In the young wine, there is an acid that tastes astringent, much like an unripe apple. Malolactic fermentation removes malic acid.

In all temperate regions, red wines retain more or less malic acid. Even if the summer is hot and the harvest is late, some malic acid remains undecomposed (see page 44). This raw, astringent acid is still present in the fermented wine, and in cool years it can become very pronounced.

During malolactic fermentation carbon dioxide gas is given off: It bubbles in the siphon.

At some point, malic acid is attacked by bacteria that transform it into lactic acid, which is milder. The acid content of the wine drops, and it tastes softer and fuller.

A Natural Process
Malolactic fermentation, initiated by bacteria, is a natural occurrence, which is sometimes referred to as a biological acid decomposition. In many grape regions it occurs spontaneously in the springtime. In those places, for

malolactic fermentation to begin, all the winemaker has to do is to open the windows and let the warm spring air in. With rising temperatures inside the winery, the fermented wine once more becomes active. First it gives off a very fine spray, then bubbles—certain signs that something is going on under the surface.

What exactly does happen remained unclear for a long time.

Stability Is Reached Only after Malolactic Fermentation
Shortly before World War II, at Bordeaux University's Institut Oenologique, scientists finally explored the exact chemical reactions involved in malolactic fermentation, or MLF, as it is called. Under the microscope, bacteria were detected that were able to multiply in an acid environment and needed no sugar to do so. It turned out that there are three lactic acid bacteria, *Pediococcus, Leuconostoc,* and *Lactobacillus.* In Europe, these are present in the vineyard, mixed in with the yeasts. They are also present in the cellar and in the fermentation vats. (The porous walls of an empty wooden cask can hold five liters of liquid, mixed with yeasts and bacteria.) Lactic acid

bacteria are usually dormant. They only become active at temperatures over 68°F (20°C), that is, usually not till the weather turns warm.

Once active, the bacteria attack acids, mostly malic acid, and in the case of *Pediococcus* and *Leuconostoc,* exclusively malic acid. They do not touch glycerin or tartaric acid.

Since wine is not stabilized before the malolactic process is complete, modern wineries heat the cellar after the completion of fermentation to initiate the process, which takes about two or three weeks. After it is completed, the wine contains no more malic acid.

Inoculation with Bacteria
In many grape regions of the world, but especially in California, South Africa, and Australia, lactic acid bacteria are not present in sufficient numbers, or are altogether absent. To have a malolactic fermentation at all, the young wine has to be inoculated with selected, cultivated strains of bacteria. This procedure is sometimes followed in some European locations as well. What counts is that the wine should reach the bottle without any trace of malic acid in it. Otherwise, there is a danger that it will ferment in the bottle. A typical indication of such bottle fermentation would be the cork moving under the pressure of the carbon dioxide generated.

Malolactic Fermentation of White Wines
Malic acid is also present in white wines. Those from cool regions contain more, those from warm regions less. Yet most makers of white wine avoid malolactic fermentation altogether: they are grateful for each gram of acid their wine contains. Acids give white wines life, freshness, and finesse. In young white wines, acids are especially indispensable. Along with some fruity tartaric acid, a few grams of malic acid are perfectly acceptable. Biological acid decomposition is practically never used even on Rieslings, which show high acidity despite late ripening, be it in Alsace, Germany, or Austria.

With certain other white wines, nevertheless, MLF is now the rule. The practice was started with white burgundies made of white chardonnay grapes and white bordeaux made of sémillon and sauvignon. Today it includes almost all chardonnay wines that are fermented in small casks, whether in Italy, Australia, California, or Chile. Occasionally only half of the vintage is submitted to malolactic treatment, so that not too much acidity is lost.

Sunshine from a Bag of Sugar

Enhancement or travesty? By enriching the fermenting must with sugar, the wine's alcohol content is heightened.

In ideal climates, perfectly ripe grapes could be harvested every year. And wines would harmoniously balance body and alcohol content to our satisfaction. In cool-climate areas, however, the winemaker has to compensate for nature's shortcomings and artificially enhance the alcohol content of his wines.

In cool, sunless years, grapes build up very little sugar. As a result, the wines of that vintage have a low alcohol content. They are light and feel thin to the palate. Great wines with strong aroma and character can become disturbingly unbalanced. So it is not surprising that winemakers add sugar to the must or to the fermenting wine. As far as the yeasts are concerned, sugar from a bag is the same as the glucose or fructose that developed in the grapes. In other words: at the end of fermentation, the wine is as dry as ever.

To raise the alcohol content of 100 liters of wine by one percentage point, 2.4 kilograms of sugar has to be added to the fermentation.

Chaptalization Has Repeatedly Saved Winemakers

Chaptalization is the process of adding sugar to the wine in order to increase its alcohol content. The name goes back to the French scientist and politician Jean-Antoine Chaptal (1756–1832). As minister of the interior under Napoléon, he was very concerned about the decline of the French wine industry in the period after the French Revolution. It

occurred to him that wines could be enriched by the addition of either sweet must or raw sugar. The surge of enthusiasm this policy generated was repeated at the end of the nineteenth century in Germany and described by the chemist Ludwig Gall. In *his* time, numerous winemakers from the Mosel area had to give up their vineyards and emigrate because for several consecutive rainy summers there had been no point in harvesting grapes at all. Gall tells us how the enrichment of sour must through the addition of sugar made possible the creation of harmonious wines in these rainy years, and that to the joyful Mosel winemakers it was "sunshine out of a bag."

Misuse of Chaptalization

Chaptalization is practiced in most grape-growing areas of the world. Only in warm regions—California, South Africa, and Chile—do the wine laws forbid it; of course, in those regions it is not needed. On the contrary, some of the best producers try to decrease the content of alcohol in their wines by 1 percent by volume by special methods. European wine laws have also set clear limits on the practice. In the coolest regions, designated Zone A—that is, England, Luxembourg, Mosel-Saar-Ruwer, and Württemberg—white wines may be enriched by 3.5 percent by volume, red wines by 4.0 percent. In Zone B, which includes Champagne, Alsace, and Baden, the limit is set at 2.4 percent. In zone C, Bordeaux and Burgundy, the limit is 2.0 percent.

Nonetheless it does happen that wines from Zone C are enriched—in good years and without need—only to give them more weight. The winemakers of Burgundy and Switzerland are known for their generous hand with sugar. In these locations, many small wines are built up to offer more alcohol than nature had originally intended.

In Italy chaptalization must be done not with sugar but with sweet grape must. This Italian law is violently opposed by nearly all producers of fine wine, since the addition of must from grapes other than those of the region can alter the taste of a wine beyond recognition. Another danger worries politicians of the European Union: the temptation exists to drive the vines to overproduce and then chaptalize, enhancing the deliberately weakened wine.

Reverse Osmosis

In 1989 a new method for concentrating the must and thus avoiding adding sugar was developed in France. The procedure, called reverse osmosis, consists of withdrawing water from the wine, which automatically concentrates its flavor compounds and its alcohol. Reverse osmosis involves dividing a tank into

Bags of sugar in a large winery.

two chambers by means of a semiporous membrane. One half contains water, the other half, wine. When pressure is increased in the wine chamber by the use of pumps, water molecules are driven through the membrane from the wine into the water chamber. Reverse osmosis is used mostly in the Saint-Emillion and Pomerol regions and has made it possible for dense, concentrated wines to be made there even in rainy years. The procedure is so expensive and involved that only a few great Bordeaux châteaus can afford it.

12 Residence

8 Old *cuvier*

9 Guesthouse

Stations in the Production of Wine

The carefully planned process of red wine production is mirrored with perfect clarity in the physical plan of the châteaus of Bordeax. From the reception of the crop at one end to the processing of the pomace at the other, each activity has its fixed place within the total château system.

1 Reception of red grapes: Must weight is automatically measured.

2 Destemmer-crusher *(fouloir-égrappoir):* The red grapes are destemmed, crushed, and transported via underground conveyor to the fermentation tanks.

3 New fermentation cellar *(cuvier):* Separated by variety, the crushed grapes are fermented in stainless steel tanks. In the first phase of fermentation, the automated fermentation tanks turn over their content at least twice a day to achieve optimum extraction of tannins.

4 Computer board: Fermentation temperature is automatically monitored. At 86°F (30°C), the cooling system is activated.

5 Microvinification: In small stainless steel tanks, the cellar master can experiment on selected lots, to attain better extraction, for example.

6 White wine fermentation cellar: Many Bordeaux châteaus make small amounts of white wine, in addition to their reds. After pressing, the white grape must is fermented in small oak barrels.

7 Tank presses *(pressoirs):* When fermentation is complete, the wine goes to the presses, where the free run *(vin de goutte)* is separated from the press wine *(vin de presse).*

8 Old *cuvier:* Red wines used to be fermented not in stainless steel but in large, open, wooden vats. Even today, some of the best châteaus swear by these traditional fermentation vessels. Others have turned their old *cuviers* into museums.

9 Guesthouse with dining rooms for visitors and grape pickers.

10 First-year cellar *(chai):* After pressing, the young wine is pumped into small *barriques,* where it undergoes malolactic fermentation. It then matures for eight to twelve months in the small oak barrels, which hold exactly 225 liters.

11 Second-year cellar *(chai):* In its second year, the wine is pumped via subterranean pipes into another cellar. Here it matures another year, and is clarified in the process.

12 Residence and garden of the château proprietor.

13 Bottling plant: After one and a half to two years, the wine is bottled; before that, it receives a small dose of sulfur and a light filtration. This ensures that it is free of all haze.

14 Bottle storage: The filled but unlabeled bottles are stored in bays within the cellar's passages. The cellar masters check for loose corks and any fermentation that might occur in the bottles.

15 Case storage and shipping: Depending on château policy, 50 to 80 percent of each vintage is sold immediately upon official release. The remainder stays in reserve at the château. Before being crated, the wine is labeled.

16 Pomace collection: The pomace is composted and sold to a distillery.

17 Tasting room: All the larger châteaus have a tasting room, where visitors can sample the new vintage.

An Inside Look at

a Wine Estate

15 Case storage

16 Pomace collection

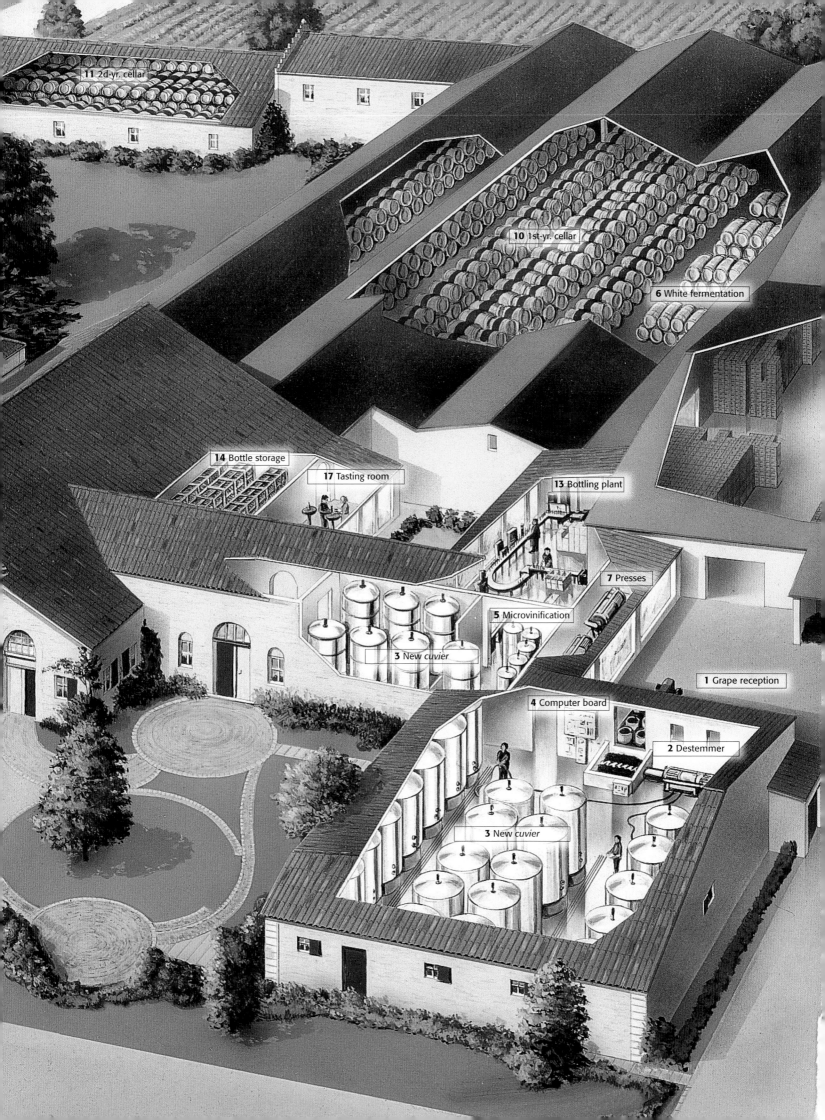

11 2d-yr. cellar

10 1st-yr. cellar

6 White fermentation

14 Bottle storage

17 Tasting room

13 Bottling plant

7 Presses

5 Microvinification

3 New *cuvier*

1 Grape reception

4 Computer board

2 Destemmer

3 New *cuvier*

Easy Does It

High-quality grapes can be made into a superior white wine only if the winemaker treats them gently and proceeds with swiftness and caution. It takes a special knack. Even in the pressing one can make a number of mistakes.

After their delivery, white grapes are traditionally first destemmed. This is accomplished in the destemmer. Thanks to the centrifugal force of the rotating cylinder, the grapes are torn from the stems and flung outward through the cylinder's perforations. Some of the grapes remain intact, while others are cut open by the sharp edges of the openings—depending on the setting used. The grapes are then pumped into the press. The juice that runs off without pressure is called the free run, and will ultimately produce the highest-quality wine. But no producer can afford to use only the free run. It amounts to only about a third of the juice contained in the grapes. To obtain what remains in the cells, it is necessary to press the grapes.

Pressing

The actual pressing is now done in modern hydraulic tank presses. A tube inside the cylinder containing the destemmed grapes is inflated, pressing the grapes against the wall. The wall is perforated, so that the juice can run off into a vat beneath the tank. At first only gentle pressure is applied. Half the cells in the flesh of the fruit are broken at a pressure of only 1 bar. Gradually the pressure is increased, so that the remaining juice can be expressed.

Do White Grapes Have to Be Destemmed?

A hundred years ago practically all grapes were pressed and fermented with their stems. Since the invention of mechanical desstemmers, white grapes in nearly all the world's growing regions are destemmed before crushing. This to say that the stems are separated from the grapes and only the grapes themselves are pressed. In this way all contact between the must and the stems is avoided. Destemming helps in creating limpid wines. There are other advantages, however: the winemaker can dispense with crushing the grapes, for the paddles of the destemmer break open the skins, liberating some of the juice. In the case of high-quality white grapes, this must—along with its skins—is sometimes left to macerate in the catch basin

White wine can be pressed in two ways. Normally, the grapes are run through the destemmer, pressed, and the must is fermented in a steel tank. Where whole-grape pressing is practiced, the grapes go into the press right on delivery.

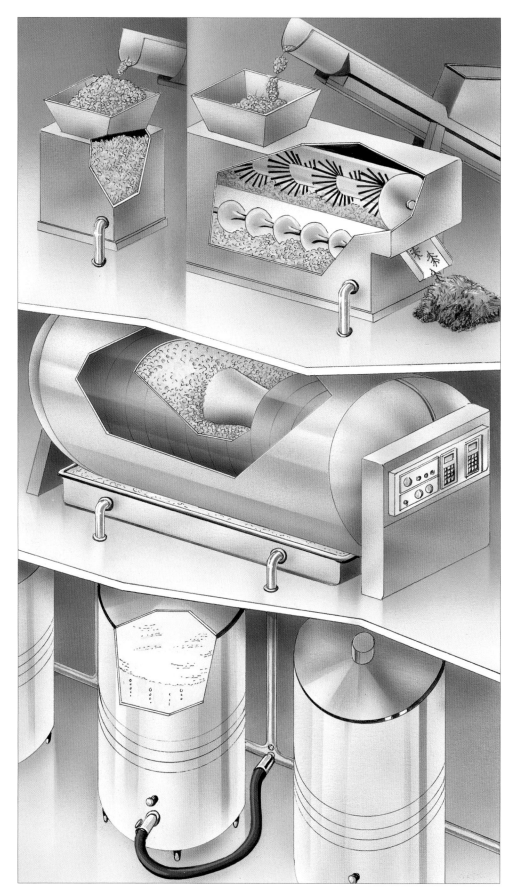

of the destemmer for a few hours before being pressed. The presence of stems would make this maceration on the skins a complete impossibility, as they would transfer to the wine unpleasant phenolic substances and unwanted plant juices. These would be noticeable as bitter, astringent tannins in the finished wine.

Whole-Cluster Pressing

In certain grape-growing regions, destemming is deliberately skipped; this is the case in Champagne. Many late sweet grapes are also pressed without destemming. In these cases, any crushing of the grapes is avoided, so as to prevent the transfer of phenols to the must. Upon arrival in the winery, the grapes are immediately subjected to pressing.

Some whole-cluster pressing is increasingly used in normal white wine production because it puts less stress on the grapes and because the stems create channels within the compacted pulp that allow the must to run off more quickly. As a rule, only part of the vintage is treated by this method, however, and even that only in good years.

Pressing whole clusters with their stems is the norm for sparkling wines, and is also practiced for some still white wines.

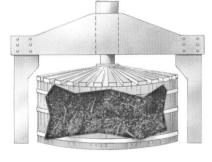

Basket Press

Vertical basket presses are constructed on the same principle as the winepresses of old. Their disadvantage is their generally small capacity, which makes them unsuited to modern, large-scale winemaking. For making quality wines, however, the basket press is newly in vogue. Some of the most famous makers of Champagne, for example, use the large Marmonier basket presses, which hold over 8,800 pounds (4,000 kg) of grapes, for their best wines. The first 570 gallons (2,500 liters) form the *cuvée,* the highest-quality must, filling ten barrels of 205 liters each. The second pressing *(taille)* yields 615 liters (three barrels).

Screw Press

Within the horizontal screw press, two round plates, mounted on screws at either end, move in on one another, pressing the grapes between them. The perforated walls of the cylindrical press allow the must to escape. The cylinder is closed, and the air can be withdrawn from it so that pressing can take place in an oxygen-free atmosphere. Since in relation to the amount of grapes in the press the two press heads are small, considerable pressure has to be used to extract the juice. The screw press is seldom used for white wines.

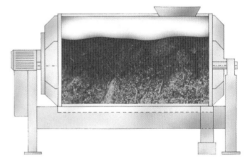

Tank Press

Tank presses work pneumatically: air is pumped into a plastic bag, the bladder, within the press chamber. When inflated, it presses the grapes against the perforated walls of the tank. As the berries break open, their juice flows off through the holes. Tank presses use considerably less force than screw presses. Their screen walls also keep small pieces of pulp and skins out of the must, solids that would be highly undesirable in white wines, for which this type of press is ideally suited. Tank presses are used in virtually all white wine production today.

From Cloudy to Crystalline

Press must is relatively viscous, cloudy, and of a yellow-green color. It has to be clarified before fermentation.

Composition of White Grape Must	
70–85%	Water
15–27%	Sugar
0.3–1.8%	Tartaric, malic, succinic, and lactic acids
0.3–0.6%	Potassium, nitrogen, phosphorus, and other minerals
.01–0.2%	Tannins
.03–0.5%	Amino acids, protein
under .01%	Vitamins, aldehydes, higher alcohols

Before the must of white grapes can be fermented, it has to be rendered less viscous. The technical terms for this thinning of the grape must are clarification and fining. These procedures have to be used with care since they could result in a thin, one-dimensional wine without body.

The must that flows from the crusher is yellow-green, viscous, and cloudy. It contains particles of pulp, fragments of skin, pieces of stems, soil, and other unwanted solids. Many winemakers fear that unless they clear the must of every bit of this solid matter the wine will suffer. For this reason, they resort to fining *(collage)*.

Among the fining agents used are enzymes, which dissolve pectins. Pectin is what makes the must so thick. Pectin is present in all must, and the later the grapes are picked, the more pectin there will be. High viscosity slows down the precipitation of solids.

Removing the pectin thins the must. It can be clarified faster and fermented sooner.

In large wineries, quick clarification is crucial if only because they have such enormous quantities of grapes to process in a short time. But smaller wine estates also insist on quick processing and fermentation. Because it is low in phenols, white grape must is very vulnerable to oxidation. It can turn brown and lose freshness very fast. Timely fermentation lowers the danger of oxidation.

Unclarified Musts

Much controversy surrounds the business of clarification. In the past, all white wines were fermented unrefined, with the risk that they remained cloudy. Even today, some of the most respected white wines are made virtually without clarification, among them Meursault, Puligny-Montrachet, and Corton-Charlemagne. It is true that the must of these wines is relatively clean to begin with, because the grapes are carefully selected and crushed very gently. Furthermore, these wines are made largely of free-run must.

Not all white wines have the stature of white burgundy. As a rule, some fining of the must is necessary, especially in years when a high proportion of the crop has been affected by rot. In fining, however, it is important to avoid destroying components of the must that add to the distinction of the wine. Ambitious winemakers always try to limit their fining to the absolute minimum necessary.

Settling

The simplest and most natural method of clarification is settling *(débourbage)*. The freshly crushed must is pumped into a settling tank, where it rests for a day. After only a few hours, a good portion of the solids has sunk to the bottom. The natural enzymes in the must do not split the pectins, or do so only partially. Thus the must retains its viscosity to a large extent. After twenty-four hours, all solids have precipitated, and the must has clarified itself.

For this procedure to work, the must has to be cooled to from 41 to 32°F (5° to 0°C), so as to prevent fermentation from setting in. In cool wine regions, it is sufficient to place the settling tank outdoors, since autumn nights are cold. The drawback of settling as a method of clarification is that the must has to be treated with sulfur dioxide to prevent oxidation. Only with high-extract must that has undergone a short maceration on the skins and is high in phenolics, is the danger of oxidation negligible.

Other Clarification Methods

Where the possibility of cooling the must does not exist, other clarification methods have to be used. The must can, for example, be fined by the addition of bentonite. Bentonite precipitates the proteins but does not remove the cloudiness. For this reason, many winemakers swear by mechanical clarification. Centrifugal, rotary-drum vacuum filters can clarify 2,270 gallons (10,000 liters) of must in an hour. The must is immediately ready for fermentation. The risk of oxidation is slight; the use of sulfur dioxide is unnecessary, or the amount used can at least be kept at a minimum, since the must has air contact for a very short time, certainly much shorter than in a settling tank.

The disadvantage is that centrifugation may remove valuable compounds from the must, such as colloids. These polymers often contribute class to fine white wines, lending them a body, longevity, and complex structure that simple wines do not have. Yeasts are also lost through the centrifugal action of the separator or through the suction of the vacuum filter. Pure cultured strains of yeast will then have to be used to begin fermentation. Winemakers with high aspirations may prefer to use their ambient wild yeasts, which contribute to the formation of the wine's character.

Diatomite

Many large wineries and cooperatives use rotary-drum vacuum filters only as a first step in the clarification of the must. It is then pumped through a thick filter. Solids and other materials remain stuck in the convoluted channels between the filter's particles. Large quantities of must can be clarified quickly by this method. The filtering material used is diatomaceous earth, which is made up of the fossilized skeletons of unicellular algae.

The Separator

Chamber or plate separators work centrifugally to separate heavier, solid particles from the liquid must. Must can contain as much as 15 percent solids. The clarification of the must depends on the speed of rotation: at 10,000 rotations per minute, the must is clarified more thoroughly than at, say, 4,000 rotations per minute. In comparison to settling, which is the gentlest method of clarification, the separator puts more stress on the must.

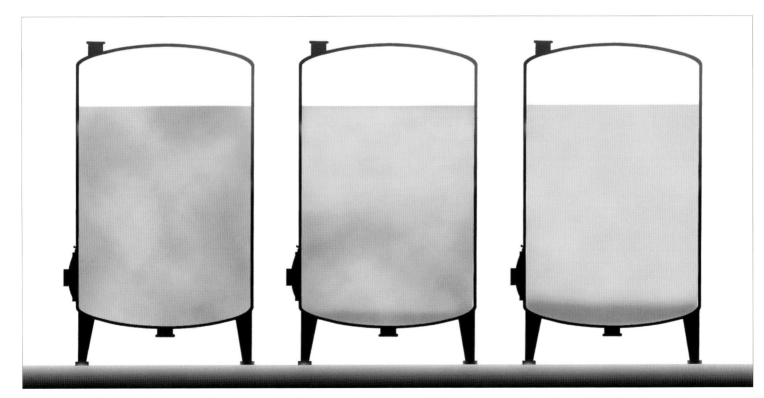

After 3 hours: Solids and clouding begin to sink toward the bottom of the settling tank.

After 8 hours: A portion of the must, which has been cooled to 41°F (5°C), is already clear.

After 24 hours: All cloudiness has precipitated; the must is clear and can be pumped into the fermentation tank.

Tingling Freshness, Bracing Aromas

Thanks to modern cooling technology, white wine can now be made in warm wine regions, even under a hot sun, as here on New Zealand's North Island.

The fermentation of white wines has been revolutionized in the last thirty-five years. The possibility of cooling the must artificially, thereby slowing down fermentation, has created a new type of wine: fragrant, fresh, and pure of tone.

For many makers of white wine in the past, a naturally cold fermentation cellar was almost as indispensable as a good vineyard. It made possible the controlled fermentation of white wine without intervention. A controlled fermentation process is so important because white wines depend much more on primary aromas than red wines do. These being volatile, they can easily be lost when fermentation temperatures rise so high that alcohol begins to evaporate.

How Cooling Is Achieved
Cooling down the must became possible with the introduction of stainless steel tanks. These can cool fermenting wines in one of two ways. The very simplest method consists of running cold water down the outside of the tank. The more expensive and more efficient method involves a double-walled tank, with cooling coils in the space between the walls. In such a tank it is possible to maintain just about any chosen temperature, even if it is standing outdoors in the sun.

Temperature-Controlled Fermentation
At a temperature of around 59°F (15°C), grape must will begin to ferment in about two days. Soon the yeast is working so hard that temperatures at the core of the liquid reach 64 to 68°F (18 to 20°C), and will rapidly mount to 86°F (30°C) if the cooling mechanism does not click in. By maintaining lower temperatures, refrigeration ensures controlled fermentation. Today, most white wine is fermented at 59 to 64°F (15 to 18°C). This new process is called temperature-controlled or cold fermentation.

New White Wine–Producing Nations
The possibility of cooling down the must has radically changed the world map with respect to white wine production. Today fresh-tasting white wines can be made in even the warmest wine regions of the world. Spain, Sicily, Aus-

tralia, South Africa, Chile, and California have all benefited from this new freedom. Of course, a great investment in cooling technology is required. The fermentation rooms of many wineries look like refineries, with batteries of stainless steel tanks, humming coolers, and gleaming chromium pipes through which the wine is pumped from one tank into another.

Acidification

A lively, fruity acidity is especially important in wines that have undergone cold fermentation. Yet it happens again and again that wines from hot grape regions do not offer enough acidity, despite early grape harvests. Both in hot growing regions and in warm northern summers, natural acids can fall below 4 grams per liter. Then it makes sense to enrich the must by adding citric or malic acid. This process, called acidification, is sanctioned by law and routinely practiced in Australia, South Africa, Chile, and California. In Europe, acidification is seldom resorted to, and it is in fact illegal to acidify chaptalized wines.

Disdain for "Tank Wines"

Today's white wines are unquestionably superior to the raw, harsh, partially oxidized vintages of the past. Yet not all wine connoisseurs love the new wines. Wine snobs may contemptuously refer to them as "tank wines" because their taste is too one-dimensional and because often it is difficult to identify the grape variety or the region that produced

---

Cold Fermentation

The limitless possibilities offered by cooling inspired oenologists in the 1970s to experiment with fermenting some wines at 54, 50, or even 46°F (12, 10, or 8°C). In such cold environments, yeast grows very slowly. Must fermentation is correspondingly slow and long. The result: extremely fresh, polished, attractive wines with a crisp aroma—just the things for a new class of wine lovers, who want uncomplicated wines and place particular value on explicit variety characteristics. This process is called cold fermentation.

Cold fermentation is only possible using certain specific strains of yeast that are active at low temperatures. In addition, the must has to be well clarified. Very thoroughly fined must, however, is poor in pectins—that is, carbohydrate polymers—which have the ability to fuse molecules, adding viscosity to wine and thereby giving it body. Wines poor in pectins have little body and are too easy to drink. Thus cold-fermented wines are seldom faceted and complex. Their aroma structure is little altered by the transition from the juice stage to the wine stage. The wines are grapey, but not winey. A typical example of a cold-fermented wine is the Italian pinot grigio.

---

them. Moreover, since fermentation often takes place in enclosed, oxygen-free tanks, the resulting wines are all the more susceptible to oxidation once they are bottled. They change in the bottle relatively quickly, and taste old. In other words, these wines have to be enjoyed while they are young.

The initial enthusiasm for highly controlled fermentation has in recent years subsided among those winemakers who want their product to be more richly faceted, more imposing. They continue to seek ways to obtain wines that are visually brilliant and yet offer more content.

There are white wines that are fermented at up to 77°F (25°C) and are unharmed by such treatment. The higher the temperature the stronger the reaction of the carbohydrate compounds, which carry the aroma, with other substances. This changes the taste of the wine. The primary fruit aromas are then joined by the complex, sometimes bizarre fermentation aromas found in some chardonnays, sauvignons, and viogniers.

Extended Skin Contact and Cryomaceration

Sometimes white grapes are not pressed, but only crushed. Must and skins subsequently remain together for a few hours to release the aromatic substances from the skin and give the wine more structure. The white must is cooled to 32°F (0°C) to prevent it fermenting. Cryomaceration, by contrast, refers to the freezing of whole grapes. They subsequently enter the press at 21°F (−6°C). As the water in the must freezes first, only a highly concentrated extract high in sugar is gained. This method, similar to the process for ice wine *(Eiswein)*, is applied in many countries to produce sweet dessert wines. However, they never reach the quality level of genuine ice wines or sweet, botrytized wines.

Maceration on the skins: A short contact with the skins transfers flavor compounds to white wine must.

The Kiss of Wood

The triumphant success of fresh, fruity white wines, the fashion for cold fermentation, the growing reliance on cultured yeasts—these developments have given many a winemaker cause for reflection. Many of them are searching for ways to make different wines. In the process, they have rediscovered the wooden barrel.

Before there were stainless steel tanks, all wine was fermented in wooden barrels. Thus it is not an innovation when many of today's

The main difference between a wooden barrel and a stainless steel tank, in terms of fermentation, is that in the former, temperature cannot be controlled. Heated to 73 to 77°F (23 to 25°C), fermentation will necessarily take a different course. New ester complexes are formed, which structure the wine quite differently than cold fermentation would. The wine loses some fruit and develops fermentation aromas. These can be lactic (like cheese), tea- or tobacco-like, vegetative (like hay or bell peppers), or like caramel, butter, or

this biological acid decomposition (see page 76), the wine is mellower and has more body. Because of their greater sensitivity to heat and cold, oak barrels make malolactic fermentation much easier than a large stainless steel tank would. All the winemaker has to do is to heat up the cellar.

Barrique Seasoning
After fermentation, wine is frequently matured in small oak barrels. Since wood is porous, it provides a slight but steady supply of oxygen to the maturing wine. Thus a slow oxidation of the wine can take place. It matures more quickly than in a low-oxygen environment and develops greater complexity of aroma. This is particularly true of wines that are allowed to lie on their lees for a few months. Resting on the lees imbues the wine with some extra taste nuances, which can be intensified by stirring the lees. In French this is called *bâtonnage.*

Misuse of Wooden Barrels
Not every white wine is suited to oak barrel fermentation and maturation. This method was devised for heavy wines, rich in substances. Le Montrachet, Haut-Brion *blanc,* a grand Pouilly-Fumé—such wines will reach a more complex ripeness, receiving a delicate vanilla tone from the oak and a freshness from the lees.

This is not true of medium-heavy or light wines. Slow oxidation tends to tear them apart, and the oak flavors can literally overwhelm the wine. Unfortunately, many winemakers continue to use oak barrels even for light wines, their desire to produce a white wine of international stature overriding their understanding that to achieve that goal, they need better grapes, a better location, and a different attitude.

Wines rich in substance benefit from fermentation in small oak casks.

winemakers once more entrust their wines to them. What is new is that this development involves mostly *barriques,* or small oak barrels. These are not simply fermentation vessels; they influence the development of the wine in a fundamental way.

Barrique Fermentation
It used to be that white wines were fermented in small oak barrels only in Burgundy and Bordeaux, though in the more distant past this was the case in Champagne as well. If many winemakers in other wine-producing nations are now taking up the custom, it is because they are impressed with the individuality of these French wines. Chardonnay, especially, is frequently, if not always, fermented in *barriques.*

butterscotch; they increase the complexity of the wine's range of tastes.

It is true that if fermentation temperatures rose much higher than those mentioned, harmful bacteria would be activated. This danger is not great, however, since the wooden surface of the barrel conducts the cold of the fermentation cellar to the wine. Since a *barrique's* wall surface is relatively large in terms of the small volume of liquid the barrel contains, it is a sufficiently efficient means of cooling it.

Malolactic Fermentation
Wines fermented in small oak barrels often undergo malolactic fermentation as well. This occurs right after the alcoholic fermentation, or even during it. Its result is to decompose the malic acids present in the new wine. After

Traditional Barrels
Traditional wooden barrels ten or twenty years or older have virtually disappeared from cellars and wineries. You can still find them occasionally in Alsace, in Austria, and in Germany. The value of such barrels, which do not affect the taste of the wine anymore, is unquestionable. Cleaned regularly on the inside, they can yet impart some nuances to the wine. Coated inside with half an inch of argol (a deposit of tartrate crystals), they can be used for the same functions as stainless steel tanks. Their outside carvings serve to beautify many a cellar.

Exquisite as French Oak

For hundreds of years, wine barrels have been made of the wood of various trees— chestnut, acacia, cherry, nut pine, palm, red cedar, and eucalyptus. Yet no wood is as suited to maturing wine as the wood of the oak tree.

Oak is harder and denser than most other woods. The sweet, fragrant tannins of the wood can support the aroma of fine wines perfectly. For this reason, since the seventeenth century oak barrels have been preferred for the seasoning of wine. But oak trees grow slowly. They have to be at least eighty years old before they can be used, and their trunk must be at least half a yard thick.

Three Major Sources of Barrel Oak

Although worldwide there are 300 species of oak trees, only a few can be used for making wine barrels. They are *Quercus sessilis, Q. robur,* and *Q. peduncolator,* all European trees, and the American white oak *(Quercus alba),* a native of North America. Up to World War II, European red wines matured in barrels made of wood that came from Poland, Latvia, and Estonia. Today there are three major sources of oak: France, above all the forests of central France and of the Vosges; the former Yugoslavia, Slovenia, Croatia, Bosnia-Herzegovina, and Serbia, where the Slavonian oak grows; and the United States, which has established itself as a source of oak in recent years. The wood of the American white oak is highly esteemed in Australia and Spain, and increasingly so in the south of France. Austria and Germany are of marginal importance as far as supplying oak wood is concerned.

French Oak

French oak is today generally accepted as being the best. Not only is it aromatic; the high quality of its aroma cannot be equaled. Of course, it is expensive, and only the producers of very valuable wines can afford to use French oak. It is made mostly into *barriques, pièces,* and other smaller barrels.

French oak is so expensive for several reasons. First of all, the extensive French oak forests are subject to very restrictive silviculture. Moreover, the most valuable oaks grow only in a few regions, where the soil is not too moist and contains no iron. Even more important is that working with French oak is more labor-intensive and requires more wood than working with either American or Slavonian oak. This is because French oak cannot be sawed; it must be split by hand (see page 104). Since splitting is only possible along the fibers, the yield is very limited, and there is much waste.

Slavonian Oak

Slavonian oak consists almost exclusively of the species *Quercus peduncolator.* Since ancient times it has been used to make barrels, especially large barrels that hold from 130 to 3,960 gallons (5 to 150 hl). These are traditionally used for Italian wines, such as Barolo, Brunello di Montalcino, and Chianti. The structure of the fibers of this species of oak is somewhat coarser than that of French oak, and its aroma more neutral. The management of the forests of the new Balkan republics is, of course, not as strict as that of France. It happens again and again that trees are felled too young. Later, they transfer their harsh tannic acids to the wines. Or the wood may be sawed, not split, and this will eventually cause leakage in the barrel. Hungary, Romania, the Ukraine, and Russia are also standing in the wings, ready to take the stage as suppliers of barrel oak.

American Oak

The wood of the American oak is considerably harder than that of the European *Quercus* species, and much easier to work. It is very aromatic oak, which has proven to be well adapted to maturing red wines with an intense palate, made of grapes such as shiraz (syrah) or tempranillo. For delicate, elegant wines, however, it has too powerful an effect. Consequently, for wines of this type, French oak is preferred, even by many American winemakers. The United States has the greatest stands of white oak in the world. Barrel oak is usually cut in Minnesota, Pennsylvania, or other eastern states, but it also grows in Oregon, and some stands are found in California.

The Most Significant Stands of Oak in France

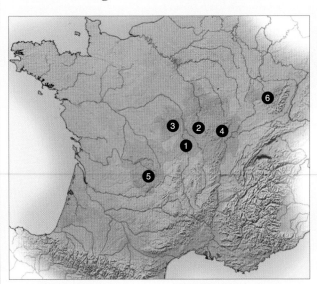

1 Allier: Département *in central France, on the banks of a tributary of the Loire of the same name. The oaks grow in poor soil. Their wood is highly valued for its fine pores and its sweet, vanilla-scented tannins. The best stands in Allier are Tronçais, Gros Bois, and Dreuille.*

2 Nevers: *This city on the Loire, in the département of Nièvre, is famous for the fine-pored, tight-grained oak that grows there. Its tannins are somewhat more intense than those of Allier oak, but they are also very soft and sweet.*

3 Cher: *Around the city of Bourges, in the central French* département *of Cher, the oak trees have fine pores, narrow fibers, and tight grain. The wood has slightly more tannin than Allier oak, but it is at the same time very elegant, and highly regarded.*

4 Burgundy: *The mixed stands of oak vary in quality in the forests that straddle the départements of Yonne, in the north, and of Rhône, in the south. The wood can sometimes be hard and tight-grained, sometimes coarsely pored, with harsh tannins.*

5 Limousin: *The extensive oak forests of the départements of Creuse and Haut-Vienne grow in calcareous, fairly fertile soils. The grain of the wood has large pores, and the tannins are easily leached out of it. It is used primarily for maturing cognac.*

6 Vosges: *The oak here grows on the western reaches of the Vosges Mountains in the département of the same name. The wood is very tight-grained, small-pored, and intensely fragrant; it is slightly reminiscent of Allier oak.*

The Precise Art of Aeration

Practically all wines have to undergo a period of maturing before they are bottled. This is true for red as well as for white wines. Maturation can be as short as a few weeks. It can also extend over several years. The French refer to this maturing process as *élévage.* During *élévage,* the talents of a vintage are developed and its flaws minimized or removed. The grapey taste that young wine exhibits just after fermentation is transmuted into the aroma of wine.

This change is in part brought about by the addition of minute amounts of oxygen, which affect the wine subtly but profoundly. This process is called aeration. The amounts of oxygen involved are so small that the process could also be described as storing the wine with as little oxygen contact as possible. *Elévage* can take place in a wooden barrel, in a stainless steel tank, or in the bottle. Frequently, the winemaker opts for a combination of all three. Some wine maturation processes do not involve oxygen at all.

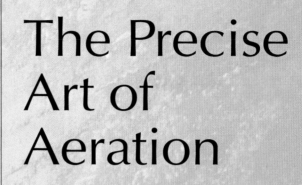

Controlled Exposure to Air

After the end of fermentation we have wine, but it is not potable. It tastes raw and harsh, and needs maturing, which amounts to resting in a vessel with a controlled oxygen supply.

Oxygen is regarded as the enemy of wine. It makes it age fast, and in the end will kill it. Yet wine cannot mature completely without oxygen, either; the proper development of wine requires at least a little of it. It is difficult to say just how much oxygen is required for the wine to mature: as little as possible, as much as necessary. Red wines require more oxygen

lose their dark red color and, as they lighten, take on purple or garnet red tones.

The fragrance of the wine also changes. Hydrocarbon compounds, carriers of the primary aromas, combine with oxygen molecules to create more complex aroma compounds. Tannins are also very quick to react with oxygen. They merge under aeration with other phenolic compounds, so that as well as the pure fruit tones new aromas are formed, such as earthy or spicy tones.

Polymerization
Polymerization is the name given to the fusion of phenols under aeration. The word sounds

tannin molecules keep combining until they have become insoluble in any liquid and are precipitated as sediment on the bottom of the bottle.

Reductive Seasoning
Storing wine virtually without oxygen carries with it the danger of reduction. Reduction means that the wine, because of lack of oxygen, cannot react or reacts only in limited ways. The result is that the malodorous chemical compounds that are present after every fermentation (like hydrogen sulfide and mercaptans) cannot be neutralized. Wine that is stored in a virtually oxygen-free vessel, be it a stainless steel tank or a barrel, develops disagreeable smells reminiscent of rotten eggs or the cowshed. The winemaker who practices reductive maturation can avoid these flaws by aerating the wine at the end of fermentation, after it is drawn off the lees.

Oxidized Wines
Too generous an oxygen supply has a harmful effect on the wine. Contact between alcohol and oxygen causes acetaldehyde to be formed. Dissolved in wine, this substance tastes flat and stale. The wine is then referred to as "oxidized": it has a sherry or Madeira tone, typical of opened bottles that have been allowed to stand too long.

Just how fast wine will oxidize is best illustrated by some numbers. Let us assume that a barrel is not completely filled, so that the surface of the wine has contact with air. If the exposed surface is one square meter, then in one hour, 150 cubic centimeters of oxygen are dissolved in the wine. That means that in a few days, the entire barrel will be oxidized. To prevent this disaster, the winemaker has to keep his barrels topped up, that is, filled all the way to the bung, assuming the barrel stands bung up. He also has the option of pumping nitrogen into the empty space, to act as a protective gas that keeps out oxygen. If he uses stainless steel tanks, he can make use of the inner lid, which can be lowered onto the wine's surface within the airtight tank, providing effective protection against oxygen.

Primary air contact: Wine receives most of its oxygen while being pumped from one container to another.

than white ones, which are unable to bear more than a tiny amount.

Chemical Reactions
After fermentation wine contains many components that will react with oxygen. The anthocyanins, for example, are responsible for the color of the wine. Like all phenols they react very quickly with oxygen, producing some changes. White wines will shift from an initial straw color to golden yellow; red wines will

complex, but it describes an essentially simple process. Small, short-chained phenol molecules combine to form larger ones. In this manner, tannin polymers and the more complex tannin polysaccharides are generated. All this polymerization has a significant impact on the aroma of the wine. The larger molecular structures give the wine delicacy, clarity, and elegance. They soften the young wine's initial harsh attack into complexity and elegance. As maturation continues, the

Esters—Elements of Maturity
Some important maturation processes take place in wine without the presence of oxygen. Esterization is the most significant of these. Esters, organic compounds generated when alcohol reacts with acids, are formed when

Secondary air contact: The wine has some contact with oxygen thanks to the small air bubble behind the bung.

then let them finish aging before they release the bottles for sale. Spain's prestigious Bodegas Vega Sicilia, which used to age its wines for up to seven years in wood, now bottles them at the latest after four years, but holds the bottles in its cellar for up to twenty years. This is an extreme example; it would make no sense at all except in light of the Spanish tradition to sell wines only when they are mature and ready to drink. It does, however, serve to illustrate the worldwide trend toward cutting short barrel maturation in favor of bottle aging.

Precisely speaking, bottle aging (*viellissement en bouteille*) is a process of refining. In the bottle, oxygen contact is significantly less than in the barrel. A certain period of bottle aging definitely makes for more balanced wines, their aromas better melded and their tannins and acids better integrated. In other words, the wine becomes more harmonious. Bottle aging is—in the first few years—largely a reductive process, that is to say, it happens practically without oxygen.

In some wine regions, laws forbid bottling certain wines before their statutory number of years in the barrel have passed. Production statutes enacted twenty or more years ago may stipulate that a wine has to be in the barrel for one, or two, or two and a half years before bottling. In some areas of Italy, the updating of such laws began only a few years ago, as for example in Brunello di Montalcino.

the wine is fermenting. Ethyl acetate, one of the most common esters in wine, is a product of acetic acid and ethyl alcohol; it is this ester that imparts to wine its fruity aroma. After fermentation, esters continue to build, as succinic and malic acids combine with alcohol. This process mellows the acids, so that after a few years the wine often tastes milder. At its peak, a wine exhibits an optimum balance among acids, esters, and alcohol.

Bottle versus Wooden Barrel
Long barrel storage brings with it the danger that the wine will be weak and tired, its freshness lost. To avoid this pitfall, more and more producers bottle their wines early and

The Danger of Excessive Air Contact
Air can enter the wine at three basic stages in the process of barrel aging: through the porous wood of the barrel, through the narrow neck of the bunghole, and during racking, the necessary transfer from one barrel to another. The most oxygen is taken in while the wine is being pumped into another barrel; the least, in the barrel.

- For each liter of wine that passes through tubes to another vessel, 3 to 4 cubic centimeters of oxygen are absorbed. If the wine is racked four times in its first year, one liter would receive 12 to 15 cubic centimeters.
- The total oxygen intake through the bunghole is 15 to 20 cubic centimeters per year.
- Between the staves of a wooden barrel, 2 to 5 cubic centimeters of oxygen enter the wine and are dissolved in it.

Third contact with air: Only traces of oxygen reach the wine through or between the staves of the wooden barrel.

The Final Polish

Before bottling the wine, the winemaker has to make sure that it is stable. Stable means that it is free of opacity or sediments, and will remain so. It may not start fermenting again and it may not contain any compounds that will alter it in the future.

White wines have to be stabilized in a relatively short time, since most of them are already on the market the February or March following their harvest. Stabilization is a process that consists of many distinct steps and begins long before bottling. It starts with the clarification of the wine. The aim of clarification is to free the wine of suspended debris so that it becomes, in the language of winemaking, optically clear. Next, steps have to be taken to protect the wine from later microbiological changes. In the past, wine was pasteurized to achieve this end. Today the same end is reached through filtration and separation or, more gently, through cooling and settling.

First Racking and Clarification
Stabilization begins with the clarification of the young wine after the alcoholic fermentation has ended. The wine is separated from most of the yeast, which has settled as a thick sediment on the bottom of the fermentation vessel. To be exact, the precipitated solids consist of dead yeast cells, bacteria, crystals of tartrate, bits of grape skin, and fragments of fruit pulp. This layer is called the lees. The more or less clear wine above the lees is racked off into another barrel. This first racking thus includes a clarification. By the way, it always involves deliberate oxygen contact in order to aerate the wine.

Not infrequently, this first clarification is fairly complete, especially if the wine was filtered or centrifuged as it was transferred. This procedure does stress the wine considerably, however, and while it may be a reasonable method for mass-produced wines, it is not appropriate for precious and expensive ones.

Yeast Maceration
Many winemakers with high aspirations emphasize the slow clarification of their wines. They delay the first racking so that the young wine can rest on the yeast for a few weeks. This allows additional tannin aromas to enter the wine, which make it fuller and more delicate. Wines that profit greatly from yeast maceration are those that were fermented in small wooden barrels. They are destined for a malolactic fermentation in any case, and the bacteria to initiate that process are located in the lees at the bottom of the barrel. For this reason, the yeast is regularly stirred with a stick, a *bâton,* which is why in Burgundy they call this stirring *bâtonnage. Bâtonnage* also aerates the wine, to lessen the risk that it will take on off odors. Only after this is the wine racked.

Cold Stabilization
It is common practice to place white wines that have been racked off the yeast into the

First racking of the wine: Fermentation is complete, and the wine needs aerating.

coldest part of the cellar, or to cool them down to 32°F (0°C) in a stainless steel tank. At such low temperatures, excess tartaric acid is precipitated and sinks to the bottom of the vessel in the form of crystals of tartrate, or argol. This procedure greatly reduces the danger that the wine will precipitate argols at a later date, in the bottle, where they could alarm uninformed consumers by their resemblance to splinters of glass. Argols consist of potassium hydrogen tartrate and represent neither an impurity in the wine nor a threat to its taste or aroma.

Fining White Wines
Just because a wine is clarified does not mean it is stable. It contains numerous organic compounds that could react under some external conditions and exert a deleterious effect on the wine. Proteins dissolved in the wine can normally be detected only under the microscope; but, left in the wine after it is bottled, they can coagulate when exposed to warmer conditions, as may prevail, for example, on a wine dealer's shelf. To remove them, the wine has to be fined.

Fining *(collage)* has as its purpose the precipitation of esters and other dissolved polymers in a solid form, so they can sink to the bottom of the vessel and thus be separated from the liquid. The most frequently used fining material is bentonite, a clay earth consisting of hydrated silicon and aluminum oxides suspended in water and added to the wine. Proteins in the wine adhere to the bentonite particles and sink to the bottom. Another approved fining agent is isinglass, which, like bentonite, leaves no trace on the taste of the wine.

Fining to Improve the Taste

Fining also serves to remove the possible faults in taste or aroma that wines will sometimes exhibit after fermentation. Among the substances used to fine in these situations are small amounts of charcoal or gelatin (to counteract the odor of hydrogen sulfide), or more rarely, yeast, tannin, calcium alginate, or potassium ferrocyanide (for the removal of heavy metals). All of these substances are officially permitted as fining agents (see page 99). All are odorless and have no taste of their own. It would be more appropriate to look on them as a form of intervention than of fining, however, since they all serve solely to "repair" improperly fermented wines. Faults in aroma and taste are always the result of mistakes in vinification.

The Second Racking

About eight weeks after the first racking, the new wine is racked again, this time without oxygen contact. This racking serves to draw the wine off its fine lees. The smallest particles that had still been suspended in the wine—the last of the yeast cells, small argol crystals, the precipitates created by fining materials—have had time to sink to the bottom of the vessel. If the lees were very coarse after the first racking, there will have been more fine particles left in suspension.

Some white wine producers like to macerate their wines on their fine lees for a long time. The labels of some French muscadets explicitly state that they were developed *sur lie;* but many producers of Riesling wines in Germany and Austria take maturing *sur lie* for

granted and do not bother to mention it. By the end of this maceration, most of the suspended materials are on the bottom of the vessel. Above the lees, the wine is clear. A third or fourth racking is seldom required; filtration before bottling will remove whatever last traces of opacity might be left. Now the wine is not just brightly polished, it is stable.

What Happens to Empty Barrels?

Barrels that will be unused for a long time, perhaps not till next year, have to be filled with water or a mixture of wine and water so that the staves do not dry out and contract, rendering the barrel leaky. In some wine regions, some of the yeast lees are added to the water. The reason is that within the lees live some of the bacteria necessary for malolactic fermentation. In this way the bacteria are rescued as a barrel is "prepared" for next year. The best way to treat an empty barrel, however, is to fill it with wine, or else to retire it. Small oak barrels are retired after four or five vintages have matured in them.

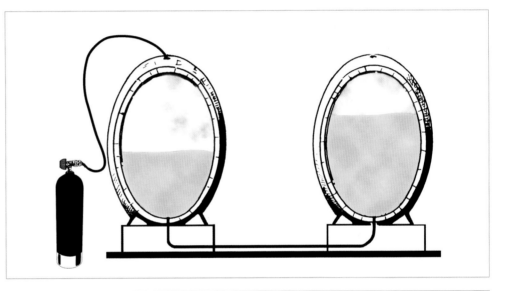

Above: Pumping wine into a new barrel without oxygen contact. Nitrogen or carbon dioxide gas is released into the top portion of the old barrel from the pressurized gas tank. The gas presses the wine through the hose on the bottom of the barrel into the bottom of the new barrel, which was first filled with the same gas. As the wine rises in the new barrel, it displaces the gas, which escapes through the bunghole. Below: Transferring wine with oxygen contact. The wine is drained from the first barrel, and the pump delivers it to the top of the second barrel.

Precipitated argol crystals.

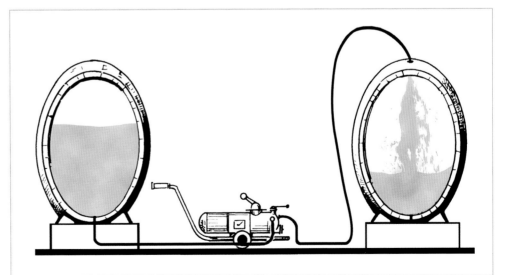

A Move Does Wonders

As with white wines, stabilization of red wines occurs during _élévage_. It extends over a longer period of time, however, than that of white wines because red wines are brought to market later.

Even before it is put in the barrel, red wine undergoes one stabilization: during malolactic fermentation, all malic acid is transformed into lactic acid, so that this fermentation cannot start again in bottle. Clarification and further stabilization then take place during maturation.

Racking the Wine

The wines of Bordeaux are traditionally racked four times in their first year. This changing of barrels is called _soutirage_. Its purpose is to free the wine from the sediments that accumulate on the bottom of the barrel. Besides the yeasts, bacteria, and other microorganisms, the lees of red wine contain argol and mineral salts, which could go back into solution later when the wine is exposed to higher temperatures. With each racking, less sediment is precipitated. In its second year the wine is almost clear. It is sufficient to rack it three times, or maybe only twice.

The Dangers of Frequent Racking

The red wines of other regions (with other barrel sizes) are not racked as frequently as those of Bordeaux. Each pumping operation stresses the wine. The pressure of the compressor and the unavoidable agitation can separate out some compounds, which is not desirable. The chemical balance of the wine is disturbed. At the first racking, it is important to aerate the wine; at that stage, the threat of oxidation is minimal. The wine is not yet saturated with carbon dioxide. Subsequent rackings usually take place in the absence of oxygen. The loss of wine caused by evaporation of its water content through the capillaries of the wood is minimal (1 to 2 percent per year), provided that the atmospheric humidity of the cellar is maintained around 85 percent. Bubbles of air around the bung are due primarily to the contraction of the fluid in winter. It is therefore important to keep the barrels filled right to the bung after each racking and

Fining of red wine: Into each barrel, the beaten whites of two eggs are introduced. Suspended particles in the liquid immediately bind with the egg white and sink to the bottom.

to top them up regularly. Every winemaker sets aside a barrel of wine for use in topping up *(ouillage).*

Fining Red Wine

Like white wine, red wine has to be rendered chemically stable, or fined. This includes removing a portion of the colloids suspended in the liquid. Colloids are the finest particles in the wine, mainly tannins, anthocyanins and other phenols, and proteins. Unless removed, they would separate out slowly later and leave a heavy sediment in the bottle. The average consumer would refuse to buy such wines. But even valuable wines made for connoisseurs need some fining to separate out unstable tannins and anthocyanins, as well as heat-sensitive proteins. After the next racking these compounds can then be removed as part of the lees.

Fining Agents

Frequently, the clay-rich mineral earth called bentonite, and less often diatomaceous earth, kaolin, and charcoal, are used, and also products containing egg white–gelatin, isinglass, and more rarely, albumin and casein. All of these materials are available in powder form. Often fresh chicken eggs are cracked open and their whites added to the barrel. Within minutes, the beaten egg white fuses with tannins and pigments, forming large-flaked colloids that are easily removed. Bentonite, which is well suited to binding with proteins, is used with care in red wines because it attacks tannins. The substances listed leave virtually no trace in the wine. In the past, whole milk and animal blood were also used for fining.

Filtering

Filtering wine is another means to render it stable. White wine is usually filtered when it is racked off the yeast; red wine, when maceration is over. Filters are usually made of rough layers of cellulose, calcium alginate (fossilized, pebbled algae), or perlite (a glasslike filter material made mostly of aluminum silicate). These filters remove the large particles from the wine. They replace sieves and cloth, simple methods that had been in use since the Sumerians first began filtering their wines.

Normally, wine is not filtered again until it is bottled. For this fine filtering, membranes are used nowadays. These consist of sheets of porous synthetic material that catch any remaining invisible particles suspended in the wine. With white wines and young red wines, a last fine filtration is necessary. In the case of red wines that have undergone lengthy *élévage,* it is a matter of judgment, since these wines have largely clarified themselves by means of settling.

The Pros and Cons of Filtration

Today, some producers of very valuable red wines try to manage entirely without filtration, with a view to preserve all of the wine's important flavor compounds. In this practice there always lurks the danger that later, in the bottle, the wine will not develop along optimal lines. Producers take this risk to be able to maintain the very best quality possible. Thus some of the most famous wines in the world are brought directly from barrel to bottle, as for example, some of the wines of Burgundy. It should be mentioned here that a strong, powerful cabernet sauvignon suffers less in filtration than a delicate, fragrant pinot noir. It all depends on the experience of the winemaker.

Topping up the barrel after racking.

Fining Wine

Fining wine serves to free it of the smallest residual particles and make it clear. To refine wine, albumin- or clay-rich substances are introduced into the barrel, to which the suspended particles bind through surface attraction or flake development, become weighed down, and sink to the bottom, where they can be removed. The wine is thus clarified and rendered "pure." Permitted fining agents are bentonite, kaolin earth, silica, tannin powder, gelatin, egg whites, fish bladder, casein (milk powder), and albumin (powdered eggs).

After refining, the wine must be filtered to remove these precipitated substances. Any possible residues impair neither the taste nor the purity of the wine. But albumin-content fining processes can cause allergic reactions, and since 2005 all wines fined with them must have an appropriate notice on the label–whether or not there is any residue in the wine.

It All Depends on the Dosage

Practically all wines on the market are "sulfured." If they were not, they would quickly oxidize and turn to vinegar. Naturally, sulfur is not an element that can be added to wine without great care. It can cause serious trouble. The rule is that the dosage must do no harm to either the wine or the consumer.

Sulfur was used as a means of preserving wine as far back as the ancient Greeks. It prevents wine from oxidizing. A wine that contains some sulfur will therefore present clean, clear aromas, while one that has not been treated will taste weak, lack freshness in its aroma, and quickly turn brown. The amounts of sulfur used are so minute that they cannot be tasted or smelled. The effects of sulfur on health are also practically nil. Although sulfur in large quantities can be a

other natural components of wine. Sulfur can be introduced in the form of a gas, as a liquid solution, or, as potassium disulfide, in a small tablet. The winemaker's task is to add just enough sulfur dioxide to his wine to ensure that it stays fresh as long as possible but not so much as to affect the wine's natural aromas. Naturally, the sulfur will not last forever. During aging it continuously decreases and is eventually all used up. At that point, oxidation will turn the wine to vinegar.

When Sulfur Is Added

At one time barrels were treated with sulfur before they were filled with wine. Today the wine is sulfured instead at three points during its production: at the must stage (with or without skins), after fermentation, and before bottling.

Adding sulfur to must serves to curtail the enzymes, namely oxygen-transferring oxi-

The first addition of sulfur: After fermentation all wines receive a light dose.

poison, headaches and nausea are much more likely to be due to high alcohol consumption, heartburn, and stomach upset than sulfur intolerance. In Australia and the United States, labeling laws require that a sulfur warning appear on the bottle.

How Sulfur Works

Hardly any substance reacts with oxygen more swiftly than does sulfur. This reaction preempts all attacks by oxygen on any of the

des. After fermentation, sulfur serves to neutralize the acetaldehyde that is formed in the wine when alcohol reacts with oxygen and that gives wine a disagreeable staleness. As for the final addition of sulfur, its purpose is to preserve the wine in the bottle.

The Culprit: Acetaldehyde

The main reason for adding sulfur is to bind acetaldehyde. Without this step, no wine can survive. The amounts added are small, be-

Château Latour 1956: Great red wines need little sulfur. Their tannins "eat up" oxygen.

tween 10 and 30 milligrams per liter. White wines, being more susceptible to oxidation, need a bit more sulfur, red wines a little less. Occasionally, even smaller extra amounts of sulfur may have to be added during *élevage,* in special cases where the wine goes through another brief fermentation, generating further acetaldehyde. Sulfur does not react with acetaldehyde alone; it also binds with other components of wine, namely, benzyl-racemic acid, the keto-acid group, and glucose. Thus sulfur can alter and detract from the aroma of wine. Makers of good wine attempt to keep the addition of sulfur to an absolute minimum.

Sulfur, Bound and Free
Sulfur occurs in wine in either bound or free form. Bound sulfur has already reacted with acetaldehyde and other components of wine. It is undetectable to the senses and has no effect on health. This is not true of free sulfur,

which is present as sulfite— that is, as a salt— or as sulfuric acid. It is this free sulfur that can sometimes be smelled and have adverse effects on health if the wine contains too much. Healthwise, then, it is solely a matter of how much free sulfuric acid is in the wine.

Adding Sulfur before Bottling
After fermentation, only as much sulfur is added as is needed to bind the acetaldehyde. It is at the bottling stage that wine makers add that sulfur which is meant to protect the wine from any oxidation in the bottle. This is called free sulfur. White wines contain between 34 and 45 milligrams of free sulfuric acid per liter; red wines need only 20 to 35 milligrams. Sweet late wines contain the most, at 60 to 80 milligrams. Less sulfur is required in wines made of healthy grapes, in which rotten grapes were rare in the harvest. Careful vinification can also reduce the amount of acetaldehyde generated, and thus, the need for sulfur. Of the total amount of sulfur contained in wine, free sulfuric acid represents only about 20 percent, bound sulfur, 80 percent.

Wines Low and High in Sulfur
Up to now, no effective substitute has been found for sulfur. It is therefore impossible to make sulfur-free wines without sacrificing quality or durability. Some winemakers, especially in the United States, nevertheless use ascorbic acid before bottling instead. Ascorbic acid, or vitamin C, also has antioxidant properties; but unlike sulfur, ascorbic acid does not inhibit enzymes and so cannot be substituted for the sulfur that is added to grape juice.

It is important to keep the total amount of sulfur in wines as low as possible. To minimize the amount required it is essential to process newly picked grapes quickly. If the producer is able to turn them into must while they are still healthy, he can eliminate the need to spray the grapes themselves with sulfur. Unfortunately, mass production in hot regions, where the trip from vineyard to winery is long, still makes spraying mandatory, although the quality of grapes is definitely impaired by it.

Second addition of sulfur, at the bottling stage.

Sulfur in tablet form: It goes into the wine, not the barrel.

Maximum Legal Sulfur Content Permitted for the Member Countries of the European Union (milligrams per liter)	
Dry red wine (up to 5 g of sugar)	160
Dry white wine (up to 5 g of sugar)	210
Dry white wine (over 5 g of sugar)	260
Spätauslese	300
Auslese	350
Beerenauslese, Trockenbeerenauslese, ice wine, sweet wines	400

All a Matter of Aging

The wooden barrel is the most frequently used container for aging wine. The barrel's most significant feature is that it allows the wine to breathe. The steady supply of oxygen it provides speeds the process of polymerization. This in turn makes the wine softer, more harmonious, more complex.

It is above all red wine that is aged in wood. While most white wines lose freshness and are made stale by lengthy storage in wood, red wines are not damaged by the oxygen that reaches them through the staves of the barrel. Because of its high phenolic content, red wine can stand oxygen, even needs it to mature well. Looked at in this way, aging is nothing but the slow oxidation of the wine.

Barrel Size

The amounts of oxygen that pass through the staves of the barrel are very small. Just how small depends on the size of the barrel. Size is of critical importance for the timing of the aging process. One thousand liters of wine held in one large barrel have half as much wood contact as 1,000 liters divided among four 225-liter barriques. It follows that small-barrel aging is only appropriate for wines so high in phenols that they are able to withstand the intense aeration. Bordeaux's *premiers grands crus,* the great red wines from the Spanish Priorato, a few California cabernet sauvignons, and the best of the Australian shiraz wines can age in these small barrels, in good years, for twenty-four months. A light pinot noir from Alsace would probably show the first signs of tiredness after no more than six months, but in large wood barrels it can be aged for a longer period. The best Italian Brunello is aged in large casks for as long as two to three years, and some of the greatest Barolos for five years, without suffering any damage.

The size of the barrel is what matters. In small barrels, the wine has more intense contact with the wood, in large ones, less. The smallest of the commonly used barrels are the barriques (near right and below). These are from Bordeaux and hold exactly 225 liters. In Burgundy they are a little smaller, holding 205 liters. In the Portuguese Douro Valley they also employ small barrels to store port. They are called pipes (right); they hold either 550 or 580 liters.

The Thickness of the Wood

The size of the barrel also determines the thickness of the barrel's staves. The larger the barrel, the thicker they have to be to hold the weight of the liquid contents. So that they do not burst from the pressure of the weight, barrels are held together by metal bands. The staves of a 50-hectoliter barrel that are 4 inches (10 cm) thick let only very small amounts of oxygen pass through them. The staves of the small *barriques* are less than 1 inch (2.5 cm) thick, and thus allow much more oxygen through. This explains why small barrels promote faster aging.

The Effect of New Wood

Aging in a small barrel has yet another effect on the wine. The tannins of the wood are dissolved and transferred to the wine, altering its taste to a greater or lesser degree—at least, as long as the barrels are new. The amount of tannin involved is not insignificant. In its first year, a *barrique* transfers about 200 milligrams of tannin to the wine it holds. This corresponds to about one tenth of the tannins from the grape skins. Oak tannins are in any case very different from those of grape skins; for one thing, they are not polymerized and so do not change with the age of the wine. They also consist of different carbohydrate compounds. Oak tannins add to the bouquet of the wine their typical notes of vanilla, roasted hazelnuts, cloves, and caramel. Unfortunately, some of these notes may not enhance the wine's own aroma, but overwhelm it.

After three or at most five years of use, the influence of a wooden barrel is down to zero. Commercial wineries simply use oak chips or even chemical essences to add oak tones to their wines, but serious winemakers eschew such measures.

Along the Rhine, many a German Riesling ages in old barrels called Stückfässer (right), which hold 1,000 liters. On the Mosel, the customary size is the double Stückfässer, which holds 2,000 liters. Other regions use the half Stückfässer (500 liters). Traditional red wines are aged in old barrels of oak, chestnut, acacia, cherry, or other wood (left). Huge barrels can hold 150 hectoliters; very small ones 7.5 hl.

Barrel Making—An Ancient Craft

Many old coopers' tools have been replaced by machines, like the adze and the croze, which were once used for carving the groove, called the croze, into which the barrel head is fitted. Opening used barrels to remove the argol from the inside of the staves and to give the barrel a new scorching are also jobs the cooper (tonnelier) takes on.

Splitting the Wood

Quartering the log along the fibers of the wood is not done by hand anymore; a mechanical splitting tool is used. Splitting has the advantage over sawing that the cell structure of the wood is not damaged. It is nonetheless often true that oak logs are not quartered any more, but are sawed into staves right off, producing less waste.

Storing the Wood Outdoors

Building a barrel is a matter of technique; storage of the wood is a factor that determines the quality of the barrel. Traditionally it has been the rule to store oak under the open sky for three years, to let the sun dry it and the rain wash out the sharp tannins as well as the polysaccharide and glucose. Today most barrel wood is dried artificially in ovens, shortening the whole process to three to twelve months.

Assembling the Staves into a Barrel

The size of the staves for a barrique is determined according to a mathematical formula. The wood is then trimmed and sawed, and the individually shaped staves are put together without glue. That the edges of the staves fit tightly is assured by the wine itself: it makes the wood swell so that the liquid cannot escape.

"Toasting" the Barrel

Before the bottom is fitted in, the barrel has to be toasted, the technical term for the scorching of the inner walls. The burning changes the chemical structure of the wood and later imparts to the wine a roasted tinge. Depending on the wines that the barrel is made to hold, it receives a light, medium, or heavy toast.

Fitting the Hoops

After the heads have been fitted into the barrel, the temporary iron hoops are removed and permanent metal hoops are placed around the body of the barrel. They hold the barrel together and guarantee that it will not spring apart under the weight of the wine. The bung hole is then drilled into the thicker bung stave.

Artificially Wooded Wine

Oak chips instead of barrels: Roasted wood shavings and powder add aroma to the wine.

Globalization of the wine market is proceeding apace. To cut costs, winemaking procedures are being simplified and the amount of time required for aging radically curtailed. Many of the new cellaring techniques can no longer be reconciled with traditional notions of wine production.

Increasing numbers of wine suppliers on the world market have led to stiff competition. Overseas wine-producing countries are imposing new wine styles on the European market. For their part, Europe's wine-producing countries are being threatened with overproduction and are defending themselves by striving for new levels of quality. Everyone's goal is to offer wine as cheaply as possible, and thereby secure a market share. Unfortunately, quality is all too often sacrificed, and often the term "quality" is simply redefined to bring it into harmony with the new imperatives. This is mainly a matter

of simplifying cellaring procedures to save money. Winemakers are experimenting with various ways of attaining the desired quality even when the vine does not provide it.

Aging in Oak Barrels

High-quality red wines are traditionally aged in new, small oak barrels. The virtue of such barrels, also called *barriques*, is that the wine's tannins react with the tannin in the wood, which "softens" them, making the wine more durable and stabilizing its color. The downside is that the wines take on the slightly sweet aroma of the tannin, reminiscent of vanilla, roasted coffee beans, or cedar. The woody taste can be quite strong, especially in the first years, yet many younger consumers do not find the woody tone a drawback at all. On the contrary, they prefer it. To them it has become a typical characteristic of a high-quality wine. Therefore, more and more producers have turned to aging their red wines in small

oak casks. Good red wines may have profited, but others have definitely been denatured by *barrique* aging.

Artificial Wood Taste from Chips

Feeling the need to satisfy the taste preferences of consumers, the wine industry has tried to deliver the wines consumers expect. But *barriques* are expensive and aging in them takes between eight and eighteen months. Moreover, large air-conditioned cellars are required to store them—unprofitable for simple, lower-priced red wines. Some time ago shrewd oenologists hit upon the idea of suspending netting bags of inexpensive oak shavings—so-called chips—in the steel tanks in which the wine is fermented or aged. This way the wine takes on the aroma of oak even if it is not meant to be especially durable and does not require its tannin. It is simply a matter of cost: *barrique* aging automatically makes a wine at least two dollars more expensive, whereas aging with chips adds only a few cents a bottle. While still young, the resulting wines are indistinguishable.

Stave Technology

Another way of imparting artificial aroma is even less expensive: stave technology. Thin oak slats are mounted in a metal frame that is placed in the steel tank. The slats are constantly washed by liquid while the mash ferments. The amount of wood surface in contact with the wine is considerably greater than with chips, and the oak aroma imparted is correspondingly stronger. Handling the staves is simple, and the cost of the oak is modest; the staves–like chips–are byproducts of barrel-making. The oak aroma of stave and chip wines is identical to that of *barrique*-aged wines, and even in the laboratory it is impossible to tell whether a wine was aged in a wooden barrel or in a large steel tank with oak chips. Outside Europe the use of alternative oak is therefore allowed. Europe's wine authorities forbid the use of "pieces of oak," as they are officially called. Chips and staves, they argue, do not promote aging, they simply add aroma; accordingly, they are not part of traditional cellaring techniques and cannot be allowed. Since to date–and presumably in the future as well–it cannot be determined whether a wine was aged in oak barrels or provided with aroma artificially, it will be impossible to enforce such a ban much longer without handicapping European wine producers. Ultimately, aging in *barriques* also results in aromatic wines, whether or not this is desired.

Micro-oxygenation

The cost advantages of producing aroma with "pieces of oak" are in part owing to the reduced amount of time required for aging. Instead of spending a year or more in the barrel, stave and chip wines take on the desired oak flavor in only eight weeks. Of course, at that point the wine is still not mature. To hasten maturing, winemakers frequently employ the technique of micro-oxygenation developed in Bordeaux. Tiny quantities of oxygen (roughly ten milliliters per liter per day) are infused into the freshly fermented wine. The introduced oxygen helps to remove unpleasant fermentation gases and faulty notes. Also, the bitter tannins polymerize, becoming softer and integrating

New barriques*: Too expensive and difficult to make for inexpensive, everyday wines.*

Stave technology: Thin oak slats are inserted into a steel tank.

Artificial Concentration

Modern oenology attempts to influence the nature and character of wine not only during aging, but even during the vinification process itself. With technology it is possible to achieve more concentrated wines, especially reds. The oldest form of concentration is racking (or saignée). In it a portion of the liquid is removed from the mash so that the concentration of color and tannin in the remaining portion is increased. A trickier method is vacuum steaming, which takes advantage of the fact that in a vacuum, water begins to vaporize between 10 and 25°C. This water vapor is captured, condensed, and let off into a water tank. The remaining must is more concentrated. Since the vacuum vaporizer only draws out water and does not add foreign substances, the wine is still a natural product. This concentration method can be used for both white and red wines. Using another technique it is also possible to withdraw water from the wine by reverse osmosis (see page 77). But like vacuum vaporization, it is involved and expensive. In any case, artificial concentration only makes sense if the must is of high quality. If it is not, its negative features (insufficient ripeness, for example) are only accentuated.

the wood flavor. In other words: the aging processes to which wine is traditionally exposed in the breathing barrel can be speeded up in the steel tank through oxygenation. The wine is then fully mature in only a few months. Winemakers are not in complete agreement about micro-oxygenation. Although it may cut the cost of simple wines, it is not appropriate in the aging of high-quality wines.

Wines for No Special Occasion

Champagne, port, and sherry have one thing in common: they owe their creation to special circumstances or happy chance. For port, it was the War of the Spanish Succession; for sherry, a crime, namely the raid on Cadiz by Sir Francis Drake. For Champagne, it was a series of coincidences; the discovery of sparkling wine in France happened about the same time as the development of pressed glass in England.

Asked on what occasion she drank Champagne, Mme Lily Bollinger replied: "I drink it when I am happy, and I also drink it when I am sad. Sometimes I drink it when I am alone. In company I drink it, for sure. Even when I have no appetite, I like to take a little glass of it. And when I do have an appetite, of course I reach for it. But otherwise, I do not touch it—unless I am thirsty." Many have followed the example of the grand old lady, and many still do. But a few Englishmen have found Champagne to be decadent: "I forego Champagne, and henceforth at my domestic hearth I shall partake only of humble port." But that is history. Today, the English drink both—and sherry, besides.

The Realm of Effervescence

The first time he drank a sparkling wine, Dom Pérignon exclaimed: "I am drinking stars." The monk from the abbey of Hautvillers near Reims did not invent Champagne, but he did understand what the bubbles are for: they heighten the taste of the wine.

Champagne is the most famous sparkling wine in the world. Its fine effervescence and its delicate taste have made it into the symbol of exalted French taste in wines. Champagne grows in the *département* of Marne (about 93 miles [150 kilometers] northeast of Paris) and in four neighboring *départements*. It is the most northerly and the coolest wine region of France. Only a wine that grew there may call itself Champagne, and only if it was made according to the bottle fermentation method.

How Sparkling Wine Is Made

Sparkling wine is the result of a second fermentation of the still wine. This happens when the finished wine is bottled and a small amount of wine, yeast, and sugar (24 grams

The widow Nicole Clicquot had the idea of turning Champagne bottles in order to loosen the yeast.

per liter) is added to the bottle. Immediately, the yeast begins to ferment the sugar in the bottle. After one or two months, the fermentation is complete, and the wine's alcohol content has been raised by 1.2 percent. This bottle fermentation, like any other, produces carbon dioxide. The gas cannot escape because the bottle is closed airtight by a crown cork. The carbon dioxide remains dissolved in the wine.

Disgorging

The bottles are stored in the cellar, horizontally, on top of one another, so that the dead yeast cells settle in the belly of each bottle. Depending on the type of sparkling wine, it now rests for a period of from nine months to five years on its lees without being moved. This maceration on the lees *(tirage)* is important for the wine: it keeps it fresh, and the yeast lends it a series of complex flavor compounds.

After resting on its lees, the Champagne will have to be cleared of the yeast. To accomplish this, the bottle is plunged headfirst into a freezing solution. The yeast, which has accumulated in the neck, freezes into a single icy lump. Immediately, the crown cork is removed and with the release of pressure the yeast is shot far out of the bottle. The wine is now clear, and the bottle is swiftly recorked for a final time. This process is called disgorging.

Riddling

Before disgorging, however, the yeast deposits have to be moved to the neck of the bottle. The widow Clicquot had the idea of drilling holes into her kitchen table and standing the bottles in them, upside-down, before disgorging them. Today, the bottles are placed at a slight angle into a riddling rack *(pupitre de remuage)*, so that the yeast can slowly slide into the neck. Even though Champagne yeast is chosen for its large-grained sediment, it will adhere slightly to the walls of the bottle and has to be dislodged. Every day, the bottles in the riddling rack are turned slightly to loosen the yeast. It takes twenty-one days to move all the yeast into the neck of the bottle.

The *Dosage*

After disgorging, sparkling wine is clear. To avoid losing too much carbon dioxide, the bottles are corked and labeled immediately. Before this, however, the wine receives an addition of sugar syrup dissolved in wine. This *dosage* has two effects: it restores the level of the wine in the bottle, which had been lowered somewhat by the disgorgement of the yeast, and it also sweetens the Champagne a little. Almost all standard Champagnes and nonvintage sparkling wines are given this final dose *(liqueur d'expédition)*, containing more or less sugar, to harmonize the taste of the wine. Since these wines usually contain

more acid than normal, even after the addition of some sugar, they still taste dry *(brut)*. Only valuable vintage Champagnes or sparkling wines from other regions that have rested on the lees for long periods, are corked without *dosage. Brut nature, dosage zéro,* or *pas dosé* will then be printed on their labels. The pressure of the carbon dioxide in the bottle amounts to five or six atmospheres, which corresponds roughly to the pressure in the tire of a car.

Assemblage

Eighty percent of all Champagne is marketed without vintage. This means that it is blended from two or more vintages. Blending several base wines into a homogeneous, harmonious wine is called *assemblage.* Mainly, three grape varieties are blended. Often older vintages of pinot noir and chardonnay are used, wines that have had a chance to mature in steel tanks for twelve to twenty-four months. Occasionally the winemaker will reach for still older, valuable reserve wines in order to add nobility to his *assemblage.*

Connoisseurs believe that the ability to create a great *assemblage* is the true mark of a great Champagne house. What is involved is the ability to taste and evaluate hundreds of wines, so that the end result is 5 or even 10 million bottles of wine of uniform quality—the number of bottles a large house will release. Only about 20 percent of total production is marketed as vintage Champagne.

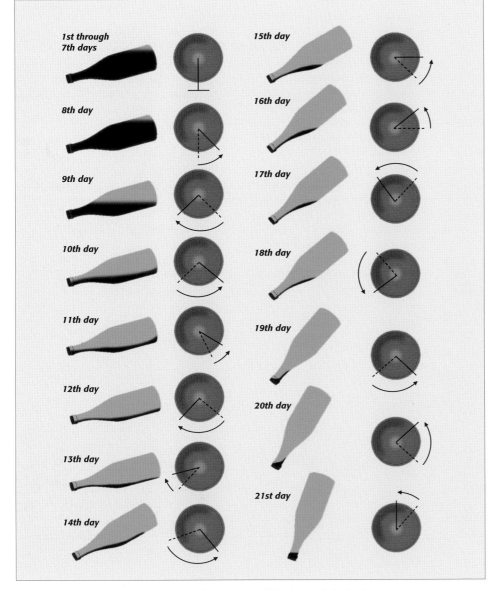

The system of riddling: For three weeks, the Champagne is riddled by hand. The bottles are turned at a certain angle each day, and at the same time tilted.

All sparkling wines that undergo bottle fermentation have to be riddled . . .

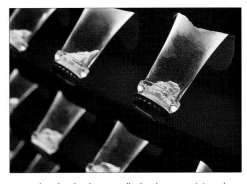

. . . so that the dead yeast cells that have precipitated are collected in the neck of the bottle . . .

and the wine can be disgorged in an icy bath, freed of every trace of yeast.

Plenty of Kinds of Bubbly

The First Wine Master

It was Dom Pérignon (1639–1715) who realized that a wise blending of wines from different varieties and vineyard lots can yield a far better end product. The discovery of sparkling wine, however, took place in London, not in Champagne. While around 1650 the French still stoppered their wine bottles with oil-soaked rags that allowed air to enter into them, the merchants of England were already using corks. The fizz from any unwanted fermentation that happened in these airtight bottles could not escape, so the carbon dioxide remained in the wine. When the bottle was opened, the wine would foam. Deliberate bottle fermentation was attempted in Champagne for the first time about 1700. It was not very successful; most of the bottles exploded. Only after the English could deliver stronger bottles to France did bottle fermentation become viable.

DOM PÉRIGNON

Dazzled by the brilliant aura of Champagne, producers of sparkling wines the world over have imitated the technique of its bottle fermentation. Few winemakers can be said to be masters of the high art of making sparkling wine. Those few, however, have proved that it is possible to make high-class sparkling wines outside of Champagne, from the same grapes or using other varieties.

Champagne is traditionally made of three kinds of grapes: white chardonnay and two red varieties, pinot noir and pinot meunier. The latter two are made into white wine by fermenting them without their skins. Thus the color of the skins does not enter the wine. Pinot noir gives Champagne its fullness, chardonnay gives it finesse, and pinot meunier gives it fruit.

Assemblage

Before fermentation in the bottle can begin, the three wines have to be melded into one wine. *Assemblage* is the name given to this blending. During *assemblage*, it has to be decided in what proportion the three wines should be blended. Much skill and experience in wine tasting is required for this job. Often dozens of wines in different vats and barrels have to be tasted to decide whether and in what proportion a wine should enter the final blend. For this reason, *assemblage* always involves several people. The proprietor, the sales director, and other good palates are invited to taste the blend and, if necessary, to change it.

Styles of Champagne

Assemblage determines the style of a Champagne house. Bollinger traditionally uses a high proportion of pinot noir. Billecart-Salmon adds more chardonnay. High-class Champagnes usually also contain a small amount of older wines. Krug's *grands cuvées* always include at least six different vintages. Selecting them is part of the art of *assemblage*.

Champagne does not necessarily have to include three wines. It can be made out of a chardonnay alone *(blanc de blancs)*, or out of pinot noir alone *(blanc de noirs)*; rose Champagne is made of pinot noir grapes alone. A Champagne house depends for its success very largely on its *assemblage*.

Sparkling Wine: Crémant, Spumante, Cava, Sekt

The art of making sparkling wines is no longer the sole province of the producers of Champagne. California and Australia now make some first-class sparkling wines out of chardonnay and pinot noir grapes. Italy also produces a few very high-class spumantes. In France itself, sparkling wines are made in northern and southern Burgundy, largely out of chardonnay grapes. These wines made outside the Champagne region are called crémants.

In addition to Crémant de Bourgogne, the list includes Crémant de Loire (made mostly of chenin

Many great Epernay Champagne houses store their wine in natural subterranean limestone cellars with passages that extend for miles.

Champagne: The view from the Montagne de Reims over the little village of Ville-Dommange. On its slopes grows a steely chardonnay.

blanc), Crémant de Die (made of clairette), Crémant d'Alsace (made of pinot blanc, pinot gris, pinot noir, auxerrois, and Riesling), Crémant de Limoux (made of blanquette), and Crémant de Bordeaux (made of sémillon, sauvignon blanc, and muscat). Some of these are the equal of Champagne. Austria and Germany make Sekt; nineteenth-century Sekts were the most important competition for Champagne. Today, some of them reach the level of a good Champagne, even though they are made of different grapes (in Austria Grüner Veltliner, Welschriesling, and Riesling; in Germany predominantly Riesling). The same goes for cava from the Penedés, Spain's best-known sparkling wine. The fame of the red Russian Crimea Sekts has faded since the revolution of 1917.

Prestige Cuvées and Vintage Sparkling Wines

In addition to their standard sparkling wine, which represent a blend of vintages produced in large quantities, most great Champagne houses also make limited quantities of highest-quality cuvées. Some famous prestige cuvées are "R.D." and "Grande Année" (Bollinger), "Louise Pommery" (Pommery), "Cristal" (Roederer), "La Grande Dame" (Veuve Clicquot), "Comtes de Champagne" (Taittinger), and "Nicolas François" (Billecart-Salmon). These wines consist of first pressings, contain a large component of reserve wines, have rested on their lees, and can be expected to last twenty to thirty years. Similar claims can be made for vintage sparkling wines.

A marmonnier is the traditional basket press of Champagne. It holds 5,280 pounds (2,400 kg) of grapes, which are pressed uncrushed; the maximum amount of must obtainable from one lot is 1,500 liters. The first 900 liters are the cuvée—the highest quality. The next 350 and 250 liters are the second and third tailles.

Other Methods of Making Sparkling Wine

Bottle fermentation with long years of aging and the subsequent processes of riddling and disgorging are labor-intensive and expensive. For these reasons, experts have devised simpler, less expensive methods for making sparkling wines. None of these seem to be able to deliver the fine bubbles of the *méthode champenoise.*

The Charmat Method

The second fermentation of the base wine takes place under pressure in large stainless steel tanks. The yeast deposits are removed before bottling by filtration. This industrial method was invented in Bordeaux; it is well suited to simpler sparkling wines, such as the Italian prosecco, spumante, and many German Sekts.

Transversage

After bottle fermentation, as with Champagne, the bottles are opened; their contents are then poured into a tank. The yeast is filtered out, and the wine is bottled under pressure. This method was developed in the United States and is also used there for high-quality sparkling wines.

Carbonation

Without a second fermentation, the wine is injected with carbon dioxide from a tank and bottled under pressure. The wines so made are not sparkling but fizzy (*frizzante* in Italian, *pétillant* in French).

Dosage for Sparkling Wines (grams of sugar per liter)

Brut nature, pas dosé, dosage zéro, naturherb	up to 3
Extra brut	under 6
Brut	under 15
Extra dry	12–20
Dry	17–35
Mild	over 50

"The Englishman's Wines"

Port: The Most Important Styles

Ruby

Dark ruby red, sweet as jam, this port is aged four years. Ruby represents the greatest bulk of all port sold; it is always blended from base vines of various vintages.

Tawny

These mahogany-brown ports are usually aged longer than ruby, and can in some cases be assembled from small lots of wines that are twenty, thirty, or forty years old, in which case, they are very fine. Tawny port is ready to drink and should be enjoyed soon after opening, as it oxidizes easily.

Colheita

This tawny port is made of a single vintage and is barrel aged at least seven years, usually more. LVP (late-bottled vintage) is vintage port from a lesser year, usually aged four years. Though it can be very good, it often turns out to be just a better Ruby.

Vintage Port

This wine is only made in "great" or "very good" years. It is aged for two years in wood and then requires twenty to thirty years in the bottle before reaching its acme of perfection. It represents 1 percent of total port production.

White Port

White port only rests on the skins for a short time or is made of one of the few white grape varieties that grow on the Douro. It is aged for a maximum of eighteen months in a tank and is somewhat less sweet, sometimes almost dry. Its alcohol content is 17 percent per volume. About 15 percent of all the port made is white.

Vintage port has to be laid down to age at least for twenty years to be enjoyable, but tawny port is ready when it reaches the market.

Topping barrels in which tawny port is aging. Evaporation accounts for 3 percent per year.

Port and Madeira were invented by English wine merchants, and once were particularly appreciated by the intellectual upper class. Since winters are long in the British Isles and the colleges of the eighteenth century were unheated, scholars liked to warm themselves with port or Madeira. In this age of central heating, their tastes have changed somewhat: these wines are drunk for enjoyment alone.

Port is a sweet red wine that is fortified by the addition of wine spirits. The result is a heavy, intoxicating wine, opaque in color, with an alcoholic strength of 19 to 22 percent. In its way it is of unmatched greatness. Port comes from the terraced slopes above the Douro River in the north of Portugal. The wine gets its name from the city of Porto on the lower reaches of the river. On the riverbank opposite the city are the warehouses of the great port merchants. This is where the wine is aged. The English influence is still very strong in the port wine market. The warehouses are called lodges; the firms have names like Cockburn, Taylor, Dow, Sandeman, or Graham. And though it is now sold all over the world, port is still considered "the Englishman's wine."

How Port Is Made

Forty-eight varieties of grapes are used in the production of port, of the over one hundred varieties that still grow in the Douro Valley. Most of these are red varieties. In the past they were crushed by foot treading in large wooden troughs *(lagares)*, but now the work is accomplished by hydraulic presses. The must ferments on the skins, but after only one or two days the fermentation is stopped by the addition of 77 percent wine brandy. The wine is racked off the lees while it still contains 40 to 60 grams of unfermented sugar per liter. In the spring, the wine is taken in tank cars to Porto and stored in barrels with a capacity of 520 liters, called pipes. The wine then

the wine is kept at 104 to 122°F (40 to 50°C) for several months. It is heated either by the immersion of heating units or by heating the *estufas,* the so called "oven rooms." This heat treatment speeds up the maturation of the wine and caramelizes the sugar. Madeira needs maturity very badly; it comes with both high tannin content and high acidity, including a lot of volatile acid, which can be detected in the bouquet. Madeira's taste ranges anywhere from chocolate sweetness to rancid dryness.

High-Class Madeira is Rare

Most Madeiras made might just be good enough for cooking, but there are a few high-class wines among

The English may have invented port and Madeira, but they are drunk around the world.

In the vineyards of the Douro, around one hundred varieties of grapes are grown; many of them can be used for port.

ages at least two, but in some cases as long as twenty or even forty years.

The Making of Madeira

Madeira is also a fortified sweet red wine. It comes from the island of Madeira, where they make it largely out of the tinta negra mole variety of grapes. Qualitatively, it is a middling variety that was only resorted to after the phylloxera catastrophe. Unlike port, Madeira undergoes a special heat treatment after it is spirited. In bricked-up concrete tanks, in stainless steel, in glass carboys, or in wooden vats,

them. Most of these grow at altitudes of 5,900 feet (1800 m), on mountain terraces increasingly planted with old white varieties—sercial, boal, malvasia, and verdelho. These white wines get their dark color from the heat, but they are usually allowed to ripen slowly without being artificially heated. They are put down to age in 600-liter pipes under the roofs of the dealers' lodges, where it is cool in winter and very hot in summer. These vintage Madeiras, or *vinhos de canteiro,* have aromas of malt and caramel, vanilla, sweet almonds, raisins, and dried fruit. They are among the longest-lived of wines.

Madeira: The Most Important Styles

Standard Madeira is blended of several vintages, and even when it is labeled Extra Dry it retains a marked residual sweetness. Most Madeiras, however, are more or less sweet wines. The best are made from the noble grape varieties and carry their names on their labels.

The Generally Accepted Hierarchy
Finest (3 years)
Reserve (5 years)
Special reserve (10 years)
Extra reserve (15 years)
Vintage (at least 20 years)

Sercial
A relatively light, usually moderately dry Madeira with a lively acidity, Sercial is a fine aperitif wine. It needs aging and is almost dry when old.

Verdelho
This aromatic, strong wine from the north side of the island is dry to moderately sweet and has a fine nose of nuts. It is very long-lived.

Boal
Boal is a dark, caramel-colored wine with a rich and fragrant bouquet. It has a definite sweetness and tastes slightly "burned." Also called Bual.

Malmsey
Malmsey is the rarest, sweetest, darkest Madeira, made exclusively of malvasia grapes that grow on the southern slopes of the island. The full taste is carried by the alcohol, which mellows the lemony freshness of the acidity.

Southern Fire

Soleras *in one of the bodegas of Jerez: Fino, amontillado, and oloroso are the finest types of sherry.*

duction figures. First it is fermented like any other white wine and laid down to age in barrels called butts. In the barrel, a unique grayish yellow film of *flor* yeast builds on the surface of the wine. It grows and grows, until it forms a waxy cover over the wine, essentially closing off its air supply. *Flor* makes for the critical difference between sherry and other fortified white wines. It leaves characteristic flavor nuances of bitter almonds in the wine, for which it is carefully tended. *Flor* yeast is sensitive to high alcohol levels, for example, and it is for this reason that fino sherries are spirited with small doses at a time and seldom have more than 15 percent alcohol.

Similar treatment is given to manzanilla, the fino variant from the neighboring city of Sanlúcar de Barrameda, not far from Jerez, on the mouth of the Gualdalquivir. Manzanilla is more delicate than fino. The natives of Sanlúcar drink it with fish and crayfish.

The white wine used for making sherry is flat and lacks interest. Only after it has been transformed by aguardente, the brandy that is added to it in small amounts, does it reveal its full, unmistakable flavor and inimitable fire.

There are many variants of sherry. It comes bone-dry or wholly sweet; it can be dark or light; it can be strong or low in alcohol. There are two basic types, the straw-colored, dry fino and the dark oloroso. These two basic types are the starting point for dozens of variations to be found on the market, ranging from syrupy liqueurs to refined, nobly aged dry wines.

Fino and Manzanilla

Fino, from the region of Jerez de la Frontera, is the classical dry sherry, even though it is not on top of the list of sherries in terms of pro-

Amontillado

In the hot summers of Andalusia, even the roomy warehouses of the sherry dealers heat up. In the heat, the layer of *flor* on the wine can break, since the *flor* yeasts do not like heat. Air reaches the wine and oxidizes it, and fino becomes amontillado, developing more fullness and an amber coloring. A real amontillado, then, is a fino that aged without *flor*

A fino sherry with its unique flor yeast layer: Under the flor, the sherry ages practically without oxygen.

Solera

In the sherry bodegas the butts are ranged up to five high. The highest butts contain the youngest wine, called criadera; the bottom layer is the oldest. This wine is called solera. Two or three times a year, 20 or 30 percent of the wine from the solera butts is siphoned off; it is ready. These butts are replenished with newer wine from the first criadera, immediately above. These butts are in turn topped up by still newer wine from above. Thus the younger wines are gradually blended with the old.

Tasting sherry is a celebration: The venencia *was developed to remove small samples of sherry from under the* flor *cover in the butt.*

Its outcome is to blend young wines with older, aged vintages, so that in very old manzanillas, there may be as many as nineteen different vintages. Although the system guarantees that all the sherry bottled at any time will be of the same style and quality, it was developed for a completely different reason. In order to keep the *flor* yeast alive, older butts have to be replenished with younger wine at regular intervals. This is necessary since alcohol content goes up as the wine ages under the yeast; new wine, lower in alcohol, has to be added to dilute it, or the yeast will be killed by the alcohol.

Palo cortado: This rare, high-class sherry consists of numerous small samplings of oloroso from the solera. Since sherry is normally marketed as fino or oloroso, it is hard to find.

Pale Cream: A light, commercial sherry, sweetened with *mistela*.

Manzanilla pasada: An extremely fine, fully matured manzanilla that has rested under the *flor* for only a short time. It displays a salty note.

Raya: This modestly sweet sherry-type wine, made of dried grapes, is practically never bottled but used only for blending.

yeast protection and is completely dry: a fantastic potion, with a fine aroma of oranges and hazelnuts. Genuine amontillados are very rare, since most makers of sherry do not wait for the accidental collapse of the *flor* cover but deliberately promote it. One way to do this is to raise the alcohol content of fino to 16 percent, so the yeast dies. The wine is then blended in the *solera* and sweetened with *vinos dulces,* the sweet reserve. The most commonly sold amontillado is medium dry.

Oloroso

Oloroso is a sherry without *flor* yeast. The wine's alcohol level is raised to 18 percent after fermentation, so that no yeast can develop. Thus oloroso ages with oxygen contact, and this oxidative aging process imparts a dark caramel color and a pungent flavor, with a tinge of dried fruit. Since the long years in the *solera* mean that some liquid will evaporate (3 to 6 percent per year per butt), the alcohol content can exceed 23 percent. Olorosos are by nature dry sherries. Very old olorosos are in fact among the most exquisite and most costly of all. In practice, most oloroso is cut with sweet must and reaches the shelves of supermarkets as "cream sherry." The best *mistela,* as the intensely sweet blending wine is called, is also known as PX, as it is made of dried Pedro Ximénez grapes. These used to be grown widely in Jerez, but are now hard to find. Sherry producers have acquired the right to use PX grapes from outside their legal region, namely from Montilla-Moriles.

The *Solera* System

Another unique feature of sherry production is its system of aging, which is called *solera*.

Drying Pedro Ximénez grapes, imported to Jerez from the neighboring Montilla-Moriles region.

The Great
Wine Nation

France has been wine's great teacher. No country has contributed to the development of truly great wines to the same extent that France has. A two-hundred-year tradition of excellence as vigorous as ever—what other country in the world can boast of that? To this day, Bordeaux, Burgundy, and Champagne continue to bring forth wines of un-equaled quality, and all indications are that this country in the heart of Europe will continue to make great wines in the future. Yet France includes 300 wine regions, and the brilliant names of the three best-known ones sometimes seem to throw a shadow on the others. Great teachers always attract disciples, and many of those who came to France from California, Australia, Chile, and Spain have learned their lessons well, as have grape growers and winemakers deep in the provinces of France. In short, France's fame shines as brightly as ever, but there are corners of the country where changes are due.

France and Its *Terroir*

It is a basic tenet of French wine philosophy that wine is an expression of the soil and the climate combined. This conviction is summarized by the word *terroir*. The notion may appear obvious, but it is by no means accepted everywhere else in the world. French wines are made in strict accordance with this concept.

Nowhere is French wine philosophy implemented with greater care than in the making of the country's top-quality wines. What would pinot noir be without Burgundy? Without the well-drained gravel soils on the banks of the Gironde, what would the potential of cabernet sauvignon be? Today these two varieties are grown worldwide, but only here do the wines made from them achieve the wealth of expression attained in their native regions. Quality is achieved by human intervention, but the character of grape varieties and the greatness of their wines are entirely in the hands of nature. Hervé de Villaine, director of Domaine de la Romanée-Conti, summarizes this view: "Truth lies in the vineyard, not in man."

Assemblage and Varietal Wines

The wine regions of France differ in many respects. In the south and southwest of the country, red wines are considered to require careful blending of several grape varieties. This gives them much greater complexity and reduces the variation from vintage to vintage. Châteauneuf-du-Pape, for example, is permitted to use thirteen different grape varieties.

By contrast, in the north, most wines are made from a single variety; this is the case along the Loire, in Chablis, in Savoy, in Beaujolais, in Alsace, and above all, in Burgundy. There, even individual plots within a vineyard are fermented separately, except perhaps in the case of simple village wines. The *premiers* and *grands crus* ("first growths" and "great growths," or lots) are picked, fermented, and bottled vineyard by vineyard. Only in Champagne is *assemblage*, as blending is called, the rule: traditionally, Champagne consists of various amounts of pinot noir, chardonnay, and pinot meunier.

The Emperor Probus and the Beginning of Wine

The first grapes were probably brought to France around 600 B.C. by Greek settlers who planted vineyards between Marseilles and Banyuls, near the present border with Spain. The systematic expansion of viticulture was started by the Romans during their administration of Gaul. First, they planted the well-populated valley of the Rhône River. In the second century they reached Burgundy and Bordeaux, and in the third, the first grapevines sprouted along the Loire. French winemaking began, according to historians, with the Emperor Aurelius Probus (232–282 A.D.), who ordered that vineyards be planted throughout the Roman province of Gaul. His orders were implemented with enthusiasm. Although the emperor was later clubbed to death by his own soldiers, viticulture flourished in Gaul. In the fourth century, it reached Champagne in the north.

The Rise of French Wine

The expansion of viticulture through the land went hand in hand with the spread of Christianity. The Benedictine and Cistercian missionaries saw it as their duty to establish vineyards around their cloisters to supply the wine for the Eucharist. The monks soon came to appreciate the intoxicant properties of their wine, as did the country's secular rulers. By the end of the Middle Ages, the rising class of urban burghers had become involved as well.

As early as the twelfth century, French wines were part of a lively trade with England, and soon reached Scotland, Holland, and Germany. Rising demand for the precious potions was ample inducement to plant more and more vines. Viticulture expanded so mightily that by the beginning of the seventeenth century vineyards covered three times the area they do today.

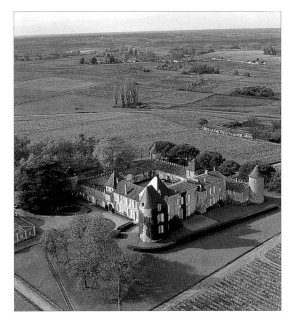

Château d'Yquem: The most famous sweet wine of France.

After the French Revolution, the domains of the nobility were taken over by the middle class. During the period of secularization, the same thing happened to the estates of the Church. In Bordeaux, it was mostly the members of the parliaments who were able to establish themselves as owners of the Médoc vineyards. In 1855 the Bordeaux chamber of commerce established a classification of the Bordeaux châteaus on the order of Emperor Napoleon III. It is valid to this day.

White Wine Paradise

Champagne is the northernmost wine region of France. The general fascination with Champagne has obscured the fact that great white wines and sparkling wines are also made along the Loire.

The vineyards that supply the base wines for Champagne are spread over a large area. Some vineyards over 62 miles (100 kilometers) to the south of Reims are a part of this AOC region. Ninety-five percent of its area is stocked with the three Champagne varieties, namely, chardonnay, pinot noir, and pinot meunier. About three-quarters of the Champagne's vineyards are divided equally between the last two varieties; chardonnay covers about 25 percent. The special quality of the wines of this region is due to the cool climate and the extremely infertile, calcareous soils, which allow grapevine cultivation only with regular fertilization.

The great Champagne houses that control the market together own only about 10 percent of the vineyards of the district, and have to purchase the bulk of their grapes. The vineyard communes of Champagne are officially classified and ranked on a scale from 80 to 100 percent according to quality. Vineyards rated from 90 to 99 percent comprise the *premier cru* category; 100-percent vineyards are *grands crus*. Thus, a 99-percent vineyard proprietor will receive 99 percent of the highest officially set price for his type of grapes. The best chardonnay grapes grow south of the Marne, around the villages of Chouilly, Cramant, Avize, Oger, and Mesnil. The best pinot noir comes from Bouzy and Ay.

Brand-name, or nonvintage, Champagnes always consist of a blend of many *crus* and several vintages, which is why their labels can show no specific vintage. The *prestige cuvées* and vintage Champagnes tend to be very long-lived and capable of great refinement. A small amount of the wine of the Champagne region is sold as still red or white wine.

Nantais

The Pays Nantais, around the city of Nantes, produces a wine that complements the cuisine of the Atlantic coast: Muscadet. It is an inexpensive, simple wine, but its freshness and tangy flavor enable it to stand up to the seafood dishes served in the region.

Sur lie is seen on many labels, meaning the wine has rested on its lees. The muscadet variety, also called melon de Bourgogne, has little taste, a deficiency that had inspired winemakers long ago to leave the young wine on its lees until it was bottled. In this way, it picks up some flavor compounds and a little sparkle. The bulk of the region's wines, however, never spends time on its lees; it is simply pepped up with carbon dioxide. The Maine-et-Sèvre district, to the east of Nantes, makes the most satisfying wines.

Coteaux du Layon

In this large appellation south of the Loire, two extremely fine sweet wines are made from late-harvested grapes: Quarts de Chaume and Bonnezeaux. Depending on the vintage, they can be as opulent as a sauterne and as racy as a Beerenauslese.

Savennières

The tiny appellation of Savennières makes very good, concentrated, dry chenin blanc wines in the subdistrict of La Roche-aux-Moines. It also is known for an extraordinary wine, the Coulée de Serrant. It has achieved cult status among connoisseurs and is one of the best and most long-lived white wines in the world.

Anjou

The district around the city of Angers is traditionally known for its aromatic, fruity red wines; they are made of cabernet franc grapes and are relatively affordable. Frequently they contain small amounts of cabernet sauvignon and other varieties. This is true, for example for the substantial Anjou Villages, the Saumur-Rouge, and the Saumur Champigny.

A specialty of Anjou is its semidry rosés, Cabernet d'Anjou and Rosé d'Anjou, which latter can be made of cot (the local name for malbec), gamay, and other local grape varieties. Not everyone can appreciate the special flavor of these wines.

Champagne vineyards; Prince Philippe Poniatowski, the producer of one of the best long-lived Vouvrays.

In Sancerre and Pouilly grow the best sauvignons of the upper Loire.

For some time now, the growers of Anjou have been planting white varieties, especially chenin blanc, which is fermented into large quantities of Saumur Mousseux, a fine sparkling wine made according to the classic method of bottle fermentation. This is available for a price far below Champagne levels. The still Saumur Blanc, a strangely unknown wine of this region, is also very good. Like the sparkling wine, it often contains some sauvignon and chardonnay in addition to chenin blanc. Finally, throughout the whole of Anjou and Touraine, chenin blanc, cabernet franc, and other varieties are made into the Crémant de Loire.

Touraine

This rather large region around the city of Tours on the Loire produces many simple red, white, and rosé wines from many grape varieties. The sub-appellations of Bourgueil and Chinon are known for their aromatic, uncomplicated cabernet franc wines, which should be enjoyed when young. In the vicinity of the little town of Vouvray, chenin blanc vineyards (locally, the grape is called pineau de loire) make the local white wines. They can be dry, semidry, or sweet. Sometimes they are insignificant, sometimes delicious. Moreover, though they seem strangely unknown, they are so durable as to seem immortal. Some wines are made into the elegant sparkling Vouvray Mousseux.

Sancerre

Named for the village perched high above the upper Loire, Sancerre combines a pungent simplicity with the fragrance of gooseberries and peppers. Since the appellation extends over several communes with different soils, the character of the wine changes with its locality. Sancerre is always a pure varietal wine, made of sauvignon blanc grapes.

Pouilly-Fumé

The wines of the appellation Pouilly-Fumé, situated across the river from Sancerre, are more dense, more powerful, and more distinguished, at least at their best. In the district's pebbly and lime-rich soils, the sauvignon blanc grape can reach its optimal expressiveness. Because of the high flint content of the soil, many wines exhibit a smoky personality. Of the few vineyards with flint in the ground, quite a number grow the chasselas grape, which is fermented into the lighter, simpler Pouilly-sur-Loire.

From Alsace to the Beaujolais

Many everyday wines and a few top-quality ones are grown in eastern and southeastern France; among the latter are the whites from Alsace.

Travelers exploring the wine route from Thann in the south to Marlenheim in the north might imagine that they are on the German, not the French side of the Rhine. They will find small, comfortable villages with many half-timbered houses, *Weinstuben,* where there is singing and swaying in unison, and German road signs and restaurant menus. They will be served wines with German names like Riesling, Gewürztraminer, and Edelzwicker.

French When It Comes to Wine
Getting to know the people of Alsace, one soon learns that they are indeed French. Their vineyards are classified by soil quality and microclimate. The variety is less important than assuring each grapevine the best possible site. Each *grand cru* represents only one variety. Should another grape also happen to grow there, its name may not appear on the label.

Alsatian wines also are completely dry. The only thing Alsace has in common with German conditions is that it is a large appellation. On the label it is called Alsace AC. It extends for 93 miles (150 kilometers) along the foothills of the Vosges Mountains and covers 14,500 hectares of vineyards.

Alsace Topping
The permissible yields per hectare in Alsace are the highest in France. Yet Alsace regularly

Jura wine grower with a young vin jaune.

The village of Turkheim in Alsace, with Grand Cru Brand *in the background..*

produces some of the most delightful white wines in France. When vineyards are in a good location, the Riesling is the king of vines even if it mostly yields high-alcohol wine (many Alsatian vintners like to supplement it with sugar). Sylvaner, the second most common variety of grape, yields substantial wines. Tokay (pinot gris) and the fine Gewürztraminer are heavy-but inimitably full-bodied. The latter is mostly offered as dry or *vendange tardive* (high-grade late harvest) or as *grains nobles* (from grapes dried on the vine). In Alsace, pinot blanc is a simpler wine. Apart from these, small quantities of chasselas, muscat, and a light pinot noir are produced. All these wines have to consist purely of the grape varieties stated. Only the Edelzwicker is a blend of several varieties.

Jura
The mountain chain of the French Jura runs along the Côte d'Or, on the west side of the Saône River. The vines grow mostly on limestone. The Jura district is small, containing only about 1,500 hectares of vineyards. The best-known wine of the region is Arbois, which can be red, white, or rosé. The red wines are made from the pale red poulsard variety, while the whites come from chardonnay, with occasional additions of savagnin, to give the wine more aroma and a flavor of nuts. Fermented as a varietal, the savagnin grape produces the

famous, though rare, *vin jaune,* a sherrylike wine aged for six years under a layer of *flor* yeast. The best known producer of *vin jaune* is Château Chalon, which has its own appellation.

Beaujolais
Beaujolais belongs to Burgundy, but it is the only part of this wine-growing region where no pinot noir is grown, only the gamay variety, which yields a light, fruity wine that does not bear the slightest resemblance to burgundies. It is one of the most reasonable red wines in France, produced in huge quantities—almost 170 million bottles, more than is produced by the rest of Burgundy put together. In and around Lyon, locals drink virtually no other wine. The secret behind this success also lies in the way the wine is made. Some of the grapes are fermented with carbon dioxide (see page 74), which gives the wine its fruitiness. This is most striking in Beaujolais Nouveau, which is released on the third Thursday in November. In view of the commercial success of this wine, it has been forgotten that a Beaujolais grown in the northern part of the region, where the soils consist of granite, porphyry, and slate, is a rich, full-bodied wine that ages well. On its label, it bears the name of one of the ten villages where it is produced: Saint-Amour, Juliénas, Chénas, Moulin-à-Vent, Fleurie, Chiroubles, Morgon, Régnié, Brouilly, or Côte de Brouilly.

Chablis and the Unknown Burgundy

There is more to Burgundy than the Côte d'Or. A few excellent red and white wines do grow outside this wine-growing area. Most of them are relatively unknown. Just one has escaped anonymity: Chablis.

Chablis

Chablis grows near the city of Auxerre, around 112 miles (180 km) south of Paris. It is named after the idyllic town of the same name, which has almost 3,000 inhabitants and lies on the River Serein, hardly more than a small creek. The finest Chablis is rich (but never as heavy as the white burgundies of the Côte de Beaune) and has a sophisticated mineral bouquet with a hint of flint and blossoms. Its ability to age is mostly overestimated. Even the best Chablis should be drunk within five to ten years, when it begins to take on its sweet, slightly nutty aroma. Simple Chablis— the mass of wines in this appellation—unfold their charm in the first three years.

Chablis and the Wooden Cask

Chablis is made from chardonnay grapes. Considering the relatively northern location, the grapes do not reach the same high degree of ripeness as Meursaults and Puligny-Montrachets. Apart from this, the region is often cool right into spring, with night frosts occurring in April and May (these frosts, incidentally, are the greatest hazard to winegrowing in Chablis). This makes Chablis steelier and more acidic than the wines in southern Burgundy, as do the soils, of very chalky clay, which lend it more of a mineral bite than sheer richness. Chablis is the only chardonnay wine that traditionally matures in a concrete or steel tank, although a number of producers feel it would be better to ferment and fully ripen it in small wooden casks. There are producers in favor of this, like Dauvissat and Raveneau, but also traditionalists like Durup and Michel against it. But the wines of both camps are among the best in the appellation.

More and More Chablis

In Chablis, grapes are grown on 5,300 hectares, and this area is growing. A not inconsiderable proportion of Chablis vineyards were pastures twenty-five years ago. The wine from these is marketed as *petit Chablis*, rather flattering for a wine that has little resemblance to the genuine Chablis. The genuine Chablis AC accounts for 75 percent of the wine from this region and can taste exceptionally good. On paper, the *premiers crus* (739 hectares) are better, although their quality does not always justify the higher price due to the expansion of the cultivated area. From the seven *grands crus* (97 hectares), all on the large hillside facing the town of Chablis, comes Chablis in perfection.

Côte Chalonnaise

The Côte Chalonnaise extends south of its border with the Côte de Beaune, near the city of Chalon. It lacks the glitter of the Côte d'Or, but it brings forth some remarkable wines. The most important is Mercurey, named after the village to the south of Chagny. This pinot noir wine may be a bit rougher than the burgundies that grow farther to the north, but it also has more body and more strength. The red wines from the neighboring village of Givry can be equally good. Rully, just a few miles south of Chagny, is known above all for its white wines, which are made from chardonnay grapes. These wines have more fruit and are considerably lighter than those of Chassagne-Montrachet. Much of the white wine made in southern Burgundy is used to make Crémant de Bourgogne.

Mâconnais

This wine district surrounding the city of Mâcon on the Saône is known for agreeable, palatable white wines from chardonnay grapes, marketed as Mâcon Blanc or Mâcon Villages. They do not show the fullness of the white burgundies of the Côte de Beaune, but they are good buys. The very best of them grow on the limestone hills in the neighborhood of the little village of Pouilly-Fuissé, after which they are named. Pouilly-Vinzelles and Saint-Véran also offer above-average quality.

In addition to chardonnay, some gamay is also grown. Its wine is called Mâcon Rouge, and it is one of the few red wines that carry on the tradition of the gamay grape, which once dominated vineyards throughout Burgundy.

Aligoté de Bourgogne: This strong, sturdy white wine, made from the aligoté grape that grows in the south of Burgundy, comes from the village of Bouzéron, which has its own appellation controlée (AC). It is a delicate, rather full-bodied wine, its quality widely underestimated.

Bourgogne Rouge, Bourgogne Blanc: The red wine is a simple pinot noir in which grapes from anywhere in Burgundy are permitted. It is a glorified everyday wine, now rough, now soft as velvet, depending on the maker. Similar things can be said of the white wine, made of chardonnay grapes.

Bourgogne Passetoutgrain: Made everywhere in Burgundy, this is a hearty, simple red made of gamay blended with at least a third pinot noir. It is served young.

From Pouilly-Fuissé in southern Burgundy comes an ample, earthy wine with great aroma, made of chardonnay grapes.

Wines Like Velvet and Silk

Vineyards around the village of Puligny-Montrachet produce legendary white wines of unequaled excellence.

The Côte d'Or is the jewel among Burgundy's wine districts. It extends from Santenay in the south, through Beaune, almost all the way to Dijon in the north. In spots where calcareous layers of soil surface, some of France's best grapes are grown.

Nuits-Saint-Georges

The town of Nuits-Saint-Georges is the commercial center of the Côte de Nuits. Numerous large *négociant-éléveurs* have their headquarters there, for example, Joseph Faiveley and Moillard. The vineyards are on the slopes above the town; they are planted exclusively with pinot noir grapes. Nuits-Saint-Georges and the neighboring Prémaux-Prissey can boast of no *grands crus*, but they have all the

more *premiers crus*, some of them with wines that are very near the *grand cru* level. Some of these are Clos de la Maréchale and Clos Arlot, and above all, Les Saint-Georges and Les Vaucrains. They are relatively light in color but powerful on the tongue, and they have a smoky sweet-oak aroma.

Vosne-Romanée

The vineyards of this dreamy little town comprise the heart of the Côte de Nuits. Nowhere are the wines more velvety, more fragrant, more flavorful, more complete. The *grands crus* cluster in the core of the slope, around Romanée-Conti. They are wholly or partially owned by the Domaine de la Romanée-Conti, except for La Grande Rue and La Romanée. The wines of Echézeaux are outside the district, but they are counted as part of Vosne-Romanée.

Vougeot

Clos de Vougeot, with its 50 hectares of vineyards, is the largest *grand cru* of the Côte de Nuits. Completely surrounded by a wall, it reaches from the château all the way down to Route Nationale 74. Only the wines of the upper portions of the district have *grand cru* status, while those from the lower reaches

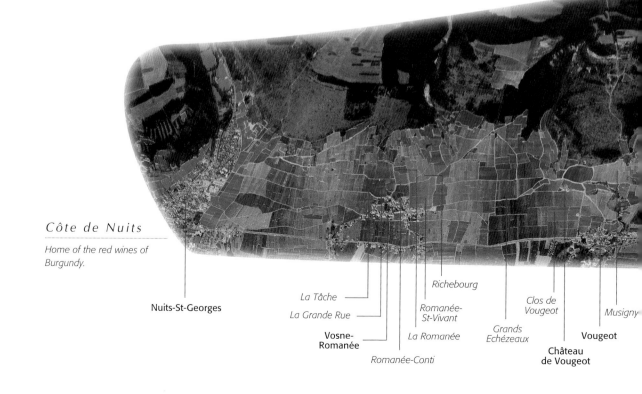

Côte de Nuits

Home of the red wines of Burgundy.

Nuits-St-Georges

La Tâche

La Grande Rue

Vosne-Romanée

Romanée-Conti

Richebourg

Romanée-St-Vivant

La Romanée

Grands Echézeaux

Clos de Vougeot

Château de Vougeot

Vougeot

Musigny

only merit a higher rank of commune (village) classification. Since ownership is dispersed among a large group of winemakers, there are differences in the quality of production.

Chambolle-Musigny
Situated right at the base of the Côte, the commune of Chambolle-Musigny delivers relatively light but tremendously fragrant wines. In no other wine can you taste the fascinating bouquet of pinot grapes as clearly as in these —a sweet smell of irises underlain with a rougher aroma of plums. The two top growths are Les Musigny, which yields incredibly tender wines (a portion of this location is stocked with chardonnay), and Les Bonnes Mares. In addition, two *premier crus*, Les Amoureuses and Les Charmes, stand out above the rest in the area.

Morey-Saint-Denis
The *grands crus* are all situated above the road that passes through the town. Clos de Tart and Clos de Lambrays make rather light, elegant wines, while Clos Saint-Denis and Clos de la Roche exhibit the stature and firmness of the Chambertin wines.

Gevrey-Chambertin
The largest wine commune on the Côte de Nuits is Gevrey-Chambertin. The ocean of grapevines reaches from the edge of the forest, across Route Nationale 74, down into the plain. Wines from these lower vineyards are simple and have little charm. The *grands crus,* which are all located toward the top, are classified according to exposure to the sun into several *climats.* The wines that grow there are considered masculine, meaty, fiery—in short, the most powerful Burgundy reds. There are some differences among these wines: Chambertin and Clos de Bèze are the most ebullient representatives of the *grands crus;* Mazis-Chambertin is the most velvety.

Other locations also offer very good, but less homogeneous wines. Among the *premiers crus,* Clos Saint-Jacques, behind the village, is worthy of special mention. Its wine is of highest *grand cru* quality—and it is not a franc less expensive, either. The commune wines of Gevrey-Chambertin can also be of very high quality. It is best, however, to taste them before making a purchase, since the district is known for its limitless grape production.

Fixin
This wine commune on the northern end of the Côte de Nuits has some *premier cru* locations that in no way lag behind those of its neighbor, Gevrey-Chambertin. The village of Brochon has no appellation of its own. The wines all are part of the AOC Gevrey-Chambertin.

Bonnes Mares

Clos de Tart

Clos St-Denis

Clos des Lambrays

Clos de la Roche

Charmes-Chambertin

Chambertin

Latricières-Chambertin

Mazoyères-Chambertin

Griottes-Chambertin

Chapelle-Chambertin

Chambertin-Clos de Bèze

Mazis-Chambertin

Ruchottes-Chambertin

Clos St-Jacques

Chambolle-Musigny

Morey-St-Denis

Gevrey-Chambertin

White Wines of Overwhelming Fullness

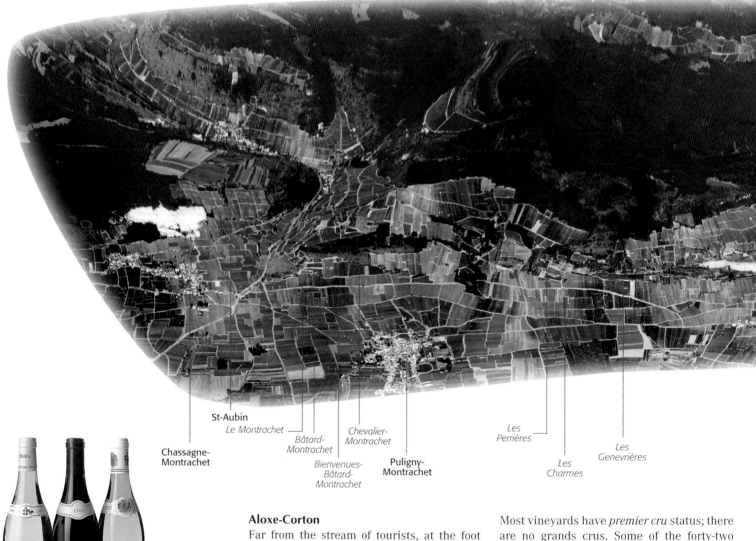

St-Aubin
Le Montrachet
Bâtard-
Montrachet
Chassagne-
Montrachet
Bienvenues-
Bâtard-
Montrachet
Chevalier-
Montrachet
Puligny-
Montrachet
Les
Perrières
Les
Charmes
Les
Genevrières

Most of the Côte de Beaune is planted with pinot noir grapes. Yet many of its communes are famous primarily for their white wines.

These white wines, made exclusively from chardonnay grapes, have achieved world fame under the generic name of "white burgundy." The best among them are as heavy as red wines, and at the same time offer amplitude and great longevity.

As for the red wines of the Côte de Beaune, they are compact and rich in nuances, but they do not have the depth that the wines of the Côte de Nuits can reach.

Aloxe-Corton

Far from the stream of tourists, at the foot of Mount Corton, lies the little village. From there, you cannot see over the wooded peak of the mountain. Almost the entire slope is covered with *grands crus* vineyards, the highest bordering right on the forest. In sunny locations, they are planted with chardonnay, which is fermented into the famous Corton-Charlemagne: a full, heavy white wine with a nutty vanilla bouquet. The red Corton is a robust, long-lived wine, reminiscent of a good Gevrey-Chambertin.

Beaune

The famous historic wine capital of Burgundy, Beaune is the trading center of the Côte d'Or. Each year famous wine auctions are held there that establish the price of the new Burgundy vintage. The town is surrounded by vineyards–a total of 400 hectares. Beaune is thus the largest wine-producing community in the entire Côte d'Or.

Most vineyards have *premier cru* status; there are no grands crus. Some of the forty-two *premier-cru* vineyards, almost all of which produce red wines, yield wines with a great deal of character and elegance. Differences between the *premiers crus* are only very slight. They range from light, delicately fruity wines from sandy soils (Les Teurons or Les Grèves, with the famous vineyard L'Enfant de Jésus, for example) to full-bodied, robust wines from more calcareous soils (like Clos de Mouches).

Pommard

Pommard is an appellation consisting of roughly 300 hectares of vines, more than half of them with *premier cru* status. They are planted exclusively with pinot noir. From the best vineyards come soft, mildly fruity wines similar to those of the *premiers crus* of Beaune, with the exception of the vineyards of Epenot and especially Rugien, which produce wines with more depth and fire.

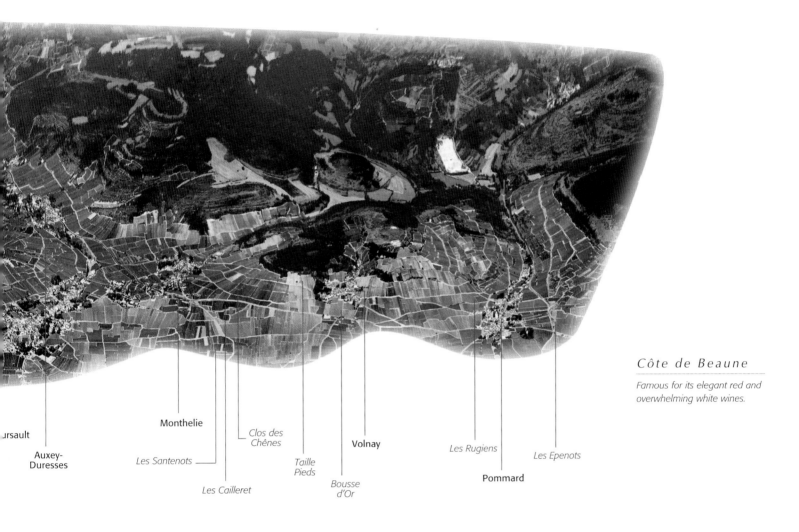

Monthelie

Clos des
Chênes

Volnay

Les Rugiens

Les Epenots

ursault

Auxey-
Duresses

Les Santenots

Taille
Pieds

Pommard

Les Cailleret

Bousse
d'Or

Côte de Beaune

Famous for its elegant red and
overwhelming white wines.

Volnay

Though not especially compact, the wines of
Volnay are uncommonly filigree with a
delicate fruit that are among the smoothest of
the Côte de Beaune. More than half of the
vineyards, totaling some 230 hectares, are
designated *grand crus*. They are all planted
with pinot noir. The vineyards Santenots and
Les Plures, belonging to Meursault, also come
to the market as Volnay.

Meursault

Meursault is an important white wine appellation between Beaune and Puligny-Montrachet
in which the chardonnay grape yields world-
class wines. This is true not only of the *premier
crus* Genevrières, Perrières, and Charmes,
which make up roughly a fourth of the
appellation's area, but is also true in part of the
simpler communal wines. They are elegant
and soft, but profound, extremely long-lasting,
and never overloaded. A total of 370 hectares
are planted. Reds are also produced, but only

in small quantities. The soils are a mixture of
hard, pebbly chalk and sand.

Puligny-Montrachet

This is the mecca of white wine lovers:
Montrachet, Chevalier-Montrachet, Bâtard-
Montrachet, and Bienvenues-Bâtard-Montrachet
—the four *grands crus*—are the headiest and
richest white wines of Burgundy, so opulent that
in some years they run the danger of seeming
overloaded. With 14 percent alcohol and their
tremendously rich body, they can last twenty
years, or longer. The neighboring vineyards
also yield full and incomparably fine white
wines with great staying power. Especially
worthy of mention are the *premier crus* Les
Pucelles, Les Combettes, and Les Folatières.

Chassagne-Montrachet

The white wines of this district resemble the
fullness of those of Puligny-Montrachet, and
have a steely impact. This applies to the tiny
grand cru Criots-Bâtard-Montrachet and also

to the finest *premiers crus* of Clos de la Maltroie
and Les Ruchottes. The red wines are earthy,
rough, and without great finesse.

Santenay

The sleepy little village of Santenay makes
delicious, easy-to-drink pinot noirs that do not
pretend to be among the great wines of
Burgundy. They are velvety-soft and mellow
with a delicate aroma of raspberry and cherry.

Saint-Aubin

This small appellation borders directly on
Chassagne-Montrachet but includes only 145
hectares, a third of which enjoy *premier cru*
status. Connoisseurs prefer its white wines,
made exclusively from chardonnay grapes.
These wines are known for their strength and
body rather than their great finesse. The red
wines, which make up roughly 40 percent of
production, are somewhat less smooth and do
not quite equal the best pinot noirs from the
Côte de Beaune.

Vines above the River

Dark syrah grapes yield the Hermitage wine (below, the mountain of the same name).

The Rhône Valley is the best-known wine region of France. Its wines, incomparable for their fullness and fire, impress more by their forcefulness than by their finesse. The connoisseur distinguishes between the northern and southern Rhône. The north is the home of the syrah variety and of the more prestigious vineyards.

Côte Rôtie

The wines of the Côte Rôtie owe their special quality to an unexpected turn the Rhône River takes at the city of Vienne. On 200 hectares of steep riverbank stocked with syrah grapes is born the most forceful, most outstanding wine of the Rhône. To tame the animal strength of its aroma and its wealth of tannins, it may be blended with up to 20 percent of the white viognier grape. Subzones of the appellation with different soils are called Côte Blonde and Côte Brune. These two wines are traditionally blended with each other, but some of the best winemakers bottle them individually.

Hermitage

At Tain, the Rhône once again takes a twist, creating a sloping bank with a direct southern exposure. A legendary red wine, Hermitage, grows there. Usually, it is produced as a varietal syrah wine. Its intense aroma of chocolate, its raspberry fragrance, and its longevity (it is not ready to drink for ten years) have made it famous all around the world. The appellation is only 125 hectares in size, and the wine is correspondingly expensive. Hermitage Blanc is a rare white wine made of marsanne and roussanne grapes.

Cornas

This, the third great red wine of the Rhône, comes from a small appellation south of Tain. Made only of syrah grapes, it can equal a Hermitage. It is distinguished by its earthy aroma, its raspberry nose, lots of sweetly rough tannin, and a very long life expectancy.

Crozes-Hermitage

This is the largest region of the northern Rhône, producing syrah wines that range in quality from excellent to nondescript. The white Crozes-Hermitage is made of marsanne and roussanne grapes.

Saint-Joseph

This is the lightest syrah wine of the region, fruity, delicate, and ready to be drunk when young. The grapes grow on light sandy and pebbly soils.

Condrieu and Château Grillet

These two white wine appellations of the northern Rhône, one small, the other tiny, are known for expensive, high-quality wines. Connoisseurs are in awe of them. In Château Grillet there is but one producer; in Condrieu, but a handful.

Red Wines Ablaze with Fire

South of Valence, the landscape becomes flatter and takes on a Provençal flavor. After Monpellier, grapevines again border the Rhône. Here the grenache grape predominates, though it does not hold the same monopoly that syrah has in the north.

Côtes du Rhône
Côtes du Rhone is a huge region, encompassing almost the entire Rhône valley. The main wines produced are simple but tasty red Côtes du Rhône, fermented of practically any of the grapes that are planted in the region—mostly grenache, carignan, mourvèdre, cinsaut, and syrah, with a few white varieties as well. Wines of the Côte du Rhône-Villages classification tend to be a bit more significant.

Gigondas
This small appellation in the back country of the valley offers wines with good substance, made mostly of grenache grapes. They tend to taste somewhat raw at first, but turn very soft in time. The best are harmonious, intensely tasty wines, with good aging potential.

Vacqueyras
The neighboring village to Gigondas, Vacqueyras has its own AOC. Its wines have a higher proportion of syrah grapes and are, therefore, more powerful.

Châteauneuf-du-Pape
This fiery, alcohol-rich red wine grows on particularly stony ground around the town of that name, onetime seat of the papal court. Apparently the stones serve to reflect heat during the night. Yet the region seems warm enough, or many wines would not reach alcohol levels of 14 percent. The best Châteauneuf-du-Pape wines are without doubt majestic, their full body equal to their alcohol content. Grenache grapes predominate in these wines, and twelve other varieties are permitted, including some white ones. Naturally, not all winemakers use all of them. Unfortunately, the majority of the wines are merely heavy without being particularly fine.

Tavel and Lyrac
These two small districts have made their name mostly with heavy rosé wines the color of onionskins. They may be made from just about any Rhône variety. In Lyrac, the same grapes are made into a light, easy-to-drink red wine.

Côtes du Tricastin and Côtes du Luberon
These two large districts extend deep into the hinterland of the Rhône. They offer simple wines, much like Côtes du Rhône but lighter and more varied because they incorporate local grape varieties. The two districts also make white and rosé wines.

Summer pruning on the Côte du Rhône: The abundant growth of the vines is curtailed.

For the élévage of Châteauneuf-du-Pape, small, aged oak barrels are customary.

The Champs-Elysées of Wines

Ch. Cos
d'Estournel

Ch. Cos
Labory

Marbuzet

Ch. Montrose

Ch. Calon-Ségur

St-Estèphe

Saint-Estèphe

*On the graveled high
plateau are vineyards that
produce austere wines
with strong tannins.*

France owes its reputation as the top producer of exquisite wines predominantly to Bordeaux. The triple basis for the success of Bordeaux's red wines consists of soil, quality vines, and a tradition that goes back hundreds of years.

By a considerable margin, Bordeaux is the largest wine region of France. With over 117,000 hectares of productive vineyard area, the region is subdivided according to the size and quality of each vineyard plot. The most famous vineyards are located along the Gironde: on the right bank, such names as Saint-Emilion and Pomerol; on the left bank, Médoc and Haut-Médoc. Here are grown the most significant red wines in the Bordeaux region, if not in the world.

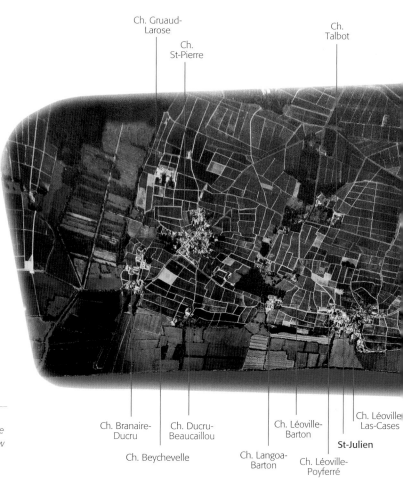

Ch. Gruaud-
Larose

Ch.
St-Pierre

Ch.
Talbot

Ch. Branaire-
Ducru

Ch. Ducru-
Beaucaillou

Ch. Léoville-
Barton

Ch. Léoville
Las-Cases

Ch. Beychevelle

Ch. Langoa-
Barton

Ch. Léoville-
Poyferré

St-Julien

*Pauillac
and
Saint-Julien*

*These two villages on the
Gironde are the heart of the
Médoc. The wines that grow
here are of incomparable
depth and finesse.*

Haut-Médoc

The wines that grow on the elevated, pebbled slopes of the left bank of the Gironde are the most illustrious bordeaux. Here cabernet sauvignon, merlot, and cabernet franc predominate. Almost all the wines of the region are made of these grapes.

Saint-Estèphe

A former fishing village on the Gironde, Saint-Estèphe lent its name to its wine. It is situated at the tip of the Haut-Médoc, where heavy clay forms the base of the soil. The wines of Saint-Estèphe are regarded as the most austere of the region, dark and imbued with tannins. They open up very slowly, but are said to "explode" with good taste later on.

Pauillac

A port and commercial center, Pauillac is the heart of the Haut-Médoc. Here you find the deepest layers of gravel; three outstanding châteaus are located here, more than in any other appellation in Bordeaux: Lafite-Rothschild, Mouton-Rothschild, and Latour. Their vineyards are right next to the river, living proof of the saying, "A great wine has to see water."

The wines of Pauillac are the most opulent and the most polished of the Haut-Médoc. They have the densest tannin structure, without seeming overloaded. The tannins themselves are extraordinarily fine and soft, at least in good years. Moreover, they tend to be the most durable wines of Bordeaux. Even in the hinterlands, where the soil has a high admixture of sand and clay, the wines produced are full, muscular, and at the same time refined. Normally, the wines here contain 65 to 74 percent cabernet sauvignon. Experts claim that in Pauillac, cabernet sauvignon reaches its optimal expression. Nonetheless, its proportion has in recent years markedly decreased in favor of the softer merlot grape.

Bottles of wine at Château Pontet-Canet, a cru classé of the fifth rank, in Pauillac. It is among the best of the fifth-class estates.

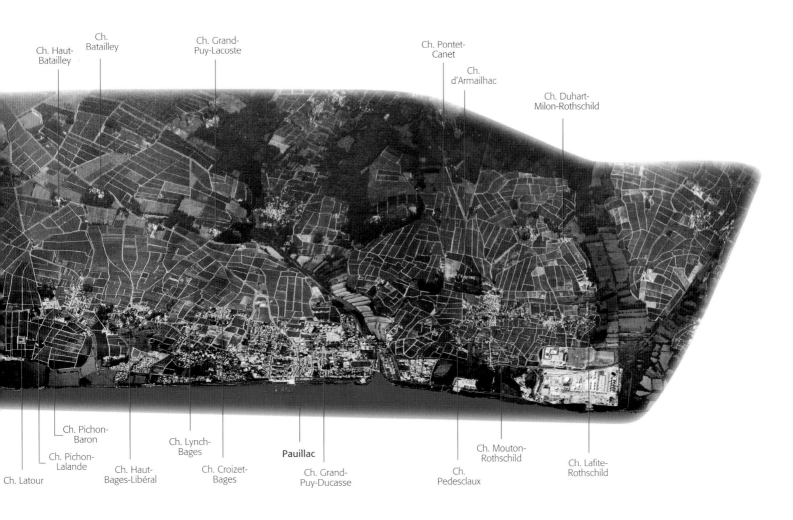

Refinement and Zest

Château Margaux, number one in the Margaux region.

Saint-Julien

Saint-Julien is separated from Pauillac only by a narrow little stream. Thus the vineyards of Château Latour are adjacent to those of Léoville-Las-Cases, the outstanding wine of the little community of Saint-Julien. It consists of little more than a cluster of vineyard workers' houses and almost a dozen châteaus. What is important here, however, is the soil. Much of the district is situated on slightly gravelly hills, right on the riverbank; these low hills have excellent drainage, a very important criterion of quality in the Médoc. Nonetheless, Saint-Julien has no *premier cru*, but experts agree that Léoville-Las-Cases has long ago reached that level of excellence; the great number of so-called "second-class" vineyards here attests to the general quality of the location and of the wines of Saint-Julien. These may not be quite so compact and durable as those of Pauillac, but they have more flavor and elegance. Merlot and cabernet franc are more strongly represented in them than in most of the wines of Pauillac. Léoville-Las-Cases even adds 2.5 to 5 percent petit verdot, a grape that is normally only grown in Margaux.

Margaux

The village of Margaux lies at the southern end of the Haut-Médoc; the appellation is relatively large, encompassing the neighboring communes of Issan, Cantenac, Labarde, and Arsac. The soils of Margaux are no less well drained than those in other parts of the Gironde, but they are very infertile and poor in nitrogen. The wines, though not among the most full-bodied Bordeaux, are the noblest and most fragrant. Their delicate, flavorful, smoky fruit, their elegant, perfectly integrated tannins, and their tendency to achieve a perfect balance between alcohol, acid, and body—all this has given them a world reputation.

Margaux

Produces elegant and silky wines that are nevertheless structured.

Ch. Giscours

Labard

Ch. Dauzac

Château Prieuré-Lichine grapevines in Margaux. The appellation produces the most elegant wines in the Médoc.

It is true that in Margaux one finds numerous wine styles and large differences in quality, but given the very large number of châteaus and the extensiveness of the region, which encompasses many different kinds of soils, this is hardly surprising. One lone peak soaring above all the rest is Château Margaux, the sole *premier cru* in the appellation. The second-rank classification is quite uneven, and the third and fourth encompass very large differences in quality. At the same time, there are in Margaux a goodly number of *cru bourgeois* wines, which are practically of *grand cru* quality. Margaux wines are based on cabernet sauvignon, but during *assemblage* the wines added are not just merlot and cabernet franc but always some proportion of petit verdot, which adds its extremely dark color and acids to the wines.

Ch. Brane-Cantenac
Ch. Cantenac-Brown
Ch. Rauzan-Gassies
Ch. Marquis de Terme
Ch. Ferrière
Ch. Rausan-Ségla
Ch. Durfort-Vivens
Ch. Lascombes
Soussans

Ch. d'Alesme-Becker
Ch. Prieuré-Lichine
Issan
Margaux
Ch. d'Angludet
Ch. Boyd Cantenac
Ch. Kirwan
Ch. d'Issan
Ch. Malescot St-Exupéry
Cantenac
Ch. Palmer
Ch. Margaux
Ch. Desmirail

Listrac and Moulis

These two small commune appellations in Margaux's back country belong to the Haut-Médoc and make powerful, fine wines, though sometimes they can be slightly rough.

Pessac-Léognan

Both places belong to the great region of Graves, which extends to the south of Bordeaux all the way beyond Sauternes, along the left bank of the Garonne. Pessac is actually situated within the city limits of Bordeaux, and boasts the only *premier cru* of the appellation, Château Haut-Brion, as well as the outstanding châteaus La Mission-Haut-Brion and Pape Clement. There are also some less significant wine estates and Château Laville-Haut-Brion, which is known for its white wine. Léognan, which is situated farther south in a diverse landscape of forest and vineyards, grows delicate, quite fruity wines on meager, very sandy soil; these do not achieve the many-layered durability of the wines of the Médoc.

Graves

Almost all the wine estates south of Bordeaux make some white wines from sauvignon blanc, sémillon, and a little muscat. These wines, usually fermented in small oak barrels, have such rich body and such high potential for refinement that they are considered among the noblest wines in France.

Sauternes

In the southern end of Graves lies the small district of Sauternes, famous for its heavy, sweet wines derived from sauvignon blanc and sémillon. Even more important in creating these special wines than the soil around the small village of Sauternes is botrytis, or noble rot, which appears almost every year to infect a large portion of the grapes because of the vineyards' proximity to the little stream Ciron. The most illustrious Sauternes is that from Château d'Yquem. The healthy, unbotrytized grapes are fermented—as everywhere else in the district—into dry, full white wines with great body, and marketed as Graves.

Barsac and Cérons

The two appellations north of Sauternes make somewhat lighter, less opulent sweet wines, especially Cérons. While a good Barsac is not far from a Sauternes, a Cérons does not approach its class. In the north of Barsac, the very lightest of sweet wines are made.

Built on Sand: The Realm of Merlot

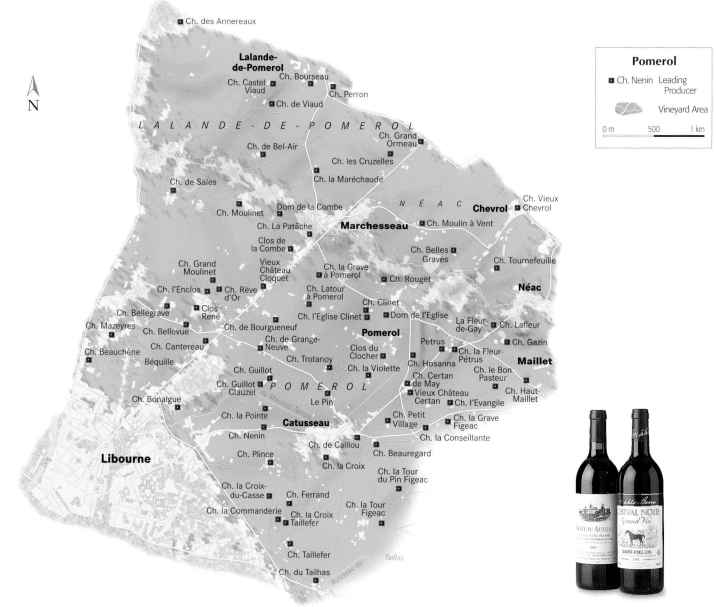

N

Pomerol

■ Ch. Nenin Leading
            Producer

Vineyard Area

0 m   500   1 km

Ch. des Annereaux

Lalande-de-Pomerol

Ch. Castel Viaud
Ch. Bourseau
Ch. Perron
Ch. de Viaud

L A L A N D E - D E - P O M E R O L

Ch. de Bel-Air
Ch. Grand Ormeau
Ch. les Cruzelles
Ch. de Sales
Ch. la Maréchaude

Ch. Moulinet
Dom de la Combe
N É A C
Chevrol Ch. Vieux Chevrol

Ch. La Patâche
Marchesseau Ch. Moulin à Vent

Clos de la Combe
Ch. Belles Graves
Ch. Tournefeuille

Ch. Grand Moulinet
Vieux Château Cloquet
Ch. la Grave à Pomerol
Ch. Rouget
Néac

Ch. l'Enclos   Ch. Rève d'Or
Ch. Latour à Pomerol
Ch. Clinet

Ch. Bellegrave   Clos René
Ch. l'Eglise Clinet   Dom de l'Eglise
La Fleur-de-Gay   Ch. Lafleur

Ch. Mazeyres
Ch. Bellevue
Ch. de Bourgueneuf
Pomerol
Pétrus   Ch. la Fleur-Pétrus   Ch. Gazin

Ch. Beauchêne
Ch. Cantereau
Ch. de Grange-Neuve
Clos du Clocher
Ch. Hosanna
Ch. le Bon Pasteur
Maillet

Béquille
Ch. Trotanoy
Ch. la Violette
Ch. Certan de May
Ch. Haut-Maillet

Ch. Guillot
P O M E R O L
Vieux Château Certan
Ch. l'Evangile

Ch. Guillot Clauzel
Le Pin
Ch. Petit Village
Ch. la Grave Figeac

Ch. Bonalgue
Ch. la Pointe
Catusseau
Ch. la Conseillante

Ch. Nenin
Ch. de Caillou
Ch. Beauregard

Libourne
Ch. Plince
Ch. la Croix
Ch. la Tour du Pin Figeac

Ch. la Croix-du-Casse
Ch. Ferrand
Ch. la Tour Figeac

Ch. la Commanderie
Ch. la Croix Taillefer

Ch. Taillefer

Ch. du Tailhas
Taillas

The northern bank of the Dordogne consists of gravel intermixed with sand and, in parts, with heavy clay. This is the habitat of the merlot vine. The wines made from its grapes are consistently heavier than those of the Médoc.

Saint-Emilion

In Saint-Emilion, the wines are traditionally half merlot, half cabernet franc. Within this appellation there are really two different planting areas: the high plateau of fine gravel sand and the slopes *(côtes)* around the village, where a sandy limestone underlies the soil. This is where the majority of the châteaus are located. Their wines are ample and spicy, with fruit that is often "sweet," or

at least very pronounced. They are not as many layered or as durable as the wines of the Médoc. Château Ausone is the only *grand cru* Class A in this district.

The wines of the high plateau are stronger, and they have a spicy mineral aroma. They often contain more cabernet franc, and not infrequently a portion of cabernet sauvignon. The only *premier cru* Class A is Château Cheval Blanc, which contains 66 percent cabernet franc. Figeac, one of the best B-class châteaus, contains as much as 70 percent.

Pomerol

The border between Saint-Emilion and Pomerol runs through the vineyards. The small district of Pomerol, practically unknown as recently

as the 1950s, is an extension of the gravel plateau of Saint-Emilion. After Libourne, the soil becomes more sandy, while toward the north it turns into clay.

The proportion of merlot in the wines of Pomerol varies between 50 and 90 percent. Château Pétrus, the star among wine estates, has the highest merlot content with 95 percent, the rest being cabernet franc. Cabernet sauvignon is rarely encountered in Pomerol. The wines here are the most extravagant, heaviest red wines in Bordeaux—and rare to boot, since the district is so small. Aside from Pétrus, the highest prices are fetched by Le Pin, Lafleur, Trotanoy, and L'Evangile—a secret classification by wine lovers.

N

France's Viticulture in Numbers

Acreage under vines:
895,000 hectares
Wine production:
47–50 million hectoliters
Annual wine consumption per capita: 56 liters

The Ten Most-Planted Grape Varieties

1. Merlot	red	12%
2. Grenache noir	red	11%
3. Carignan	red	10.6%
4. Ugni blanc	white	10.1%
5. Cabernet sauvignon	red	6.3%
6. Syrah	red	6.1%
7. Chardonnay	white	4.3%
8. Cabernet franc	red	4.2%
9. Gamay noir	red	4.1%
10. Cinsaut	red	3.4%

French Wine Law

French wine law is strictly hierarchical: the larger the area of provenance of a wine, the lower its position in the pyramid of quality.

Vins de table, table wines: These simply give France as their provenance.

Vins de pays, "country wines": These represent large regions, such as the southwest or a certain *département*.

Vins délimités de qualité supérieure (VDQS): These are wines of higher quality and of specified smaller regions, which meet stricter requirements than *vins de pays*.

Appellation d'origine contrôlée (AOC): Quality wines from narrowly defined districts. These meet very strict production standards.

The wine districts themselves are also hierarchically arranged. The smaller the district, the more strictly is its production circumscribed. The rules for a whole region (e.g., Côte du Rhône) will be structured quite generously. Below them are the smaller districts (e.g., Haut-Médoc). Then come the communes (e.g., Pauillac). In Burgundy, even smaller subdivisions are observed. These vineyards or plots may have AOC status, such as Beaune *premier cru* "Les Amoureuses" or Echézeaux *grand cru*.

Map labels (Saint-Emilion):

Ch. Gazin, Ch. le Bon Pasteur, Ch. l'Evangile, Ch. Haut-Maillet, Ch. la Conseillante, Ch. la Grave Figeac, Ch. Corbin Michotte, Ch. Corbin, Ch. Haut Corbin, Ch. Grand Corbin Manuel, Ch. la Tour du Pin Figeac, Ch. Cheval Blanc, Ch. la Dominique, Ch. la Croix-Toulifaut, Ch. la Tour Figeac, Ch. Ripeau, Ch. Chauvin, Vachon, Ch. Vieux Fortin, Ch. Figeac, Bézineau, Sarrensot, Ch. La Fleur, Merissac, Ch. du Tailhas, Ruisseau du Taillas, Ch. Petit-Figeac, Ch. Haut-Segottes, Ch. Rol Valentin, Ch. Moulin du Cadet, Ch. Cap-de-Mourlin, Ch. Dassault, Ch. Rocher Bellevue Figeac, Ch. La Marzelle, Ch. Grand Barrail, ST-EMILION, Balau, Ch. Larmande, Clos de l'Oratoire, Ch. Yon-Figeac, Mède, La Gomerie, Ch. Fonroque, Ch. Petit Faurie de Souchard, Ch. Laroze, Ch. Clos des Jacobins, Ch. Cadet-Piola, Ch. Soutard, Ch. Franc Mayne, Ch. Grand Mayne, Ch. Coutet, Ch. Balestard la Tonnelle, Le Rivalon, Le Dôme, Ch. Beau-Séjour Bécot, Clos Fourtet, Ch. la Couspaude, Ch. Bellevue, Ch. Villemaurine, Ch. Trottevieille, Ch. Tour Fonrazade, Ch. Angélus, Ch. Canon, Ch. Bergat, ST-CHRISTOPHE, Fonrazade, St-Emilion, Ch. la Clotte, Ch. Beauséjour Héritiers, Ch. Gracia, Ch. Pavie Macquin, Ch. Haut Barde, Ch. Roylland, Duffau-Lagarrosse, Ch. Ausone, Ch. Magdelaine, Ch. de Valandraud, Ch. Troplong Mondot, Ch. Belair, Ch. Moulin St.-Georges, ST-LAURENT, Ch. Fonplégade, Ch. Pavie-Décesse, La Mondotte, Ch. l'Arrosée, Ch. la Gaffelière, Ch. la Clusiére, Ch. Canon-la-Gaffelière, Ch. Pavie, Ch. le Tertre Roteboeuf, Ch. Larcis Ducasse

Saint-Emilion
- Le Dôme — Leading Producer
- Vineyard Area
- 0 m — 500 — 1 km

Other Wine Districts

Lalande de Pomerol: Adjacent to Pomerol on the north, Lalande de Pomerol makes wines that are good but somewhat rustic and have nothing in common with Pomerol, except the name.

Fronsac: Fronsac is a region traditionally planted with merlot, cabernet franc, and malbec. Its wines are lighter than those of Saint-Emilion.

Entre-Deux-Mers: Between the Garonne and the Dordogne lies a region of white wines: simple but tasty and very reasonably priced. They are derived from sauvignon blanc, sémillon, muscat, and ugni blanc. The district also produces some good red wines.

Premières Côtes de Bordeaux: In this district, which stretches along the right bank of the Garonne, opposite Graves, some ambitious investors have settled in the last few years. In gravel and calcareous soils the merlot vine thrives, and in some instances yields quite excellent red wines.

Château Gazin in Pomerol.

Mass Production, Unrecognized Excellence

Jurançon: An unknown wine grows at the foot of the Pyrenees.

The southwest is the quiet province of France. Only a little of its wine production travels beyond its borders, but that little deserves attention. By contrast, the Midi is the home of mass production—and of many new, extremely ambitious winemakers.

The part of France called the southwest lies between the Massif Central and the Pyrenees. In this wooded, hilly countryside, grapes are grown in many locations, and in a few of them the wines reach the quality of quiet greatness. The grape varieties grown are as strange to the visitor as the landscape itself.

Cahors
The river Lot meanders through deep clefts in the valley floor, past the city of Cahors. The district produces dark red wines, which in the nineteenth century rivaled those of Bordeaux. Made of malbec grapes—locally called cot or auxerrois—they are usually blended with the smoother merlot and tannat grapes. A few gorgeous wines are the pride of the district.

Jurançon
Jurançon is an amber-colored, dry or sweet wine made of gros manseng, petit manseng, and courbu grapes, which grow around Pau. It is hard to find, but once found, it is a revelation.

Madiran
This sharp-edged, tannin-rich red wine always needs a few years to become drinkable. It is often obstreperous, but never insignificant.

Midi
What is called the Midi is mainly the coastal plain between Marseilles and the Spanish border. The region, once discounted as an area of mass-production, is now considered the most dynamic wine region in France. By reducing maximum yield, Roussillon, Languedoc, Minervois, Fitou, and Corbières are now producing a large number of good, fruity red wines (from grenache, carignan, cinsaut, mourvèdre, syrah, cabernet sauvignon, and merlot). Vintners in the mountainous hinterland, especially, make concentrated, velvety wines. In addition to red wines (85 percent), a few spicy and elegant white wines are produced (from picpoul, clairette, bourboulenc, marsanne, and roussanne), as well as a very small percentage of rosés.

Banyuls
The red wines of this tiny appellation at the farthest southern end of the Midi are as heavy as they are noble and sweet. They faintly recall the quality of port.

Other Wine Districts

Gaillac: The best-known wine of the southwest, Gaillac is simple in quality and varies widely from place to place in color and in taste.

Pécharmant: The best red wine in Bergerac is made mostly of bordeaux varieties. The other Bergerac wines, whether white, red, or rosé, tend to be pretty simple.

Monbazillac: The sweet wines of this small appellation in Bergerac could conceivably be as good as those of Sauternes, but they seldom are.

Irouléguy: Located in the French Basque country, Irouléguy grows tannat, cabernet sauvignon, and cabernet franc grapes. They are fermented into good red and rosé wines that can well stand on their own.

Béarn: Including under its AC many red wines of the southwest, Béarn shelters such names as Madiran, Jurançon, Pacherenq-du-Vic-Bilh, and Irouléguy.

Tursan: The white wine of this small appellation is excellent, and many interesting red tannat wines are made here as well.

Blanquette de Limoux: Another interesting white sparkling wine, made of mauzan and chardonnay grapes. It is also made in a *crémant* version.

From Pale Rosés to Strong Reds

Provence is a vacation land. Most of the wine made in the region has always been consumed there. What is required of a vacation wine is not the highest standard, yet some winemakers have shown that Provence is capable of great wines, especially red ones, and their example has inspired others.

For years, Provence was identified with the pale red or onionskin-colored Rosé de Provence, still considered by many to be the typical wine for a Mediterranean vacation. And no wonder; it is produced all over the region, in Cassis, Bellet, and Bandol as well as in the large appellations of Coteaux Varois, Coteaux d'Aix-en-Provence, and Côtes de Provence. Each appellation makes, in addition to red and white wines, rosés, and these usually represent the largest percentage of its production.

It used to be that these rosé wines were all vapid, coarse, and much too heavy (14 percent alcohol), without any hint of finesse. The changes that have occurred in the region are most clearly seen in this same Rosé de Provence: most are now fresh, light, fruity, and furnished with a mild, winy acidity. Not only have fermentation techniques improved but the varieties planted have in part changed, and the time of harvest has been advanced.

Côtes-de-Provence
This large appellation has an impressive wine industry: enormous quantities of simple mass-produced wines are made, as well as a few

Harvesting cinsaut grapes at Le Luc: Soil, sun, and light are the most important factors for quality wines in Provence.

high-class reds, whites, and rosés. The latter come from dynamic and ambitious winemakers who want to bring out the best in the traditional wine varieties of the region. These are also actively experimenting with varieties from outside the region, like viognier, cabernet sauvignon, merlot, and syrah.

Bandol
Around the city of Bandol cluster the vineyards that make the best red wine in Provence. The mourvèdre grape expresses its virtues no-

where better than in this little enclave of red in the kingdom of rosé. The mourvèdre wine is assembled together with various grapes of the region. Bandol wines are ample, fiery, and, despite their tannins, gentle and spicy. They gain in quality and refinement upon resting in the bottle for several years.

Palette
There are only two producers in this very small appellation near Aix-en-Provence. Both make high-class red wines, excellent rosés, and fine white wines. Always expensive, they are also always good.

Corsica
Though most of the island is still largely focused on table wines of the simplest sort, in the last few years several vineyards have attained AOC status and set about improving the quality of the island's wines. Red and white wines from Patrimonio and Ajaccio have already reached amazing levels.

Vines near Propriamo on Corsica: Along with the simple vin de pays, a few excellent AOC wines are now made.

In Love
with Wine

Italian wine and winemaking have changed more profoundly in the last thirty-five years than in the previous three centuries. Gone is the mixed viticulture of grapes, olives, and fruit trees. In the vineyards, the vines are planted in separate plots, by variety. The grapes are harvested one variety at a time and fermented separately, not as before in mixed batches.

In the fermentation cellars even more has changed. Above all, temperature-controlled fermentation has brought new levels of quality. In a warm, often hot country, this amounts to a revolution. Angelo Gaja, winemaker of Barbaresco and one of the first to make wines of international stature, claims that "temperature control is the most important oenological achievement since the invention of the wooden barrel." Overall, the updating of viticulture and cellar management has led to an unimagined increase in quality, a wave of success that originated in the late 1960s in Tuscany, moved to the Friuli and Piedmont, and has now carried with it all the wine regions of Italy.

A Short History of Modern Italian Wine

Italy is the world's largest producer of wine, turning out on the average 60 million hectoliters per year. Wine consumption within the country, however, is declining steadily. The Italians are good winemakers, but indifferent wine drinkers.

Most of the wine made comes from the mass-production areas of Apulia, Sicily, Latium, and the Veneto. The product, a modest table wine, is largely either purchased by European wineries for blending purposes or removed from the market as surplus wine by the European Commission (the European Union's administration) and sold, to be distilled into industrial alcohol.

Italy has taken steps to expand its quality wine production in an effort to counteract the general tendency to make oceans of table wine. The DOC *(denominazione di origine controllata)* and DOCG *(denominazione di origine controllata garantita)* statutes contain limits on grape yields, and the relative proportion of DOC wines has risen to 19 percent of total production since the 1980s. In other words, the amount of wine sold by the tank is decreasing, while the number of bottles is going up, and with it, quality.

To confuse wine lovers, some of the best wines of the land are sold as table wines with imaginative names. The reason for this is that the makers of these wines cannot or will not adjust to the wine laws, which are inflexible and in some ways even seem to oppose quality production methods. By declassifying their wines voluntarily to *vini da tavola,* these winemakers retain the freedom to experiment freely with new methods.

Italian Wine Began in Greece

The history of Italian viticulture goes back to the ancient Greeks, who explored the Mediterranean around 1000 B.C. and began colonizing its shores. In their colonies they planted grapevines. It was in Sicily and Calabria that the first Greek trade outposts in Italy were established. From there, grapes slowly encroached on the rest of the peninsula. At the latest in the seventh century B.C., the Etruscans in Tuscany were making wine and trading with it. By the third century, when the Carthaginian general Hannibal attacked Rome, grapes were cultivated throughout the whole of southern Italy. The most famous wine of that period was the Falerno.

Decline Under Foreign Rule

The expansion of the Roman Empire brought grapes first to northern Italy and then across the Alps, to France and Germany. With the invasion of the Goths and Lombards, viticulture collapsed. With the high culture of the Renaissance, wine also experienced a new flowering. Great wine houses, like Frescobaldi and Antinori, were established at that time.

After the collapse of Medici rule in the sixteenth century, when Italy fell under the control of the Spanish Hapsburg dynasty, wine production once more went into a decline. Because of the political upheavals that followed, until the nineteenth century only regional pockets of wine production could maintain themselves. Then the phylloxera louse and two world wars did their part in destroying the vineyards. The real revival of Italian wine began only around 1960.

Bacchus and Amor: Wine and love are connected in mythology, just as wine is linked to reverence for the gods.

Land of Red Wine and Truffles

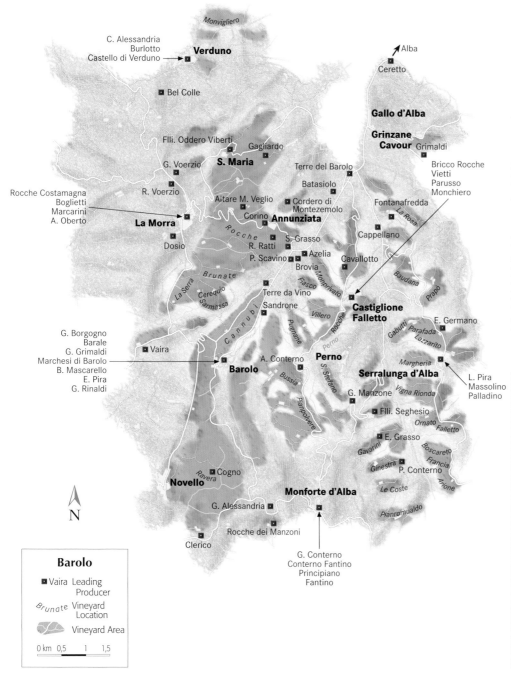

the wine's flavor is rough and fruity, but over the years it develops a many-layered bouquet, which recalls wilted flowers, forest floors, and sweet cloves. The wine's color, a not very dark cherry red or scarlet, should not mislead one into thinking that this is a light wine. In fact, Barolo and Barbaresco can show a 14 percent alcohol content in a good year.

Barolo

Barolo, a small district, lies southwest of Alba and encompasses eleven villages and their lands. The most important of these are Serralunga d'Alba, Monforte d'Alba, Castiglione Falletto, La Morra, and Barolo itself. Vineyards are planted as high up as 1,640 feet (500 m). The wines are very powerful and delicate at the same time. At the earliest, they may be released

Barolo is traditionally aged in large, old oak barrels.

Piedmont: A Highly Ambitious Wine Region

Piedmont is a rural wine-growing region and one that is extremely ambitious. It is famous for its Barolo and Barbaresco wines, which enjoyed a glittering rebirth in the 1980s, having experienced a similar wave of wild success in 1860, when Italy was unified. In the 1990s, Barolo and Barbaresco have been joined in the limelight by Barbera and several other, less well known wines.

Barolo and Barbaresco are two of Italy's most significant wines and belong to the small group made solely from the nebbiolo grape. Nebbiolo is an old native variety, probably from the valley of the Aosta; it is planted practically nowhere but in Piedmont. It thrives best on the eroded, calcareous soils intermixed with clay common in Langhe around the city of Alba. There the variety brings forth a full-bodied wine, strong in tannins, with an unmistakable character. When it is still young,

after three years, and only after they have aged two years in wooden barrels. Traditionally they spend much longer in the wood, in large casks made of Slavonian oak, because Barolo is so high in tannins. In recent years, *élevage* in small barrels or *barriques* has become popular. Barolo had in the past been called a "tannin whip," but now, at least some of the Barolo produced has been improved and refined through the choice of good sites, better clone selection, careful fermentation, and crop reduction.

Barbaresco

The vineyards of Barbaresco start in the northeastern outskirts of the city of Alba and extend over three communities: Treiso, Neive, and Barbaresco. The district is even smaller than that of Barolo, with production practically never exceeding 2.5 million bottles. The vineyards are at somewhat lower elevations than those of Barolo, and their soil tends to be lighter and sandier. For this reason, the wines are less ample than those of Barolo. Most of them express more fruit than tannin. Yet in Barbaresco's top locations, the wines are as opulent and heavy as any in the neighboring district. Barbaresco wines are also aged in large Slavonian oak casks, and have to stay in wood for at least one year before they are marketed in their second year. Despite their proximity to Barolo, the winemakers here have remained conservative, and fewer Barbaresco wines reach top quality levels. The very best, however, do not lag behind in fullness and durability.

Barbera

The barbera vine is the most widely planted in Piedmont. Especially in the province of Asti and around Alba it is very common. Barbera d'Alba is made as a second wine by many vineyards: of medium body, poor in tannins, but distinctly fruity. The barbera variety's best performance is achieved in Monferrato, as the hill country to the north and south of Asti is called. In the calcareous, sandy soil there, some powerfully structured wines are made, palatable, with an alcohol level of 13 to 14 percent. They were once aged in large wooden vats, but recently winemakers have had great success with *barriques*.

Other Wine Districts in Piedmont

Gattinara: Gattinara, a village near Vercelli, has given its name to a powerful nebbiolo that lacks the finesse of most Barolos.

Ghemme: A mighty but somewhat rustic nebbiolo wine from the village of Ghemme, in the immediate vicinity of Gattinara.

Roero: This up-and-coming grape district on the north side of the Tanaro River is well known for its delicate white Arneis and its red Roero. The latter is a nebbiolo wine that tends to turn out lighter than barolo and Barbaresco, but can be very fine indeed.

Gavi: Gavi is a hilly white-wine zone to the southeast of Alessandria, where the cortese grape yields light, slightly acidic wines.

Moscato d'Asti: The entire southern half of the Monferrato hill country is included in this district, where the sparkling wines Asti and Moscato d'Asti are made.

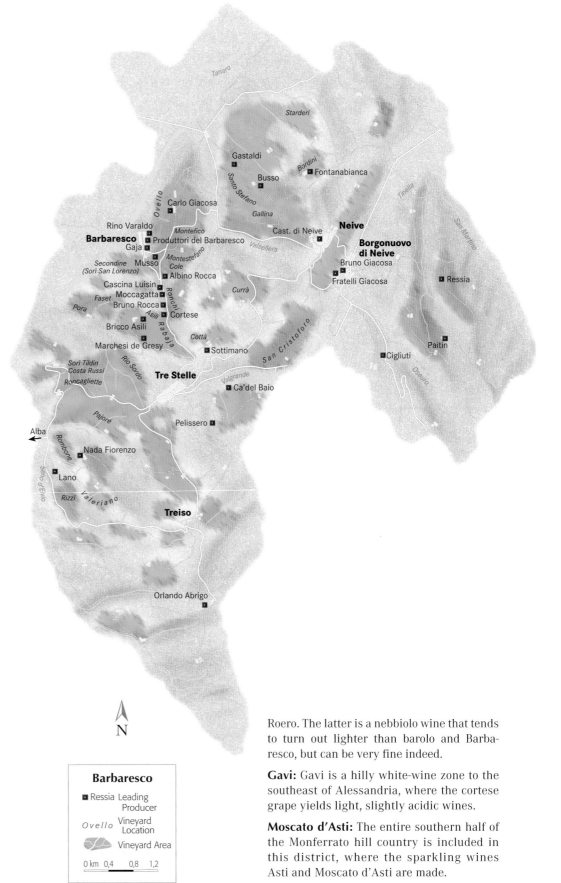

Barbaresco

◼ Ressia Leading Producer

Ovello Vineyard Location

Vineyard Area

0 km 0,4 0,8 1,2

New Wines from Ancient Vineyards

Viticulture in the Alto Adige (South Tyrol) is almost 2,000 years old, but today's wines have nothing in common with the ancient ones.

Franciacorta

The small region between Brescia and Lago d'Iseo belongs to Lombardy. It has recently been brought to the attention of wine lovers by some courageous and enterprising winemakers who have improved its sparkling wines, now rightfully regarded as Italy's best. Most of these are made from chardonnay and/or pinot nero (the Italian name for pinot noir) grapes, for which the calcareous soils of the area provide ideal growing conditions. The spumantes of Franciacorta are not only among the top sparkling wines of in Italy; at their best they compare well with good Champagne, even if they are fruitier and less steely. The chardonnay grapes are also made into an excellent still wine. The red Franciacorta Rosso is blended of several varieties, such as cabernet, barbera, nebbiolo, and merlot.

Alto Adige or South Tyrol

In this wine district, which is predominantly German-speaking but belongs to Italy, the Vernatsch or schiava grape is the most commonly planted, accounting for 55 percent of all vineyard land. It is made into ordinary, extremely simple wines that fuel the conviviality in local pubs. Both private growers and the cooperatives that process over 80 percent of the grapes are endeavoring to give more space to the old local varieties, Traminer, Weissburgunder (pinot bianco, or pinot blanc), and Lagrein. At the moment, the most interesting wines in the district are made from chardonnay and sauvignon. Merlot and pinot nero are used in reds that are not always a complete success. Cabernet sauvignon ripens only in a few locations, but when it does ripen, it makes a fine wine, rich in tannins.

Trentino

Trentino has become Italy's most important cultivation area for chardonnay and pinot grigio. The char-

Pergola training system in Valpolicella: Much supermarket wine, little classical Valpolicella.

donnay is largely used by Italy's spumante industry; the pinot grigio is used for simple, light everyday wines. Only in exceptional cases are these varieties made into fine wines. Local varietal wines are fermented from marzemino and teroldego grapes. At their best, they are concentrated, aromatic, and characterful, but usually they are rather average.

Valpolicella

The wine region of Valpolicella, which extends down into the plains, is still devoted to mass production. Only in the hilly zone of Valpolicella Classico are some light, meltingly fruity wines with some real character produced. These are usually made from three varieties: corvina, molinara, and rondinella. A very small portion of the district's production is represented by the fiery Amarone, a wine partially made of dried grapes, fully fermented, with an alcohol content of 14 to 17 percent. This is a specialty of Verona, and in some instances can be a grand wine.

Breganze

In this tiny district, which encompasses the environs of the village north of Vincenza, one producer is responsible for all good wines. Maculan makes excellent chardonnay, cabernet sauvignons, and dessert wines (Torcolato, Dindarello, Acininobili). The rest of the area's production is respectable but unimposing.

Friuli

The Friuli's warm, Mediterranean climate has during the last twenty-five years turned it into a booming wine region for both red and white wines. Some very good wines grow in the lower zones of the hilly Collio, around Gorizia, in the Colli Orientali, around Udine, on the meager gravelly terrain of Grave, and in the red soils of Isonzo. The white wines from this area have a very good reputation. Because of their rich body and their fresh, fruity primary aroma, they are often said to be Italy's best.

Many of the older local varieties have in recent years been replaced by chardonnay and sauvignon. The native tocai grape is still the one most commonly planted in the Friuli. This tocai has nothing to do with the Hungarian wine or with the Alsatian grape variety: it is indigenous to Ischia. Tocai wines age quickly and tend to be of average quality.

More interesting wines are made out of ribolla and pinot bianco (pinot blanc). Verduzzo and picolit, which yield mildly sweet dessert wines, are of only local importance. The red wines of Friuli have in recent years taken a turn for the better. People are beginning to talk about valuable merlots and, more rarely, cabernet sauvignons. Small amounts of very fine wines with a rough earthiness are also made from the old regional grapes, schioppettino, pignola, tazzelenghe, and refosco.

Soave

Although this district, located east of Verona, is known mostly for its mass-production white wines, a few remarkable white wines are being made in the hill zone of Classico, around the villages of Soave and Monteforte. The producers include Pieropan, Anselmi, Pra, Bolla, and a few others. The main Soave grape variety is garganega. Because of its thick skin, it is also used for a delicate sweet wine called Recioto.

Other Wine Districts

Bianco di Custoza and Gambellara: These two wine regions extend along the southern end of Lake Garda. They specialize in simple, clean white wines, made mostly from garganega and trebbiano grapes.

Lugana: South of Sirmione on Lake Garda in Lombardy, the wine region of Lugana makes white wines that are relatively substantial and full-bodied, using trebbiano grapes.

Grape harvesting in Collio, in Friuli: The source of ample white wines and tannin-rich reds.

Red Wines of Spare Elegance

Map: **Chianti Classico**
- ■ Lilliano Leading Producer
- Vineyard Area
- 0 km 1,5 3 4,5

N

Tuscany — A Mythic Cultural Landscape

The area between the Apennines and the Tyrrhenian Sea is one of the most beautiful and best-preserved landscapes in Europe. A 120-mile carpet of hills stretches between its northern and southern boundaries, threaded with winding streams, dotted with medieval villages, and covered with oak forests. Vineyards are found almost everywhere, though there are few contiguous growing areas.

One-third of Tuscany falls into the wine district of Chianti. This includes many subzones, including Chianti Classico, and also a few indigenous wine zones, such as Brunello di Montalcino or Vino Nobile di Montepulciano.

Great Chianti

The Chianti district extends from Pisa in the north, past Florence and Siena, all the way to Montalcino in the south. It is divided into seven subzones, of which only one has any claim to fame: Chianti Classico, between Florence and Siena. The other zones are: Chianti Rufina (around Pontassieve), Chianti Colline Pisane (Pisa), Chianti Montalbano (Carmignano), Chianti Colli Fiorentini (Florence), Chianti Aretini (Arezzo), and Chianti Colli Senesi (southern Siena). All of these subzones are classified as the very highest quality, DOCG (see page 155), even though for the most part, they are relatively simple red wines. Since the term Chianti encompasses the seven subzones, producers can decide whether they want to market their wine as simple Chianti or as a Chianti with designated origin. The quality requirements for simple Chianti are the loosest, those for Chianti Classico, the most constraining. One thing all Chiantis have in common is that they must use primarily sangiovese grapes. At their very best, they are concentrated wines with dry, astringent tannins and a fine aroma of raspberries: wines of spare elegance.

Chianti Classico

The hill country between Florence and Siena is considered the heart of the Chianti. It is made up of nine communities. All their wines are made exclusively, or at the very least 85 percent, from sangiovese grapes. Recently revised Chianti Classico statutes prescribe that the remaining 15 percent may consist of canaiolo, malvasia nera, mammolo, or other native varieties. In addition, alternative varieties like merlot and cabernet sauvignon are permitted. White varieties (previously 6 percent) are no longer permitted. The previous Chianti formula was set down around 1860; the white grapes served to make the wines ready for marketing at a younger age.

Hardly a Unified Wine District

Chianti Classico is not a uniform wine zone. In the north, around San Casciano and Greve, the wines are more fragrant, their tannins more delicate than in the south. Castellina, Gaiole, Radda, and Castelnuovo Berardenga, at the southern edge of the zone, yield more powerful wines, with stronger tannins. They can be a bit rougher, as well.

Within the area, the wines vary according to location, altitude (up to 2,300 feet [700 m]), and soil structure. In lower-lying vineyards, the soil tends to be mixed with sand and fine gravel, and brings forth delicate, elegant wines. In higher locations, where a clay-rich loam is predominant, as in Galestro, or the ground is calcareous sandstone, as in Alberese, more muscular wines are made.

The New Wines

Since the beginning of the 1980s the quality of Chianti Classico has improved considerably. Private investors with plenty of capital have bought up estate after estate and introduced modern production methods. They have reduced yields, increased plantings of sangiovese vines, and experimented with alternative varieties. Ultimately, their wines no longer met the production requirements of Chianti or Chianti Classico. Some were fermented exclusively from sangiovese grapes without the addition of white (or other red) grapes, which was strictly prescribed at the time. Others contained varieties that, up to that time, had not been provided for in the

The medieval village Volpaia in the Chianti Classico.

production of quality Tuscan wines: cabernet sauvignon, for example, merlot, or other international varieties. These new wines were good, to be sure, even better than the traditional ones, yet they could not carry the name Chianti on their labels. As a result, they left the estates as simple *vino da tavola* (table wine) under a made-up name.

The End of *Vino da Tavola*

The dicey situation arose that the best wines from Tuscany ("Super Tuscans") came to the market in the lowest wine category provided for by European law. The winemakers were by no means upset. Since legislators made only few demands on table wines and had imposed few restrictions, winemakers could experiment all they wanted. Things changed only in 1997 when makers were forbidden from marketing table wines with vintage dates. (The vintage is essential for high-quality wines.) At the same time, the new category of IGT wines was created: wines typical of a geographical region. The category required wines to show the vintage, and the boundaries prescribed were generous. These provisions were flexible enough to include all the "Super Tuscans." The requirements for Chianti and Chianti Classico were revised at the same time. They can now be produced without white grapes and can even be made exclusively from sangiovese. Accordingly, varietal sangiovese wines have returned to the heart of the Chianti.

The Chianti is a hilly landscape with stony soils.

The Resurgence of Sangiovese

Villa di Capezzana, the center of the small growing region of Carmignano, west of Florence.

Chianti Rufina

To the east of Florence, near Pontassieve, there is a small wine zone that was incorporated into the Chianti region in the 1930s. Before that it had made its own wine under the designation Rufina. The grape combinations permitted for Rufina are the same as for other Chiantis, but the special soils of the area—sandstone and clay-marl—catapult the wines made there into a class of their own. They are somewhat stronger in tannins, but their fruit is delicate, and the best of them are the equals of any Chianti Classico. The DOCG zone includes a mere 600 hectares, and top producers are few. Pomino, formerly part of Chianti Rufina, now has its own DOC.

Carmignano

In 1932 this small grape-growing region to the west of Florence became a part of the Chianti Montalbano zone, but in 1975 it once more achieved independent status. Carmignano wine is made from sangiovese

and canaiolo grapes, with 10 to 20 percent cabernet sauvignon added. Since its vineyards are at a lower elevation, the wine is less acidic than a Chianti Classico, and because of the sandy quality of its soil, it never achieves the same full body. Carmignano is one of the four Tuscan wine zones named an outstanding growing region by the Grand Duke of Tuscany as early as 1716.

Bolgheri

A small town on the Mediterranean coast some thirty miles south of Livorno, Bolgheri has given its name to a small, very dynamic red wine region. A single wine has made the region famous: Sassicaia. It was Italy's first varietal cabernet sauvignon, and ever since it was first produced in 1968 it has enjoyed high esteem worldwide. The success of this wine has encouraged a number of winemakers to grow cabernet sauvignon in Bolgheri, as well as merlot, petit verdot, and syrah. These have gradually replaced the sangiovese vines that were formerly heavily represented in this

coastal area. Today Bolgheri is considered one of the best cabernet regions in Italy. The success of its wines has unleashed a veritable wine boom along this narrow strip of coastline. Although they were previously marketed as vino da tavola, since 1995 they have been labeled either Bolgheri DOC or Bolgheri Superiore DOC. Only Sassicaia has the right to call itself Bolgheri Sassicaia DOCG. The new designation of origin is very flexible, to be sure. Even sangiovese-based wines (at least 30 percent) can use it. In addition, Bolgheri Rosato and white wine are produced, mainly from the varieties vermentino and sauvignon blanc.

Montescudaio

An ancient Tuscan growing region in the hinterland of Cecina, Montescudaio has seen the arrival of increasing numbers of new investors in recent years. Traditionally it has been known for its sangiovese grapes, which yield a supple, fruity wine without a strong backbone of tannin. To foster the production of denser, more durable wines, the DOC statute was changed in 1999; now only 50 percent sangiovese is required. The rest can be made up of cabernet sauvignon, merlot, and other international varieties. As a result, a few remarkable reds have been introduced, for example La Regola and Sorbaiano. Castello del Terriccio markets its wines as Rosso della Toscana.

Val di Cornia

This wine region on the Mediterranean coast extends from Piombino, past Campiglia Marittima, to well beyond Suvereto. The wide valley opens to the sea and enjoys a warm, Mediterranean climate in which merlot and cabernet sauvignon are especially successful. Grapes from the rust-red, mineral-rich soil of the higher valley elevations produce wines that are among the best in Italy. For this reason the Val di Cornia has attracted a great rush of new winemakers and investors who have devoted considerable capital and great dedication to wine production. In the area around Suvereto, wines can be fermented from single-variety grapes. Sangiovese, ciliegiolo, and montepulciano (also some malvasia nera and colorino) are the varieties traditionally grown in the region. White varieties are also cultivated in small quantities: traditionally trebbiano Toscano, biancone, and ansonica, but recent years have seen increases in pino bianco, chardonnay, and clairette. The red aleatico vine, from which a sweet Passito wine is produced, has recently become especially popular with winemakers.

Morellino di Scansano

This wine is produced in southern Tuscany around Grosseto, made from sangiovese grapes with small additions of local varieties such as canaiolo, colorino, ciliegiolo, and alicante, and more recently merlot, cabernet sauvignon, and syrah. In the past, Morellino di Scansano was a simple wine, softer than a Chianti but without the fullness of a Brunello di Montalcino. Since the region has seen the arrival of numerous foreign investors, its producers have become more ambitious. New vineyard owners have planted quantities of merlot, syrah, and cabernet sauvignon in addition to sangiovese, so as to be able to ferment them as varietals or bottle them as *cuvées* (even with the inclusion of sangiovese). These wines are then marketed as Maremma Rosso IGT. A majority of these wines are still being developed. The growing region is large and not very homogeneous. The lower areas close to the sea experience high temperatures and have sandy soils that produce simpler wines.

Other Wine Regions

Vernaccia di San Gimignano: This well-known and very popular white wine is from the medieval town of the same name. It is made from vernaccia grapes and is a simple, refreshing wine that has a high alcohol content in its best qualities. Since it was awarded DOCG status in 1994, it has been allowed to add 10 percent of other varieties. The San Gimignano red must have at least 50 percent sangiovese grapes, while the other half may be cabernet sauvignon, merlot, or other recommended varieties.

Cortona: This growing region around the city of Cortona has become a center for experimentation with new vine varieties and new wines. Pinot bianco, chardonnay, grechetto, Riesling, Italico, and sauvignon blanc are permitted in the white wines; in the reds, in addition to sangiovese, producers can use cabernet sauvignon, merlot, syrah, gamay, and pinot nero, either as varietals or *cuvées*.

Parrina: A growing region in the extreme south of Tuscany near Orbetello, Parrina produces a rather supple, fruity sangiovese wine, some of it cut with merlot and cabernet sauvignon, and also white wines from trebbiano, malvasia, and ansonica.

Chianti Montespertoli: The newest subzone of the Chianti, this region has a centuries-old wine-growing tradition and was an important wine trading center early on. Since 1997 it has had the right to its own designation of origin. The village of Montespertoli lies eighteen miles south of Florence in the valley of the Pesa. Its vineyards are therefore among the lowest in the Chianti. It produces a supple, not-too-corpulent Chianti that is mainly distinguished by fruitiness and freshness.

Montecarlo: This old white wine region is near the town of the same name west of Florence and, in recent years, has been increasingly planting red varieties including sangiovese, canaiolo, ciliegiolo, colorino, and malvasia nera, which form the basis of the DOC reds, and, above all, merlot and syrah. The tradition of white vines has not been abandoned, although the lower areas at the foot of the Apennines yield rather simple wines. Since the Napoleanic Wars, sauvignon blanc, roussanne, pinot grigio, and pinot bianco have been native to Montecarlo. However, it is trebbiano Toscano that traditionally forms the basis of the region's white wines.

San Gimignano: A medieval city in the Chianti known for its vernaccia wines.

The Discovery of Sweet, Soft Tannins

Montalcino

The grapes for Brunello di Montalcino grow on the slopes of this little town in southern Tuscany.

Sant'Angelo in Colle   Castello la Banfi   Col d'Orcia

ing area. Its tannins are sweeter and softer, too, and its acidity is lower. It ages for at least two years in wood–traditionally a large barrel made of Slavonian oak. Only after four years can it be marketed. Not every Brunello lives up to the new fame–or the new price–of these wines. A wine of excellent quality and relatively reasonable price is the secondary wine of the area, the Rosso di Montalcino. Like the primary wine of this district of southeastern Tuscany, it is a pure brunello, but it ages in wood for only one year.

Brunello di Montalcino

Internationally, Brunello is Italy's most esteemed DOCG red wine, ample and muscular with a lot of soft but powerful tannins. It is a varietal wine, made of a variant strain of sangiovese grapes called brunello. The success story of the wine is grounded in this clone of the sangiovese grosso vine, which was isolated and propagated in the middle of the nineteenth century by Ferruccio Biondi-Santi. Until the 1960s the Biondi-Santi family held a virtual monopoly on Brunello. Since then over a hundred firms, mostly bottling plants, have been established in the region, and the area planted with brunello grapes has more than doubled since the early 1980s. In addition to the large wine producers and the private growers with capital who have moved into the area, more and more farms have begun bottling their own wines.

Brunello is a heavier wine than Chianti Classico. This is due to its more southern grow-

Cellar of the wine estate Il Greppo of Biondi-Santi: Brunello ages for three years in wooden barrels.

Vino Nobile di Montepulciano

The second significant wine of southern Tuscany is Vino Nobile di Montepulciano, which ripens on the slopes around the little medieval town. The grapes it contains are primarily sangiovese—locally known as prugnolo gentile—canaiolo, and to a small extent, mammolo. The wine district is only half as large as Brunello; it has sandier soils, and because it is farther from the sea its climate is cooler and more temperate. These are the reasons why a Vino Nobile never quite attains either the fullness of Brunello or the density and elegance of Chianti Classico. Nonetheless, the best Vini Nobili are worthy representatives of the sangiovese grape variety. The less favored locations deliver the grapes for the secondary, simple but delicate Rosso di Montepulciano or the even less complex Chianti Colli Senesi.

Montecucco

A new, up-and-coming growing region in southern Tuscany, Montecucco rests on the slopes of Monte Amiata between Montalcino and Grosetto. The best of its wines, when fermented solely from sangiovese, come close to a Brunello di Montalcino. They are then called Montecucco Sangiovese. In contrast to this wine, the Montecucco Rosso can consist of a maximum 40 percent merlot, syrah, cabernet sauvignon, and other international varieties.

Montalcino: Lovely, forested hill country, which brings forth great red wines.

Torgiano

The fame of Torgiano is largely attributable to the Lungarotti family, who exert control over much of the vineyard area around this little village on the Tiber. They were among the very first to establish quality standards for their wines, setting an example with their Riserva Monticchio, which they age for ten years (mostly in the bottle) before they release it for sale. The simple Torgiano is an unpretentious but delicate wine. Its basis is sangiovese, but 30 percent canaiolo enhances it with an expressive, fruity flavor.

Montefalco

Perhaps the best Umbrian wine comes from the hills around the small city of Montefalco: Montefalco Sagrantino. The sagrantino grape yields a many layered, traditionally somewhat fiery but today rather compact wine that is ruby red in color and has a lot of mellow, bittersweet tannin. It is produced as a varietal. A somewhat simpler wine is the Montefalco Rosso, made up of sangiovese (60 to 70 percent), sagrantino, and whatever other varieties one chooses.

Orvieto

The most important white wine region of Umbria, Orvieto produces large quantities of simple white wines of commercial quality. The main varieties grown are trebbiano and Grechetto. Vineyards that have planted chardonnay and sauvignon produce better qualities. For several years now, more ambitious winemakers have turned more and more to red varieties.

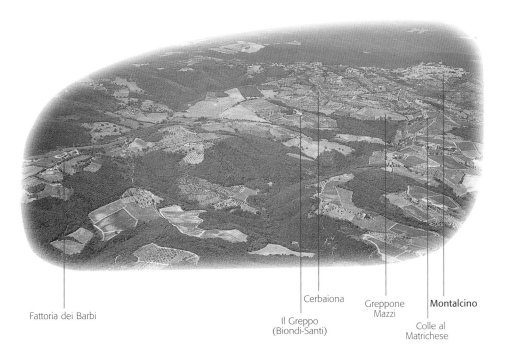

Fattoria dei Barbi

Cerbaiona

Il Greppo (Biondi-Santi)

Greppone Mazzi

Montalcino

Colle al Matrichese

New Messages from the Hot South

Evening light over the hills near Montecarotto, in the Marches, home of verdicchio and of the red wines made of montepulciano grapes.

Montefiascone

In northern Latium, near the border with Tuscany, lies the wine district of Montefiascone. It has become known for its white wine called Est! Est!! Est!!! This rustic, unexciting wine is made of trebbiano grapes. Its industrial producers have in recent years been joined by some smaller enterprises that have taken this local wine in hand with good success. Since then, merlot grapes have been introduced to the district, and they are doing well.

Frascati

Frascati, which belongs to the region of Latium, is a mass-production area outside Rome, whose output mainly consists of modest, watery white wines made according to a simple formula. A few producers have recently started marketing wines with more substance and delicate fruit.

Rosso Conero

South of the port of Ancona, within the reach of cooling sea breezes, grows a full, fiery red wine. Its name is Rosso Conero, and it is made from montepulciano grapes. Although it may contain up to 15 percent sangiovese, this does not add any particular quality to the wine, since the warm climate of the Adriatic does not suit that variety. Rosso Conero used to be made fiery and somewhat rough, but careful fermentation methods have recently begun to lend it a remarkable finesse. Unfortunately, only about a dozen winemakers offer this high quality.

Verdicchio

Verdicchio, the most important wine of the Marches region, grows in calcareous soil intermixed with clay. This white wine enchants not with its lively acidity but with the richness of its body. Only the industrial variants of verdicchio are slim wines. The characteristic qualities of verdicchio are fullness, fragrance, and complexity. This is certainly true of Verdicchio dei Castelli di Jesi, and even more so of Verdicchio di Matelica. Both of these wines have their own DOC and are fermented as varietal wines from the grape that gives them their name.

Apulia

The sheer wealth here of known and nameless red DOC wines–some ordinary, some middling–makes it difficult to select individual areas for special mention. The uniformly warm climate that prevails in the region and the suitability of the soil to grape cultivation mean that quality is essentially in the hands of the vintner. Almost all red wines contain the main

Temple of Segesta in Sicily, surrounded by old vines.

variety of the region, negroamaro ("bitter black"), and malvasia nera and montepulciano grapes occur in many. Especially interesting are the wines made of the uva di Troia grape, now being replaced in many places; it is made, for example, into Castel del Monte and Cerignola. The indigenous primitivo variety has recently also been fermented into some great, dry red wines.

Calabria

This forgotten wine region in southernmost Italy makes very few good wines. These grow only in the back country of the port of Cirò, and are powerful, tannin-rich red wines that faintly recall Barolo, but do not have that wine's durability or finesse.

Campania

This is a classical wine region of Italy, one that produces a great number of solid white and rosé wines in the Mediterranean style. The most significant red wine is the Taurasi: a heavy wine with strong tan-

nins and expressive fruit. It grows around the city of Avellino. The white Fiano is another wine with an unmistakable personality.

Basilicata

At the foot of Monte Vulture, a dead volcano, the aglianico grape is planted on small terraces scattered about the slopes. It is fermented into Aglianico del

Volcanic ash on Pantelleria, island of sweet wines.

Vulture, one of the most beautiful red wines of southern Italy.

Sicily

Sicily, an enormous wine region, is perceived mostly as a mass-production area. Very few producers have come near to realizing the qualitative potential of the island. The very first to do so were the governmental winery of Duca di Salaparuta in Casteldaccia, the estates of Count Tasca d'Almerita in Scalfani Bagni, and the marsala maker Vecchio Samperi. Many producers have tried to catch up with these pioneers by making fresh white and rosé wines in the contemporary style.

Sardinia

Sardinia produces light, fresh summer wines made of vermentino, nuragus, malvasia di Sardegna, and sauvignon grapes. It also makes substantial red wines, in recent years adding to the old varieties cannonau, malvasia nera, sangiovese, and cabernet sauvignon with great success.

Italy's Viticulture in Numbers

Acreage under vines:
856,000 hectares
Wine production:
42–51 million hectoliters
Annual wine consumption
per capita: 48 liters

**The Ten Most-Planted
Grape Varieties**

1.	Trebbiano	white	11.6%
2.	Sangiovese	red	10.0%
3.	Barbera	red	5.5%
4.	Merlot	red	3.7%
5.	Negro amaro	red	3.6%
6.	Montepulciano	red	3.6%
7.	Primitivo	red	2.0%
8.	Dolcetto	red	1.2%
9.	Prosecco	white	0.8%
10.	Pinot bianco	white	0.8%

Italian Wine Law

Denominazione di origine controllata e garantita (DOCG): Controlled and guaranteed provenance, the highest rank in the Italian wine pyramid. Since 1983, only a few wines have attained it. As a rule, this level sets many restrictions, including caps on production yields, more severely than DOC.

Denominazione di origine controllata (DOC): Controlled provenance, a designation awarded since 1964. This law contains regulations concerning borders of grape districts, permitted varieties, methods of vinification, and time of release for sale. At this time, about 19 percent of Italian wines are designated DOC.

Indicazione geografica tipica (IGT): A regional wine category introduced in 1997 that corresponds to *vin de pays*. Requirements for minimum alcohol content and maximum production per hectare are below those of DOC. The labels may show variety, region, and vintage.

Vino da tavola (VdT): Table wine with minimal quality requirements. It has to be unspoiled and suitable for marketing. On the label, only color, area of provenance, and alcohol content may be given, not the vintage.

More Than Just Rioja

In terms of acreage devoted to grapes, Spain is the largest grower in the world; in wine production it stands third, after Italy and France. Because of the dry conditions that predominate in much of this land, Spanish grapes bear very lightly. Moreover, Spain tends to stick to its traditions, some of which go back not just to the nineteenth but to the eighteenth century. For example, in no other grape country in Europe are vines planted as far apart as in Spain.

During the 1960s, the Spanish wine industry experienced an unparalleled overhaul. Unfortunately, this has resulted in mass production and a lessening of quality standards. Only very recently has contemporary, quality-oriented winemaking entered Spain. The quality revolution began not in Rioja, Spain's internationally known wine region, but in many small, unheard-of districts around the country.

La Coruña

San Sebastián

Ribeira Sacra

Ribeiro

Bierzo

Rías
Baixas

Valdeorras

Rioja

Navarra

Somont

Vinho
Verde

Ribera del Duero

Toro

Porto

Rueda

Porto e Douro

Madrid

Bairrada

Dão

Ribatejo

La Mancha

Valencia

Utiel-
Requena

Bucelas

Colares

Lisboa

Valdepeñas

Yecla

Carcavelos

Jumilla

Alicante

Setúbal

Alica

Cartagena

Montilla-
Moriles

Sevilla

Málaga

Jerez

Málaga

Clinging to Honored Tradition

Today Spain is one of the most dynamic wine nations in the world. Yet most regions of the country are still dominated by grape varieties that for fifty or a hundred years have granted a secure income to wine growers by delivering high yields and making few demands.

Two Spanish grape varieties are still dominant— airén among the whites, garnacha (grenache) among the reds. Both yield modest, simple wines. Traditional methods of winemaking, however—late harvest and fermentation without temperature control—are a thing of the past. Cooperatives dedicated to industrial mass production now largely control Spanish winemaking. In their hands, many white wines are both thin and heavy. Red wines are usually high in alcohol and low in acid.

Only the new generation of winemakers that stepped on the scene in the 1980s and 1990s is trying to make changes. These pioneers have moved viticulture from the hot regions of the country into cool ones, and they have invested heavily in cellar technology. The result: fresh, clean white wines and concentrated red wines with substance, neither overaged nor poor in acids. These wines are beginning to set the new Spanish wine styles.

From the Carthaginians to the Arabs

Grapes have been cultivated on the Iberian Peninsula for 3,000 or 4,000 years. Spain's first wine boom occurred after the Phoenicians had founded the city of Cádiz and after the Romans and Carthaginians had set up a lively commerce around the Mediterranean, that is, around 200 B.C. Rome consumed a lot of wine from Baetica (Andalusia) and Terraconensis (Tarragona). After the Arab conquest of Spain, viticulture was discouraged, but it was tolerated. Although the Prophet had forbidden the enjoyment of wine, the wine tax was something the emirs and caliphs did not want to abolish completely.

Wine in More Recent History

After the reconquest of the peninsula by the Christians in the fifteenth century, winemaking once more experienced a renaissance. Jerez and Málaga became the most important Spanish wine regions. In 1587 Sir Francis Drake raided Cádiz and carried off 2,900 pipes (barrels) of sherry. Soon thereafter, the wine trade with England began, and Spanish wine production began to flourish. It was not till the second half of the nineteenth century that the wine industry's fortunes changed: powdery mildew and phylloxera wiped out the vineyards from Catalonia to Málaga. The one region preserved was Rioja, which, because of its remote situation, was hit by phylloxera at a time when its vines had largely been grafted onto resistant American stock (1900 to 1910). Numerous bordeaux growers roamed Rioja in search of viable replacements for their destroyed vines. Although the French visitors brought their *barriques* and introduced new cellaring techniques, the Spanish wine industry could not recover given the devastation of civil war and two world wars.

Decline and Revival

In the 1950s, winemaking experienced a revival thanks to the formation of many wine cooperatives. The new producers concentrated on producing simple table wines and bulk wines for export. Quality was completely lost. Only sherry and rioja experienced a boom in the 1960s. Since the 1980s, however, Spanish winemakers have been trying hard to close the gap between their own wines and those of the rest of Europe. In Catalonia, Old Castile, and a few other wine regions of northern Spain, young wine entrepreneurs and investors have mounted a quality offensive of staggering proportions.

The wines of Marqués de Murrieta embody the aristocratic style of the Rioja. These wines are completely traditional, with enormous longevity. The '59 Castillo Ygay spent twenty-five years in wood. The owner of the estate, the Conde de Creixell, has since shortened the required time for barrel aging.

Quality Revolution in the North of Spain

The phylloxera blight of the last century and the industrial mass production that began after World War II have decisively slowed the expansion of quality winemaking on the Iberian Peninsula, but now Spanish winemaking is experiencing a surge of vitality unequaled elsewhere.

Bodegas Raimat in Costers del Segre: As well as tempranillo, they grow cabernet sauvignon, merlot, and chardonnay.

Costers del Segre

This viticultural oasis near the city of Lleida is famous because of the presence of the ultramodern, top-quality wine producer Raimat. The Raimat vineyards make wines that are among the very best of the new generation. They are located in the cold highlands, where the summers bring such droughts that the vines can only survive with the aid of a system of irrigation canals. In addition to the traditional varieties parellada, macabeo, and tempranillo, they successfully grow chardonnay, merlot, cabernet sauvignon, and pinot noir.

Penedès

The cool hill country south of Barcelona is mostly known for cava, the popular Spanish sparkling wine, which is made according to the bottle-fermentation method from the white varieties macabeo, xarello, and parellada. Since 1988, chardonnay has also been permitted. The first cava was made in 1872 by the pioneer winemaker José Raventos, using the Champagne method. His winery, Cordorníu, is now known across the country. Cava has to rest on yeast for at least nine months; vintage cava, for four years.

The light-colored chalk and clay soils that produce cava also produce a strong still white wine with emphatic fruit. It is made of the three cava varieties. Red wines are also made from cariñena (carignan), garnacha (grenache), and monastrell. Miguel Torres is the best-known winemaker of Penedès, and was the first to introduce contemporary viticul-

tural methods to Spain, in the 1970s. His estate in Villafranca makes noble red wines from cabernet sauvignon. Young avant-garde growers in the region have also had good results with merlot.

Priorato

This little region includes only nine villages, which are located in the mountainous back country of Tarragona. Most of the vineyard area is planted with cariñena grapes, which are made into dark, alcohol-heavy, but simple red wines. Since the end of the 1980s, however, a dozen top grape growers have settled in the Priorato; they have begun to honor the traditional garnacha grape and also to plant some cabernet sauvignon. From these varieties outstanding, extremely individual, and durable wines are made, which are among the best and the most expensive in Spain.

Rioja

The Rioja region is 74 miles (120 kilometers) long and follows the banks of the Ebro river. The area is justly famous for its deep red, spicy wines, which in their *reserva* and *gran reserva* forms have aged for decades and acquired an incredible finesse. It is true that more than half the wine of the region is sold when it is young.

The region consists of three subzones: Rioja Alavesa in the west extends north of the river Ebro; Rioja Alta follows the south

side of the river into the rising hills; and east of Logroño, the Rioja Baja subzone begins. This is the hottest and driest of the zones, producing wines with an alcohol content of up to 15 percent. A typical rioja wine consists of 80 percent tempranillo grapes, with the rest usually made up of part garnacha and part cariñena. With special permission, it is possible to add cabernet sauvignon and merlot as well. The wines are aged in small barrels, called *barricas*, that hold 225 liters; they are made of American oak. The quality of rioja wines varies enormously; many lack body, and many are overmatured. The rioja boom of the 1960s promoted mass production. Today there are 100 large bodegas that bottle rioja and thousands of small wineries that, despite severe summer droughts, frequently harvest far more than the legal limit of 11,000 pounds (5,000 kg) per hectare.

Only in the last few years have some wineries begun to establish their own vineyards in order to be able to control the quality of their grapes. White riojas are more and more frequently entering

Many riojas age in small barricas of American oak, such as these at the Bodegas Palacio.

the market as fresh, fragrant, young wines. The traditional wood-aged *crianzas* and *reservas* still exist. They constitute about 20 percent of production and are today fermented mostly from macabeo grapes, and only occasionally from the traditional malvasia variety.

Navarre

Simple but delicate rosé wines from garnacha grapes have helped to make this region famous. These wines are still made in great quantities, yet more and more vineyards are replacing garnacha with the considerably more refined tempranillo grape. From this variety it is possible to make well-constructed red wines that can seriously compete with riojas. Cabernet sauvignon and merlot are also planted with good results. Navarre is among Spain's most upwardly mobile wine regions.

Somontano

Somontano runs along the southern slopes of the Pyrenees in the region of Aragón. At 2,100 hectares it is one of the smallest wine regions of Spain, and it is also one of the newest, established only in 1985. In the cool, rainy mountain climate, excellent white wines are made from chardonnay and chenin blanc. In the lower, warmer areas, the old Spanish varieties monastrell and garnacha are more

and more frequently joined by cabernet sauvignon, merlot, and pinot noir. These varieties yield elegant red wines with good substance, which have received much attention in the last few years.

Ribera del Duero

The most significant wine region of Castilla y León is east of the city of Valladolid, along the banks of the Duero River. It is about a fourth the size of Rioja, with only 12,750 hectares of vineyards. In terms of quality, however, the Ribera has become a serious rival to Rioja. The primary variety planted in the Ribera is tempranillo, called tinto fino or tinto del país in this region. Its vineyards rise all the way to 2,950 feet (900 m). In the past, they produced simple rosé wines. Today tempranillo yields powerful, dark red wines of great finesse and durability. Bodegas Vega Sicilia is the most famous estate of the region, adding to its wines cabernet sauvignon, merlot, and malbec grapes. Most of the newly established bodegas follow its example. Others continue to

ferment only tinto fino, among them Pesquera, the second most famous bodega of this zone. It was the success of these two producers' wines in the 1980s that sparked the spectacular development of this region, where sugar beets can still be found growing beside the grapevines. Climatically speaking, the lonely Ribera is a land of extremes: long, frosty winters and short, dry summers, which do not produce large grape yields.

Rueda

For a hundred years this region that extends around the city of Rueda in the southwestern Valladolid had been forgotten by the outside world. Now things are about to change. For centuries, only the sugary palomino grape was planted in the region, for making sherry-like wines. Since the 1980s, growers in the area have been replacing palomino with another traditional variety, the verdejo grape. It forms the basis of today's light, dry white wines from this area. Rueda Superior must consist of at least 60 percent verdejo; the rest is part viura, part sauvignon.

Toro

This is a small enclave of good red wine production east of the city of Zamora. Toro is a full-bodied, fiery wine, made entirely from tempranillo grapes.

El Bierzo

This region is located in the northwest of Spain, near the border of Galicia. Although it is still very traditional at this time, its cool climate guarantees it a great future, especially for elegant red wines.

Rias Baixas

Galicia is well-situated for growing white wines because of its damp, Atlantic climate. Its southern district, between the city of Cambados and the Portuguese border and known as Rias Baixas, is therefore considered to be Spain's best white wine region. Ninety percent of the vines in the area are of the albariño variety, which produce fresh, slightly spicy wines that are valued highly within Spain itself, sold at high prices, and exported only in very small quantities.

New Wines in the Hot South

In Jerez, Pedro Ximénez grapes, used for sweet sherries, are dried in the sun before being pressed.

known for its mild, glowing red wines. Formerly it almost only produced white wine, mainly from airén vines. Even its few red wines were once made up of as much as 90 percent airén. Ten percent of tempranillo (locally called cencibel) was enough to give the wine color and tannin. More recently cencibel and international varieties like cabernet sauvignon and syrah have taken over the vineyards. Today's red wines are produced from them, either as varietals or *cuvées*. The majority are flavorful, uncomplicated wines that can be marketed relatively inexpensively. However a few producers are aging their Valdepeñas as a reserva in new, small oak barrels.

Jerez

Sherry is the most important wine in Andalusia. There is nothing in the world to compare to it, in terms of either character or production. It can be produced from the three white varieties palomino, Pedro Ximénes, and muscat d'Alexandrie. Dry sherry is in fact produced from up to 90 percent palomino grapes. It is grown in the province of Cádiz, near the sea, where despite the high temperatures prevailing in Andalusia there is always a cool breeze flowing in from the Atlantic. The center of sherry production is the city of Jerez de la Frontera. The highest quality sherries are attained from its white albariza chalk soils. What makes sherry unusual is that it is spiked with brandy to give it a higher alcohol content to match its opulent body. In recent years the growing region around Jerez has shrunk by half, as the worldwide demand for sherry has declined. Instead, simple whites and reds are being produced. But among connoisseurs the wine continues to enjoy a unique reputation.

La Mancha

The bleak, lonely highlands southeast of Toledo constitute Spain's largest wine regions. Although the sun is fierce and water scarce, huge amounts of modest, mass-produced wine come from this part of New Castile. Famous for its windmills and Don Quixote, La Mancha is nevertheless changing from a growing region for mass-produced white wines (until the 1990s 90 percent of the vineyard area was planted in the drought-resistant airén vine) into Spain's largest red wine region. As before, airén is the main variety, but by 2006 it had been replaced in nearly half of the total area by cencibel. Well-known producers from other growing regions have now established themselves in La Mancha, and are setting new standards of quality with their varietal wines from cencibel, cabernet sauvignon, syrah, and petit verdot, which show the potential of the region. Roughly half of the total area (200,000 hectares) is the DO zone of the same name.

Valdepeñas

This city on the high plain of La Mancha gives its name to an extensive growing region at an elevation of 2,300 feet (700 m). With some 303,000 hectares in vines, the region is now

Other Growing Regions

Jumilla: An extensive, hot region in the hinterlands of Alicante dominated by the red monastrell vine. It is generally made into fiery, heavy red wines with a powerful aroma. For a long time the vintners of Jumilla specialized in mass yields, but after an infestation of vine pest in the late 1980s they reconsidered, and many of their wines have become considerably more refined. Along with those of the neighboring growing regions of Yecla and Alicante, the wines of Jumilla are among the least expensive in Spain.

In the hot growing regions of central and southern Spain, progress begins with stainless-steel tanks, which make it possible to control the temperature during fermentation.

Yecla: This town in the mountains of Murcia lends its name to a small growing region of only 4,500 hectares. Its dark, expressive red wines are derived from the native monastrell grape, also from garnacha, tempranillo, cabernet sauvignon, merlot, and petit verdot. They are powerful wines with a distinct fruit, similar to those from Jumilla. In recent years they have gained in importance.

Alicante: A growing region of roughly 14,000 hectares that is made up of two sections far apart from each other: Vinalopó and La Marina. Its specialty is Fondillon, a wine made from monastrell grapes that have been dried on the vine like raisins. Along with these wines produced by the solera process, red wines are derived from the same grape: heavy, fiery wines that are generally of only modest quality. In addition, there are a few muscatels. In recent years a few producers have been fermenting respectable reds.

Utiel-Requena: A large growing region in the hinterland of Valencia that produces strong red wines made from tempranillo and bobal grapes. These include both dark, fruity, heavily structured reds and delicately fruity rosados fermented from bobal exclusively. But recently bobal has been appearing not only in blends and Rosé Furore; more and more vintners have turned to it for the production of a light, elegant, single-variety red wine.

Montilla-Moriles: This area produces wines from the Pedro Ximénes grape that are comparable to sherry in style and quality, but are considerably less expensive and always dry. A considerable percentage of its grapes is sold to Jerez to be used for sweet Olorosos—a practice that is allowed.

Binissalem: Mallorca's most important growing region, with full-bodied, fiery red wines from manto and negro, in part from tempranillo and monastrell.

Spain's Viticulture in Numbers

Acreage under vines:
  1.2 million hectares
Wine production:
  32–41 million hectoliters
Annual wine consumption
  per capita: 34 liters

The Ten Most-Planted Grape Varieties

1. Airén	white	19.2%
2. Garnacha	red	8.8%
3. Tempranillo	red	6.6%
4. Monastrell	red	5.0%
5. Macabeo	white	3.6%
6. Bobal	red	3.0%
7. Pedro Ximénez	white	1.4%
8. Mencía	red	0.9%
9. Moscatel	white	0.9%
10. Palomino	white	0.8%

Spanish Wine Law

Denominación de origen (DO): Quality wines from specific growing regions. Wines from precisely defined districts with a special Consejo Regulador that oversees production and marketing and ensures that specific standards of quality are met. An even 50% of Spain's wine production has DO status.

Denominación de origen calificada (DOCa): Qualified quality wines. First awarded to Rioja wines in 1991.

Vino de la tierra (VdlT): Regional wine. Wines from a specific growing region that does not have DO status.

Vino de mesa (VdM): Table wine. The grapes come from several different regions.

Spanish Wine Designations

According to long-standing Spanish tradition, wines are only released when they are ready to drink. Accordingly, a sophisticated system has been developed by means of which the consumer can tell the age of a red wine by studying the label:

Joven: 1 year
Crianza: 2 years
Reserva: 3 years
Gran reserva: 5 years

Land of Secrets

The terraced landscape of the Douro: Hot summers and cold, rainy winters characterize the climate of the river valley that gives us port.

Portugal is not just Mateus Rosé and port. The country boasts 500 native grape varieties. True, many of these are destined for mass-produced wines, sweet to the palate. But there are also a number of reds and whites of distinct character. Just how good Portuguese wines can be will only be known in ten years' time.

Portugal is a country in the process of change: a new era has already begun, the old era has not yet ended. Inland, the old order still prevails: red grapes are fermented with their stalks and without mechanical aids of any kind. The wines thus produced are mighty, tannin-loaded, and raw. They pucker the palate and take years and years to become drinkable. And then there are the clean, fresh, fruity white wines, sweetened at bottling with a few grams of sugar, that go forth to conquer the world markets.

Thus, a land of contrasts: in the cool Atlantic climate of the coast, light wines like *vinho verde* ("green wine," sold shortly after fermentation) triumph. The continental climate of the rest of the country, with its hot summers, adds heaviness to wines. At their best, these are like port.

Historically, Wine Follows Trade

In ancient times, grapes were planted on the Iberian peninsula by the Phoenicians, the Greeks, and the Romans. The thriving wine industry stagnated during the Moorish occupation but did not quite perish. After Portugal's independence in 1385, it entered into a lively trade relationship with England. From the Minho River, which today forms the border between Spain and northern Portugal, regular shipments of wine were dispatched across the Channel. At that time, port did not yet exist.

Port as a Means to Success

Port only came into existence after 1693, when the English king set such high tariffs on French wines that English wine dealers were forced to find replacements for the well-loved French red wines they had been importing previously. This of course took time. In the meantime, in 1678 an English wine dealer sent his two sons to Portugal. They traveled up the Douro, deep inland. Near Lamego they met a winemaking priest who had the habit of fortifying the local red wine with brandy while it was still fermenting. The result, a sweet red wine of great alcoholic strength, suited the palate of the English, who loved heavy red wines. Soon, all along the Douro, warehouses were built to ensure ample reserves. To prevent fraud, in 1756 the borders of the port wine region were established (see page 112). In the eighteenth and nineteenth centuries, Madeira, named after an Atlantic island off the Portuguese coast (see page 113), rose to equal prominence.

All this trade came to a virtual end when phylloxera and downy mildew destroyed the vineyards of Portugal. Only in the 1930s did the industry begin to be rebuilt, jump-started by the establishment of numerous cooperatives. When Portugal joined the EU in 1986, the country already had a variety of wine regions. Thanks to the great success of Mateus Rosé, the winemakers of Portugal have never looked back.

Vinho Verde

Vinho verde, quantitatively the most important wine of Portugal, comes from the north. This "green wine" comes in two versions: red and white.

The red *vinho verde* is reserved, astringently tannic, and pretty well unknown. Few examples of it ever leave the country, while the white *vinho verde* is, after port, the country's leading export wine. A light wine, slightly refreshed by carbon dioxide, it has an alcoholic strength between 8 and 10 percent. Often it also contains a few grams of residual sugar. It is marketed quickly and consumed equally fast.

The *vinho verde* region comprises the province of Minho, from Porto to the Spanish border. This is a cool, rainy part of Portugal; for this reason, it is densely populated and studded with vineyards, where many white grape varieties grow. Thus *vinho verde* may consist of any number of varieties, in any combination—pederñao, trajadura, avesso, and loureiro, for example. The most valuable variety is

Vinho verde: *Because of the damp soil and the danger of rot, the vines are trained along high wires.*

alvarinho (the Spanish albariño), which is cultivated in the far north, near the border with Galicia. Its wines, which are 13 percent alcohol, usually remain within the country. In the past, *vinho verde* was always submitted to a malolactic fermentation, which generated the carbon dioxide. Mass-produced *vinho verde*, which now represents 90 percent of production, has carbon dioxide added.

Douro

The port wine region, on the upper reaches of the Douro, lies 60 miles (100 km) east of Porto, with the center of wine production at Pinhau. The terraced vineyards extend far into the countryside. They are planted on eroded slate soil that is able to store moisture, so that the vines can survive the dryness of summer (see page 27). It is not generally known that half of the Douro's production consists of unfortified red wines. The best known is Barca Velha, made by the port house of Ferreira and rightly considered to be Portugal's best red wine.

Bairrada

Two hundred years ago, the wine region around the city of Agueda was still world-famous for its red wines, sold after they were fortified. As an independent region, Bairrada only became known again in the last fifty years. It now makes mighty, enormously durable wines with strong tannins from the thick-skinned baga grape, which form the base of numerous Garrafeira blends bottled by the large wine houses. The Bairrada region also makes small amounts of a robust, acidic white wine from the bical grape.

Dão

Northeast of Lisbon is the up-and-coming Dão wine region, traditionally known for its heavy red wines made of diverse varieties, such as Touriga Nacional, tinta rouriz, bastardo, and jaen. Many Dão wines are still fermented with their stalks, and so tend to be harsh and bitter. At their best, however, these wines can have finesse and class.

Other Wines

Carcavelos: Carcavelos is a sweet, fortified dessert wine made from white grapes. It was a favorite in England a hundred and fifty years ago. Today, the tiny production region has been almost completely swallowed up by Estoril, a beach resort outside Lisbon.

Bucelas: This small region north of Lisbon makes a white wine much praised in Portugal but really rather simple. It is made from arinto grapes.

Ribatejo: Out of this large region comprising the countryside behind Lisbon come scores of mass-produced wines; nevertheless, a few of the Ribatejo wines are quite remarkable.

Colares: Colares is a thick, almost black wine, much sought after in Portugal. It is vinified from ungrafted ramisco grapes, which grow in sand dunes west of Lisbon.

Portugal's Viticulture in Numbers

Acreage under grapes:
260,000 hectares
Wine production:
5-6 million hectoliters
Annual wine consumption
per capita: 46.3 liters

Most-Planted Grape Varieties

In Portugal there are no precise estimates of grape varieties and acreage devoted to them. The most important red grapes are alfrocheiro preto, tinta roriz (aragonez), baga, Caselão Frances (Periquita Mortága), Touriga Francesca, Touriga Nacional, and verdelho (gouveio). Dominant among white grapes are alvarinho, arinto, avesso, azal branco, bical, encruzado, Maria Gomez (Fernão Pires), loureiro, and trajadura.

Portuguese Wine Law

Portugal was the first wine country in the world to establish the boundaries of a growing region by law to prevent wine fraud: the port-wine region along the Douro. That was in 1756. Today Portugal has five wine-growing zones with thirty-two quality wine-growing regions. Twenty-six of these enjoy DOC status (*denominação de origem controlada*, comparable to the French AOC system). In six regions, wines are given the IPR designation (*indicacão de proveniência regulamentada*, corresponding to VDQS wines). There are also eight areas producing *vinhos regionais* (corresponding to French *vins de pays*). The remainder are labeled *vinho de mesa* (table wine). Today Portugal produces more quality wines than all other categories put together.

Portugal's Wine Designations

Verdes: Young wines that are consumed right after fermentation.
Maturo: Mature is a term used for all wines that are not verdes.
Garrafeira: Label for a top wine that has aged for a long time, often for ten years, in the barrel or in the bottle.

The Elegant Lightness of Wine

Germany counts among the smaller wine-producing nations. The acreage devoted to wine in Germany is only 8 percent of that in France, and the total amount of wine made is not much more than that produced in Romania. Nonetheless, Germany is a special wine nation. German vineyards lie close to the fifty-first parallel, right at the extreme northern edge of the grapevine's climatic range. In the relatively cool, continental climate that prevails, grapes can reach full ripeness only in a few spots. This circumstance does not imply that German wines are at the bottom of the quality scale. On the contrary: as French Champagne clearly proves, wines produced in marginal regions often have a special finesse and character. Moreover, Germany has at least one indigenous grape variety that is rightly counted among the noblest in the world, Riesling. The wines made from this variety in Germany have no equivalent anywhere else.

Wines Hard-Won from Nature

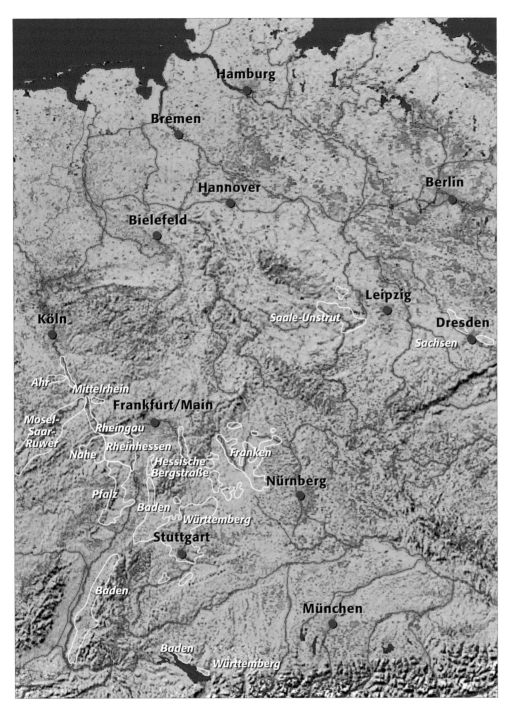

No other country has suppressed its viticultural history as completely as Germany. No other European country has made as many viticultural mistakes as Germany. No other country clings to its mistakes with such uncanny stubbornness. These tragedies notwithstanding, there are some winemakers who produce some great wines.

Grapevines were brought to Germany by the Romans. In the third century A.D., the poet Ausonius speaks about the grapevines along the banks of the Mosel; whether these were Riesling is not known. In late medieval times Elbling and Silvaner grapes were known and widely planted. A variety called "Ruesseling" was mentioned for the first time in the fifteenth century; the significance of the Riesling vari-

ety, however, was not recognized till much later. In 1787, the bishop-prince of Trier, Clemens Wenzeslaus, decreed that Riesling vines should be planted along the Mosel. With that, the golden age of wine began all over Germany. In the nineteenth century Rieslings from the Rheingau were the most expensive wines in the world. London vintners charged as much for one bottle as for seven bottles of Château Lafite. Of course, only the wines from the best locations were accorded such honors—for example, Erbacher Marcobrunn, Schloss Johannisberger, and Rauenthaler Baiken. Not until the industrial revolution, when country people moved off to live in the cities, did German wine production start to decline.

After World War II, viticulture was expanded without any thought being given to differences in quality between various vineyard areas. Instead, a hierarchy of quality wines was created that embodied a purely superficial concern with the criteria of good quality. Nothing has changed in the last fifty years in German wine policy; on the contrary, again and again average wines are given higher quality ratings in order to give them a better marketing position. The modest stature that German wines do have today is due solely to the commitment to quality of certain individual winemakers, who, faced with administrative obstacles, nevertheless persist in their pursuit of excellence.

Palatinate

The Palatinate is Germany's second-largest growing region—23,600 hectares in vineyards—and a cornucopia of hearty, drinkable wines. Most of the white wines come from Müller-Thurgau vines, most reds from Blauer Portugieser. The region is producing increasing numbers of high-quality wines. In the warm south, Spätburgunder and Dornfelder—the latter in alarming quantities—are being planted more and more. The most important red wine variety in terms of quantity is still Blauer Portugieser. In all, a fourth of the vineyard area is planted with red grapes. The greatest potential for quality lies in the northern half of the region: the Mittelhaardt. This elongated hilltop, with its limestone gravel, clay, basalt, sand, and red sandstone soils, extends from Grünstadt in the north nearly to Neustadt in the south and is one of Germany's best Riesling areas. Towns like Kallstadt, Ungstein, Wachenheim, Deidesheim, Forst, and Gimmeldingen are famous for their strong Rieslings. In addition to Rieslings, some outstanding Weiss-

Vineyard landscape in the Palatinate: A cool climate for elegant white wines.

burgunder, Grauburgunder, and quantities of Müller-Thurgau, Kerner, and Silvaner are cultivated in the gravel, clay, and sandstone soils of the more level areas extending onto the Rhine plain.

Nahe

The Nahe is a small river that rises in the Hunsrück and flows into the Rhine. It has given its name to a small wine-growing region planted mainly with Riesling, which accounts for one-fourth of its area, but also with Müller-Thurgau, Silvaner, and Weiss- and Grauburgunder. Red varieties are represented only in small quantities; Dornfelder and Blauer Portugieser constitute the majority of them. With roughly 4,400 hectares of vineyards, the Nahe is no longer small, but neither is it too large. It is highly heterogeneous, as none of the vineyards are contiguous. This is reflected in its large number of varieties and in its very different types of soil. Along the upper Nahe, between Monzingen and Traisen, the area is composed predominantly of porphyry, melaphyry, and red sandstone. At Bad Kreuznach one encounters weathered sandstone soils overlaid with clay and loam. The lower Nahe is characterized by slate and

quartz. The types of wines produced are equally varied. The very best of them are as good as any in Germany. The fact that they do not enjoy a special aura is because the region does not have a distinguished history. Up until 1930 its wines were generally sold as "Rhine wines." Only later did the Nahe emerge as an autonomous growing region.

Rhine-Hesse

Germany's largest wine region (more than 26,000 hectares in vines), Rhine-Hesse has boundaries so widely drawn that it produces completely different wines in both style and quality. On the fertile loess loams of the backcountry, especially in the Wonnegau between Alzey and Worms, hearty Müller-Thurgaus (roughly 25 percent of the growing area) are cultivated along with a few outstanding Rieslings (roughly 10 percent). Silvaner is well represented in this region as well (roughly 11 percent), yielding good table wines with a hint of fruit. The main Silvaner area lies in Rhine-Hesse's southern tip near Worms, the home of Liebfraumilch. This thin wine, produced from Müller-Thurgau, as well as Kerner, Scheurebe, Bacchus, Silvaner, and other less high-quality varieties, is regularly

sugared and still accounts for roughly a fourth of the region's wine production. To the dismay of Germany's quality winemakers, it continues to be what foreigners think of as German wine. Riesling is mainly grown along the Rhine around the towns of Nackenheim, Nierstein, and Oppenheim. Some of Germany's loveliest Rieslings grow in the red-sandstone soil along the river. They have an almost symphonic fullness and incomparable finesse. Since they are more powerful and fuller, but have somewhat less acid than Mosel Rieslings, they are often finished very dry. In recent years red wine production has greatly increased in Rhine-Hesse: more than 20 percent of the vineyard area is now planted with red varieties. Dornfelder especially has been newly planted, and has, because of modest qualities for the most part, contributed to a drop in the price of this wine. But many winemakers are also trying to capitalize on the red wine trend with Blauer Portugieser, cabernet sauvignon, and merlot. The king of the red wines is still the Spätburgunder, however. In the few good red wine vineyards of this growing region, near Ingelheim, for example, impressive qualities are achieved.

The Present Troubles of a Famous Wine

Lorcher Bodenthal-Steinberg

Johannisberg

Klaus

Hölle

Mittelhölle

Schloß Johannisberg

St. Nikolaus

Mittelheim

Höllenberg

Assmannshausen

Rheingau

Where the Rhine flows from east to west, on the slopes facing due south, some of the best Riesling wines in the world are produced.

Berg Schloßberg

Berg Roseneck

Berg Rottland

Rüdesheim

Mäuerchen

Fuchsberg

Geisenheim

Rothenberg

Kläuserweg

Jesuitengarten

Hasensprung

Schloß Vollrads

Winkel

Jesuitengarten

Lenchen

Oestrich

Rheingau

The Rheingau is a small (3,100 hectares of vineyards) but illustrious wine region west of Frankfurt. It extends from Hochheim past Wiesbaden, Eltville, and Rüdesheim as far as Lorch. Its chalky loess slopes fall south toward the Rhine and produce powerful white wines, the best of them extremely fine; an island of phyllite shale near Assmannshausen yields light red Spätburgunder with a delicate fruit, some with an almond note. Riesling covers 88 percent of the vineyard area. Unlike Mosel Riesling, most of it is finished semidry. There were already vineyards around Johannisberg Castle and the Eberbach monastery in the thirteenth century. At the beginning of the twentieth century London's wine connoisseurs would pay as much for a bottle of the best

Rheingau—then known as "hock"—as for a Château Lafite. Today, by contrast, Rheingau wines are inexpensive, but the best of them are still among the world's great white wines. Communities like Rüdesheim, Oestrich, Hattenheim, Erbach, Kiedrich, and Rauenthal continue to have good reputations. However, as a result of far too large harvests, there are also any number of mediocre wines produced. Local marketing from taverns and street fairs has had a negative effect on quality as well.

Mittelrhein

The central Rhine area incorporates a region some sixty miles long to the left and right of the river. It extends from Lorch in the south to Königswinter in the north. The good reputation of this less well-known region is based

on its fizzy, slightly acidic Riesling with a faint mineral taste. Cool cellars ensure that the wines often preserve a natural residual sweetness due to incomplete fermentation. Because of the high acidity, this slight, often scarcely detectable sweetness is exquisite. In any case, the best Rieslings are hardly outshone by the famous wines of the Rheingau. Muller-Thurgau and Kerner are also well represented in its vineyards. Wine growing is only possible on the few slopes or side valleys of the Rhine. They are almost always steep-terrace vineyards covered with shale, oriented to the south, difficult to reach, and maintained by hand. Because of a shortage of labor, many vineyards have been allowed to grow wild in recent years. Today there are only roughly 700 hectares still

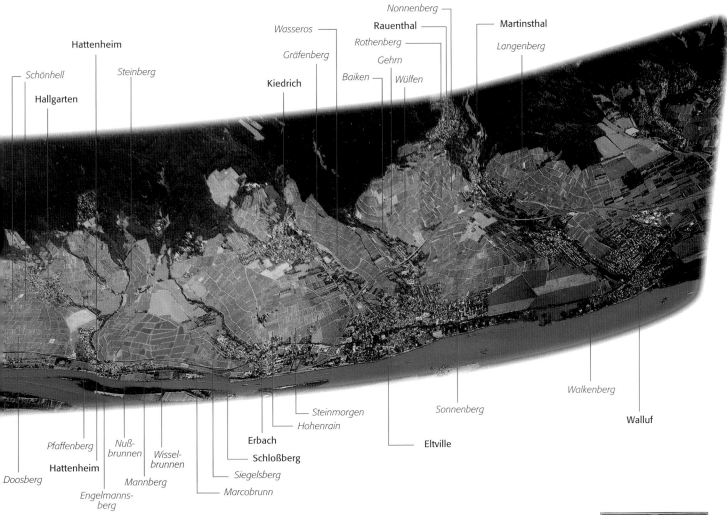

Schönhell
Hallgarten
Hattenheim
Steinberg
Wasseros
Gräfenberg
Kiedrich
Nonnenberg
Rauenthal
Rothenberg
Gehrn
Baiken
Wülfen
Martinsthal
Langenberg

Doosberg
Pfaffenberg
Hattenheim
Nuß-brunnen
Engelmanns-berg
Mannberg
Wissel-brunnen
Marcobrunn
Siegelsberg
Erbach
Schloßberg
Hohenrain
Steinmorgen
Eltville
Sonnenberg
Walkenberg
Walluf

planted with vines, and that number is decreasing.

Ahr

The Ahr lies clearly north of the 51st Parallel, which is often considered the natural boundary for wine growing in Europe. But surprisingly, the Ahr is one of Germany's warmest growing regions. Especially on the steep slopes, with their heat-capturing, weathered slate soils, high temperatures dominate well into fall. These unusual climatic conditions explain why red wine has been produced along the Ahr since time immemorial. Roughly 83 percent of the vineyard plantings, which are small and often laid out like gardens, consist of red varieties. By far the most important is the Spätburgunder, from which velvety, at times opulent wines with a sweet, fruity fullness are produced, the best of which are among the country's top reds. In recent years increasing quantities of Frühburgunder have also been cultivated. The amount of the less-imposing Blauer Portugieser is being reduced. White varieties make up only a small portion of the 525 hectares of vineyard area. Riesling clearly predominates. The region is named after the small Ahr River, which meanders through the Eifel, then flows into the Rhine south of Bonn. In the upper, narrow reach of the valley between Altenahr and Marienthal grow filigree, delicately fruity wines. However, from the loess clay soils of the broader lower section from Walporzheim to Heimersheim come full-bodied, more opulent wines.

Steely Rieslings with Resounding Acids

Piesport: The best wines come from the steep plantings above the banks of the Mosel.

Mosel-Saar-Ruwer

The Mosel, with its high, steeply sloping banks carpeted with vineyards, is one of the most impressive wine landscapes in the world. Riesling is most at home between Koblenz and Trier. The slate and schist soils store heat, nourishing very light, delicately spicy, and steely wines with thunderous acidity that stand in a class by themselves. A majority of the vines are still "root-true," that is, they have not been ennobled. Depending on the soil, their aroma changes from peach to apricot to juniper underlain with a slatey note.

Unfortunately, the region's legal boundaries have been drawn much too widely, including the higher ranges of the Hunsrück and Eifel and far beyond the steep riverbanks, where frequently even Müller Thurgau does not fully ripen. Grapes are also grown on flat or hilly sites in the bends of the river, but they never reach the quality of wines from the steep slopes. So today the Mosel produces both high-quality, world-class wines and a flood of simple, unsophisticated wines. Riesling is the most important variety, but makes up only a little over half (55 percent) of the growing area. It is followed by Müller-Thurgau, Elbling, and Kerner. The best Riesling vineyards are found along the central Mosel between Ürzig and Leiwen. The finest, most filigreed Rieslings, with their wonderfully delicate, winey acid, grow in slate soils. Only a third is marketed dry. Most wines, especially the Spätlesen, are fruity and mild. In the last few years

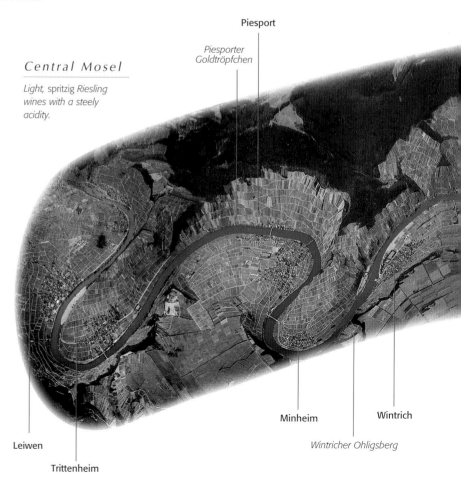

Central Mosel

Light, spritzig *Riesling wines with a steely acidity.*

Piesport

Piesporter Goldtröpfchen

Wintrich

Wintricher Ohligsberg

Minheim

Leiwen

Trittenheim

some wines from the lower Mosel between Cochem and Koblenz have excited attention. This part of the Mosel, because it is not yet completely consolidated, is also called the "Terrace Mosel." The Ruwer, a small tributary near Trier, also produces delicate, acidic Rieslings. As a rule, the wines of the Saar have the steeliest acids. Germany's best ice wines come from there and so do great Beerenauslesen and Trockenbeerenauslesen. Altogether, the Mosel-Saar-Ruwer area has shrunk to 9,300 hectares of vineyards.

Saxony

Saxony is the easternmost and second-smallest of Germany's thirteen growing regions. There are now 445 hectares of vineyard, and more are being added all the time. They lie in the Elbe Valley between Meissen and Dresden. Despite cool mean annual temperatures, the Elbe basin provides enough warmth during the growing period to ripen the grapes. The vines are rooted in stony granite and gneiss soils with isolated sprinklings of porphyry and red sandstone. Müller-Thurgau is the most common variety, covering a fourth of the growing region. But the amount of Riesling is sharply increasing, and so is that of Weissburgunder. In addition, a small amount of Traminer and, recently, Elbling are grown. In the small, elaborately terraced vineyards, one also finds small amounts of Kerner, Scheurebe, Perle, and Bacchus. The dry wines from the better locations are consistently expressive, the top ones even remarkably smooth, though at times somewhat lacking in body.

Germany's Viticulture in Numbers

Acreage under vines:
102,000 hectares
Wine production:
8-10 million hectoliters
Annual wine consumption
per capita: 24 liters

The Ten Most-Planted Grape Varieties

1.	Riesling	white	20.2%
2.	Müller-Thurgau	white	14.7%
3.	Spätburgunder	red	11.1%
4.	Dornfelder	red	8.0%
5.	Silvaner	white	5.5%
6.	Portugieser	red	4.8%
7.	Kerner	white	4.5%
8.	Grauburgunder	white	3.7%
9.	Weissburgunder	white	3.1%
10.	Trollinger	red	2.5%

German Wine Law

Depending on the vintage, 90 to 98 percent of all German wines are in the realm of *Qualitätsweine bestimmter Anbaugebiete (QbA),* quality wines of specified origin. Table wines and country wines are a minuscule part of production. Within the QbA, the *Qualitätsweine mit Prädikat (QmP)* are distinguished. The criterion for *Prädikat* ("distinction") is high natural must weight. These wines may not be chaptalized.

Kabinett: Made of ripe grapes; must weight between 70 and 80° Oechsle, varies with location.

Spätlese: Late harvest; fully ripe grapes; must weight at least 90° Oechsle.

Auslese: Select late harvest; fully ripe grapes, with a small proportion of overripe grapes; must weight up to 125° Oechsle.

Beerenauslese: Special select late harvest; mostly overripe grapes; must weight between 125 and 150° Oechsle.

Trockenbeerenauslese: made exclusively from overripe grapes; 150° Oechsle and up.

Eiswein: Ice wine; frozen grapes, harvested and pressed at 19°F (-7°C) or less; must weight at least 125 to 150° Oechsle.

The Problem of the *Grosslagen*

All German vineyards have been assigned to a *Grosslage,* a geographical unit that consists of several communities; but in terms of quality, the name of a *Grosslage* on the label means nothing.

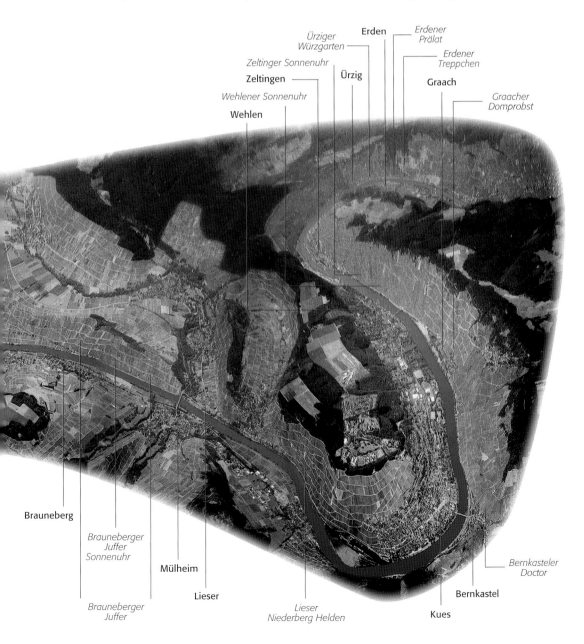

Erden · Ürziger Würzgarten · Erdener Prälat · Zeltinger Sonnenuhr · Erdener Treppchen · Zeltingen · Ürzig · Graach · Wehlener Sonnenuhr · Graacher Domprobst · Wehlen · Brauneberg · Brauneberger Juffer Sonnenuhr · Mülheim · Bernkasteler Doctor · Lieser · Bernkastel · Brauneberger Juffer · Lieser Niederberg Helden · Kues

Burgundies Among the Rieslings

As though groomed with a comb: Vineyards in the Ortenau in Baden.

Saale-Unstrut

The vineyards on the banks of the Saale and its tributary, the Unstrut, comprise Germany's northernmost growing area. It lies at roughly the same latitude as Kassel and once again comprises 650 hectares (up from 350 hectares in 1990). Surprisingly warm and dry summers provide the conditions that allow the grapes to ripen—despite a mean annual temperature of only 9°C. Müller-Thurgau and Silvaner are the main varieties. Both ripen relatively early and are adapted to the short growing season, which because of the long, cold winters often begins only at the end of March. Riesling and Traminer are found only in isolated quantities, however increasing amounts of Weissburgunder are being grown, which in the calcareous and red-sandstone soils can produce delicate wines of considerable finesse. To be sure, all the Saale-Unstrut wines are light and acidic. They are almost all dry with a tart, earthy undertone. The limited production—aside from that of one large, sparkling-wine cellar—is mostly consumed in Saxony-Anhalt.

Franconia

Franconia is not a cohesive growing region. Its vineyards are strewn in climatically favored niches along the Main, from Aschaffenburg in the west to Schweinfurt in the northeast (for a total of roughly 6,000 hectares). Because the growing area is so spread out, the soils vary considerably. Around Aschaffenburg there are weathered, primary-rock soils, along the central Main between Klingenberg and Wertheim are red-sandstone soils, and in the east, around Iphofen and Castell, are heavy gypsum marls. The center of wine growing is the "Main rectangle" around Würzburg. There again the soils are mostly shell-lime. The soil differences are reflected in the range of vine varieties. The region contains more than a dozen, among them still numerous new ones from the 1950s like Bacchus. Franconia's typical vine is Silvaner, from which neutral, fruity, earthy wines are produced that are some of the best in Germany. Riesling ripens in only a few locations, but when it does it yields high-quality wines. Many winemakers have switched to Rieslaner (Silvaner and Riesling),

from which Franconia makes aromatic, Riesling-like wines. The prominent variety is Müller-Thurgau. Franconia's wines are full of body, mostly dry (up to four grams of residual sugar), and bottled in typical Bocksbeutel (flask-shaped bottles). Although in large areas Franconia is a classic white-wine area, red varieties have now taken over more than 15 percent of the vineyards. In the last few years plantings of Schwarzriesling (Müllerrebe), Dornfelder, Domina, and Regent have sharply increased, however the wines produced from them have not managed to attain more than local importance. The best reds, as always, come from Spätburgunder, which attains its peak quality in the warm red-sandstone soils along the Main.

Hessische Bergstrasse

The Hessische Bergstrasse is Germany's smallest wine region (440 hectares in vineyards). Even so, some outstanding wines come from the west-facing slopes that fall steeply toward the valley of the Rhine around Bensheim and Heppenheim. Riesling is the main variety grown, with more than half of the vineyard area. But Müller-Thurgau and Silvaner, which produce good everyday wines, are also worth mentioning. It is important to not forget the few but fine Grauburgunder and Weissburgunder, in which the region's proximity to Baden is apparent. The majority of the wines produced in the Hessische Bergstrasse are consumed by tourists in the numerous local wine pubs and taverns, but they are also loyally bought up by natives and people from nearby cities.

Baden

Baden is Germany's southernmost growing region and the most heterogeneous. It extends from the valley of the Tauber across Heidelberg, Baden-Baden, Freiburg, and Lörrach to Lindau on Lake Constance. It comprises some 16,000

Trollinger harvest in Württemberg.

hectares of vineyards. Baden is made up of several completely independent subzones. One of these is the Kaiserstuhl, a warm, hilly region lying in front of the Black Forest, where mainly red wine is produced from Spätburgunder grapes. Many wine lovers consider it one of Germany's best. The same is true of neighboring Tuniberg where weathered volcanic soils and loess are predominant. For white wines, the winemakers prefer Weissburgunder and Grauburgunder to Riesling. In its traditional version, the Grauburgunder is marketed as a dense, alcohol-rich Ruländer, generally with a residual sweetness. Sauvignon and chardonnay have

Vineyards in Saale-Unstrut, Germany's northernmost wine area.

made inroads on the Kaiserstuhl in recent years. Another, smaller subzone is the Kraichgau, south of Heidelberg, with full-bodied Rieslings, light Weissburgunders, and "fatty" Grauburgunders that are finished somewhat dry. The best-quality Rieslings come from the Ortenau around Baden-Baden, though there the variety is called Klingelberger, not Riesling. A few outstanding Spätburgunders are also produced there. South of Freiburg the Markgräflerland begins, where the Gutedel grape makes its home, yielding a light white wine with an acidic freshness. The dominant vine along Lake Constance is Müller-Thurgau; in the northern Tauber Valley Silvaner is also grown. There wines can be marketed in *Bocksbeutel*, or flask-shaped bottles.

Württemberg

Württemberg is red wine country. More than half of its wine comes from red grapes, the majority of it a pale red Trollinger. Trollinger is not consumed at all outside the growing region, but is especially popular in Swabia: a thirst-quenching, unassuming wine that at its best is delicate, but is often also insipid.

Classic red wines are made from Lemberger, the German counterpart of Austria's Blaufränkisch vine. The most common red wine variety is Schwarzriesling (pino meunier), from which only modest qualities are produced. Hardly more successful is Samtrot, a mutation of pino meunier that is still widespread in Württemberg. In addition to the unassuming Dornfelder, in recent years increasing numbers of hybrid vines like cabernet dorio and cabernet dorsa have been planted. The results have been altogether encouraging. However, the Spätburgunder is unsurpassed in Württemberg as well when grown in the right locations. Württemberg's Rieslings are powerful, but not as fine as those from cooler regions. The 11,500 hectares of vineyards are divided into numerous subzones. The center of wine growing is the Neckar Valley around Heilbronn with its tributaries, the Enz and the Kocher. There, in red marl and shell-lime soils, a considerable amount of Riesling, Müller-Thurgau, Silvaner, and Trollinger are grown. Wine growing is also relatively well represented in the Rems Valley near Stuttgart.

A Late Commitment to Quality

The international wine markets were late in recognizing Austria as a wine producer. Even today, owing to its relatively modest output, Austrian wine is little known outside the country. But the natives consume their Grüner Veltliner, Riesling, Zweigelt, and Blaufränkisch with gusto.

Austria was one of the last wine-growing countries in western Europe to switch to the production of quality wines. After counterfeit wines turned up in major quantities in 1985, the wine market completely collapsed. Wine growers and winemakers who had committed themselves to quality emerged from that crisis even stronger than before. Strict new wine legislation was passed, and inspections were intensified. Since then Austrian wine has been on an upswing. A number of the country's white and sweet wines are world class.

Top-Quality Vintages Among Ordinary Wines

The reasons behind the recent rise of Austrian wine are its distinctly improved quality, a turn to dry wines, and the Austrian winegrowers' well-developed sense of their own *terroir*. These have led to a strong demand within the country. The pacesetters were growing regions like the Wachau and Styria, whose winemakers were the first to change their course following the scandal. Other regions followed. After 1990 Austria also began thinking about its red wine tradition. In the Burgenland especially, new vineyards were planted with Blaufränkisch and Zweigelt, new cellars established, and up-to-date winemaking methods introduced. All told, roughly 70 percent of Austria's wine is sold on the domestic market, including still a large percentage of very ordinary country or table wines, some of them charming, sold in two-liter bottles. Germany is by far the largest export market.

Weinviertel

The largest of Austria's growing regions, Weinviertel comprises more than 18,000 hectares of vineyards widely strewn between Vienna and the Czech and Slovakian borders. The majority of Austria's Grüner Veltliner comes from this region and tastes spicier—more "peppery"—than the wines from the Wachau. Welschriesling is also widely grown. Riesling, Gewürztraminer, Weissburgunder, and chardonnay are some of the local specialties. Portugieser, which yields velvety but unostentatious wines, is the dominant red variety. It is slowly but surely giving way to Zweigelt. Blauburger is also still found in numerous vineyards. The Weinviertel was the first Austrian growing region to receive its own designation of origin (DAC).

Thermenregion

This growing region—the country's warmest—centers south of Vienna on the town of Baden. It is famous for its white wine, which was formerly a blend of the two native varieties Zierfandler and Rotgipfler and was marketed under the name Gumpoldskirchner. Today Zierfandler and Rotgipfler are generally fermented as varietals. In addition, increasing quantities of Neuburger and Weissburgunder are grown. The most important wine towns aside from Gumpoldskirchner are Traiskirchen, Sooss, Guntramsdorf, and Tattendorf. In the south, around the health resort Bad Vöslau, red wine is produced: traditionally St. Laurent, Blauburgunder, Zweigelt, and Portugieser. In recent years more and more Blaufränkisch and cabernet sauvignon are also being cultivated.

Carnuntum

This is a small, up-and-coming wine region that extends from Schwechat, east of Vienna, beyond Höflein and Göttlesbrunn to the Slovakian border. It produces powerful Grüne Veltliner as well as delicate chardonnay and white wines from the various Burgunder varieties. In recent years its red wines have received increasing attention: fruity Zweigelt, lusty Blaufränkisch wines, and a few opulent pinot noirs and *cuvées*. Red wine growing has concentrated especially on the sunny south slopes of the Spitzerberg. It now accounts for half of all the vineyard area, planted more and more in international vine varieties like cabernet sauvignon and syrah.

Donauland

This growing region lies along the middle part of the Danube, from Klosterneuburg, near Vienna, beyond Tulln to Strass. Its famous wine villages are Mailberg and Grossriedenthal (ice wines), as well as the Wagram villages Engabrunn, Feuersbrunn, Fels, Engelmannsbrunn, and Kirchdorf. On the extensive, warm south slope descending to the Danube, powerful, "peppery" Grüner Veltliner is grown, also spicy Roter Veltliner, and substantial Weissburgunder. The best easily compete with the wines of the Kamptal. In the last few years more and more red wines have been grown on the Wagram as well (Zweigelt, pinot noir).

Vienna

In the northern periphery of the Austrian capital, and to a lesser extent the southern one, wine has been produced for some 2,500 years. By far the majority of it is the simple, uncomplicated Heuriger consumed in Vienna's 150 wine taverns. Grüner Veltliner is the most common vine variety, but other whites are cultivated as well. The best-known wine suburb is Grinzing with its numerous taverns, but there are also any number of them in Heiligenstadt, Nussdorf, Sievering, Neustift am Walde, and the suburbs Strebersdorf, Stammersdorf, and Jedlersdorf on the east bank of the Danube. From the very best locations there are a few isolated top-quality wines made from Riesling, yellow muscat, Grüner Veltliner, and chardonnay, as well as Zweigelt and pinot noir. In the late Middle Ages Vienna was completely surrounded by vineyards, and the wine trade was the city's most important source of income. Today only some 700 hectares are left.

The Donauland growing region: Powerful Grüner Veltiner from the steep slopes of the Wagram.

Thermenregion: Zierfandler and Rotgipfler are produced in the wine village Gumpoldskirchen.

World-Class Whites

Austria's Viticulture in Numbers

Acreage under vines:
  50,000 hectares
Wine production:
  3 million hectoliters
Annual wine consumption
  per capita: 30 liters

The Ten Most-Planted Grape Varieties

1.	Grüner Veltliner	white	36.0%
2.	Zweigelt	red	9.0%
3.	Welsch-riesling	white	8.9%
4.	Müller-Thurgau	white	6.8%
5.	Weiss-burgunder	white	6.5%
6.	Blaufränkisch	red	5.4%
7.	Blauer Portugieser	red	4.9%
8.	Riesling	white	3.4%
9.	Neuburger	white	2.3%
10.	Blauburger	red	1.9%

Austrian Wine Law

Prädikatswein: Highest rank of quality, reserved for sweet or residually sweet wines, which may not be chaptalized. Subdivided by must weight into Spätlese (minimum must weight 19° KMW), Auslese, Beerenauslese, Ausbruch, Trockenbeerenauslese, and *Eiswein* (ice wine).

Kabinettwein: Unchaptalized quality wine with a maximum alcohol content of 12.9% per volume.

Qualitätswein: wine; must weight at least 15° KMW.

Landwein: Country wine; must weight at least 13° KMW; can be chaptalized.

Tafelwein: Table wine; must weight at least 13° KMW; can be chaptalized, and there are no restrictions on production yields.

For Qualitäts- and Prädikatsweine in Austria the maximum yield is 9,000 kilograms of grapes per hectare (67.5 hectoliters). If the yield exceeds that amount the entire production is declassified to simple *Tafelwein* (table wine).

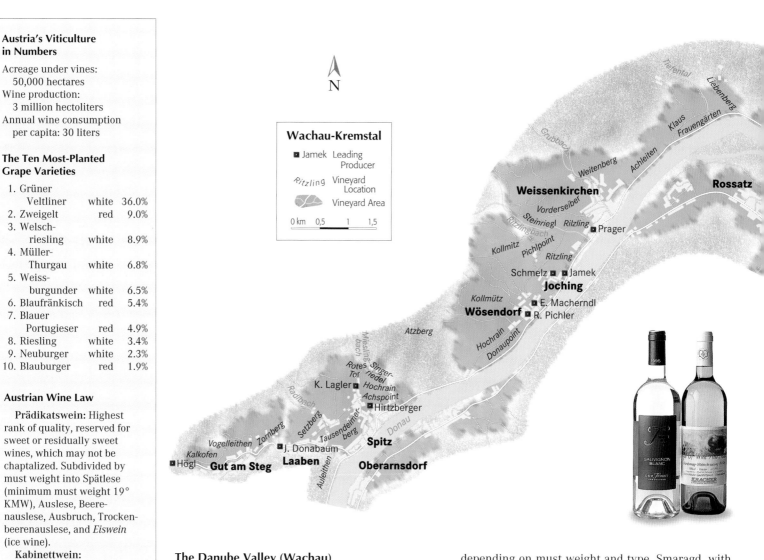

The Danube Valley (Wachau)

A small but prominent growing region along the Danube between Melk and Krems, the Wachau is one of the most fascinating wine landscapes in the world. Comprising a mere 1,400 hectares, the Wachau is characterized by small terraced vineyards, at times stacked steeply one above the other, in which world-class Grüner Veltliner and Riesling are grown on weathered primary rock. Thanks to the Danube Valley's opening to the east, the Wachau is influenced by the warm Pannonian climate, which means that, as a rule, the grapes can fully ripen and at times yield monumental wines with more than 14 percent alcohol per volume. At the same time, cool air streaming in through the side valleys of the Waldviertel assures that their acidity is preserved. In 1993 the Wachau's winemakers joined together to form the association "Vinea Wachau," with strict guidelines and their own designation system. Their quality wines, for example, are divided into the categories Steinfeder, Federspiel, and Smaragd,

depending on must weight and type. Smaragd, with its exotic fruity notes and honey tones, stands at the top of the hierarchy, though it cannot be achieved every year. To achieve such high must weights, in most years at least a portion of the grapes has to be infected with noble rot. In addition to Riesling and Grüner Veltliner, small quantities of Neuburger, sauvignon, and yellow muscat are grown.

Krems Valley (Kremstal)

The Wachau extends seamlessly into the Kremstal growing region. Its vineyards are situated in and around the Danube city of Krems and extend deep into the backcountry—both to the north and to the south. All in all, more than 2,200 hectares are planted with vines. Aromatic and meaty Grüner Veltliner and Rieslings grow partly in weathered, primary rock containing quartz and partly in heavy loess; the best of the wines made from them are fully equal to those from the Wachau. Roter Veltliner is also cultivated in isolated vineyards.

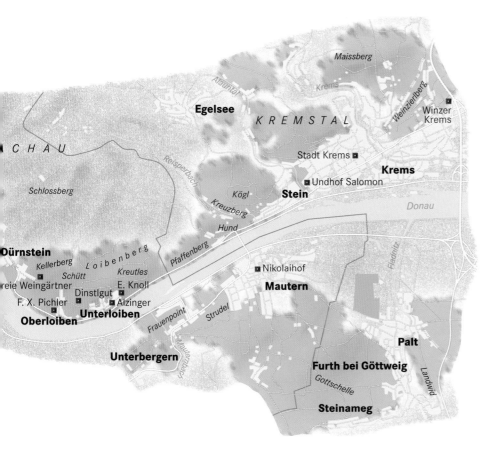

Traisental

Traisental is a small, ancient white wine area between the Lower Austrian capital St. Pölten and the village of Traisen on the Danube. On a mere 700 hectares, Grüner Veltliner, Riesling, and smaller quantities of Weissburgunder, Grauburgunder, and chardonnay are grown. The region produces aromatic wines with firm fruit and racy acidity.

Kamp Valley (Kamptal)

This growing region is adjacent to Krems, but turned away from the Danube around the city of Langenlois. It has a warm, dry climate in which Weissburgunder, chardonnay, and isolated quantities of cabernet sauvignon and other red varieties are grown. The majority of the vineyard area is nevertheless reserved for Grüner Veltliner and Riesling. In the higher elevations the soils are composed of primary rock, the lower ones of loess. The climate is characterized by large variations in temperature between day and night. The Rieslings, and especially the spicy Grüner Veltliners, measure up to the best wines of the Wachau. Instead of Müller-Thurgau, which used to be the second most important variety, increasing quantities of Zweigelt are now being cultivated.

Styria

The warm but rainy stretch of land along the Slovenian border is famous for its piquant, acidic white wines, especially southern Styria, whose leading varieties are sauvignon and chardonnay (locally known as Morillon). The steeply sloping hills around Gamlitz and Leutschach yield snappy, fresh wines and weighty, durable ones (after aging in wood barrels). The highest and coolest vineyards lie in the Sausal west of Leibnitz, where racy white wines of great elegance are produced. Recently, pinot noir is also being cultivated there with very good results. Southern Styria is warmer. The various Burgunder varieties thrive in its volcanic soils. The center is Klöch, known for its Traminer. Increasing quantities of red wine are also being produced in the southeast: Zweigelt, merlot, and syrah. Even though they do not have the fullness and tannins of the wines from the Burgenland, they enrich the selection. Western Styria is the home of Blauer Wildbacher, from which Schilcher is produced. Recently, increasing numbers of red wines have also been made from it. In all the subzones there is also a great deal of Welschriesling, Müller-Thurgau, Weissburgunder, and a little Scheurebe and yellow muscat. These may also be used for Junker, a Styrian brand wine that is bottled as early as November.

Wachau: View of the Danube from Loibenberg.

Reds and Sweet Wines of Renown

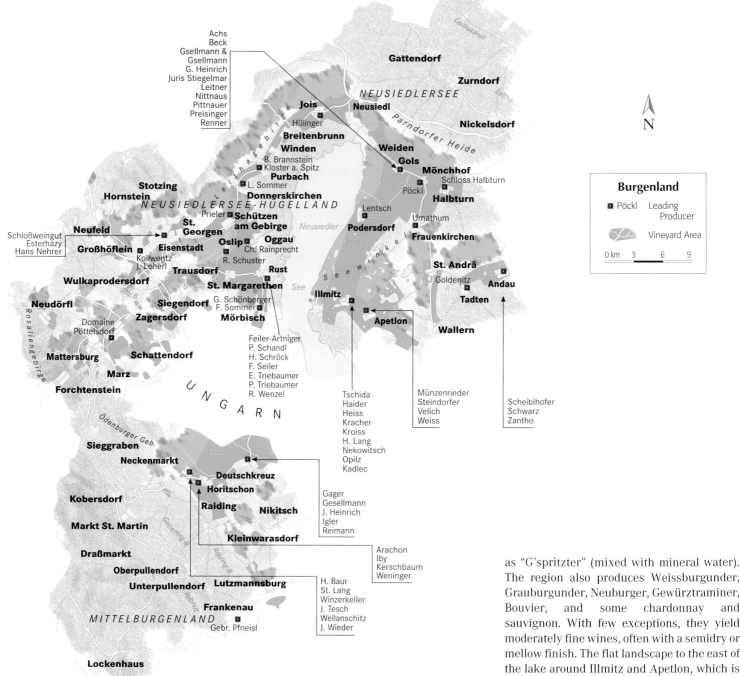

Achs
Beck
Gsellmann &
Gsellmann
G. Heinrich
Juris Stiegelmar
Leitner
Nittnaus
Pittnauer
Preisinger
Renner

Gattendorf

NEUSIEDLERSEE

Zurndorf

Neusiedl

Nickelsdorf

Jois

Hillinger

Weiden

Gols

Breitenbrunn

Winden

B. Brannstein
Kloster a. Spitz

Mönchhof

Schloss Halbturn

Pöckl

Halbturn

L. Sommer

Purbach

Stotzing

Donnerskirchen

Hornstein

NEUSIEDLERSEE-HÜGELLAND

Lentsch

Prieler **Schützen**

Umathum

St.
Georgen

am Gebirge

Neusiedler

Podersdorf

Schloßweingut
Esterhazy
Hans Nehrer

Neufeld

Oslip **Oggau**

Frauenkirchen

Eisenstadt

Ch. Rainprecht

Großhöflein

Kollwentz
J. Leherl

R. Schuster

St. Andrä

Trausdorf

Rust

Goldenitz

Andau

Wulkaprodersdorf

St. Margarethen

See

Illmitz

Tadten

Neudörfl

Seewinkel

Domaine
Pöttelsdorf

Siegendorf

G. Schönberger
F. Sommer

Apetlon

Wallern

Zagersdorf

Mörbisch

Mattersburg

Schattendorf

Feiler-Artniger
P. Schandl
H. Schröck
F. Seiler
E. Triebaumer
P. Triebaumer
R. Wenzel

Marz

Tschida
Haider
Heiss
Kracher
Kroiss
H. Lang
Nekowitsch
Opilz
Kadlec

Münzenrieder
Steindorfer
Velich
Weiss

Scheiblhofer
Schwarz
Zantho

Forchtenstein

UNGARN

Sieggraben

Neckenmarkt

Deutschkreuz

Horitschon

Gager
Gesellmann
J. Heinrich
Igler
Reimann

Kobersdorf

Raiding

Nikitsch

Markt St. Martin

Kleinwarasdorf

Arachon
Iby
Kerschbaum
Weninger

Draßmarkt

Oberpullendorf

Unterpullendorf **Lutzmannsburg**

H. Baur
St. Lang
Winzerkeller
J. Tesch
Wellanschitz
J. Wieder

Frankenau

MITTELBURGENLAND

Gebr. Pfneisl

Lockenhaus

Burgenland

Pöckl   Leading
Producer

Vineyard Area

0 km   3   6   9

N

Neusiedlersee

The largest steppe lake in Europe, southeast of Vienna, gives this growing region its name. It extends from the Jois across Neusiedl, Gols, Mönchhof, Halbturn, and Frauenkirchen as far as Illmitz and Apetlon, right to the Hungarian border. By far the majority of its production consists of white wine: mostly simple Welschriesling, which is drunk instead of Grüner Veltliner in the Burgenland as "G'spritzter" (mixed with mineral water). The region also produces Weissburgunder, Grauburgunder, Neuburger, Gewürztraminer, Bouvier, and some chardonnay and sauvignon. With few exceptions, they yield moderately fine wines, often with a semidry or mellow finish. The flat landscape to the east of the lake around Illmitz and Apetlon, which is dotted with ponds and small lakes, is famous for its grandiose sweet wines. In the moist, hot autumn climate of this "lake corner," world-class Beerenauslese and Trockenbeerenauslese are produced. In the last two decades the red varieties have also experienced a renaissance. Especially in Gols, but also in the neighboring villages of Mönchhof, Halbturn, and Frauenkirchen, red wines based on Zweigelt and Blaufränkisch are among the best wines in

The Burgenland, around the Neusiedlersee, is Austria's largest red wine growing area.

all of Austria. St. Laurent, occasionally also pinot noir, syrah, and cabernet sauvignon are supplemental red varieties.

Neusiedlersee-Hügelland

The vineyards extend from the shore of the Neusiedlersee to the foot of the Leitha Mountains. Powerful white wines with outstanding mineral content grow in loess, sand, and black soils. The varieties sauvignon, Weissburgunder, and chardonnay are especially successful, but most widespread is Welschriesling, which produces better qualities in these soils than the Grüner Veltliner found in isolated locations. The best-known wine is the nobly sweet Ruster Ausbruch. It grows in vineyards close to the lake around the city of Rust, and can be produced from all the permitted white wine varieties. In the moist, hothouse climate, large quantities of the grapes are infected with botrytis. Red wines, some of them distinguished, come from the zones farther from the lake, especially around St. Margarethen. The powerful, tannin-rich Blaufrän-

kisch wines grown in these rocky soils are among the best in Austria. Zweigelt and occasionally cabernet sauvignon and syrah also yield outstanding qualities.

Central Burgenland

This growing region south of the Neusiedlersee is Austria's most compact red-wine area. Red wines account for 80 percent of its production. The classic red wine variety is Blaufränkisch, which produces wines full of character in deep, heavy soils. They have color, tannin, and acid, and yield hearty table wines as well as long-lasting vintages. Because of their somewhat rustic character, they are frequently assembled with Zweigelt, cabernet sauvignon, or syrah into interesting cuvées. Neckenmarkt, Horitschon, Deutschkreutz, and Lutzmannsdorf are the production centers.

Southern Burgenland

This small growing region, important for its quality, lies in the country's extreme south. The majority of its vineyards lie directly next to the Hungarian border near Eisenberg, Deutsch-

Schützen, Moschendorf, and Heiligenbrunn. Traditionally, Blaufränkisch is the dominant variety, but it is supplemented by Zweigelt and a little cabernet sauvignon and other international varieties. One also encounters a few white varieties (Weissburgunder, muscat-Ottonel, Welschriesling). The wine estates are modest in size, and production is limited; this is truly idyllic wine country. One unusual product is Uhudler, which comes from a few vineyards around the village of Heiligenbrunn. It is produced from grapes from old, root-true vines from America that were planted as a precaution after the phylloxera catastrophe. They yield a legendary chaste rosé that takes some getting used to and that has a certain historic significance as a relic from a long ago era. Southern Burgenland, with fewer than 500 hectares in vines, is a very small growing region. Its importance derives from its clayey soils containing a great deal of iron, which lend a particular expressiveness to its wines. Also, one still finds a number of extremely ancient vines in the southern Burgenland.

Glaciers and Grapes

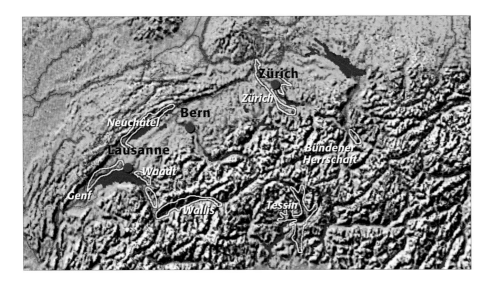

and their often unspectacular quality. If a few Swiss winemakers were not committed to achieving excellence in the face of indifference and lack of competition, no one would ever even know that fine wines of distinct character can also come out of the high mountains.

The Glitter and the Misery of Grape Growing

The history of Swiss wine production is part of European wine history. At the time of the Roman Empire, grapes were deliberately planted in the area between Basel and Windisch. All through the Middle Ages, the monks advanced winemaking techniques. In Switzerland, one landmark was the founding of the abbey of Dézaley and the establishment of the first terraced vineyards in 1142 on the shores of Lac Léman or Lake Geneva. From the beginning of the Swiss Federation (1291) to the eighteenth century, wine consumption increased steadily. Wine production also flourished until the nineteenth century, when it declined as a result of fierce foreign competition. It had completely collapsed by the turn of this century because of powdery mildew and phylloxera.

Only after World War II did the wine industry begin to recover, after grape acreage had been reduced to one-third of its former area. Economic recovery was achieved at the price of quality. Thus Switzerland produced twice as much wine in 1977 as in 1957, but total vineyard area had only increased by less than 10 percent. Pale red wines are cut with dark imported bulk wines; white wines are massively chaptalized to produce an up to 3 percent increase in alcohol.

Swiss Viticulture in Numbers

Acreage under vines:
  15,000 hectares
Wine production:
  1.2 million hectoliters
Annual wine consumption per
  capita: 43 liters

The Five Most-Planted Grape Varieties

1. Chasselas	white	35.2%
2. Pinot noir	red	30.6%
3. Gamay	red	12.8%
4. Merlot	red	5.7%
5. Riesling x Silvaner	white	4.4%
6. Chardonnay	white	1.6%
7. Sylvaner	white	1.4%
8. Pinot gris	white	1.0%
9. Gamaret	red	0.6%
10. Pinot blanc	white	0.5%

Swiss wine statutes permit growing grapes in almost all twenty-four cantons. The regulations are generous. Yields are set at 1.4 kilograms per square meter for white wines, and at 1.2 kg/m2 for red wines. This means that 84 to 110 hectoliters are harvested per hectare, too much for quality winemaking. Of course, good growers harvest significantly less.

Almost all Swiss wines are dry. In the Valais (Wallis) there are a few nobly sweet Johannisberg wines. Unfortunately, chaptalization has become common, even though in the Valais and the Rhine Valley this should not be necessary.

The Swiss are patriotic—except when it comes to wine. Most of the wines they drink come from other countries. Some explain this by saying that there are not enough Swiss wines. Others say that there are not enough good Swiss wines.

Because of the preference of the citizenry for foreign wines, the government of Switzerland felt it had to take steps to limit imports, especially imports of white wines. Since this protectionist policy was implemented some time ago, Swiss wines have had a domestic market, but internationally, the tariffs also managed to isolate the Swiss wine industry. Outside its borders, Switzerland's wines are practically never encountered. This may also be due to their high price

Terraced vineyards in Lavaux: Some of the country's best white wines come from the north shore of Lake Geneva.

Valais (Wallis)

The Valais accounts for about 40 percent of total Swiss wine production. On the steep and challenging southern slopes of the upper Rhône Valley from Visp to Martigny, some vineyards are almost vertical, others terraced into the mountainside. More than forty different grape varieties grow there, though half of the area's vineyards are stocked with the chasselas grape, known in the Valais as fendant. This variety yields powerful, full-bodied wines with a mineral or fruit character, depending on the soil.

Chamoson makes aromatic, full-bodied dry wines from Sylvaner (known here as Johannisberg) grapes. In Fully they make the spicy Petite Arvine and the exotic Ermitage, which is fermented from white marsanne grapes. In the upper Rhône Valley, more than a dozen ancient grape varieties survive in obscurity, their names known only to local growers. One-third of the wine produced in the Valais is red, mostly Dôle, which is a blend of at least 51 percent pinot noir and gamay. Pure pinot noir wines are also made.

Vaud (Waatland)

Vaud, the classic white wine region of Switzerland, is planted over 80 percent of its vineyard area with chasselas grapes. The best-known district is the picturesque Lavaux, on the north shore of Lake Geneva. The district between Montreux and Lausanne produces the finest chasselas wines in Switzerland. In this part of the country, the chasselas grape is called dorin. The best wines are marketed under the name of their community of origin: Chardonne, Saint-Sophorin, Epesses, Calamin, and above all, Dézaley.

In the stretch between Lausanne and Geneva, known as La Côte, some lighter, flowery wines are made that are almost *pétillant*. The best-known is Féchy. As for red wines, which are mostly made from gamay, they are rather modest; Salvagnin, for example, is a blend of pinot noir and gamay.

A very special region in Vaud is Chablais, south of Montreux, where the proximity of the high mountains can be felt. High above the Rhône, in places like Yvorne, Aigle, and Bex, chasselas grapes develop a harder, mineral note, reminiscent of the ample Fendant from the Valais.

Neuchâtel (Neuenburg)

The vineyards of this small district are strewn around the shores of Lake Neuchâtel. They are stocked with the ubiquitous chasselas grape and some chardonnay and pinot noir. Out of this grape the rosé Oeil de Perdrix, "Partridge's Eye," is made.

Bündener Herrschaft

This, the only important wine region of eastern Switzerland, is close to the city of Chur and known for delicately fruited, spicy Blauburgunder wines. These red wines have not only body but a fruity finesse.

Ticino (Tessin)

The Ticino is a small and relatively new region, but it is powerfully ambitious. Between Giornico and Chiasso, 90 percent of the vine country is planted with merlot. No other red wine in Switzerland approaches the best Merlot di Ticino in sheer quality.

On the steeply terraced vineyards of the Valais (Wallis), bringing the grapes into the cellar is very hard work.

Changes in the East

Vineyard in the Tokaj-Hegyalja wine region of Hungary, home to one of the world's noblest, most long-lasting sweet wines.

Tokaji Aszú and the *Puttonyos*

Tokaji, or Tokay, as it is internationally known, comes from the extreme northeast of Hungary and is fermented from the furmint, hárslevelü ("linden leaf"), and muscat blanc à petits grains varieties. To make this wine, over half of the grapes must be botrytized. While the healthy grapes are fermenting, the botrytized *(aszú)* grapes are made into a mash and added to the young wine. The more is added, the sweeter and nobler the wine. Its quality can be seen from the number of *puttonyos* on the label; 3, 4, 5, or 6. A *puttony* is a 55-pound (25 kg) container of *aszú* mash; the barrels hold 136 liters of fermenting wine. *Aszú eszencia* is the ultimate Tokay; it ferments for up to ten years.

Eastern Europe, with extraordinarily extensive vineyards, is a sleeping giant. As yet, the quality of its wine production does not reflect the size of its growing areas, but it is certain that in the future not only quantity, but also quality will come from the east. Hungary is already paving the way.

Hungary

The map of Hungary's wine regions resembles a patchwork quilt. It includes twenty-two growing areas that are merged into four major regions. North of Lake Balaton lies North Transdanubia, with a number of white wine regions as well as the red wine niche of Sopron, bordering Austria's Burgenland. There the dominant variety is Kékfrankos (Blaufränkisch). The white wine spectrum ranges from Olaszriesling (Welschriesling) to Furmint, Hársleveli (Lindenblättriger), Kéknyeli (Blaustiel), Sárgamuskotály (yellow muscat), Szürkebarát (pinot gris), Rajnai Rizling (Riesling), and Leányka (Mädchentraube) to ordinary Rizlingszilváni (Müller-Thurgau). Chardonnay and, in places, sauvignon blanc are also becoming important. The second-largest region is South Transdanubia, which produces a few very high-quality red wines, especially in the newer, highly successful red grape regions of southern Hungary, Villány-Siklós and Szekszárd.

There the most important varieties are Kékfrankos (Blaufränkisch), Kadarka, and Kékoportó (Blauer Portugieser). Nagyburgundi (pinot noir), Médoc noir (merlot), and cabernet sauvignon are also represented. Kunság, Hungary's largest wine area, lies in the Alföldi region, the low-lying plain in the south of the country. Almost all the varieties represented in Hungary are found on its warm sandy and alluvial soils along the Danube, extending to the Serbian border. Welschriesling predominates. Many wines are given a sweet finish. From northern Hungary, the fourth major region, comes the world-famous, nobly sweet Tokay. In the cooler north around Eger is the home of Stierblut, the successful Hungarian brand name wine formerly produced mainly from the red Kadarka grape, but now more often from Kékfrankos, cabernet, and merlot. The most talked about wines are the whites from Eger and neighboring Mátralja, which are produced from Leányka, Olaszrizling, muscat, chardonnay, sauvignon blanc, and sémillon.

Romania

Although Romania's vineyard area is two and one-half times the size of Germany's, it produces only half as much wine, roughly 75 percent of it white. Romania is divided into ten different growing areas. The largest is the Moldau, with more than a third of the nation's total acreage. It produces uncomplicated white and red wines, mainly from native varieties. The second-largest growing region is Walachia, which produces more than a fourth of Romania's wines. Its vineyards lie in the foothills of the Carpathians and extend to elevations of 2,250 feet. It cultivates Feteasca neagra, cabernet sauvignon, merlot, pinot noir, and Blaufränkisch. Its white wines are made from Feteasca alba, muscat-Ottonel, Feteasca regala, Welschriesling, sauvignon blanc, and Tamaîiosa romaneasca (Weihrauchtraube). An important subzone is Dealu Mare: it produces what are probably the country's best red wines. In Banat both the native Feteasca and the local Creata variety (thought of as the Banat "Riesling") are cultivated, as well as Blaufränkisch, muscat-Ottonel, Furmint, Kadarka, Welschriesling, and Portugieser. Cabernet sauvignon and merlot are making major inroads. With its sandy soils, Crisana, farther north but also next to the Hungarian border, produces simple wines, predominantly from white grapes, and, in the south near Minis, reds as well (Kadarka). Finally, there is Transylvania. This high plain in the curve of the Carpathians is also called "Romania's Piedmont" because of its continental climate and its austerely beautiful, hilly landscape. There white wine is produced almost exclusively.

Bulgaria

Even after the end of socialist rule, the traditional structures of Bulgarian winemaking were largely preserved. It is still true that thousands of small growers supply only a very few wineries that dictate what is grown. Cabernet sauvignon and merlot are highly regarded. More than half of the country's production is exported, part of it as simple cask wine, part as inexpensive brand wine. Thanks to the gradual introduction of temperature controls, Bulgaria is now able to produce modern white wines as well. Here the major varieties are chardonnay and sauvignon blanc, though traditional varieties like rkatsiteli, aligoté, misket, muscat-Ottonel, Riesling, Gewürztraminer, and ugni blanc continue to be in demand. The largest red wine regions lie in Thrace, where large quantities of cabernet sauvignon are grown in fertile soils and a warm climate. Harsovo, in the south along the Macedonia-Greek border, is one of the best red wine growing regions. Upscale wines, even some high-quality vintages, are made from the native varieties melnik (red) and keratzuda (white). In Transdanubia, north of the Balkans, the main variety is the native gamza grape, from which light, uncomplicated red wines are produced, but chardonnay, sauvignon blanc, and increasing quantities of merlot and cabernet sauvignon are also grown. The largest wine-growing regions are in the hilly backcountry of Varna, on the Black Sea. A fourth of Bulgaria's wines are made there from chardonnay, sauvignon blanc, ugni blanc, white muscat, and the native varieties misket and dimyat.

Other Wine Producing Nations

Ukraine: Because wine was proscribed during Perestroika, more than half of Ukraine's vineyards were plowed under in the 1980s. Winemaking has only gradually recovered from the shock. Famous in the past for its charming, sweet dessert wines (including the red sparkling wine "Krimskoje"), Ukraine now produces increasing quantities of dry wines (Riesling or the red Aluschta from cabernet sauvignon, monastrell, saperavi, and malbec).

Georgia: The area south of the Caucasus, in which there are more than 500 different varieties of grapes today, was considered the former Soviet Union's best wine-growing region. Many mellow wines and increasing numbers of dry wines are produced in the Black Sea in Imertia, Racha-Lechkumi, Kartli, and Kachetia.

Moldavia: This is a mass-producer with huge quantities of cabernet sauvignon and merlot as well as chardonnay, sauvignon blanc, pinot gris, and Riesling. Rkatsiteli, saperavi, and the red sereksia are survivals from the Soviet era.

Czech Republic: White wines are produced in Bohemia around the small town of Melnik, mainly from Müller-Thurgau and Gewürztraminer. The larger growing region lies in Moravia south of Brno, where Grüner Veltliner, Grauburgunder, and Welschriesling are cultivated along with Blaufränkisch, St. Laurent, and pinot noir.

Slovakia: The growing regions in this country lie at the foot of the Tatra Mountains. Good to very good fresh white wines are made from Welschriesling, Weissburgunder, Grauburgunder, Grüner Veltliner, Riesling, and Müller-Thurgau. Gewürztraminer is considered "the king of vines." Blaufränkisch, cabernet sauvignon, and Zweigelt are cultivated in the south. Three communities in the east are permitted to call their nobly sweet wine Tokay.

Vineyards at the foot of the Carpathians in Romania: Outstanding locations, modest wines.

Fresh Wind from the Warm South

Greek wine on the advance: With its volcanic soils, the island of Santorini presents ideal conditions for wine growing.

The wines from the European south had been in decline for centuries, if not millennia. In recent years they have been reappearing and providing no small number of surprises. The potential for quality wines is tremendous; the challenge is to exploit it.

Slovenia

Having long since seceded from the former Yugoslavia, Slovenia has achieved independence in terms of winemaking as well and is today one of the most flourishing wine-growing countries in eastern Europe. Because of high domestic consumption, the majority of its production enjoys only table-wine status. But continuous increases in quality have brought some of its wines to levels found in western Europe. A small percentage can now compete internationally, especially the Beerenauslese and Trockenbeerenauslese from the area around Jeruzalem. Slovenia is divided

into three large wine regions. White wines come from the valley of the Podravja, the best of which are in no way inferior to those of neighboring Austria. Furmint and Welschriesling are the most common varieties. Riesling, Traminer, chardonnay, sauvignon blanc, and pinot gris yield the best wines. The traditional wine style is semidry or slightly sweet, with younger producers preferring a drier finish. A second growing region is the area along the Adriatic coast (Primorska). On the hills of Brda, Vipara, Kras, and Koper—actually an extension of the Friulian growing regions Collio and Carso—wines of outstanding quality are produced from chardonnay, sauvignon, pinot gris, rebula, and malvasia. Red wines from cabernet sauvignon, merlot, and pinor noir are swiftly catching up to them. The traditional Slovenian red wine is the acidic Teran from the refosco grape. The third region lies in the valley of the Sava near the Croatian

border (Posavje), producing predominantly simple table wines.

Croatia

A flourishing wine country in the nineteenth century, Croatia fell into forgetfulness as a result of the phylloxera catastrophe and later political turmoil. After World War II only large, state-owned enterprises producing industrial wines were encouraged. Only since the Balkan War (1991–95) have there been renewed signs of initiative and ambition. The country is divided into two completely different growing regions: the section along the Adriatic coast with Istria and Dalmatia, and the continental section between the Sava and Drava rivers. Whereas red varieties predominate along the coast, in the hinterland whites are cultivated—in the past primarily Welschriesling, but more recently increasing quantities of Gewürztraminer, Riesling,

Weissburgunder, Grauburgunder, and chardonnay as well. In addition, dry wines are gradually replacing those with residual sweetness. In the continental zone, red wine plays only a subordinate role (Zweigelt, plavina, merlot, pinot noir). In Dalmatia, however, the red varieties predominate. Plavac mali is the most important of them. The famous red wines Postup and Dingač are made from it. Another important variety is babič, which yields velvety reds. In Istria refošk is widely cultivated, which yields the tannin-rich Teran. The white malvazija also has a long tradition here, and international vine varieties are being introduced more and more.

Greece

Although Greece was the leading wine nation in antiquity, the last two millennia have passed it by. Only since 1990 has Greece embarked on the international stage once again with a few remarkable wines. The best-known growing regions are in Macedonia (Naoussa), Thessaly (Rapsani), and the Pelopponese (Nemea for red wine, Patras and Mantinia for white). In recent years entirely new growing areas have been developed, producing outstanding white and red wines: Goumenissa and Amynteon in Macedonia, Côtes de Meliton on Chalcidice, Archanes and Peza on Crete, and an excellent dry white wine called Robola on the island of Cephalonia. More and more country and table wines are attaining real quality, though like the Italian "Super Tuscans" they do not meet the specifications for quality wine. They come from niche areas near Patras and Korakochori Elias, from Attica and Thrace. Greek winemakers are succeeding with exciting blends, assembling native varieties like xinomavro and agiorgitiko with such international varieties as cabernet sauvignon, merlot, and syrah. Old, traditional grapes like malagousia, zakynthino, and lagorthi are also being fermented by new methods. The heavy sweet wines from the Aegean also play a major role, at least in terms of quantity.

Cyprus

Wine growing is found almost exclusively on the Greek west side of Cyprus on the south and southwest slopes of Mount Troodos. The majority of vineyards are planted with white varieties, especially the native xynisteri grape, which yields moderately fruity, somewhat earthy wines, and the mass-produced red mavro. The four largest wineries, which process almost the entire production, are therefore turning increasingly to cabernet sauvignon, mourvèdre, grenache, carignan, and syrah. Large quantities of grapes are turned into liqueur wines and must concentrates.

Other Wine Producing Countries

Serbia: The white Smederevo grows on the Danube and Morava plain south of Belgrade. In the Krajina, near the Romanian border, the traditional vine is gamay. The Serbian south produces the best red wines, mostly from the prokupac grape. Some of them are mixed with gamay, cabernet sauvignon, and merlot. From the hinterland of the Sava, east of Belgrade, come simple reds and whites, most of them sweet.

Bosnia-Herzogovina: Simple, rustic red wines are produced from the red blatina, while the white zilavka yields some outstanding fruity, mouth-watering wines with mild acidity. The majority of the vineyards are found around the city of Mostar.

Montenegro: The Balkan country federated with Serbia has an important red wine variety: vranac. It yields dark-colored, fiery wines with a lot of soft tannin. The red kadarka and white krstac are also grown.

Macedonia: This small, mountainous country produces mainly table wines, and production is small though there is a wide assortment of varieties. It ranges from the Hungarian kadarka to the Serbian prokupac, the Croatian refošk, and the Montenegrin vranac to cabernet sauvignon and other international vines. Typical white vines are the native temjanika, the Serbian Smederevo, the Bosnian zilavka, and the Russian rkatsiteli.

Kosovo: This autonomous region belonging to Serbia is the home of red Amselfelder. This charming red wine is predominantly produced from pinot noir, which in this country, with its 300 days of sun a year, yields a soft wine with little acidity. Cabernet sauvignon is also found in Kosovo.

Wine growing in Greece: Traditional varieties predominate, though international ones are being planted more and more.

Wine with Unlimited Potential

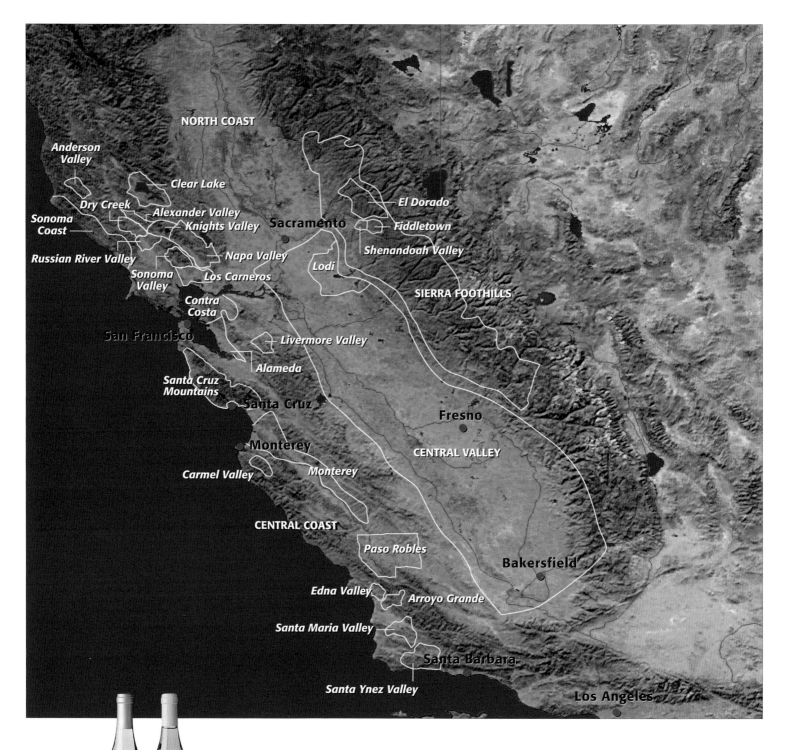

Within the last thirty years, the Napa Valley has changed from a quiet green pastureland where sheep and cattle used to graze into the most innovative and most spectacular wine region of California—a shift that had taken the wine estates of Europe about 150 years.

The wine boom on the sunny West Coast of the United States started only in the 1970s. Nonetheless, wines from Napa, Sonoma, Santa Barbara, and other wine regions of California often stand among the world's finest in tastings. The sun of California is not the only factor responsible for the success of its wine production. It was already known in the nineteenth century that the soils of the West Coast are ideally suited to viticulture. And about fifty-five years ago, research at the University of California at Davis established that the Pacific climate, in its own right, also offers ideal conditions for growing grapes.

The Beginnings of Viticulture

The history of grape growing in California begins in 1769 in San Diego. The Franciscan monk Juníperro Serra set up a series of mission stations to the north, all the way to Sonoma. Since the padres needed wine for Mass, they planted grapes at each mission. The varieties they used, such as criolla, had originally been brought to Mexico by the Spaniards. In 1782 the first wine was fermented at San Juan Capistrano. There is no reason to think that it was good.

In 1833 the Frenchman Jean-Louis Vigne established some vineyards around Los Angeles, for the first time planting varieties that he had brought directly from France. He must have made a proper wine, since his production had soon increased to a thousand gallons a year. After Mexico became independent in 1822 and the subsequent annexation of California by the United States, viticulture was continued on a large scale by some of the new settlers.

A Shift to the North

When the gold rush started in 1849, wine growers from Germany, Italy, and California saw a chance to sell their product to the gold miners in the new towns along the rim of the Sierra Nevada. Thus viticulture started its slow shift to the cooler north of the state.

The most exciting personality in the budding wine business in California around that time was the Hungarian count Agoston Haraszthy, who started his career as sheriff of San Diego and then became a distributor of table grapes near San Francisco, using imported varieties like zinfandel and muscat d'Alexandrie. Next he took a trip to Europe, returning with the seedlings of 300 different grape varieties, which he proceeded to plant in Sonoma. When his estate, Buena Vista, went bankrupt, the count decamped to Nicaragua to plant sugar cane, which he planned to make into rum. Unfortunately, he never a got a chance, as he was devoured by an alligator.

The First Boom and Phylloxera

A beginning had been made. Soon European names started to be heard in the Napa Valley: Charles Krug, Jakob Schram, and Jakob Berin-

ger. They all planted grapes. A wine boom gripped the country, only to end suddenly in 1886, when phylloxera destroyed all the vineyards. The grape louse had possibly reached California with Haraszthy's seedlings.

No sooner had a remedy been found against the blight than Prohibition struck in 1919. Its consequences for wine production were fatal. Most estates were driven to ruin. Such winemaking as there was could only be

Indian summer in a vineyard near Calistoga in the Napa Valley.

carried on for private or religious purposes. By the time Prohibition was repealed in 1933, the markets had practically disappeared, and commercial structures had been destroyed.

The Resurgence

It was only at the end of the 1960s that wine enthusiasts like Robert Mondavi and Joe Heitz settled in the Napa Valley and began making quality wines. Their efforts were supported by the oenologist André Tchelistcheff, who in 1938 had moved to California from France, where he had worked for many years

with famous wine producers. Using his extensive knowledge of modern wine management, he introduced temperature control, malolactic fermentation, and other important new cellar technology.

The sleepy valley two hours from San Francisco became a place of pilgrimage for new wine enthusiasts. In a blind tasting arranged in Paris by the Académie de Vin, in which top-notch French wines were compared with Cali-

fornia's new products, the chardonnay of Château Montelena Winery beat the best white burgundies, and one of the Stag's Leap cabernet sauvignons came out first as well. Three years later, the French gourmet magazine *Gault Millau* organized a "Wine Olympics": once more, California wines stood among the winners. A wine boom of unimagined proportions set in. While in 1960 there had been twenty wineries in the Napa Valley, now there are over two hundred thirty.

The Pride of America's Wines

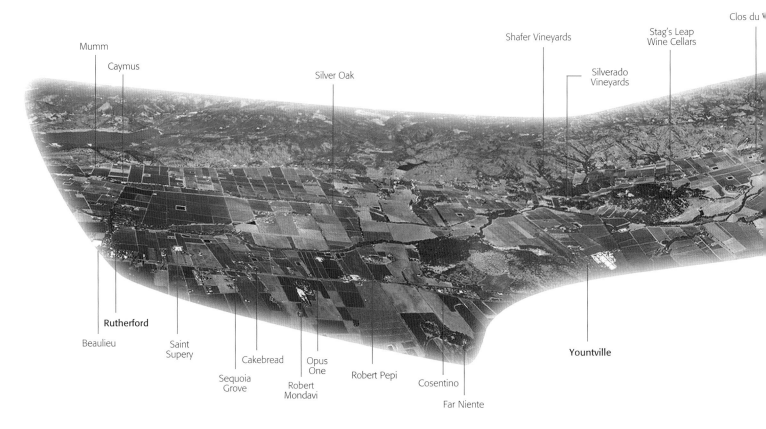

Mumm
Caymus
Silver Oak
Shafer Vineyards
Stag's Leap
Wine Cellars
Clos du V
Silverado
Vineyards
Rutherford
Beaulieu
Saint
Supery
Cakebread
Opus
One
Robert Pepi
Cosentino
Yountville
Sequoia
Grove
Robert
Mondavi
Far Niente

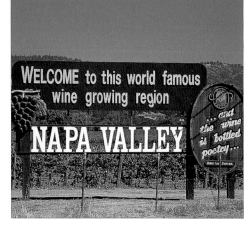

Sign at the entrance to the Napa Valley.

Carneros

The Carneros wine region is located near San Pablo Bay. The area is known for its white, sparkling, and some red wines. In this unspectacular landscape of flat hills, bordering on the Napa and Sonoma Valleys, some of the very best chardonnays and pinots of the state are cultivated. Most of the grapes are sold to Napa or Sonoma wineries. Some of these have even bought their own vineyard land in that region. Several sparkling wine producers have set up wineries in Carneros, among them some European producers, such

as Freixenet, Codorníu, Domaine Chandon, Mumm, and Taittinger (Domaine Carneros).

The red variety pinot noir also does extremely well in Carneros. With its spicy and candylike aromas, it is one of the best in all of California. It is used both to make a still wine and for *assemblage* with chardonnay by the sparkling winemakers.

Los Carneros means "sheep" in Spanish, a reference to the recent past of this area, when it was regarded as good pasture land. The cool breezes that sweep over the hills in the late afternoon cool the grapes and help keep natural acidity and fresh flavors.

Napa Valley

Napa is the apex of the American wine bonanza. All of Europe's wine knowledge and experience has been put into practice here in less than thirty years. Many of the contemporary buildings are architecturally impressive, and new knowledge, some of it purely theoretical, has been applied to the new vineyards, with the support of experts and capital from France, Germany, and Switzerland.

These new wineries are so attractive that even the renovated European wine estates seem dusty in comparison. The Napa Valley is a tourist attraction and a glittering name, though only 5 percent of California wines ac-

tually come from there. Of course, the wines are the main attraction, but the millionaires who want to leave behind a monument in the form of a winery, the eccentric inventors with amazing careers, the rich wine lovers who pay breathtaking sums at auction for the dark red cabernet sauvignon of the valley–all these people help to keep the Napa Valley in the headlines. The rather exotic flavor of the area is well conveyed by the sign at the entrance to the valley, which tells the generally matter-of-fact public, "Wine is bottled poetry," a line from Robert Louis Stevenson.

The Soil of the Napa Valley

The Napa Valley is about 30 miles (50 km) long. It extends from Napa in the south northward beyond Calistoga, into the mountains. Strangely, the temperature rises as you go north: the moist Pacific air enters from the south, but warms up and dries as it moves up the valley.

Nearly all of the Napa region's vineyards are either on the valley floor or on the foothills of the Mayacamas on one side or the Vaca Range on the other. The valley floor is heavy clay; on the slopes, the clay is mixed with gravel. In the higher, mountainous backcountry few wineries have as yet settled. Most of them are arranged like pearls strung along the

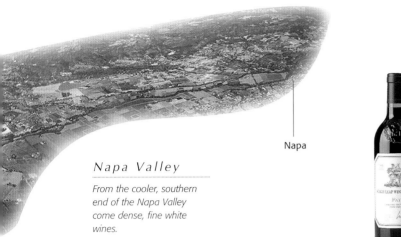

Napa Valley

From the cooler, southern end of the Napa Valley come dense, fine white wines.

Napa

Mustard blooming in a vineyard near Carneros.

two arteries that move up the valley, Highway 29 and the Silverado Trail. Some of the most interesting wineries are Robert Mondavi's Mexican-style estate; the new, blocklike cellar of Dominus; Sterling Vineyards, which looks down on the valley like a Greek monastery; Clos Pegase and the Hess Collection, combination winery and art gallery; the stylish cellar installations of Opus One; the old Ingle-nook winery, which is now called Niebaum-Coppola; and Beringer's Rhinehouse winery.

Many a great wine, however, comes out of small, unspectacular premises, such as Caymus, Mount Veeder, Stag's Leap, Shafer, or Cain Cellars, to name just a few. The soil is equally fertile everywhere, though its composition varies from plot to plot, even on the valley floor. Many winemakers do not even own any vineyards, at least not in the Napa Valley, instead purchasing their grapes from independent growers. The meaning of vineyard ownership only became clear to some wineries in the last few years, when damage due to grape pests and a few bad vintages drove prices sky-high. In February, the mustard blooms yellow between the rows of vines. Many winemakers actually make their own mustard.

Napa: A Haven for Cabernet Sauvignon

Cool Pacific breezes temper the microclimates at the south end of the valley. Up to Yountville, therefore, much chardonnay and some pinot noir are planted. North of Yountville, however, cabernet sauvignon is king. Such small enclaves of white grapes as still exist farther north are being replaced, and even southward, the tide of blue grapes is inexorably advancing. The fine-gravelled, well-drained loam is usually reserved for cabernet sauvignon, while the heavier, more clay-rich soil is planted with merlot. Napa cabernet sauvignon yields opulent, slightly peppery wines, with a bouquet of currants, many spicy notes, mocha tones, roast aromas, and a robust tannin structure. Although these wines lack the durability of the great bordeaux, they have a similar fullness and a remarkable finesse. Many blind tests have shown how difficult it is to differentiate between bordeaux and Napa cabernets. Some but by no means all the wines contain small amounts of merlot, cabernet franc, or malbec. As long as such additions amount to less than 25 percent, the label may state that the wine is cabernet sauvignon (see box, page 185).

When the Cooling Fog Rolls In

Cuvaison
Clos Pegase
Sterling Vineyards
Hanns Kornell
Frog's Leap
Burgess
Duckhorn
Freemark Abbey
Charles Krug
Beringer

While Napa is the heart of wine production in California, it is neither the first, nor the only significant wine region of the United States. Grapes were certainly cultivated earlier in Sonoma. Sonoma County consists of several subzones, and as many different wines.

Across the Golden Gate Bridge and along Highway 101, the pretty town of Sonoma can be reached from San Francisco in an hour's drive. Grapevines have been cultivated in Sonoma substantially longer than in Napa, yet Sonoma tends to stand in the shadow of its famous neighbor. It is a large region, with several climates and as many wines. The most famous wine districts are the Russian River Valley, the Alexander Valley, Dry Creek Valley, and part of Carneros. Historically, the core area remains the Sonoma Valley, which extends all the way from Sonoma to Santa Rosa. It is here in this valley that the former Agoston Haraszthy estate, Bartholomew Park, is located. Here the gigantic Sebastiani Winery has its headquarters; here we find Ravenswood, the zinfandel specialist, the small, sophisticated B. R. Cohn Winery, and the renowned Matanzas Creek Winery, with its famous merlots.

Russian River Valley

Between Santa Rosa and Healdsburg, in the Russian River Valley, the contours of the countryside are covered with vineyards. The vast majority of the vines are chardonnay, which yield a wonderfully flavored, grapefruity wine. Only on the actual banks of the Russian River, which coils through the vineyards, has pinot noir been planted to take advantage of the alluvial, pebbly soil. The natural affinity of the area for the burgundy variety, but even more for white grapes, is enhanced immeasurably by the thick fog that rolls in over the mountains almost daily from the Pacific. The moist, cool air that is blown up the open valley from the south also helps. The Russian River is the coolest district of the Sonoma region. Many Napa Valley wineries have vineyards here; many others, including the producers of sparkling wines in Carneros, buy grapes from local growers.

Dry Creek Valley

The valley of the Dry Creek lies parallel to Highway 101, in a westerly direction. In many spots the valley floor is stocked with gnarled zinfandel vines, a sure sign that wine was made here long before the cabernet boom. In the nineteenth century, Italian settlers planted grapevines, and many wine industry names here testify to the Italian ancestry of their owners: Ferrari-Carrano's showpiece of a winery, Pedroncelli's estate, justly proud of its zinfandel, the huge Simi winery, and the even more enormous establishment of the Gallo Brothers. In the remote, warm Dry Creek Valley, they grow, besides zinfandel, some cabernet sauvignon, some merlot, some syrah, but only a little chardonnay and sauvignon blanc.

where. The multiplicity of the varieties cultivated is still great, the quality often uneven. Yet without any doubt, on the clay loams that retain water, full and meaty cabernet sauvignon and merlot wines are grown, as well as some very good zinfandel. White wines are now only made in a few niches of the district.

Mendocino County

California's hot northern section has also become known for its wines. Mendocino, named after the small town on the Pacific, is far from the vine lands, however. The district only has about two dozen wineries. The area used to grow hops, but the terraced fields of the Anderson Valley are now stocked mostly with chardonnay, Gewürztraminer, and pinot noir. The valley is open to the Pacific along the course of the Navarro River, so that the summer's heat is again and again buffered by the cool ocean air.

Sparkling wine production is important in the Anderson Valley. The champagne house Roederer has set up its American branch in this area.

Along the upper reaches of the Russian River, around Ukiah, temperatures tend to be considerably higher. This district produces spicy zinfandel and muscular cabernet sauvignon wines. Small amounts of petite sirah are still cultivated, but this is now regarded as a mere reminder of the times when Mendocino County was the source of huge quantities of mass-produced, nameless jug wine. A well-known wine producer of that region is Fetzer, in Hopeland. In addition, you can find a few excellent wines from small estates.

Joseph Phelps

Helena

Napa Valley

From the northern end of the Napa Vally come heavy, full-bodied, and powerful red wines.

Alexander Valley

The Alexander Valley is in the northern Sonoma region, between Healdsburg and Cloverdale. It is the warmest district of the region. Although it used to be a mass-production area, in the 1970s quality winemaking achieved a foothold here, as else-

The underground cellar of the Kunde Winery in Sonoma.

California Viticulture in Numbers
Acreage under vines:
   224,000 hectares
Wine production:
   17–20 million hectoliters
Annual wine consumption
   per capita: 7.8 liters

The Ten Most-Planted Grape Varieties

1. Chardonnay	white	20.5%
2. Cab. sauvignon	red	13.0%
3. Merlot	red	11.1%
4. Zinfandel	red	10.9%
5. Fr. colombard	white	7.1%
6. Pinot noir	red	6.0%
7. Syrah	red	3.5%
8. Chenin blanc	white	3.1%
9. Sauvig. blanc	white	3.1%
10. Rubired	red	2.7%

Wine Laws
California wine laws are very simple. There are no restrictions on grape production; variety policy is very liberal. A chardonnay or cabernet sauvignon wine has to be at least 75 percent of that variety. Wines with a smaller varietal component must be labeled "Meritage," or, if the top wine of a winery and no more than 300,000 bottles produced, "Proprietary Blend."

The AVA Regions
In the early 1980s, some specified grape-growing regions were declared to be American Viticultural Areas. Thus, such large wine regions as Napa Valley, Sonoma County, and Paso Robles were created. Some small subregions also resulted, such as Mount Veeder, Rutherford, Oakville, and Stag's Leap—all in the Napa region. Wine from these places must contain 95 percent grapes from that area; wines from the larger region must be 85 percent from that region. In practice this means that 15 percent of the grapes can come from other regions, i.e., the hot Central Valley region.

Special Wine Designations
Jug wine: The simplest mass-produced wine.

Cooler: Fun wine, low in alcohol.

Blush: Rosé wine.

White zinfandel: A sweet rosé wine made of red zinfandel grapes.

Diverse Wines and Disneyland Too

Under the inclusive geographical term Central Coast, all the wine regions between San Francisco and Los Angeles are subsumed. This provenance is as glossy as the wines.

Southern California makes many fun and fashion wines, juicy, thin, and often pretty in their finish. Yet at the same time, some areas down south make wines that easily compete with the products of Napa and Sonoma.

The Santa Cruz Mountains

The Santa Cruz Mountains reach toward the Pacific from San Jose. The hills are partly

Southern California makes many fun and fancy wines and some genuinely outstanding ones as well.

wooded; along the slopes there are enormous, ancient trees and small, dispersed vineyards. The region produces very fine cabernet sauvignons, good zinfandels, and a few remarkable white wines. Total production, however, is small. Ridge Vineyards in Cupertino and Bonny Doon produce top wines, though with completely different philosophies.

Monterey

The dispersed vineyards of the Monterey region—near the Salinas Valley, California's vegetable garden, where the rows of broccoli and lettuce seem a mile long—are heterogeneous. For the past few years, vineyards have been established along the rim of the fertile valley. At the same time, the three AVA districts of Carmel, Chalone, and Arroyo Seco make numerous good pinot noirs and a few outstanding chardonnay wines.

Paso Robles, Edna Valley, Arroyo Grande

These three dynamic wine regions are near San Luis Obispo, a small university town near the coast. The huge Paso Robles region is famous for its excellent zinfandels, while in the Edna Valley and in Arroyo Grande—both close to the ocean—pinot noir, chardonnay, and other whites predominate. Most of the grapes from this region are nevertheless sold to wine producers in Santa Barbara County and farther north, mostly in Carneros and Sonoma.

Santa Barbara County

North of Santa Barbara, cool Pacific air moves up the open valleys of Santa Ynez and Santa Maria. The chardonnay here is crunchy, the pinot noir, vigorous and spicy. Among the leading producers are Au Bon Climat, Zaca Mesa, Qupé, Cambria, Sanford, Lane Tanner, Foxen, Fess Parker, Babcock, and Robert Mondavi's Byron Vineyards. Santa Barbara County is a booming wineland with up-and-coming varieties like syrah and cabernet franc. Some Italian and white Rhône varieties are also grown.

The Central Valley

California's most productive agricultural region, the Central Valley produces 70 percent of all California wine, and 60 percent of its wines actually grow here. Along its 500 miles (800 km), people grow everything from cauliflower to melons, including grapes, which used to be made mostly into juice and raisins but are also used in wine. E. & J. Gallo, the world's largest winery, annually makes 60 million bottles of simple but tasty wines in the valley. Near Lodi, toward the northern end of the San Joaquin Valley, we find winemakers like Woodbridge (Robert Mondavi) and Sebastiani, who are there not just to buy grapes but also to plant and ferment them. These growers are installing slow irrigation and shade-producing training systems. And the selection of grapes has changed: instead of low-quality hybrids, such as Rubired and Royalty, the new estates plant zinfandel, cabernet sauvignon, merlot, sauvignon, Gewürztraminer, and Riesling. Many of the grapes grown here are present up to 15 percent in Napa wines.

The vineyards near Santa Ynez, inland from Santa Barbara: Crunchy chardonnays and vigorous pinot noirs.

A Land in Ferment

Oregon's pinot noir pioneer, David Lett (left); large-scale irrigation in Washington's Yakima Valley (above).

Some claim that the best American wines will one day come from states other than California. In the shadow of its southern neighbor, Oregon has secretly been building its muscle for a showdown over pinot noir.

The vineyard areas of Oregon only add up to 2 percent of those of California. Wine producers with serious ambitions only began work there in the 1960s, when in California the general enthusiasm for wine had already begun. The temperate, almost European climate, with its mild winters and not too dry summers, induced some pioneers to settle south of Portland, on the Willamette River, and plant grapes. Contrary to the advice they received from wine experts at the University of California at Davis, they did not plant American hybrids but European *vinifera* grapes—chardonnay, Riesling, Gewürztraminer, and above all pinot noir. And they were lucky.

The Success of Pinot Noir

Of all the varieties, the red burgundy grape thrived best in the mild climate, and now it grows on almost half of Oregon's vineyard lands. The wines extracted from these grapes are neither heavy nor low on acids. Refined, and thus much closer to the French burgundies than most of the California wines made of pinot noir, they have a delicate fruit.

The enthusiasm of the Oregon pinot noir growers was such that a few refugees from California soon joined them. They entered into the adventure that was beginning along the Willamette, namely a commitment to a single variety; moreover, one that had never produced convincing results outside its native Burgundy.

Recently, the Burgundy wine dealership of Robert Drouhin opened a subsidiary in Oregon. Other important pinot noir producers include Elk Cove Vineyards, Bethel Heights Vineyards, and Adelsheim Vineyards. These tend to buy a large part of their grapes from local wine growers, since few of them have extensive plantings.

Certain parts of Oregon have also shown some success with chardonnay and Gewürztraminer and, in the south of the state, with cabernet sauvignon.

Washington

Washington has twice as much land planted with grapes as Oregon, but it is even less well known for its wines. Perhaps wine production is deemed as unimportant when compared to the state's main agricultural activity of growing cereals. It is surely not because the wines lack quality. The cabernet sauvignons and, above all, the merlot grapes that grow beside the warm Columbia and Yakima Rivers are of considerable quality, though not a major challenge to the wines of California. Full-bodied, heavy wines, they are never short on fullness, though sometimes they lack finesse. The leading producer in Washington State is Château Sainte Michelle, on the Columbia River, which also makes some remarkable white wines from sémillon and sauvignon grapes.

Other Winegrowing Regions

New Mexico: The hot Southwest has become known for spectacular sparkling wines that grow south of Albuquerque at altitudes above 1,000 meters, above the Rio Grande.

Arizona: From the sunny southeast near the border with New Mexico come big, flavorful chardonnays, sauvignons blancs, and zinfandels.

Virginia: An up-and-coming wine region, the mild climate here has supported grapevines for 350 years. The older, hybrid vineyards have been replaced with chardonnay, cabernet sauvignon, and merlot. These varieties yield wines of medium heaviness and a unique character.

New York State: For decades the Finger Lakes, near Lake Erie, have been famous for excellent sweet wines, as have the vineyards on the other side of the lake in Ontario, Canada.

Long Island: Some spectacular cabernet sauvignon is grown in the cool Atlantic climate near New York City.

Set for the Future

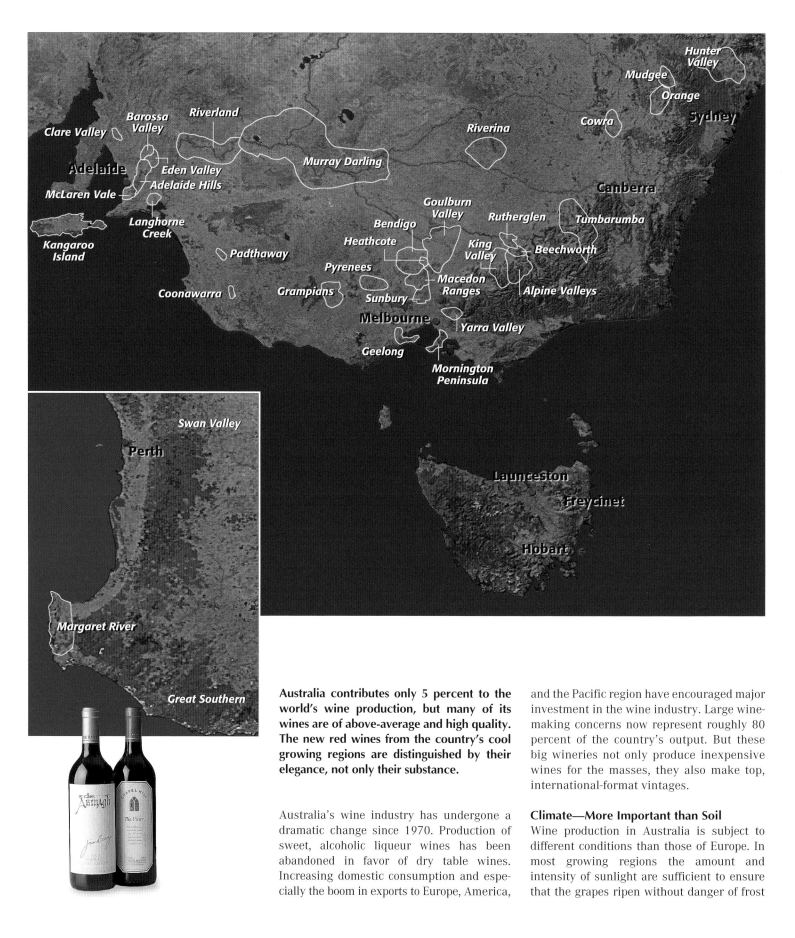

Australia contributes only 5 percent to the world's wine production, but many of its wines are of above-average and high quality. The new red wines from the country's cool growing regions are distinguished by their elegance, not only their substance.

Australia's wine industry has undergone a dramatic change since 1970. Production of sweet, alcoholic liqueur wines has been abandoned in favor of dry table wines. Increasing domestic consumption and especially the boom in exports to Europe, America,

and the Pacific region have encouraged major investment in the wine industry. Large wine-making concerns now represent roughly 80 percent of the country's output. But these big wineries not only produce inexpensive wines for the masses, they also make top, international-format vintages.

Climate—More Important than Soil

Wine production in Australia is subject to different conditions than those of Europe. In most growing regions the amount and intensity of sunlight are sufficient to ensure that the grapes ripen without danger of frost every year. There are no special growing areas comparable to *grands crus*, only climatic zones. The greatest danger is drought. In many places it is impossible to produce wines without irrigation. In recent years viticulture has increasingly withdrawn from the hot north to the cooler south. Wines from the cool-climate areas, with their fresh, fruity aromas without excess heaviness, have contributed greatly to the ascendancy of Australian wine. These areas are found in Western Australia (Margaret River, Frankland, Mount Barker), South Australia (Adelaide Hills, Eden Valley, Coonawarra, McLaren Vale), and Victoria (Geelong, Yarra Valley, Tasmania, Alpine Valleys).

Australia Produces Varietal Wines

In Australia wine is not normally the expression of a specific soil and climate, like is it in Europe, but of the vine variety. For this reason the majority of the country's wines are made from grapes from different growing areas, in some cases as many as 1,000 miles apart. They are transported in refrigerated containers and blended with wines from other regions according to strict formulas. Professionals refer to them as "multi-district blends." Most reach the market as varietals—chardonnay, sémillon, Shiraz, or cabernet sauvignon—with a generous designation of origin. To be sure, there are also many wines that come from only a single growing region, mainly from small or medium-sized estates whose wines are produced entirely, or for the most part, from their own grapes.

Australia's Winemakers

The wine industry has plenty of capital and is profit-oriented, but at the same time highly innovative and extremely concerned with quality. Penfolds, Rosemount, Hardys, Mildar, Yalumba, and others pay close attention to see that quality and price are in the right relationship. Fundamental to all the major wineries are their standard, low-price qualities, which reach the market in wholesale quantities of several million bottles. High-priced premium qualities are produced in various grades and much smaller quantities. The winemaker has to shop carefully for the right grapes. He is thus not only an oenologist, but a manager with a commercial responsibility. Australia is a world leader in the development of new growing and production techniques. Marketing, winemaking, and science are closely intertwined.

History

Australia has no indigenous vines. The British governor planted the first grapes in his Sydney garden in 1788, having brought them with him from South Africa. Three years later they bore fruit. Soon afterward winemaking was flourishing in Victoria,

New South Wales, and Western Australia, where large numbers of Englishmen had settled. The French made wine in Tasmania. In the mid-nineteenth century a number of German immigrants fleeing religious persecution settled in the Barossa Valley in South Australia and began cultivating European varieties. Syrah they called "hermitage," pinot noir "red burgundy," and white wine "chablis" or "Rheinriesling." Australians specialized in producing sweet liqueur wines—or the same ones watered down to become "Australian port." A gradual return to dry table wines began only after World War II. Increasing domestic consumption and especially the strong demand from abroad led to steady expansion of its vineyard area.

Western Australia

Wine growing began in Western Australia only in 1965 and only in the southern part of the state. The vineyards extend from Busselton, south of the capital of Perth, to the southern Indian Ocean. They are especially concentrated around the surfer paradises Margaret River and Cowaramup. Thanks to

Vineyard in the Adelaide Hills.

the cool winds from the sea, the Shiraz and cabernet have elegance and a fresh fruit despite their fullness. The sauvignons, sémillons, and chardonnays are also distinguished by snappy fruit and classic varietal aromas. Wine growing in the hinterlands of the cities of Albany and Esperance is more recent. Frankland River, Denmark, Maunt Barker, Porongurup, Manjimup, and Pemberton are small subzones that make up the Great Southern growing region. There the climate is relatively cool, so that pinot noir and Riesling are cultivated in addition to the traditional Australian varieties. North of Perth lies Swan Valley, which in recent years has seen a boom in both wholesale winemaking and tourism.

Australia's Viticulture in Numbers

Acreage under vines: 160,000 hectares
Wine production: 14 million hectoliters
Annual wine consumption per capita: 20.5 liters

The Ten Most-Planted Grape Varieties

1. Sauvig. blanc	white	29.0%
2. Chardonnay	white	23.2%
3. Pinot noir	red	18.1%
4. Merlot	red	8.0%
5. Cab. sauvignon	red	5.0%
6. Riesling	white	4.8%
7. Pinot gris	white	2.1%
8. Sémillon	white	1.7%
9. Gewürz-traminer	white	1.6%
10. Müller-Thurgau	white	0.9%

Australian Wine Law

Wines must be 85 percent of the variety and from the region of origin stated on the label. If more than one variety is named on the label, the largest component must be the one mentioned in first place. Acidifying wines is permitted, but chaptalization is disallowed. There are no legal restrictions on grape production. In quality winemaking, 60 to 90 hectoliters per hectare are harvested.

Wine Production Methods

The level of technical knowledge in viticulture and vinification in Australia is very high. The bulk of the grape crop is harvested mechanically; much of it is also pruned by machine. Red wines are often aged in *barriques:* good cabernet sauvignon in French oak, shiraz always in American oak. The best white wines undergo malolactic fermentation and are also aged in small oak *barriques.*

Minimal Pruning

After much scientific research, some wine estates have adopted the rule of pruning some varieties very lightly or not at all. After a few years of overproduction, the grapevine will regulate its own yield to about 80 hectoliters per hectare.

Home of the Wine Industry

Nearly half of all Australia's wine comes from the state of South Australia. Most of its growing regions are clustered around the city of Adelaide: almost all the large wineries are headquartered there. These growing regions close to the sea are classic cool-climate areas; the farther inland vines are planted, the higher the temperatures.

With 42.8 percent of the total vineyard area, South Australia is the country's largest growing region. Both the simplest of blending and table wines and high-class reds grow in the backcountry around Adelaide. Victoria is next with 26.3 percent, and New South Wales is third with 23.4 percent. Western Australia and Tasmania, both considered cool-climate areas, make up the remaining 10 percent of vineyard area.

Barossa Valley

The best-known South Australian growing region lies in a high, flat valley north of Adelaide. It is a warm area, known especially for its weighty, soft Shiraz, which frequently reaches more than 15 percent alcohol per volume. Many of its vines are 70, 100, even 150 years old, planted by the German immigrants who came to Barossa in 1840. In addition to Shiraz, granache and cabernet sauvignon are the main varieties, which are often blended with Shiraz. The dominant white variety is sémillon. The northeastern hilly region, the cooler Eden Valley (1,500 to 2,000 feet above sea level), is one of Australia's best Riesling growing areas, but chardonnay and a small amount of pinot noir are also cultivated there. Altogether, the vineyard area of the Barossa Valley amounts to some 7,000 hectares. More than sixty wineries have been established in the region, among them some of the largest in Australia's wine industry.

Clare Valley

Clare is a green oasis in the middle of a treeless, arid desert landscape northwest of Adelaide. It is traditionally a Riesling area. Because of the cold nights, thanks to Antarctic air streaming in from the nearby ocean, the grapes preserve their acidity, resulting in fulsome wines laced with spicy aromas and petrol tones, but still racy and with a delicate nerve (they are bottled with screw caps almost exclusively rather than corks). Red wine is grown in the warmer valleys. The main varieties are Shiraz and cabernet sauvignon. In addition, smaller quantities of malbec, sangiovese, and mataro are cultivated. As a rule, Clare wines are supple with elegant tannins.

Coonawarra and Padthaway

Australia's best cabernet sauvignon growing area lies between Adelaide and Melbourne. Its wines are dark colored, very concentrated, with fresh cassis and mint notes supported by a backbone of tannins. Coonawarra lies only forty miles from the Indian Ocean and therefore lies in the path of cool streams of air. The growing region is limited to a strip of dark red earth some nine miles long and four miles wide. The cabernet sauvignon takes on its special quality only on this *terra rossa*. In the last few years a considerable amount of Shiraz has been planted as well, which also yields excellent qualities. Padthaway, roughly sixty miles farther north, has become known mainly for its chardonnay. Many large wineries buy their grapes there before they are harvested. Now the main varieties grown on its clay and sandy soils are Shiraz and cabernet sauvignon.

McLaren Vale

This suburb of Adelaide is now probably South Australia's most important red wine region. It is known mainly for cabernet sauvignon and Shiraz. Dramatically full, almost opulent wines are made from them, with a structure similar to that of the wines from the Barossa Valley, only fresher and more aromatic. The growing region together with its bordering areas (Kangaroo Island, Fleurieu Peninsula,

Strathalbyn), also called Southern Vale, has high daytime temperatures, but lies directly on the Gulf of St. Vincent and is constantly cooled by breezes from the sea. This prevents the grapes from ripening too quickly and losing their aromas. Grenache and merlot yield top qualities, as do cabernet sauvignon and Shiraz.

Langhorne Creek

This rapidly growing wine region lies forty-five miles southeast of Adelaide next to Lake Alexandrina, a lagoon open to the Indian Ocean. The vines grow in crushed-rock soils. In this moderately warm climate almost all the internationally recognized red- and white-wine grapes are cultivated. There are few wineries, but numerous growers sell their grapes to larger and smaller wineries all over Australia.

Riverland

Australia's largest growing region lies along the Murray River near Renmano, in the midst of fruit orchards. It encompasses some 18,000 hectares of vineyards. The climate is sub-

tropical, the soils fertile thanks to frequent rains. Almost all the marketable varieties are grown there. All of the greats of the Australian wine industry buy grapes or wine there for their multidistrict blends, base wines, and even for premium qualities.

Kangaroo Island

This island just off the coast of Adelaide is known mainly for its white beaches and its unique flora and fauna. More than 20 wineries have been established here with some 120 hectares of vineyards. Elegant, spicy wines from Shiraz, merlot, and cabernet sauvignon are produced in its cool ocean climate.

Adelaide Hills

This relatively young wine region around the city of Adelaide lies in the forested Mount Lofty Ranges at an altitude of 1,300 feet and enjoys a cool climate. Its roughly forty wineries produce supple wines from chardonnay, sauvignon blanc, merlot, pinot noir, pinot gris, and viognier.

In warm South Australia grapes are harvested and processed in the cool night hours, as here in the Clare Valley.

Retreat to Cooler Regions

One of the most prestigious growing regions in Australia: The humid Hunter Valley is known for its opulent red wines from Shiraz and sémillon.

Large quantities of ordinary wine come from the states of New South Wales and Victoria, with their capitals of Sydney and Melbourne, but so does a lot of fine wine, mostly from small wineries intent on quality. In Victoria, especially, there are a number of subzones with varying soils and climates known only to professionals.

Hunter Valley

This warm, partly subtropical region has a wide assortment of wines. Its specialties are sémillon and chardonnay among the whites and Shiraz for reds. The latter thrives best on the red clay found in the lower part of the Hunter Valley (near Chessnock), while the whites, as a rule, do best on the alluvial soils in the upper Hunter Valley (near Denman). Hunter wines are traditionally weighty, high in alcohol, and distinguished by the aroma of ripe fruit. With the trend toward fresher, more acidic wines, the valley has sacrificed its position as Australia's leading wine region. Today, owing to its proximity to Sydney (100 miles), the Hunter Valley has become a getaway for city dwellers, with golf courses, stables, and luxury hotels.

Mudgee

Mudgee is a warm growing region in New South Wales, at the western foot of the Blue Mountains. Thanks to large reserves of land (and the possibility of establishing vineyards on the slopes of the Blue Mountains up to an elevation of 1,900 feet), the growing area has expanded in the past 20 years from 700 to 4,500 hectares. The main varieties grown are Shiraz, cabernet sauvignon, chardonnay, and sémillon. The majority of the grapes are bought up by large wineries outside the region.

Orange

This is a relatively young wine area in New South Wales, lying to the west of the Blue Mountains. The vineyards extend up to more than 2,900 feet and are exposed to extreme changes in temperature between day and night. In some places, the grapes cannot be harvested until May.

Tumbarumba

A new wine region that extends up to an elevation of 2,600 feet in the Snowy Mountains ski region. Since the vines were first planted in 1982, the grapes from this growing region have become some of the most sought-after in Australia. Chardonnay and pinot noir are the prominent varieties. They are sold to the sparkling wine industry.

Riverina

The largest growing region in New South Wales is Riverina. The vines grow in the moist, hot interior between the Murrimbidgee and the Lachlan River, on sandy alluvial soil that has to be irrigated year-round. Almost all the standard varieties are represented. Nearly the entire production is sold to large wineries outside the region, with only a small part of it fermented locally. Included are a few sémillons with natural botrytis that are among the best nobly sweet wines of Australia.

Yarra Valley

Because of its moderate climate, the Yarra Valley in the 1970s attracted winemakers who wanted to produce chardonnays and pinot noirs in the French Burgundy style; today a number of outstanding wines of these varieties come from the valley. Meanwhile, interest has shifted to cool-climate Shiraz and cabernet sauvignons, counterparts to the heavy, opulent reds from South Australia.

Bendigo and Heathcote

This extensive growing region, whose center Heathcote has its own appellation, has little vineyard area. The climate is warm, and wine growing is impossible without irrigation. The Shirazes are more elegant than those of South Australia, but do not have their sweetness and opulence. In addition, the region cultivates cabernet sauvignon and small quantities of merlot, malbec, and chardonnay.

Goulburn Valley

Shiraz is the traditional vine in this warm valley north of the city of Nagambie, yielding full-bodied wines that rarely present the effusive fullness of South Australian Shiraz. Cabernet sauvignon and chardonnay are also cultivated, as well as the Rhône varieties marsanne, roussanne, viognier, grenache, and mourvèdre.

Grampians

Shiraz is the most important wine from this area as well. It is produced by nearly all its wineries and yields full-bodied wines with a great deal of spice. The Grampians, formerly known under the name Great Western, is a relatively cool region with cold winds. Cabernet sauvignon does not always ripen. Riesling and Gewürztraminer are all that remain from the white wine tradition.

Pyrenees

This zone, famous in the nineteenth century for gold digging, is now known as a wine-growing region producing spicy Shiraz. The climate is warm, though temperatures are not as high as those of South Australia. A dozen small wineries have been established in and around Moonambel, producing this wine in quite respectable qualities.

Rutherglen

This area is known for heavy, sweet liqueur wines highly valued by connoisseurs. They are produced from overripe, healthy muscat or muscadell grapes (here called tokay) that are harvested in a slightly shriveled state (but without botrytis), pressed, and fermented. At from 5 to 7 percent alcohol, the fermentation is stopped by the addition of distilled alcohol so that the wines have a high residual sweetness but, at the same time, become extremely durable.

Mornington Peninsula

An even 800 hectares of vineyards are cultivated in the partly volcanic granite, partly sandy flat soils of this peninsula south of Melbourne. They blend in harmoniously with the well-tended landscape dotted with villas, parks, and pastureland. In this climate, with its typically constant sea breezes, chardonnay, sauvignon blanc, sémillon, pinot gris, viognier, and pinot noir thrive especially well.

Macedon Ranges

The wineries in this hilly growing region roughly sixty miles north of Melbourne pride themselves on producing elegant wines with a fine-grained tannin and powerful spiciness from the Shiraz grape.

Sunbury and Geelong

The small wine area of Sunbury lies northwest of Melbourne just beyond the last settlements. It has traditionally produced white wines. In the last few years, however, its wineries have begun to exploit the cool climate to create elegant, lithe reds from Shiraz and cabernet sauvignon. Geelong, west of Melbourne, also enjoys a cool, maritime climate. Growers produce outstanding fresh white wines as well as supple reds from pinot noir, Shiraz, and cabernet sauvignon in its sandy clay soils on a foundation of volcanic basalt.

King Valley and Alpine Valleys

King Valley is a new, up-and-coming growing area. Simple to good wines, including some outstanding liqueur wines, are produced in the warm part near the city of Milawa and on the fertile plain of the King River. The cooler section lies in the south at the foot of the Great Dividing Range. Large areas have been newly planted, so that there are now already 1,500 hectares of vineyards. The cool Alpine Valleys, first recognized as an official growing region in 2000, lie at the entrance to the Victorian Alps. There growers are experimenting mainly with red varieties and with chardonnay.

Tasmania

The island of Tasmania, south of Melbourne, has the coolest climate of all Australia's growing regions. Chardonnay, Riesling, and Gewürztraminer are the typical vine varieties. They yield less full-bodied wines than those on the mainland, with fresh aromas and spirited acids. Pinot noir is also grown successfully, both for red and sparkling wine. The main growing areas are Piper's River in the north, around Launceston, and Derwent Bay and Coal River in the south, near Hobart. An excellent pinot noir is cultivated in the west around Freycinet.

White wines with fresh aromas thrive in the cool climate of Tasmania.

Islands of White Sauvignon

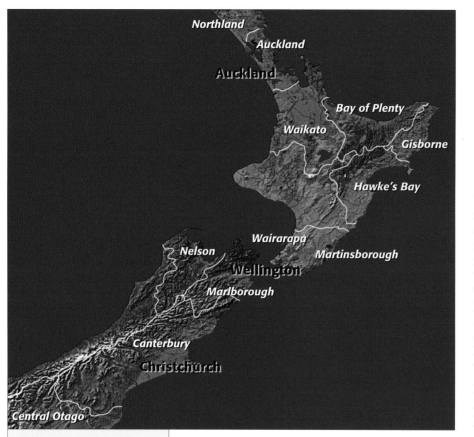

New Zealand's Viticulture in Numbers

Acreage under vines:
  16,000 hectares
Wine production: 1 million
  hectoliters
Annual wine consumption
  per capita: 10.5 liters

The Ten Most-Planted Grape Varieties

1. Sauvig. Blanc	white	27.1%
2. Sauvignon	white	23.0%
3. Pinot noir	red	12.8%
4. Merlot	red	7.0%
5. Cabernet Sauvignon	red	5.8%
6. Riesling	white	4.8%
7. Müller-Thurgau	white	3.4%
8. Sémillon	white	2.0%
9. Pinot gris	white	1.5%
10. Muscat	white	1.3%

New Zealand Wine Law

The laws in New Zealand are much like those in Australia. Grape production is not regulated. Average production for quality wines hovers around 90 hectoliters per hectare, a rather high figure, which is due to ample precipitation in some wine regions.

New Zealand is admired the world over for its spicy sauvignons and chardonnays. Within the country itself, wine has been and still is enjoyed with caution, even though wine production has increased more than twenty-fold since 1960.

For many years, only hotels were allowed to sell wine in New Zealand. Any one customer was not permitted to buy more than twelve bottles. Only since 1960 has it been possible for restaurants to offer wine with food; supermarkets have been allowed to sell it since 1990. And in 1980 there still was a law on the books that made diluting wine with water illegal.

The reason for these strange customs lies in the history of winemaking in New Zealand. The first grapevines were planted as long ago as 1819, yet the true beginnings of viticulture would wait until 1970. The years between were shaped by the effects of phylloxera, Prohibition, and the Great Depression.

The Late Discovery of the Wine

The first European *Vitis vinifera* grapes were planted in New Zealand in 1970, and the first wine to receive good reviews was made in 1984. The former favorite variety, Albany Surprise, had just then been nudged out of first place by the Müller-Thurgau grape. The

country's winemakers argued that this variety would thrive best in cool New Zealand, since it was the most frequently planted grape in Germany, which also has a cool climate. The result was a flood of light, sweet wines that inundated the market. The three largest producers accounted for 90 percent of all wine made; the remaining 10 percent was made by 150 small winemakers. The Müller-Thurgau variety remained the most-planted grape of the country until 1992, when chardonnay stepped into the lead.

Discovery of the South Island

The cool climate of New Zealand prevails predominantly on the South Island. The first grapes, however, had been planted on the warm North Island, making Auckland the center of wine production for many decades. With the spread of the Müller-Thurgau grape, the fertile Gisborne Valley became the country's largest wine district. As more demanding varieties such as chardonnay and above all sauvignon began to achieve unimagined successes, viticulture began to shift to the neighboring Hawke's Bay, and later, in the 1990s, all the way to the South Island. Today Marlborough, with its poor, stony ground and its great temperature contrast between day and night, has become New Zealand's largest and most important wine region. It is still true, though, that the best red cabernet sauvignons grow on the North Island, especially in Hawke's Bay and around Auckland.

Auckland

In the temperate, humid, and warm climate around New Zealand's capital city, red wines have traditionally been planted. The very best is cabernet sauvignon, a grape that produces especially fine wines in Matacma and on the island of Waiheke. In addition to Montana, the country's largest producer, many wealthy city folk have settled there to grow grapes.

Gisborne

Gisborne, the third-largest wine region in New Zealand, is the area where chardonnay is produced. About a third of chardonnay comes from here. Even though there are a few excellent producers, the region is devoted mostly to mass-production, and large wine producers from other parts of the country buy a lot of their grapes here. The chardonnay of Gisborne Valley produces full-bodied wines with a typical aroma of tropical fruit and mild acidity.

Hawke's Bay

Because of the drastic reduction of Müller-Thurgau plantings, the region around Napier is no longer the largest wine district in New Zealand. It is still, however, one of the best. Much chardonnay grows here, but it is the cabernet sauvignon, cabernet franc, and merlot grapes that really thrive in this area, yielding concentrated red wines, strongly flavored by oak.

Wairarapa-Martinsborough

This is a chic, small region inland from Wellington. It offers excellent cabernet sauvignons and some outstanding pinot noirs.

Marlborough

The largest and most significant wine region of New Zealand has a cool Pacific climate and stony soils. The vineyards around Blenheim are famous for piquant sauvignon wines that combine fullness with an extraordinary strong aroma. Many large wineries buy grapes from the region.

Nelson, Canterbury

This is a small and young region in the south of the island where Nelson has in 10 years doubled its vineyard area to 400 hectares. Some steely chardonnays come from Nelson, and a few interesting pinot noirs from Canterbury.

Lake Wanaka in Central Otago on South Island, one of the coolest grape-growing regions of the Southern Hemisphere.

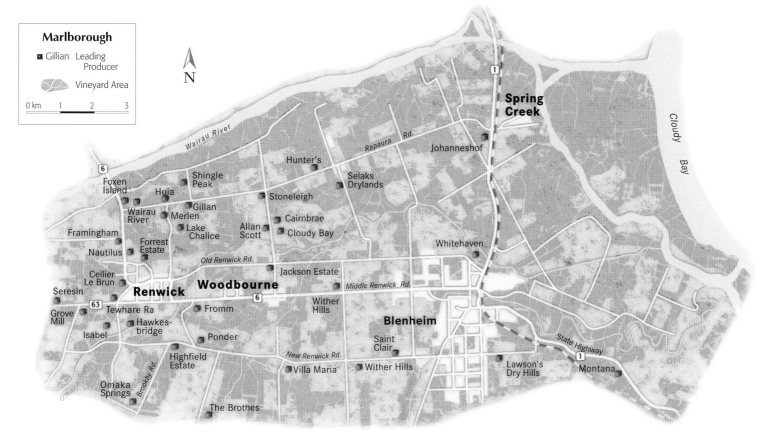

Cape of Good Wines

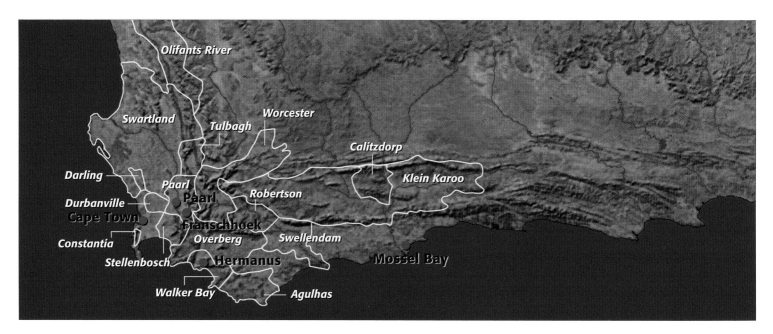

Viticulture in South Africa still has to catch up with the other new countries on the world's wine map. It only opened up to wine in the 1980s; since then, wine estates have been appearing like mushrooms. The future has just begun.

South Africa is a country in which cooperatives hold power. Thus 85 percent of wine grapes are processed by one or the other of sixty-nine wine cooperatives, most of which are members of the association of wine cooperatives, the Kooperatiewe Wijnbouwers Vereeninging (KWV). About 40 percent of the grapes processed by the KWV are distilled or made into grape concentrate.

Simple South African wines come from the hot mass-production regions of Oranje River, Olifants River, Klein-Karoo, or Malmesbury. Thanks to irrigation, these regions harvest 300 hectoliters of grapes per hectare. A large part of the wine made fills 5-liter cartons to be marketed in the areas that are inhabited by the white population of the country. The wines tend to be light and sweet.

Red Wine Instead of White Wine

Since the end of apartheid, South Africa has definitely undergone important changes. Since the mid-1980s the introduction of quality European vines has been gradually replacing the heavy-bearing native varieties. This means that the new sauvignons, chardonnays, and cabernet sauvignons are incomparably better than their predecessors. The number of private vintners and large producers is growing by leaps and bounds, and with them the percentage of red wines and the desire to produce high-quality vintages. As a result, winegrowing has increasingly retreated to the cooler regions, requiring an entirely new evaluation of slopes and growing areas.

Constantia

In 1652, the Dutch physician Jan van Riewbeek planted the first grapevines on the plateau above the bay, not far from Cape Town. Today, South Africa's oldest and most significant wine region is located there. In the eighteenth century, it was world-famous for its sweet wines; today the cool and humid climate yields palatable sauvignons and chardonnays that are among the best in the country. Some very good cabernet-merlot blends also come from the region. Three wineries dominate production in the area: the state-owned estate Groot Constantia, the future-oriented family estate Klein Constantia, and the highly ambitious estate Buitenverwachting, which is in German hands.

Stellenbosch

The most intense clustering of top-quality wine-makers is to be found in Stellenbosch, a region about 30 miles (50 km) out of Cape Town. In this pictur-esque area, which has both Dutch and English tradi-tions, the wines are predominantly powerful, tannin-rich cabernet sauvignons, merlots, and pinotages. At higher elevations, on the slopes of Simonsberg and Helderberg, the vineyards yield white wines of power, with a fruity aroma. Above all, sauvignon is planted, but increasingly also good chardonnay. The top pro-ducers are Thelema Mountains, Vriesenhof, Mulders-bosch, Kanonkop, and Morgenhof.

Franschhoek

Franschhoek is located north of Stellenbosch. This relatively warm, long valley is South Africa's most respected wine region. It is also the one most frequented by tourists. It was first settled in the seventeenth century by French Huguenots, who introduced viticulture to the area. Although just about the entire range of South African vines is cultivated here, today sémillon is a specialty of the region.

Paarl

The wine region of Paarl, located north of Cape Town, is dominated by two giant producers, KWV and Nederburg. They produce numerous wines, most of them of simple quality, as well as liqueurs, portlike wines, and brandies. The private winemakers are in the shadow of the large producers. Some of them whose vineyards happen to be in cool niches, as for example, Plaisir de Merle, make excellent red wines.

Other Wine Regions

Hermanus: In this, the southernmost wine region of the country, located on Walker Bay where the climate is cool and moist, growers are beginning to register success with pinot noir and chardonnay.

Durbanville: This region, only a few miles north of Cape Town, is a growing and promising one, especially for white wines.

Carved barrels in the Bergkelder Vinothek in Stellenbosch.

Robertson: In this warm to hot region, about two hours' drive from Cape Town, much of the wine is made by mass-production methods and tends to be simple and neutral in flavor. There are a few quality winemakers in the area, however, among them De Wetshof, Graham Beck, Springfield, and Zandvliet.

South Africa's Viticulture in Numbers

Acreage under vines:
  120,000 hectares
Wine production:
  8.3 million hectoliters
Annual wine consumption
  per capita: 9.5 liters

The Ten Most-Planted Grape Varieties

1. Chenin blanc	white	23.8%
2. Colombard	white	11.2%
3. Cabernet sauvignon	red	6.7%
4. Chardonnay	white	5.7%
5. Pinotage	red	5.5%
6. Sauvignon	white	5.1%
7. Muscat d'Alexandrie	white	4.3%
8. Merlot	red	3.6%
9. Cinsaut	red	3.6%
10. Shiraz	red	3.3%

South Africa's Wine Laws

Wine laws in South Africa are not particularly strict. "Wines of Origin" have been clearly defined since 1973, but an estate with vineyards in more than one region need only mention one of them on the label, even if the grapes came from two or more separate regions. A varietal wine need only contain 75 percent of the variety named on the label. Maximum grape production figures are nonexistent. South African wines may not be chaptalized, but they can be acidified.

The Boschendal Wine Farm in Franschoek in front of the Groot Drakenstein: Dutch and English traditions shape the wine estates.

South America's Bordeaux

An Eventful History

Chile is the oldest wine country in the southern hemisphere. As early as the middle of the sixteenth century the Spanish planted vines they had brought with them from home. In 1851 the first cabernet sauvignon vines were planted. Twenty years later exports of wine began to a Europe still crippled by phylloxera. Growth was slowed only by Prohibition (1938). The final demise of the wine industry began with the land reforms of the Christian Democratic government (1965) and later the expropriations of the socialist government of Salvador Allende (1980). In 1982 the wine market collapsed. By then the vineyard area had shrunk some 50 percent (50,000 hectares), but three years later saw a new beginning. With the help of American and French investors, new vineyards were planted and modern winemaking techniques introduced. Temperature control during fermentation opened up the possibility of producing fresh, fruit-accented red and white wines even in warm to hot growing areas. In the 1990s Chile's wine industry experienced rapid growth. Vineyard area expanded to more than 100,000 hectares. Production increased by 70 percent, exports by 300 percent. And the growth is continuing. Especially in the cool south, but also in the Colchagua Valley, vast new vineyards have been planted.

Few regions of the world have such favorable conditions for wine growing as Chile's. The climate is uniformly dry and warm, vine diseases are rare, spraying is seldom necessary, and nearly all the vineyards can be tended mechanically. The wine industry is enthusiastic. Now the country produces not only industrial wines, but also a few high-class, single-vineyard wines.

Since 1990 Chile has developed into one of the most important growing countries in the world in terms of both quantity and quality. There is ample space for vineyards, and the costs of wine production are minimal. In the past Chile was known mainly as a producer of inexpensive varietal wines, but the country has much more potential. With its first super-premium wines, Chile has shown that it also wants to star on the international wine scene. It is significant that, in contrast to Europe, the development of quality is being initiated by large wineries, not small estates. One oddity is the large percentage of root-true vines. As yet phylloxera has not penetrated the country, or at least has not shown itself to be damaging. As a precaution new vines are generally grafted onto louse-resistant support vines.

Soils and Climate

The soils consist mostly of debris washed down by rivers from the Andes. They are rich in minerals and dry. There is little precipitation, the majority of it during the winter. The Valle

Vineyards in the high Valle Central.

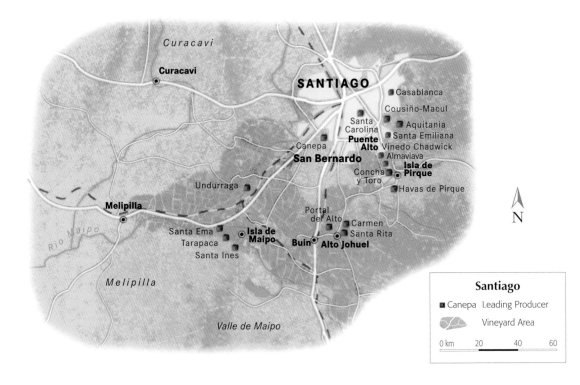

The map shows the region around Santiago, with labels including Curacavi, SANTIAGO, Casablanca, Cousiño-Macul, Santa Carolina, Aquitania, Santa Emiliana, Puente Alto, Canepa, Vinedo Chadwick, San Bernardo, Almaviava, Isla de Pirque, Concha y Toro, Havas de Pirque, Undurraga, Melipilla, Portal del Alto, Carmen, Santa Ema, Isla de Maipo, Santa Rita, Tarapaca, Buin, Alto Johuel, Santa Ines, Río Maipo, Melipilla, Valle de Maipo.

Santiago
- ■ Canepa Leading Producer
- Vineyard Area
- 0 km   20   40   60

N

Chile's Viticulture in Numbers

Acreage under vines:
  120,000 hectares
Wine production:
  6–8 million hectoliters
Annual wine consumption
  per capita: 12 liters

The Ten Most-Planted Grape Varieties

1. Cabernet sauvignon	red	39.4%
2. Merlot	red	15.2%
3. País	red	12.8%
4. Chardonnay	white	8.6%
5. Sauvignon blanc	white	7.3%
6. Carmenère	red	6.5%
7. Syrah	red	4.4%
8. Sémillon	white	1.9%
9. Pinot negro	red	1.5%
10. Malbec	red	0.7%

Chile's Wine Law

A wine law promulgated in 1985 defines the regions of origin and establishes the varieties admitted to quality wine production. There are altogether twenty-three varieties; país, one of the most common grapevines in Chile, is not among them. Almost all Chilean wines carry the name of a variety on their labels. This variety must be present in the wine to at least a level of 75 percent. The same applies to origin and vintage. Only 25 percent can be of a different vintage or origin. Chaptalization is not permitted, but acidification is allowed. There are no limits set to grape production. The average for quality wines is about 9,000 kilograms per hectare.

Central, home to 90 percent of the vineyards, is virtually an arid steppe on which wine growing is possible only with irrigation. It extends from the capital of Santiago to the city of Chillán some 240 miles to the south and is made up of four sub-regions: Maipo, Rapel, Curicó, and Maule. Each of these is further divided into a number of different subzones, and these into vineyards. In contrast to other New World countries, Chile thus has a precise system for the designation of origin. The Valle Central lies nestled between the coastal cordilleras and the Andes. Ground temperatures are uniformly warm. Only in a few places, where river valleys cut through the coastal cordilleras, do cool Pacific winds penetrate into the interior. They see to it that temperatures fall at night: a welcome cooling, for that allows the grapes to preserve their freshness. In especially cool spots even white varieties can be cultivated.

The Red Varieties

By far the majority of vineyards are planted with red grapes. Cabernet sauvignon is the most important, yielding in the higher, cooler vineyards full-bodied, tannin-rich red wines whose aromas are reminiscent of black currants, eucalyptus, and cedar wood. Varietal merlots never achieve their elegance and opulence. Carmenère, which was introduced into Chile in the middle of the nineteenth century, is making great headway. In this warm climate it yields significantly better qualities than in Bordeaux, where this variety does not always ripen and so has continued to lose ground since 1900. Up until the 1990s carmenère was confused with merlot; only then was it recognized as an independent variety. In its best qualities carmenère produces substantial wines that are rarely less than 14.5% alcohol per volume and have an aroma of leather and berry jam. They are generally blended, but also occasionally fermented as varietals. Also on the rise is syrah, which can produce delightful wines in this warm climate and dry soil.

The White Varieties

Chile's classic white varieties are chardonnay and sauvignon blanc. Roughly 90 percent of all vineyards are planted with them (although some supposed sauvignon-blanc vineyards are actually sauvignonasse or sauvignon vert; that is to say that many old vineyards are really tocai Friulano). The most important white wine zone is Casablanca, the region between Valparaiso and Santiago. In recent years white wine has also been produced somewhat farther south near San Antonio. The cooler southern growing regions around Maule are also proving to be good white wine areas. The Humboldt Current is extremely important for the climate, flowing northward off the Pacific coast and forcing streams of cold air into the interior of the country.

A Sleeping Giant

Argentina's Viticulture in Numbers

Acreage under vines:
  208,000 hectares
Wine production:
  12 million hectoliters
Annual wine consumption
  per capita: 38 liters

The Ten Most-Planted Grape Varieties

	Variety	Color	%
1.	Malbec	red	20.0%
2.	Bonarda	red	18.0%
3.	Cabernet sauvignon	red	15.0%
4.	Syrah	red	10.0%
5.	Torrontés	white	9.0%
6.	Merlot	red	7.0%
7.	Chardonnay	white	6.0%
8.	Tempranillo	red	5.0%
9.	Chenin blanc	white	4.0%
10.	Sangiovese	red	3.0%

Argentina's Wine Law
Argentina's wine legislation has no production restrictions and does not limit output per acre. Producers are free to produce as much or as little as they choose.

Salta Province (1,680 hectares): Mainly white wines, among them considerable torrontés and a little cabernet sauvignon. Most important growing areas: Cafayate and Valles Calchaquíes.

La Rioja Province (6,350 hectares): Vineyards as high as 4,000 feet, considerable torrontés. Most important growing area: Catamarca.

San Juan Province (14,500 hectares): A great deal of Alexander muscat, Pedro Ximénez, torrontés. Most important growing areas: Tulum Valley (up to 2,000 feet), Pedernal Valley (up to 4,000 feet).

Mendoza Province (75,400 hectares): Extensive vineyards with all the white and red varieties. Most important growing areas: North Mendoza (with Lavalle, Las Heras, Guaymallen, Maipú, and San Martin), Zona Alta del Río Mendoza (with Mendoza City, Lujan, Vistalba, Las Compuertas, Perdriel, and Agrelo), and Valle del Uco (with Tupungato); East Mendoza (with Santa Rosa, Rivadavia, and Junin); South Mendoza (San Rafael and General Alvear).

Río Negro Province and Neuquen (1,300 hectares): A growing area in Patagonia that cultivates pinot noir, chardonnay, Riesling, and sauvignon blanc.

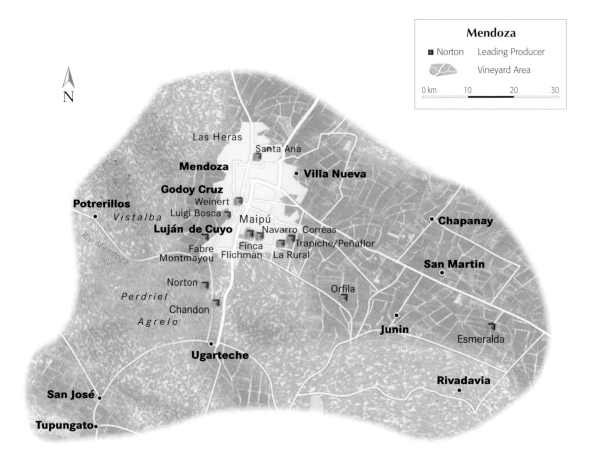

Argentina is the fifth-largest wine producer in the world, but in importance it lies far behind many smaller countries. Much has improved in Argentina's wineries in the last two decades. A large number of their wines, especially those made from the red variety malbec, have achieved international levels.

Argentina is roughly four times the size of France. Because of the tropical climate that dominates large parts of the country, wine growing is successful only in a few regions that lie in the west at the foot of the Andes. The climate there is also hot, but the nights are much cooler so the acids and sugars are not evaporated so quickly. The difference between highest daytime and lowest nighttime temperatures can be as much as 15°C. The main growing regions lie around the city of Mendoza. Almost completely destroyed by an earthquake in 1861, Mendoza was gradually rebuilt. Sheltered by 50,000 plane trees, it is the center of Argentina's wine industry. The province of the same name produces roughly 70 percent of the nation's wines.

The Highest Vineyards in the World
Mendoza lies at an elevation of roughly 2,600 feet. Most of the vineyard plantings, especially the young vines, are at elevations between 2,900 and 4,800 feet—the highest in the world. The soils are mineral-rich debris from the Andes and are completely dry. It would be impossible to grow grapes without irrigation. The water comes from the nearby Andes, led into the vineyards by an extensive capillary irrigation system.

Table Wine in Mass Quantity
Chile and Argentina have had much the same history. As in Chile, the first vines were introduced by Spanish missionaries in the sixteenth century. The first noble vines were planted in the mid-nineteenth century—as in Chile. At the beginning of the twentieth century wine production was flourishing—as in Chile. French and Italian immigrants brought vines with them and created a wine boom. But almost the entire production was consumed domestically—unlike Chile. There was no export, and Argentineans made few demands of their wines. Wine was meant for everyday consumption;

what mattered was that it be light and cheap. Little has changed to this day. More than half of the country's production is sold in domestic supermarkets; and more and more of these wines are produced from the light red missionaries' vines, criolla and cereza. During the colonial period they were virtually the only varieties.

Decreasing Wine Consumption

In the last thirty years wine consumption in Argentina has dropped from ninety liters to thirty-eight liters per person, so that the country's wine industry has had to rely on exports—and that means quality. The vineyard area has shrunk, and many plantations that produced ordinary table wines have been abandoned. At the same time, the core wine-growing region experienced a veritable boom in the 1990s. New estates were established in the hope of being able to produce good to very good quality at low cost. They have been only partially successful. For with increased production of quality wines in the southern hemisphere's other wine-producing countries, prices have fallen. Since the economic crisis at the end of the twentieth century, table wine production has once again increased significantly

Red Wines

Argentina produces roughly 80 percent red wine, the majority of it from malbec, a variety introduced from France around 1850. In the warm climate it can fully ripen almost every year and yields considerably finer qualities than it does in Bordeaux, for example. The importance of Argentinean red wine is closely tied to this variety. Production has come to exceed demand, however, so that malbec is now used in the making of table wine as well. It has even surpassed bonarda, an Italian grape that yields only average wines, but that stood unchallenged as the predominant vine variety for decades. Sangiovese, tempranillo, and barbera are other traditional varieties from which rather ordinary qualities are produced. They have now been overtaken by syrah and merlot. Plantings of cabernet sauvignon have proceeded at a rapid rate, and the best wines made from it rival those of Chile. Pinot noir is also grown at elevations of more than 3,900 feet.

White Wines

Argentina's traditional white wine variety is torrontés. It grows mainly in the north, where vineyards extend up to 6,500 feet. The vine comes from Galicia, where it is not very significant. In Argentina, however, it yields some interesting, spicy, and aromatic wines of great individuality. There are numerous types: the natives distinguish between torrontés Riojano, torrontés Sanjuanino, and torrontés Mendocino. Torrontés plantings have shrunk slightly in favor of chardonnay and chenin blanc, both of which produce outstanding qualities at high elevations. There have recently been small plantings of sémillon, sauvignon blanc, sauvignonasse, and viognier as well.

Mendoza, Argentina's most important growing region: Protected by the Andes, Mendoza harvests quantities of simple table wines and a small amount of excellent malbec.

Precious Secrets

Wine tasting is, from the technical viewpoint, an unexciting business. It is all about analyzing and forming judgments about a wine's appearance, fragrance, and taste. For a wine lover, tasting wine is a very different matter. He or she does not want to analyze. The wine lover wants to be initiated into the secrets of a wine, to be carried away by the enjoyment of it.

For the wine lover, the pleasures of wine begin with the color of the liquid in the glass, with the tears that slowly flow down the sides of it. The enjoyment ends long after the wine has been swallowed. As the Spanish painter Salvador Dalí once put it, "He who knows how to enjoy himself does not drink his wine: he tastes its secrets."

Naturally, the mind also partakes of the pleasures of wine. Knowing the origin of a wine, being aware of the special features of a certain vintage, the ability to differentiate and recall complex impressions of taste and smell: all this is part of the enjoyable and intelligent tasting of a wine. "A wine bestows a whiff of the souls of its country of origin on the person who drinks it," the late Italian winemaker Giacomo Bologna once said to me.

What the Senses Tell Us

What fascinates about wine is the diversity of its flavors. It can present aromas of peaches, black currants, cloves, butter, or dried figs. Not everything that sounds good is good to taste, but sometimes it is the bizarre aromas that lend a wine that certain something.

The aroma of a wine consists of what a person can smell and taste. Thus fragrance and taste are the most important aspects of wine appreciation. Some particularly passionate wine connoisseurs swear that its color gives them a foretaste of the pleasures they are about to enjoy. Some stress the importance of a wine's temperature, which can refresh the palate independently of the wine's taste. Some like to hear the whisper of the sparkle in champagne. Seen in this way, each wine is more than aroma; it has optical, tactile, and acoustic qualities.

Primary Aromas

The natural aromas of the grapes are considered primary. Most of them are flowery and fruity. They tend to dominate the nose of young wines; later in a wine's development, spicier notes are added.

Each grape variety has its own primary aromas. Wines made of sauvignon blanc grapes often exude a scent of gooseberries, for example, while pinot noir wines give off cherry and plum fragrances. Yet any grape variety can change its primary aromas when it is planted in a different soil, under different conditions. Thus a cabernet sauvignon from the Napa Valley will be fruitier than the same variety harvested in Bordeaux. The soil of Bordeaux is predominantly alkaline, while that of the Napa region is acidic.

Secondary Aromas

During fermentation wine acquires, in addition to its own natural aromas, some new ones. The fermentation or secondary aromas enrich the wine; they render it vinous or winy by altering its aroma profile from that of grape juice to that of wine. The carriers of secondary aromas are alcohols, acids, aldehydes, and esters. Their quality depends on the yeast strains used to turn the sugars into alcohol and on the ripeness of the grapes themselves, that is, on the amount and composition of the grape sugars. Secondary aromas are reminiscent of such things as butter, bread, mushrooms, leather, cheese, and animal smells. More unexpected flavors, such as the taste of jam or whiffs of damp autumn leaves and of the barnyard, may also be created. A great many of the secondary aromas are volatile and disappear again, often during *élevage*, sometimes in the bottle.

Tertiary Aromas

The summer after its harvest, when it begins to be warm, the aroma of wine begins to change, irrespective whether it is in barrel or in bottle. The primary aromas recede, and new fragrances form. Aromas arise that are spicy, balsamic, woody: these are the first signs of the process of aging. To the expert, from that point on the wine does not have aroma; it has "bouquet." As the wine is further aged in wood or refined in the bottle, the bouquet keeps developing. Now the wine becomes more complex, more stratified, more multifaceted.

Describing Aromas

Scientists have identified five hundred different wine aromas. If their means of measuring aroma—gas chromatography and mass spectral analysis—were more refined, no doubt they would identify many more. Most of these aromas are not subject to chemical analysis and description. Only a few aromas can be assigned chemical formulas. When attempts are made to describe aromas in language, many unexpected, even bizarre designations result. In the early 1980s, scientists on the Davis campus of the University of California tried to systematize the various wine aromas. The result was the aroma wheel. It is useful, but it has not succeeded in creating a generally accepted language of aroma.

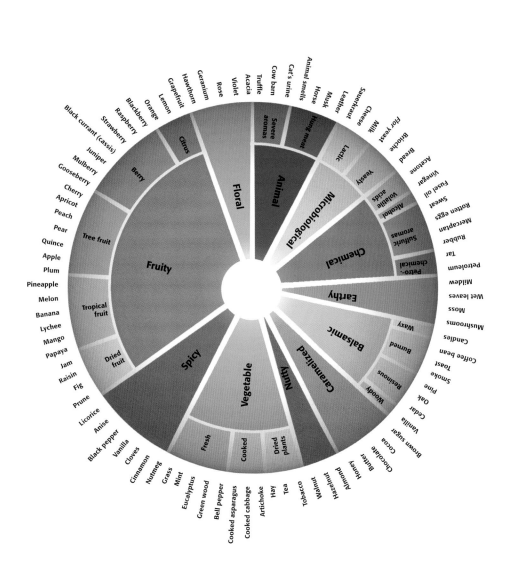

California chardonnay: Aromas of pineapple and nuts.

Red bordeaux: Aromas of cassis and cigar tobacco.

Pouilly-Fumé and Sancerre: Aromas of gooseberries and flint.

Chianti Classico: Aromas of violets, pansies, and blackberries.

Riesling from the Rhine: Aromas of apple and peach.

Red burgundy: Aromas of plums and oak.

Scoring that Extra Tenth of a Point

Informal wine tasting at Olivier Leflaive in Puligny-Montrachet. On the right, a typical professional tasting sheet for scoring wines.

Tasting Sheet

			Tasting Event	Taster	Wine	Color						
						Type						
						5	4	3	2	1	0	Multi-pliktor
Viscosity												1
Color	Clarity											1
	Hue											1
Bouquet	Cleannesit											2
	Quality											2
Taste	Cleannes											2
	Quality											2
Total assessment	Finesse											3
	Complexity											3
	Length											3
												Total:

Enjoying wine is one thing, tasting professionally, quite another. Wine tasting is work—work with very little enjoyment. For one thing, the wine is never swallowed; it is spit out. The aim is to form as complete as possible a judgment of a wine. This assessment has to make sense to others as well. Often this is difficult; sometimes it is impossible.

Noticing taste sensations and describing them is not the same as making a judgment about a wine. Two hundred years ago, the French *philosophe* and gastronome Anthelme Brillat-Savarin (1755–1826) made a very important distinction. For him, the enjoyment of wine begins with a "direct experience" of its taste. The wine touches the lips, flows slowly over the tongue, and then rolls back toward the lips. In this way, the taste is fully experienced.

Yet for a "complete experience," more is required: the mouthwatering sight of the wine, the "tears" that flow down the glass after it is rotated, and naturally, the fragrance. The fragrance initiates the direct experience. It stimulates the senses just as the touch of the wine on the tongue also stimulates them.

Tasting for Enjoyment

While the "complete experience" constitutes the basis for an assessment of the wine, it is only the final "contemplated experience" that sorts out the impressions received by the senses and permits a final judgment. A total picture of the wine—its body, length, complexity, fullness, harmony—is formed by putting together a multitude of separate impressions. This final assembling of sense impressions into an assessment is a mental activity. Brillat-Savarin was an epicure, and his first priority was always his own pleasure. Only after that, did he want to make sense of his enjoyment. His work *La Physiologie du goût* (1825; *The Physiology of Taste*) is an almost scientific inquiry into the higher pleasures, including those of wine.

Wine Tasting

Today's wine tastings tend to be a lot more sober. Enjoyment plays no part in them; they are all about assessing the wines. Without swallowing, sommeliers, vintners, and journalists taste the wines. After a wine has been "weighed" on the tongue, it is spit into a container. The emphasis is on work, not pleasure.

Wines are tasted blind; that is, without the labels being seen. This is to prevent the tasters' personal preferences and prejudices from influencing their judgments. At official tastings, as when wine awards are given, a formal tasting sheet is used. On it there is room to score wines for appearance, bouquet, taste, and overall balance. Although there are many variations on the tasting sheet, they are all constructed of the same elements. After the scores for each wine have been added and averaged, the winner is usually ahead of the rest by no more than a tenth of a point.

Tasting 150 Wines a Day

One purpose of comparing the scores of wines is to award them medals in competitions. The credibility of such awards, however, has decreased around the world since so many of them are now given out.

A more serious use of point scores is to establish rankings of wines. This is done by professional tasters, tasting commissions, and wine journalists. Wine rankings, which are usually published, have become an important sales tool. No wine magazine can afford to do without them. Wine reports based on points earned have replaced the often flowery and imaginative wine descriptions of the past.

While Europeans use a twenty-point scale, in the United States a hundred-point scale is customary. Of course the reliability of the results does not depend on the scale used but on the dedication of the tasters and needless to say on the circumstances surrounding the tasting. To perform a concentrated tasting

and evaluation of 80 wines in a single day is definitely difficult. If a taster is required to judge 150 wines a day, as is often the case, a high rate of error is to be expected.

Private Wine Tastings

Private wine tastings can easily be arranged. It is best to set a theme for them: cabernets of France versus cabernets of California, or a comparison of the ten best California chardonnays. This is what is called a horizontal tasting. When a wine tasting is structured vertically, the same wine is compared over several vintages. It is important to make sure that the wines are tasted blind, so that the objectivity of the tasters is maintained. The bottles are wrapped in paper, so their labels cannot be seen. It is also possible to pull a sock over each bottle. Whether the tasters assign points or give verbal assessments is up to the organizers of the tasting. At such events, the wines are usually drunk, not spit out.

Connoisseurs judge a wine first and foremost with the nose.

When wine tastings are logically arranged, it is possible to give serious assessments of forty to fifty wines a day.

Lovely to Look At

Wine provides a feast for the eyes. Whether a bright scarlet or a saturated amber yellow, the color of the wine has its own appeal. Not only that, color can tell us about the age, the variety, and in some cases, the condition of the wine.

White wines darken with age. Wines with a great deal of substance, those that perhaps have had a short rest on their lees, are never pale yellow but will show a lemony hue when they are still young.

In red wines, the development of color is reversed; they lighten with age, eventually showing an orange aura around the edges. After twenty years a brown tinge tends to develop in bordeaux, and even more in burgundies, which makes them almost unattractive. The color is then in sharp contrast to the taste, which, reaching its apex, develops a refined, malty sweetness.

Light yellow: Pinot grigio

Straw-colored: Sauvignon blanc

Lemon yellow: Young chardonnay

Dark red: Ribera del Duero

Ruby red: Médoc

Cherry red: Young Chianti Classico

The Problem of Color

For young bordeaux wines it is often stated that the darker their color the better they are. And in fact there is a positive relationship between the amount of pigment in the grapes and the quality of the vintage. The better the bordeaux vintage, the more saturated the color of the wine.

It is, however, impossible to jump to the conclusion that what is true of a bordeaux is true of any wine. Most red grape varieties have less pigment than cabernet sauvignon, which happens to be the major component of bordeaux wines. Other wines are lighter, even in great vintages. This does not mean they are any less good. Burgundies and Barolos are fine examples of wines that never reach the depth of color of a bordeaux or of a Spanish Ribera del Duero. Thus color as such is definitely not an indicator of quality. As a matter of fact, many dark red wines come from hot growing regions, and most wines from southern Italy, southern Spain, and Algeria, far from being superb, are used mostly for blending.

Golden yellow: Mature chardonnay

Old gold: Mature sauternes

Amber yellow: Amontillado sherry

Scarlet: Saint-Emilion, ten years old

Brick red: Barolo, fifteen years old

Light brick red: Burgundy, thirty years old

Glasses: Spiegelau

Always Follow Your Nose

Most of what we think we are tasting we are actually smelling. This is true also of wine. To penetrate all the secrets a wine holds, more than anything you need a good sense of smell.

The fragrance of wine is carried by the volatile compounds, which constitute the majority of a wine's aromas. Chemically, these volatile substances are bound to alcohol, aldehydes, esters, acids, and other carbohydrates. The more carbon atoms they contain, the more intense is their smell. Esters are the most strongly scented compounds. They are also the most volatile, even more so than the aldehydes, which smell more intensely than the alcohols. The acids are the least volatile.

The Organs of Smell

The sense of smell in humans is located in a small side chamber of the upper nasal cavity. The air stream that enters with a breath does not touch the olfactory zone directly; rather, turbulences of air carry the stimulants into the side chamber and cause the olfactory sensations to arise. The receptors for these stimulants are all located in an area not larger than a quarter inch (1.5 cm) square, called the olfactory bulb. It is covered with a moist mucous membrane, so that the molecules of scent are dissolved when they reach it. Smells are only registered in liquid form.

The nostrils, though moist within, have no olfactory function. They serve to filter, moisten, and warm up the air that is breathed in. Since the olfactory pit is open to the throat via the retronasal passage, the smell receptors are stimulated more intensely during breathing out than breathing in. This is the reason why some wines can be tasted so long after they have been swallowed.

The Olfactory Receptors

The human olfactory organ consists of about 50 million receptors, formed like minuscule hairs, that swim within the mucous membrane of the olfactory bulb. These receptors are nerves that are directly linked to the brain. They pass the stimuli they receive directly

The human olfactory nerve can differentiate up to 4,000 smells.

into the olfactory nerve, which is located just above the sinuses. This nerve path is obviously short, evidence that our human central nervous system is very closely tied to the sense of smell. The olfactory nerve decodes the stimuli it receives and forms them into the homogeneous impression of a smell. This is a necessary operation, since millions of smell receptors are stimulated at once. Scientific research has established that humans can differentiate 4,000 smells. Our memory for smells, a very important aspect of wine tasting, is a matter of training and intelligence, however, and unlike the sense of smell itself, it is subject to our will.

Olfactory Thresholds

It is rather unlikely that some people are born with a talent for wine tasting. Although the olfactory bulb varies in size from person to person, it is not its size but its sensitivity that matters. Some people react when only 100 fragrance molecules are present; others can

smell only in the presence of as many as 10,000. The perception of smells is thought to be affected by general brain activity; it depends on a knowledge of the various smells and their components and on a willingness to differentiate between them. Thus the sense of smell can be trained, at least as far as wine tasting is concerned.

There are some limits, however. People exposed to constant smells such as tobacco smoke or exhaust fumes become inured to them. In other words, the threshold of their sensitivity to smell becomes higher; their sense of smell is impaired. It also seems that the ability to smell things decreases with age. It is not known whether this is due to wear and tear of the olfactory receptors or to a lessening of concentration. It is certain that sensitivity to smell fluctuates during any one day, both with older and younger people. After breakfast, lunch, and dinner it is particularly low. People's sense of smell is most acute when they are hungry.

A Short Attack, a Long Finale

The tongue's ability to perceive tastes is very limited; it can hardly detect more than four basic tastes.

The tactile experience of wine on the tongue can give rise to a high form of pleasure. Although taste is never as multifaceted as aroma, in the mouth wine can satisfy more than one of our senses: it can slake our thirst.

The carriers of the nonvolatile flavor components of wine are sugar, acids, and phenols. Since they have no smells, or almost none, they have to be tasted. The main organ of taste is the tongue, where most of the taste receptors are located. Though there are very few taste receptors on the palate and in the throat, these are nevertheless important in drinking wine; they are stimulated by the touch, the temperature, and the astringency of the tannins, which pucker the mucous membranes. For all these sensory impressions the mouth cavity is responsible, through the activity of the trigeminal nerve. As the wine warms up in the mouth, the olfactory receptors are also given renewed stimulation. The additional aroma compounds released in this warm atmosphere rise through the retronasal passage into the olfactory pit.

The Tongue

The tongue is covered with papillae, small nipple-like protuberances that serve first of all the sense of touch. Between 200 and 400 papillae also contain taste buds. With the help of these we can perceive chemical compounds. The taste buds are distributed irregularly over the surface of the tongue, concentrated around its tip, edges, and root. In the center of the tongue hardly any taste buds are found. This renders the central portion of the tongue neutral in terms of taste.

Each taste bud contains numerous sensory cells. At their upper end, these cells terminate in a porus or pore, a taste thread, bathed in saliva. These are the actual sensory stimulators: they react to chemical substances and send the appropriate information to the brain. Children can taste better than adults because their taste buds are numerous and densely

set. After age twenty, their number decreases steadily; by age sixty, we have lost half of them.

The Taste Buds

For a long time it was believed that the tongue could taste an infinite range of flavors. Today we know that the tongue can distinguish exactly four basic tastes: sweet, salty, sour, and bitter.

The taste of wine is known to contain these basic flavors. Sweetness is in the alcohol, especially in glycol. Tartness is supplied by tartaric and lactic acid, by acetic acid, and, in some cases, by malic acid as well. While salt is a component of the acids, it is masked by other taste components and so does not usually register as a taste in its own right. Bitterness is a feature of some phenols, such as tannins.

Few taste buds are able to pick up all four flavors. Most of them detect one or two, and so the taste buds are grouped into regions of taste on different parts of the tongue.

Areas of Taste on the Tongue

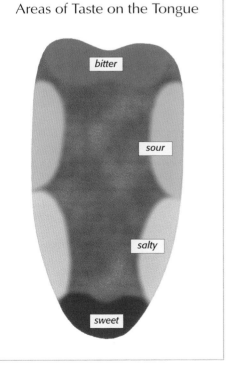

A Delicate Delight

The care of wine does not end when the wine-maker finishes his responsibilities and bottles the wine. The next task is to get the wine into the glass with its quality unimpaired. Since wine, especially fine wine, should be handled as little as possible, this is not an easy task. Between its bottling and its enjoyment there may be many months or even years, and during this time, the wine keeps changing steadily. It is changed by warm weather, by cold, by contact with oxygen, and by chemical processes that go on in the wine itself. Although wine cannot really be said to be a living being, as is often claimed, it is very sensitive. For this reason, it is important to store wine properly and to serve it correctly. To drink wine from the wrong glass is the same as sending Pavarotti on stage with a club in his mouth. Without the knowledge needed to handle fine wines correctly, a person cannot develop a feeling for the true qualities of fine wines.

Thin-Walled and Well-Shaped

Champagne and Sparkling Wines

Sparkling wines are drunk out of narrow, elongated, tulip-shaped glasses, which are high enough to allow the *mousse* or foam to build up. The little bubbles *(perlage)* must be well visible, for the eyes drink also! The chalice itself must be thin. The lips are sensitive; they like to feel the refreshing coolness of the wine.

Light White Wines

This glass, with its small diameter, is ideal for light and medium-heavy white wines, which release their floral-fruity primary aromas immediately on being opened. The small dimensions of the glass concentrate the intense aromas, while the tongue experiences mostly the melting fruit flavors. It is good for Sancerre, Soave, pinot grigio, Riesling Kabinett, Grüner Veltliner, and so on.

Full-Bodied White Wines

The larger volume of this glass is suited to white wines with substance, which have to breathe. Such wines have a naturally mild acidity, that is to say, they have been through a malolactic fermentation. This glass is ideal for chardonnay *(barrique),* sauvignon *(barrique),* Riesling Spätlese, Swiss chasselas, and so on.

Red Wines That Are Low in Tannins

Through the relatively large opening of this glass, the wine flows into the mouth in a wide stream, stimulating all places where fruit and acidity are felt. In other words, the wine is initially experienced not just by the tip of the tongue, where we experience sweet, melting sensations, but simultaneously by the other parts of the tongue as well. This is a good glass for burgundy wines, barbera, gamay, Blaufränkisch, pinotage, and so on.

Tannin-Rich Red Wines

The high chimney of this glass takes the concentrated bouquet of the wine right into the nose. Through the opening, which is not too large, the wine is first experienced by the tip of the tongue, so that the first impression is shaped by the taste of fruity sweetness. In this way, wines with lots of tannin are made to lose their first bitter impact. Through the thin glass, the temperature is immediately communicated to the lips—this is also part of the enjoyment. This glass is good for young bordeaux, rioja, Chianti, and so on.

Heavy Red Wines

Because of the large diameter of the glass, the wine has a lot of contact with the air. This allows the alcohol, which is at the same time a carrier of taste, to unfold. Fullness and complexity can better be expressed. At the same time the high stem prevents the temperature of the wine being affected by that of the hand. (It is necessary to hold wineglasses by their stems.) This is an ideal glass for mature burgundies, Barolo, Brunello di Montalcino, syrah, and so on.

Dessert Wines

Noble-sweet dessert wines are enjoyed sip by sip. The relative small bowl of this glass is appropriate to the small quantities that are usually served. The wine flows over the tip of the tongue to its edges, so that its extremely rich flavor can be more sharply felt, but the residual sweetness is not enhanced. This is a good glass for sauternes, Auslese, and so on.

Sherry and Port

Port, sherry, Madeira, and marsala are very full-bodied wines with an alcohol content of over 18 percent. Now, when a wine is tasted, alcohol may never obtrude, however. This small and narrow glass prevents the alcohol from evaporating and overpowering the bouquet. The opening is so small that it is practically impossible to stick one's nose into the glass. For this reason the high alcohol content is barely noticed.

Glasses: Spiegelau

Getting at It

Corkscrews are part of the basic equipment of a wine drinker. There are many strange variations: kitschy, difficult to use, impractical, bulky, and overwrought. Only a few corkscrews are both functional and simple at the same time. Each wine lover must decide which tool best suits his personality.

1. Cork Pliers

These pliers take the place of a corkscrew for bottles of Champagne and other sparkling wines. The pliers are not used to pull out the cork; it is silently twisted out of the neck of the bottle. If this tool is used carefully, the opener can prevent the wine from foaming over. Naturally, the pliers cannot be applied before the gold foil and the wire basket are removed from the mushroom-shaped Champagne cork.

2. Waiter's Friend

The most practical of all corkscrews is known by this affectionate name. With the blade attached to it, the capsule top can be cut off. Then the helix (screw) is driven into the cork, the fulcrum is placed on the edge of the bottle,

and the cork is pulled. It does require a little practice and some strength in the wrists.

3. The Capsule Cutter

Instead of using a knife to cut the top off the capsule, this cutter is placed on the edge of the bottle and given one turn. Whether the capsule is made of lead, of foil, or of plastic, the material is cut with a clean edge, and far enough down so that the liquid does not touch it when the wine is poured.

4. T-Model

The most popular corkscrew in the world, the T-model is simple, sure, and inexpensive— and difficult to handle. It takes strength to open a bottle with this tool. And when the cork pops out of the bottle with a loud bang, even the wine may be in shock.

5. The Screw Pull

This American invention is as chic as it is intelligent. The helix is elastic and loosely wound; it grabs just about any cork, even very tight ones. It can be used without a large expenditure of force. The handle continues to be turned in only one direction, and the cork is steadily moved up and out.

6. Zigzag

This somewhat cumbersome model can sometimes be found in England and the United States. The short screw is inserted into the cork. By compressing the shears, the cork can then be extracted without much effort.

7. Butler's Friend

This a very refined cork extractor. The two slim blades are worked down between the bottle neck and the cork with a rocking motion. Because they are of different length, the force used in pulling the cork is applied to it at different points. Thus gently held, it glides out of the bottle neck. This is often the only way to reach the wine in old bottles with crumbly corks.

8. Cork Remover

This tool is a rather cumbersome but effective means of removing the remains of broken or crumbly corks from the wine so that they will not flow into the glass. The four wire arms are opened and closed by means of a movable ring below the handle—pieces of cork swimming on top of the liquid can thus be grasped.

9. Lever Screw Pull

This is the fastest and most elegant way to free the bottle of its cork. One hand clasps the bottle neck with the pliers, while the other moves the lever from back to front, so that the thin, elastic helix enters the cork. Then the handle is reversed and the cork pulled out almost without any effort. Although neither effort nor skill is required to get the cork out of a bottle with this high-tech tool, it is the most expensive way to do the job.

From Alcohol Meter to Port Pliers

Serving a noble wine in an inappropriate manner is unthinkable. Yet it is equally gauche to make a mystique out of drinking wine. Apart from the glass and the corkscrew, little else is needed—except for a good wine, of course. On the whole, it is wise to select one's simple needs with care.

The arsenal of wine accessories ranges from a pocket-sized alcohol-measuring device to a pair of pliers for opening vintage port. Most of these paraphernalia are really toys: the machine for decanting old wines, the silver wine labels to be hung about the necks of decanters, the saber for opening champagne. The art of serving wine was reduced to a sensible minimum by Emile Peynaud, professor of oenology at Bordeaux University, when he said: "You take the wine off the shelf, you bring it to the desired temperature, you uncork it, and you serve it immediately." He allows that the treatment is slightly different for very old wines.

Clay wine cooler
In such a cylindrical clay container a precooled wine will maintain its temperature for a while. Before it is used, the cooler is held under cold water until the clay is completely saturated. The evaporation of the water in the clay causes the temperature of the container to drop. Thus for a while, the wine is kept cool and ready to drink.

Decanting basket
Old wines are sometimes served in such baskets so that the sediments can collect on the bottom of the bottle, which need not be agitated unnecessarily. It is an old-fashioned method, but it works quite well.

Decanting funnel
This funnel was invented to facilitate decanting old wines. As the wine is slowly poured into the funnel, the built-in screen will catch even the finest sediment. The funnel eliminates the need to watch out for the first signs of sediment.

Sparkling wine cooler

There is no better way to cool white and sparkling wines to the desired temperature than by standing them in a cooler like this, filled with ice cubes and water. Within a short time, the water carries off the warmth of the bottle. This process will cool the wine in the bottle, but not the wine in the neck of the bottle-unless it is put in upside down.

Wine thermometer

This is an indispensable tool for wine lovers. Although it is the only way to make sure that a wine is served at the right temperature, the instrument should not be used at the dining table or in a restaurant, for aesthetic reasons.

Sparkling wine stopper

This stopper will cap an opened bottle of sparkling wine. It makes an airtight seal so that the carbon dioxide remains in the liquid. The next day, the wine foams as it did when the bottle was first opened. This method is a much more effective than hanging a silver spoon into the neck of the bottle and leaving it open.

Decanting carafe for young wines

Many young wines have a disagreeable, reductive bouquet when they are first opened. Such wines should be decanted. In the process of decanting, the wine is already swirled about. The large surface area of the decanter also offers maximal contact with the air.

Decanting carafe for old wines

Ideal for old wines, this decorative, duck-shaped decanter has a very small neck. The old wine is slowly poured into the carafe, leaving the sediment in the bottle. The small opening minimizes the risk of turning an old, wasted wine through the shock of a sudden exposure to oxygen.

Relax and Enjoy

Not much is needed to enjoy a wine: a good bottle and an appropriate glass. But then the questions start: When is the right time to open the bottle? How do you serve a really good wine? When does a wine need to be decanted? Here are a few tips, not to introduce stiff rules, but to remove obstacles to enjoyable, relaxed wine drinking.

A Brief Serving Primer

As a rule, a bottle of wine is opened at the table. The foil cap that covers the cork should be cut off well below the rim, so that the wine does not flow over the cut when it is served. In this way, it is impossible for heavy metals, such as lead and tin alloys, to reach the glass.

With bottles that have been stored in damp cellars, there often is some mold found under the cap. This does not impair either the cork or the wine.

It is a good idea to give the cork a quick sniff after it has been extracted. An ailing cork has an intense corky smell, while a healthy cork will smell neutral or of wine.

Should the cork break, the corkscrew is inserted into the remainder once more, with great care. Any crumbs of cork that fall into the bottle are poured into the glass with the first few drops. This wine can then be discarded.

The host first pours himself a small amount of wine to make sure that the wine is not corky; that is, the cork has not been contaminated by molds that will affect the taste of the wine. The host then serves each of the guests, filling his own glass last.

The bottle is held not at the neck but at the belly, with the label facing up. Flagon-shaped bottles are held flat, not narrow side up.

Wine should be poured carefully, without splashing. When enough has flowed into the glass, shake the bottle with a slight twist. If you straighten the bottle too cautiously, the last drops land on the tablecloth.

The test for corkiness: Does it smell good or not?

Color as a test of age in white wines; the darker, the older.

Wineglasses must be free of water spots and should smell neutral. In other words, they must be washed in very hot water, without the use of rinsing chemicals. Then the glasses are dried by hand, to prevent water spots from forming.

The host is responsible for refilling the glasses of his guests. He has to pay attention and prevent their glasses from running dry.

A wineglass is held by the stem, not the bowl. This prevents the wine from being warmed by the drinker's body heat.

Wine is not drunk but tasted sip by sip. Taking one or at most two swallows is best, letting the wine linger on the tongue and, above all, taking time to enjoy the aftertaste. To slake thirst, water must be served with meals.

Any dinner is enhanced when more than one wine is served before it ends. As a general rule, the change is made from white to red wines. Two red or two white wines can also be served, instead. Before dinner, an aperitif may also be offered, and afterward a dessert wine. A dinner is not, however, a wine tasting.

New glasses have to be provided for any change from white to red wine. The same goes for the change to the dessert wine. For two similar red or white wines, the same glasses can be retained.

Old wines that need to be decanted should be brought up from the cellar two days before they are to be served. They should be stood upright to allow the sediment to settle to the bottom. Old red wines can also be placed in a bottle basket, from which they can be served as well. In that case, the host has to watch that no sediment is poured into the glasses with the wine.

As a rule, old wines are decanted directly before they are served. Young wines, which are decanted to breathe, should be poured into a carafe two to four hours before being served. If you want to dispense with decanting, open the bottle one or two hours before serving the wine, to let it breathe.

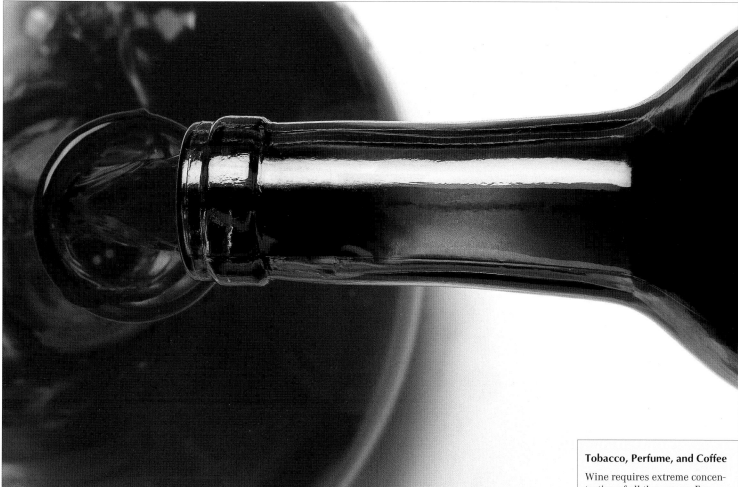

Decanting an old red wine: Like a thin thread, the sediment flows into the neck of the bottle—time to stop pouring the wine into the decanter.

Why Wines Are Decanted

Pouring a wine carefully from its bottle into a carafe is called decanting. Only two kinds of wine need to be decanted: very old red wines, which have formed a sediment in the bottle, and heavy but still young red wines, which are improved by some air contact before they are served.

The reason for decanting old wines is simply to leave the sediment behind in the bottle so that it does not enter the glasses when the wine is served. The sediment, which was built up over the years the wine was in bottle, consists mainly of tannins that have separated out. Although the taste of the wine is completely unaffected by the sediment, the deposit itself has a bitter taste. The only exceptions to this rule are old burgundies: their sediment is good and can be enjoyed with the wine. In other words, old burgundy wines need not be decanted.

With very old wines, decanting has to be done with very great care. Exposure to oxygen after years of airtight development can shock such wines

into sudden oxidation and make them completely undrinkable.

How Wines Are Decanted

The simplest tool for easy decanting is a funnel with a fine strainer in the bottom, where the sediment will be caught. A funnel is by no means indispensable, however. Experienced wine drinkers place a lit candle beneath the neck of the bottle as they pour the wine into the carafe. In the light of the candle, they can see when the sediment reaches the bottle neck and can stop pouring. The deposit stays in the bottle.

Decanting Young Wines

It is much more important to decant young wines, rich in tannins, because they need air in order to unfold their aroma and to dissipate any reductive and unpleasant smells. For young wines like this, use carafes with a large surface and a long neck, which swirl and air the wine as it is decanted. With heavy white wines, decanting can also be advantageous.

Tobacco, Perfume, and Coffee

Wine requires extreme concentration of all the senses. For this reason, it is not possible to smoke when tasting wine. This is true even when wines are tasted for a meal.
• Smoking does not impair the capacity to taste wine, but it disturbs the other participants. Moreover, the taste buds need at least fifteen minutes to regenerate after a cigarette.
• Before going to a wine tasting one should, if at all possible, avoid perfume or aftershave lotion, or should use these fragrances with extreme restraint. The scent of cosmetics interferes with the enjoyment of wine.
• Coffee puts greater stress on the tongue than tobacco. Coffee should never be drunk before a tasting; if necessary, it should be taken only after the wine tasting is over.
• Flowers also detract from the enjoyment of wine. This is particularly true of intensely fragrant ones, like lilies of the valley or roses.

How Much Wine Goes in Each Glass?

A wineglass should be at most half filled. Only with sparkling wines do you follow a different rule, for here a full glass allows you to admire the effervescence.

Filling a beer glass to the etched line is a sign of a conscientious bartender. Filling a wineglass that full is a faux pas. A full wineglass hampers your enjoyment, and it is the surest giveaway that your host is a wine novice. Many restaurants set a bad example when serving wine by the glass, but that is no excuse.

It is difficult to enjoy wine from a brimming glass. There is no room for the bouquet to collect, and it immediately dissipates. Often it is not even possible to drink from a full glass, certainly not if you grasp it correctly—by the stem—to raise it to your lips. The full bowl is too heavy, the gripping surface on the stem too small. To drink without spilling requires a deft balancing act. To be safe, there is nothing to do but grasp the glass by the bowl and lift it that way, leaving unsightly fingerprints that will become clearly visible—at the latest—once the glass is empty. Moreover, the warmth of your hand is immediately transferred to the wine, and its temperature rises, especially if you hold it very long. All efforts to serve the wine at the proper temperature are thus a waste of time. This is especially true of white wines, which rise from 50°F (10°C) to 55°F (13°C) from the warmth of the hand faster than a red wine from 64°F (18°C) to 70°F (21°C) (see page 233).

The Right Amount

White-wine glasses, which are generally smaller than red-wine glasses, should be at most half filled. Only then does the wine's aroma stay in the glass and not immediately disappear. Whether the wine in the glass amounts to a cup or half a cup is immaterial from the point of view of taste. The wine's aroma develops just as well with a small amount as with a larger one. What matters is the size of the glass. If very large glasses are used, you should serve more rather than too little. With glasses that hold only a small amount, you will have to pour more frequently. Good restaurants get around this by serving open wines in a half-pint (quarter-liter) pitcher. Guests receive the guaranteed amount, but can pour it out as they please. With red wine it is a different story. Red-wine glasses are larger, as a rule, and should be only roughly a third full. At least, that is the rule of thumb; smaller red-wine glasses of the kind used in many bistros, however, may be filled to the halfway mark. More is a no-no—even though many fans of wine bistros think otherwise.

The Exceptions: Sparkling Wines

Only with sparkling wines is it acceptable to fill glasses fuller. Depending on the type of glass—a narrow champagne flute, for example—they can even be three-quarters full. This is more to do with appearance than taste; the more wine in the glass, the greater the pleasure in watching the bubbles rising to the surface. After all, it is the effervescence that shows the connoisseur the quality of a sparkling wine. Sparkling wines fermented in the bottle, like

A "drop stop" helps you serve wine without drips—a useful accessory for wine lovers.

champagne, develop very tiny bubbles that rise upward like beads on a string. In tank-fermented sparkling wines, like most Sekts, the bubbles are larger and more irregular. Especially expensive vintage champagnes and prestige cuvées, many of which have aged in the bottle for three, five, or more years, are served in glasses that are not so tall but have a greater diameter. They require time to "breathe" after the bottle has been uncorked. Here it is sufficient to fill the glass halfway full or at most two-thirds. This still gives you a chance to delight in the effervescence.

Serving Tips

Wine is not soda water. You don't simply splash it into the glass; you pour it gently, slowly and carefully, soundlessly and not in a great surge. To this end it helps to grasp the bottle in the middle of the belly and tilt it slowly over the glass. This way you can control the flow. Note that the label should always face up. You only look clumsy if you grab the bottle by the neck, and it is difficult to control the flow of wine if you do. Even if you pour correctly, there is a chance that you will spill the last drops. Those who have failed to master the necessary twist should think of using a pouring aid: a small piece of silver foil rolled into a cylinder and inserted into the neck of the bottle. These are sold in wine shops under the name "drop stop" and cost only pennies. With them you will no longer have spots on the tablecloth or unwanted gushes of wine.

Argol crystals in the glass: What looks like ground glass or sugar crystals is calcium tartrate. This is simply the precipitated acid of a white wine. Argol has no effect on quality; in fact, it shows you that the wine is a pure, lively vintage.

What to do with opened bottles?

Designer bottle stoppers are meant to prevent the wine from losing its bouquet. A cork does the same thing.

With a pump, it is possible to remove the oxygen from the bottle. A wine stays fresh somewhat longer in a vacuum.

Private Preserve, a nitrogen gas you spray into the opened bottle, is the most effective way to keep a wine fresh.

The champagne cap forms an airtight seal. The carbon dioxide cannot escape, and the sparkling wine stays fresh.

Serving and Drinking Temperatures

Most white wines are drunk too cold, most red wines too warm—which means that they cannot be fully enjoyed. If wine is to be enjoyed at the proper temperature, a few preparations—or tricks—are required.

Every wine has its own ideal drinking temperature. For white wines it is around 50°F (10°C), for red wines around 64°F (18°C). There are deviations, to be sure, depending on the type of wine. You can certainly drink simple, light white wines a few degrees cooler, and sparkling wines should be served at 46°F (8°C). The cooler these are, the lovelier the effervescence in the glass. Strong, full-bodied white wines would suffer at such a temperature; you could not fully appreciate their fullness and complexity. They need to be somewhat warmer, say 54°F (12°C). The notion that red wines should be drunk at "room temperature" is mistaken. Today's rooms hover around 70°F (21°C), and often they are even warmer. At this temperature you taste mainly the alcohol and glycerin in the wine, not the fruit, and as a result you lose an important facet of the taste. The ideal drinking temperature is 64°F (18°C), but light, fruity red wines can even come to the table at 61°F (16°C). Those who are used to drinking their red wine somewhat warmer may require a period of adjustment, during which time a wine thermometer is essential. Using one frequently soon gives you a sense of whether a wine is too cool or too warm.

Chilling White Wines

What do you do when your cellar is too warm and the white wine isn't cool enough? Perfectly simple: you remember to fetch the wine from the cellar in time to put it in the refrigerator. If you need to chill it even faster, an ice bucket is the only solution. In ice water it will drop at least ten degrees (5°C) in a matter of ten minutes or so. The French verb for rapidly chilling a wine (or Champagne) in an ice bath is *frapper*. You do need to add water to the ice, for it is a good conductor. Putting a pinch of salt in the water can speed up the process, though; salt causes the ice cubes to melt faster and release their cold. If there are no ice cubes available, your only recourse is the freezer compartment of your refrigerator. Only use this to cool the wine a few degrees, however, for if it stays in the freezer longer than ten or fifteen minutes it will be cold, to be sure, but also half frozen. In an emergency you might even use an ice bucket or the freezer compartment for a red wine that is too warm.

Warming Red Wine

When red wine comes from the cellar, it is often too cold to be enjoyed at once. The professional term for quickly bringing it up to drinking temperature is *chambrer*. If you failed to take the wine from the cellar soon enough, you will have to do something. It used to be that you simply placed the wine on a radiator, but that heats only the wine at the bottom of the bottle, not the rest. A better method is to lay the bottle in a container of lukewarm water. The wine inside will reach the desired temperature in only a few minutes. But be careful: red wine is always served a degree or two cooler than proper drinking temperature, as it quickly warms in the glass. And another thing: don't even think of warming wine in the microwave; the bottle will immediately explode.

Still the best method for keeping white wine cool, even in summer, is placing it in a bucket of ice water.

Chambrer: After a few minutes in lukewarm water, a cellar-cool red wine reaches drinking temperature.

Frapper: Like white wines, red wines can be cooled in an ice bucket if they are too warm.

Frapper: If necessary, wine can also be chilled in the freezer compartment, but only a few degrees.

Country of Origin	Drinking Temperatures for White and Red Wines						
	42°F (6°C)	46°F (8°C)	50°F (10°C)	54°F (12°C)	58°F (14°C)	61°F (16°C)	64°F (18°C)
France	Vin de Pays Rosé	Champagner Bourgogne Blanc Sancerre Saumur Muscadet Chablis Bordeaux Sec Rosé de Provence	Pouilly Fumé Chablis Grand Cru Meursault Gewürztraminer Riesling Grand Cru Tavel Rosé Lirac Rosé de Provence Sauternes (sweet)	Puligny-Montrachet Montrachet Corton-Charlemagne Musigny Blanc Tokay d'Alsace	Vin de Pays Beaujolais Primeur	Vin de Pays Mercury Mâcon Rouge Chinon Beaujolais Cru all Burgundies Bordeaux Superieur Madiran Côtes-du-Rhône	Médoc, Haut Médoc, Pauillac, Margaux, St-Emilion, Pomerol, Graves, Cahors, Côtes de Languedoc, Côtes de Roussillon, Côtes de Provence, Chateauneuf-du-Pape, Côte Rôtie, Hermitage
Italy	Prosecco Frizzante Galestro Pinot Grigio	Prosecco Spumante Südtiroler wines Chardonnay (without wood) Soave Gavi Arneis	Chardonnay Barrique Verdicchio Frivli white wines	Marsala Vin Santo	Kalterer See Valpolicella Bardolino Lambrusco	Chianti Vino Nobile Rosso di Montalcino Barbera d'Alba Merlot del Piave Pinot Nero Südtirol Lagrein Cabernet Friaul Sangiovese di Romagna Valtellina Rosso	Chianti Riserva Brunello di Montalcino Aglianico di Vulture Taurasi Barbera d'Asti Barbaresco Barolo Amarone Südtiroler Merlot
Germany	QbA süß Weißherbst Winzer-Sekt	QbA/Kabinett Jahrgangs-/ Lagen-Sekt	Spätlese/ Auslese trocken Beerenauslesen	Grauburgunder Auslese	Trollinger	Spätburgunder Dornfelder Lemberger	
Austria	G'spritzter	Grüner Veltliner Riesling Welschriesling Neuburger	Ausbruch, Beerenauslesen	Smaragd Wachau Sauvignon Steiermark		Blauer Zweigelt St. Laurent	Blaufränkisch
Switzerland		Fendant, Aigle Epesses	Œil de Perdrix			Blauburgunder Dôle	Merlot del Ticino
Spain	Rosado	Albariño Cava		Sherry		Valdepeñas	Rioja, Ribera del Duero, Tinto Navarra, Priorato
Portugal	Vinho Verde				Port Madeira	Ribatejo	Alentejo, Dão, Bairrado
New World	White Zinfandel	Sauvignon Blanc	Fumé Blanc	Chardonnay Barrique		Pinot Noir	Cabernet Sauvignon, Zinfandel, Shiraz, Pinotage, Malbec

Corkiness and Other Faults

The French aroma researcher Jean Lenoir has put together aroma samples for the twelve most common wine faults. The set, called "Le Nez du Vin," is available in all specialty wine shops.

There are two kinds of wine faults: real ones and imaginary ones. The most common real wine fault is corkiness. Imaginary wine faults are often the result of aromas the consumer is unfamiliar with and which he intuitively rejects.

What is called a wine fault may be a permanent flaw, a temporary problem, or even a vague suspicion. Typical wine faults are: a bouquet of hydrogen sulfide, a rotten-egglike gas produced by yeast as a byproduct of fermentation; mercaptans, a skunklike smell caused by hydrogen sulfide's reaction with other components of the wine; or a disagreeable mousy note after the wine has been swallowed, due to faulty yeast action. These flaws are all temporary. Contamination that clears up quickly sometimes appears in young wines that have been submitted to reductive maturation and were insufficiently aerated before they were bottled. As a rule, this contamination will subside after the wine has been exposed to air for some time. Therefore the way to deal with such faults is:

In a restaurant you can send back a wine that tastes or smells of cork.

• Let the wine stand for five to ten minutes in an open glass; often the disagreeable smell will dissipate;
• If not, let the wine stand in the open bottle for twenty-four hours and try it again;
• If that does not work, give the wine another six months or a year in the cellar, to complete the aging process.

Permanent Faults

A serious fault in wine is the presence of residual sulfur from excessive additions of sulfur during winemaking, betrayed by a biting, slightly prickling sensation in the back of the nose. It is particularly obvious in acidic wines.

In addition, some abnormalities of aroma are not subject to treatment; they cannot be removed. Wine can smell moldy or stagnant because it was stored in contaminated barrels, and it can take on the smell of geranium leaves if it is contaminated by bacteria during fermentation. These flaws should of course have been caught by the winemaker and corrected then and there.

Volatile Acids

One fault more likely to occur in heavy, alcohol-rich wines is an excess of acetic acid, or ethylacetate, in the wine. In the bouquet, a typical note of nail polish can be detected if this is the case. (Small amounts of acetic acid are always present in wine; but it should never reach levels over 1.5 grams per liter.) Acetic acid is made by vinegar bacteria that react with alcohol. Volatile acids in the bouquet are more common in red wines and in chardonnay from warm growing regions and in good years. Sweet wines are also predisposed to develop a higher vinegar component. It is true that volatile acid is not experienced as a fault by all wine drinkers. With some wines, for example Unico from Vega Sicilia, volatile acid was considered a trademark of quality for years.

Corkiness

A wine that smells or tastes of cork is without a doubt flawed. The smell or taste of cork is not a temporary thing; it will get stronger. A corky wine cannot be enjoyed. Usually it is in the bouquet that the more or less disagreeable corky smell is detected; often the corkiness can also be tasted. In most cases it is caused by trichloranisol (see page 227). Visually, the cork will appear quite perfect.

What should the consumer do when he is faced with a corky bottle of wine?

- In a restaurant, the wine can be rejected (but only if the bottle was not first half finished!).
- Wine dealers and vintners do not replace one bottle of corky wine. If we are talking about three bottles of the same wine, the matter can be negotiated. If the entire case of a wine is corky, the dealer would be expected to replace it, even if the terms of his business state otherwise.
- When purchasing simple, everyday wines, it is best to choose bottles with screw tops or caps: they constitute a form of insurance against corky wine.

Levels of wine in old bottles

fill level (hf)
into neck (in)
top shoulder (ts)
high shoulder (hs)
middle shoulder (ms)
low middle shoulder (lms)
low shoulder (ls)

Other Real Wine Faults

- Cloudiness in red or white wines (excepting, of course, stirred-up sediments).
- White wines with a sediment; it does not necessarily mean a faulty wine, but it is sufficiently unusual to indicate this possibility.
- Older white or red wines with a little carbon dioxide; this indicates spurious bottle fermentation.

Watching the Level

With increasing age, a wine's level drops as the result of evaporation in every bottle. When buying old wine, it is therefore essential that you check the level of the wine in the bottle. The catalogs of serious auction houses scrupulously record the level in bottles that are twenty or more years old. To this end the wine experts have developed a special set of abbreviations:

hf (high fill)

in (into neck)

ts (top shoulder)

hs (high shoulder)

ms (middle shoulder)

lms (low middle shoulder)

ls (low shoulder)

For twenty-year-old wines the fill level "high shoulder" is normal. Down to "top shoulder" there is no great risk that a long-lived wine will be undrinkable. It only becomes critical when the level has sunk as far as "middle shoulder," when the increasing amount of air in the bottle hastens the oxidation of the wine. Wine in such a bottle needs to be drunk immediately. At auctions there are discounts for bottles with this fill level—unless the wine is fifty years old, that is. In this case "middle shoulder" is in fact a good indicator. If the level has sunk down to the "low middle shoulder" or "low shoulder," there is a serious danger that the wine has gone bad. Only a very few tannin-, alcohol-, and acid-rich wines are still enjoyable when this level has been reached. The drop is greater in dry cellars than in damp ones; the dry air causes the cork to shrink, allowing the wine to evaporate faster.

Bottle Sizes

Larger bottles *are very popular among wine collectors and investors. First, they serve as showpieces in any collection. Second, the wine ages better in larger bottles. The oxygen that penetrates into the bottle is distributed through two, three, or more times the amount of liquid than in a normal-sized bottle. Certain aging processes take place in the wine even without contact with oxygen, of course, as for example through the formation of esters. These maturing processes are independent of the bottle size. If that were not the case, wine in a bottle sealed with sealing wax would stay forever young.*

1) Called a jeroboam if filled with champagne
2) Commonly used in Bordeaux (4.5 liters until 1978)
3) Called a methusalem in Champagne

normal bottle	magnum	double magnum	jeroboam	impériale	Salmanasar	Balthasar	Nebukadnezar
0.75 liters	1.5 liters	3 liters(1)	5 liters (2)	6 liters (3)	9 liters	12 liters	15 liters

Ensuring a Tight Seal

Cork is an almost perfect wine seal. It closes the bottle efficiently, allows only minimal amounts of oxygen to pass, and has a neutral taste. Yet it is expensive. Depending on quality and length, a cork costs between $.10 and $.75. And unfortunately, it does not guarantee perfect security to the wine.

As far back as the Romans, natural cork was used to seal containers of wine, along with other materials such as resin and tar. It was only after the bottle was invented, however, in the seventeenth century, that cork began to be accepted everywhere.

Not all cork is equally good at delivering what it appears to promise. It happens again and again that bottles will leak or, much worse, that the wine will

tensive plantings of *Quercus suber*. Sardinia and Corsica have large stands of cork oak and their own cork industry; much of the cork that is harvested there does not come from natural forests, but grows in plantations. In southern France and North Africa, cork forests are not intensively exploited.

As a rule, trees are 25 to 30 years old when they are stripped of their bark for the first time, and it takes 10 years for the bark to grow back. If the tree reaches the age of 150 years, it will be stripped eleven times on average.

The Composition of Cork

Cork consists of the dead cells of woody tissue, called suberin. These cells are filled with nitrogen and they are absolutely water- and airtight. Thirty

Corks are stamped out at right angles to woody channels, the lenticels, so that air cannot penetrate the cork itself, but can only push itself past it.

take on a disagreeable, corky taste. And no wonder, since scientists have counted over fifty volatile substances present in cork that can react with wine. Many wine producers also believe that the quality of corks has declined as the number of bottlers has risen. They are considering alternatives, and have found at least one: stoppers made of silicon.

Where Natural Cork Grows

Cork is harvested from the bark of the cork oak, *Quercus suber*, which grows mostly in the warm countries around the Mediterranean. Portugal is the greatest exporter of cork; southwestern Spain also has ex-

to forty thousand such cells are found in a cubic centimeter of cork. Any contact between the wine and oxygen cannot take place through the cork itself; it must occur through the space between cork and bottle neck. The better the quality of the cork, the better the seal created. First of all, the suberin of the best cork is very elastic and can adhere tightly to the glass. Secondly, corks are cut against the grain of the lenticels, the dark, woody rills within the cork, so that no channel will run along the length of the cork, letting through significant amounts of oxygen. Cork is most brittle along the lenticels, by the way; this is where a cork

From the outside, there is no sign of TCA infection in a cork, which could make the wine taste corky. Altogether, fifty volatile substances in natural cork can cause off aromas in wine.

can break most easily. Valuable corks are those that have very few lenticels.

How Corks are Made

After the cork bark is stripped off the trees, it is dried outdoors for at least half a year. Afterward, it is boiled and disinfected. Now the tricky work begins: selecting those pieces that are suitable for the manufacture of wine corks. About half the harvest will be used for corks. The remainder will be worked into cork wallboards, flooring, and other building-related products.

The chosen plates of cork are cut across the line of the tree's growth into strips exactly as wide as the corks will be long. These strips are bleached (today this is done by using hydrogen peroxide), and the

A valuable 60-millimeter cork with few pores: Suitable for red wines that have to be stored securely for long periods of time.

of wine, which is completely harmless. In fact, a cork infected by TCA looks immaculate to the eye.

Since the mid-1980s, cork has not been bleached in chlorine. Not that corkiness has therewith vanished from the wine lover's world. Chlorine is everywhere—in tap water, in various chemicals that protect wood, and on and on. Very small amounts can contaminate cork. Unbleached corks can also be attacked by invisible mildews *(Aspergillus, Penicillium)* present in the warehouses of cork dealers and in the cellars of many winemakers and vintners. In some cases, the substance causing the corkiness is not TCA.

Silicon as a Cork Substitute

With a steadily growing number of bottles filled with wine each year, cork, especially good cork, is now in

A champagne cork: The top is made of compressed cork chipboard, the bottom is a piece of natural cork.

Cork harvesting in Portugal: The bark is split open . . .

. . . and peeled off the trunk by hand.

A press cork, made of compressed cork chips: It lacks the elasticity of natural cork, but is cheaper.

corks are stamped out. So that the corks will be easier to push into the bottles, they are covered with a film of paraffin or silicon.

The Source of the Corky Smell

A wine that smells or tastes of cork is faulty. The usual cause is a substance called trichloranisol (TCA), the result of a reaction between the chlorine solution used to bleach corks and the phenols naturally contained in the cork itself. When it happens that TCA is then attacked by an invisible mildew, the offending smell is generated. The mildew in question, by the way, has nothing whatever to do with the mold that forms on the outside of the cork on a cellared bottle

short supply. For table wines and country wines as well as for those quality wines that do not require long storage, bottles are more and more frequently closed with a screw cap. The use of the silicon stopper is also on the increase. This is built much like a cork, but made of polymer foam with many airtight, elastic cells. When it is compressed in the bottle neck, it does not stretch downward or upward, at least in good-quality silicon stoppers. The retro-pressure (the term used for the force exerted by a compressed cork onto the neck of the bottle) of silicon stoppers is also close to that of a natural cork. Wine cannot escape with this type of stopper, but air can penetrate the bottle to some extent.

A silicon stopper: Air- and watertight, inert to wine, and elastic, this stopper is used for many simple consumer wines.

The Oxygen Problem

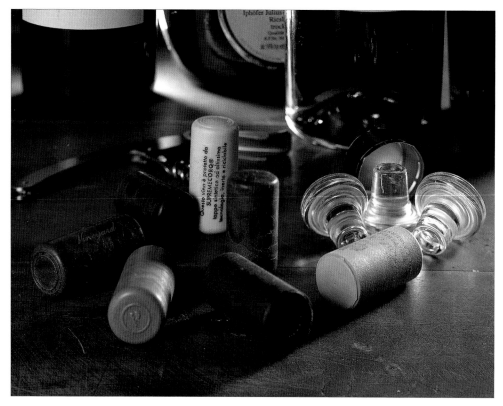

New stoppers: Silicone stoppers, screw caps, and glass stoppers.

Glass Stoppers

The glass stopper was invented by a German dentist. It resembles the glass stoppers used with whisky and cognac carafes. The only difference: the stopper seals by means of a plastic ring so that no oxygen can penetrate the bottle. To ensure that the glass stopper (brand name: Vino-Lok) stays tight, a tin or plastic cap is placed over it. Once that protector is removed, a slight pressure with the thumb suffices to loosen the stopper. There is no longer any need for a corkscrew. The stopper is hygienic, and there is no chance of corkiness. It is also aesthetic. Wine drinkers readily accept it even though it doesn't make the typical "pop" when removed from the bottle. The largest disadvantage to this stopper is that it has not been tested over long periods of time. It is not known whether the wine will stay fresh even after several years. The contact surface between the plastic ring and the liquid is minimal, to be sure, but whether it can withstand the wine's alcohol, acids, and phenols remains to be seen. For the moment the glass stopper is a viable alternative for wines meant to be consumed within three to four years.

Cork quality is declining owing in part to inadequate precautions on the part of the cork industry and cork suppliers and in part to improper hygiene at wineries. The search is on for alternative stoppers. But screwcaps and stoppers of polymer or glass also present problems.

According to recent estimates, cork failures now run between 5 and 10 percent, and they are rising. It is not always a TCA problem that ruins the drinker's enjoyment. More and more "masked" corkiness with unspecific moldy notes are appearing, supporting the suspicion that other substances besides chlorine are reacting with the phenols of the cork and are responsible for the malign changes in the wine. Scientists and wineries are therefore searching desperately for alternatives to natural cork, and they have come up with some. The only question is whether the new, alternative wine stoppers can fulfill the expectations placed on them. There is a lot to be said for alternative stoppers, but whether they can take the place of natural cork is an open question.

Synthetic Stoppers

Synthetic bottle stoppers are already widely used. They look like corks, but are made from elastic polymers that can be compressed and press tight against the glass wall of the neck of the bottle, so they are leak proof. Even so, air can be exchanged just as with natural corks. Synthetic stoppers can be pulled out of the neck of the bottle with a normal corkscrew. Wine drinkers can still enjoy the satisfying "pop" when they pull free. Most drinkers have accepted synthetic stoppers—only for simple wines, to be sure, which are drunk within two to three years. Longer-lived wines are only rarely sealed with synthetics. Extensive studies at the research institute in Geisenheim have confirmed the functionality and safety of synthetics, but they are not suited for longer storage. Wines with synthetic stoppers break down sulfuric acids faster than those sealed with natural cork. Moreover, it is impossible to test all the products on the market, and every manufacturer uses a different formula. Some use carbon-based polymers, or polyethylene; other synthetic stoppers are made of silicone. Some products reach the market without softening agents, some with. All of these affect the research results.

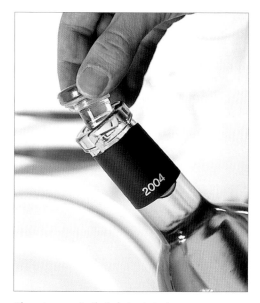

Glass stoppers: Aesthetic but untested.

Screw Caps

These stoppers have proved effective for bottles of spirits and fruit juices for years now, but the demands made on wine stoppers are different. Preliminary experiments with screw caps have shown that wine oxidizes faster. The traditional seals in screw caps are fine for foodstuffs, but they do not prevent the influx of oxygen. Not so the new ones: in them tinfoil is sandwiched into the seal. These Stelvin Caps, as they are called in trade, do not permit any exchange of gases. Since they are covered with a normal capsule, the purchaser cannot recognize them as screw caps. Many winemakers view the Stelvin Cap as the best and safest alternative to natural cork—for white wines and red, ordinary table wines, and high-priced ones. But Stelvin Caps also present problems. The wines cannot be reduced too much because unpleasant-smelling gases that

Screw cap: Carries hope for the future.

develop later in the bottle can no longer escape through the air-tight cap. They require less sulfur, since no oxygen can penetrate into the bottle. For this reason the extraction of tannin from red wines can be more moderate. The tannin, which instantly reacts with oxygen and binds it, no longer determines the durability of the wine. The results are fruitier aromas and a more elegant style. The stopper therefore alters the style of the wine.

No Air Left to Breathe

Wine does not require oxygen to mature in the bottle.

Oxygen is wine's greatest enemy. It rapidly causes it to lose its freshness. It expedites oxidation and hastens spoilage. In short, oxygen kills the wine. For this reason every winery sees to it that as little oxygen enters the bottle as possible. Modern bottling plants rinse the empty bottles with nitrogen before they are filled with wine then immediately seal them with a cork. In the gap between the fill level and the face of the cork (commonly thirty millimeters) there is therefore a lot of nitrogen and little oxygen. This oxygen is immediately bonded by the free sulfur in the wine and cannot cause any damage. Over the course of time, to be sure, tiny quantities of oxygen penetrate through the cork or between the outer wall of the cork and the glass. As long as there is still free sulfur, this oxygen is rendered harmless. But at some point the penetrating oxygen can no longer be bonded. It reacts with the wine and begins to alter it. At first the anthocyanins polymerize with the oxygen molecules, and the wine changes color. Red wine turns an orange brown, white wine a golden yellow. The hydrocarbon molecules, which carry most of the aroma, bond with the oxygen. Fruity aromas grow weaker, and aromas of wax, leather, tobacco, and licorice come to the fore. The composition of the fatty acids changes under the influence of oxygen. Furfural, an aldehyde that smells like almond oil, and eugenol, a monoterpen with the flavor of fresh clover, increase. The tannin in red wine reacts violently with oxygen. Before it can attack other substances, it is "devoured" by the tannin, which becomes weaker in the process. Oxygen also alters the microbacterial condition of the wine. Vinegar bacteria multiply. Once they exceed a certain level, the wine threatens to "turn." Finally, the oxygen even attacks the alcohol. Moldy-smelling aldehydes are produced—unmistakable signs of the wine's gradual demise. Are all of these processes negative? According to the old school, wine requires oxygen to mature, though only in small quantities. It is a matter of balance. Natural cork, which allows only minimal air to pass through it, thus represents the ideal bottle stopper to representatives of this school. With the development of the new air-tight screw caps, this notion has been put into question. Alan Hart, a scientist at the large Australian winery Penfolds, recently presented investigations which stated that a wine that is stored under

"Anaerobic" process of maturing in an airtight bottle.

"anaerobic" conditions (with an improved, gas-proof screw cap) also undergoes a process of maturing, only more slowly than wine sealed with a cork stopper. After seven years the screw-cap wine proved to be considerably fresher than the cork-stoppered wine. Hart's conclusion: "Oxygen is not a necessary element in the maturing of the wine." In other words, there is an "anaerobic" maturing process undergone even by wines provided with a screw top and, thus, an airtight seal.

Please Do Not Disturb

Jens Priewe's wine cellar: Plenty of every-day wines, many higher-quality wines, and some outstanding vintages.

1. Grüner Veltliner, Sauvignon Steiermark.
2. Alsatian Riesling, pinot blanc, Gewürz-traminer *vendange tardive.*
3. Chablis, white burgundy.
4. Diverse French white wines: Saumur, Savennières, Pouilly-Fumé, Tursan.
5. German Sekt, Italian spumante.
6. Muscadet, Fendant.
7. Young and mature California chardonnays.
8. Sicilian and Calabrian white wines.
9. Mature German Rieslings.
10. German Beerenauslesen, ice wines.
11. Older, white Graves, Ygrec, Australian dry sémillon.
12. Old Riesling Auslesen.
13. White burgundies: Chassagne-Montrachet, Bienvenue-Bâtard-Montrachet, Corton-Charlemagne, Meursault.
14. Wachau Riesling Smaragd.
15. German dry Riesling Spätlesen.
16. Coteaux d'Aix-en-Provence, Côtes-de-Roussillon, Cahors.
17. Cornas, Côte Rôtie, Hermitage.
18. Old red burgundies: Chambertin, Corton, Chambolle-Musigny, Romanée-Saint-Vivant.
19. Diverse South African and New Zealand wines: pinotage, chardonnay, sauvignon.
20. Lucky finds: 1932 marsala, Canadian ice wine, Heitz Fay Vineyard 1974.
21. Old Barolo, Barbaresco.
22. Mostly bordeaux, not yet ready to drink.
23. Sauternes, some in half bottles.
24. Diverse sweet wines: Vin Santo, Banyuls, Tokay, Acininobili, Noble Rot No . . .
25. Lucky finds: Argentinian malbec, New Zealand pinot noir, Hungarian Gewürz-traminer.
26. Vintage port, white port, oloroso sherry.
27. Rioja, Ribera del Duero, Priorato.
28. California cabernet sauvignon, Oregon pinot noir.
29. Minimax thermometer, hydrometer.
30. Bordeaux, almost ready to drink.
31. Young Barolo, Barbaresco.
32. Chianto Classico, Riserva.
33. Brunello di Montalcino.
34. Red burgundies: Gevrey Chambertin, Vosne-Romanée, Mercurey.
35. Australian cabernet sauvignon, shiraz.
36. Older "Super Tuscans" in magnum bottles.
37. Magnums of burgundy and Barolo.
38. Young "Super Tuscans" in magnum bottles.
39. Bordeaux in double magnums.
40. Champagne, spumante, various white wines in magnums.

"I am, like so many other people today, a man of eclectic tastes in wine. In the last twenty years, I have acquired numerous small lots of various wines; seldom have I bought large quantities of any one wine. Thus I am able to choose between several wines at any one time, according to my current mood or the taste of the moment.

"My cellar is rather simple: wooden shelves supported by brick columns. On the wall I have a hydrometer and a minimum-maximum thermometer. I do not keep a cel-lar book. I generally know what my shelves hold. And I would not like to give up the sudden pleasure of discovering a wine I did not know I had in my collection."

serve wine only when they have guests. Then there is the faction that drinks quite a lot but feels that anything costing more than five dollars a bottle is only for snobs. Finally, there are people who own only priceless vintages, which they are so in awe of that they wouldn't dream of drinking one. Gazing at the labels gives these collectors all the buzz they need. All these people have one thing in common: they need space in which to store their wine.

Cellar or climate chest?
The size and type of a wine cellar should reflect a person's drinking habits. The person who collects wines but drinks little needs a large cellar, but the person who consumes no more than 100 bottles a year could get by with a cellar niche. But take care: wine should not be stored in a room where there are bicycles, rubber tires, paints, an oil tank, or strong-smelling foodstuffs. If there is no suitable space, it pays to buy a climate chest (see page 231).

Storeroom size
Those who drink a bottle of wine a day will find a climate chest barely adequate–unless, that is, they buy their wines in small batches. As a rule they will need a storeroom, but how big? The size depends not so much on the quantity of wine consumed as on whether they want to age their wine or drink it young. Those who enjoy young wines and prefer not to wait will have a higher turnover in their cellar and require less shelf space. Patient wine lovers who buy bottles they have no intention of opening for years will need the corresponding extra storage space. With cleverly arranged shelving, it is possible to accommodate up to 500 bottles in less than twenty-one square feet.

Getting the right mix
A well-appointed cellar has a workable mix of red and white wines, young wines and old ones, of varied provenance and characteristics. It should also have some port, some sherry, some nobly sweet specialities, and some sparkling wines–at least in small quantities. Larger bottles should also be part of a wine collection. On the other hand, wine drinkers who tend to be pack rats need to remember that every year brings a new vintage.

To achieve ideal conditions, one has to build a wine cellar deep underground. Very few of us can afford to do this. Nor is it necessary, since somewhat less than ideal storage facilities will do the job–to let the wine rest peacefully until it is mature–very nicely. And what does *mature* mean? An estimated 80 percent of all wine today is consumed within the first two years. Special wine cellars are therefore needed only for a small percentage of those wines to be stored for five or ten years or more.

How much wine do you need?
People's wine consumption varies. Some wine drinkers consume a bottle a day, others that amount at most over a weekend. Still others

Alternatives to the Classic Wine Cellar

Under the proper storage conditions a long-lived wine can take years, even decades, to fully mature.

Many wines, though not all, need time to develop. For that reason it is worthwhile to lay in a smaller or larger supply of wines and store them for five or ten years or even longer. The cellar is not necessarily the best place for these; a climate cell or a climate chest does just as well—if not better.

What to aim for

Wine ages best at a constant temperature of around 54°F (12°C). The bottles need to lie in a place that is free of vibrations and as dark as possible. Light triggers chemical reactions in wine, especially white wine. Smells can also have a negative effect on wine stored for a long time, which is why a kitchen cupboard or a corner of the garage is unsuitable for storing wine. The space should not be too dry. A humidity level of 80 percent is ideal. For comparison's sake, the humidity in the average home is around 60 percent. Cellar rooms with heating ducts passing through them have similarly low humidity levels. In such spaces corks

dry out and loosen, allowing the wine in the bottle to evaporate more quickly and the oxygen that replaces it to oxidize what is left. Humidity of more than 80 percent does no damage to corks, but it encourages the formation of mildew on labels. This has no effect on the wine's taste, of course, but it does reduce the resale value of a wine bought as an investment.

Optimizing the wine cellar

Unfortunately, finding the ideal wine cellar is extremely difficult. Thus it comes down to providing the best storage conditions you can in the space available to you. For example, you can rest your shelving units on a rubber base to minimize vibrations. You can easily black out cellar windows by either covering them with metal foil or bricking them up. You should reclose wooden cases after removing a bottle so that the remaining bottles continue to lie in the dark. Cardboard boxes are not as good for storing wine; the cardboard absorbs any moisture in the air, and damp car-

Climate chest: The interior is divided into various zones. At the top it stays at 64°F (18°C) for red wines; at the bottom at 46°F (8°C) for white and sparkling wines. Humidity can also be regulated.

Climate cells are spaces insulated from heat and light that are closed with special climate-control doors. They can be set up in a cellar or in some other room in the house.

tons are likely to cave in if stacked, leaving you with broken bottles. A humidifier is a good idea if the cellar is too dry, but it is often sufficient to keep a bucket of water in the space.

Regulating the temperature

The most important requirement for storing wine is a constant temperature. It does not really matter whether this is 46°F (8°C), 54°F (12°C), or 61°F (16°C). A wine will mature with no problems, even over a longer period, at any of these temperatures. Variations in temperature, for example between winter and summer, are another matter. If the cellar is only 46°F (8°C) in winter but reaches 61°F (16°C) in summer, the wine never comes to rest. In summer it expands, in winter it contracts. Fluctuations of 8°F (4°C) over the course of a year are bearable. These are found even in the best cellars in Bordeaux, where wines lie undisturbed for decades, or even more than a century.

Climate chests

Ideal conditions are found only in climate-controlled surroundings such as those provided by a climate chest for wine. A climate chest differs from an ordinary refrigerator in that the temperature can be set to range from 42°F (6°C) to 64°F (18°C); the lower temperature is maintained in compartments for sparkling wine, the higher one in those set aside for red wines. These temperatures will vary by only one degree (0.5°C). In a normal refrigerator the temperature constantly fluctuates by 4°F (2°C) or more—too much for long-term wine storage. The humidity is automatically regulated, and vibration is minimized. The only disadvantages: a climate chest rarely holds more than 120 bottles, and it costs a lot of money.

Climate cells

If you want to store more than 120 bottles, you might consider installing a climate compartment, or cell—a sealed room closed with a climate-control door—wherever there is space. The door unit functions much like a climate chest. It creates an ideal climate inside the cell. The smallest prefabricated cells require a mere 21 square feet and can hold some 500 bottles. If you move, you simply dismantle the cell and reinstall it in your new house or apartment. If you have a sealed room in your cellar, all you need is a climate-control door to maintain a constant temperature in the space. Any heat sources in the space must be insulated beforehand, of course.

Factors That Determine a Wine's Durability

Wine Type: Tannin-rich red wines and acidic white wines generally have greater longevity than simple fruity wines low in acid.

Provenance: Wines from specific regions can improve in the bottle over long periods of time: top red wines from the Rhône, from Bordeaux, from the *grand cru* vineyards of Burgundy, from the Ribera del Duero and Rioja in Spain, from Barolo and Barbaresco in the Piedmont, and from prime vineyards in Tuscany. Especially long-lived white wines are the best white burgundies, Rieslings from Germany, Gewürztraminer and pinot gris from Alsace, top-quality Grüner Veltliner from Austria, and nobly sweet wines from all over the world.

Vinification: Red wines that fermented for a longer period on their skins and wines that have been aged in small oak casks can continue to improve, as a rule, longer than the same wines without these advantages.

Producer: Certain producers are known for deliberately producing long-lived wines: the Leroy Winery in Burgundy, for example; in Bordeaux, some of the great Grand Cru Classé; in the Ribera del Duero, the Bodegas Vega Sicilia; the Ridge Winery in Santa Cruz; and Bruno Glacosa in the Piedmont.

Grape variety: Only a few of the world's vines are capable of producing long-lived wines—but by no means are all wines from these varieties capable of great longevity.

Vintage: A wine from a small vintage is generally ready to drink earlier than the same wine from a banner year.

Cork: A tight cork with few lenticells (the dark, woody rills within the cork) protects the wine during long aging.

Sulfur: Every wine is sulfured before bottling. In wines intended to age for a long time, it is important that the dosage of free sulfur be large enough. It should bind the oxygen in the bottle and any that seeps in later. Too much free sulfur prevents a wine from developing, and renders it unpalatable.

Grand Cru with Dividends

The 50 Blue Chips of Wine

France
Château Mouton-Rothschild
Château Lafite-Rothschild
Château Latour
Château Margaux
Château Haut-Brion
Château d'Yquem
Château Ausone
Château Cheval Blanc
Château Léoville-Las-Cases
Château Pichon Lalande
Château la Mission Haut-Brion
Château Ducru-Beaucaillou
Pétrus
Château le Pin
Château l'Evangile
Château l'Eglise-Clinet
Château Lafleur
Romanée Conti/Dom.Rom.-Conti
La Tâche/Dom.Rom-Conti
Montrachet/Dom.Rom.-Conti
Montrachet/Comtes Lafon
Musigny/Comte de Vogue
Clos de Vougeot/Domaine Leroy
Richebourg/Méo-Camuzet
Châteauneuf-du-Pape/Rayas
Hermitage La Chapelle/Jaboulet
Hermitage/Jean-Louis Chave
Cornas/Auguste Clape
Côte Rôtie La Mouline/Guigal
Montus Cuvée Prestige/Brumont
Champagne Clos du Mesnil/
Krug
Champagne Grand Cru/Sélosse
Champagne Vielles Vignes/
Bollinger
Champagne Cuvée S/Salon
Champagne Cristal/Roederer

Spain
Unico/Vega Sicilia
Pesquera Res. Janus/
A. Fernandez

Portugal
Vintage Porto/Taylor's

Italy
Sassicaia/Tenuta San Guido
Ornellaia/ Tenuta dell'Ornellaia
Solaia/Marchesi Antinori
Sori San Lorenzo/Gaja
Barolo Ris. Monfortino/
G. Conterno

Australia
Grange/Penfolds
Hill of Grace Shiraz/Henschke

California
Opus One/Robert Mondavi
Dominus/Christian Moueix

Austria
Grüner Veltliner Smaragd M/
F. X. Pichler
Grande Cuvée/Alois Kracher

Germany
Riesling Eiswein/Egon Müller

Wine auctions are an important marketplace for the trade of premium wines.

Enjoyment has a value. And that value rises as more people clamor for the particular enjoyment. The wines of the world are therefore not only enjoyed, they are collected for the profit derived from their increasing value. The best of them are like blue-chip stocks that can earn their owners impressive gains—assuming that the investors know what they are doing.

Wine prices have risen dramatically in the last twenty years, prices of long-lived premier wines especially. This increase in value has definitely exceeded the yield from fixed-interest bonds, and certain top vintages have outperformed the stock of many a successful corporation. In view of these trends, it is no wonder that a number of wines have become sought after by speculators, attracting the interest of people who have no intention of drinking them. To such people wines are an investment they hold on to for a time, then dispose of to take the profit. So it happens that today some of the world's best wines are traded on the stock market like blue-chip investments.

Classic Bordeaux

The classic wine to invest in is Bordeaux. It is prized like no other wine in the world. Worldwide demand for Pétrus, Château Mouton-Rothschild, and other first-class vintages has often caused their prices to increase by up to 100 percent in the first year after their release. It is not uncommon for the best of the second-tier wines, such as Château Léoville-Las-Cases and Château Pichon Longueville de Lalande, to rise in value by 50 percent. It was only in the late 1990s that the boom subsided somewhat. The starting prices had become so high that there was scarcely any room for gains.

Wine Futures

The original sale of young Bordeaux wines is done by subscription *en primeur* through dealers. That means that investors acquire the wine while it is still lying in the barrel at the château. To be precise, they buy only vouchers against later delivery, for the châteaux only release their wines after three years. For his early payment and blind trust in the wine's quality, the buyer enjoys a favorable price. In the language of the stock market, such vouchers are called "futures," and they themselves are traded. Their value may have doubled by the time the wine is released, but it can also fall, of course, if the wine or the vintage fails to meet expectations. In any case, it is not uncommon for wines to have changed hands a number of times even before they are placed on the market.

Vintage Instead of Château

According to an old wine dealer's rule, it is Bordeaux's vintages that are sold, not its wines. In other words, it is the stature of the given year that essentially determines the wine's future value. Nineteen-eighty-two, 1986, and 1990 were vintages that made money for wine investors who bought early. The quality was excellent, and the châteaux's opening prices were relatively low. Within a year they rose almost 100 percent. In the 1990s the price of select 1982 wines rose by nearly 1,000 percent. But it can also go the

other way. The 1995 and 1996 vintages, even those from the famous châteaux, brought little pleasure to investors. Prices for many of them are still at their relatively high starting level. Investors who bought the 1997 early on even lost money; the vintage's quality was overrated, and prices have dropped accordingly. To be sure, certain châteaux buck the trend by offering good quality even in poor years. The goal of the investor is to sniff these out from the enormous number of wines available.

Relying on the Experts

Early buyers of Bordeaux rarely taste the wines themselves, but rely on expert opinion. In the first weeks of April in the year following the harvest, the Bordelais châteaux open their doors and offer a preliminary sampling of their young, still unfinished wines to dealers and critics whose judgment will determine the price of the wine when it is released. The best-known and most influential of these wine critics is the American Robert Parker. A wine to which he accords 99 or 100 points can double its price in a day. A rating of less than 85 points amounts to a virtual trashing—at least among classified Bordeaux. In addition to Parker, who publishes his own newsletter on wine, the *Wine Advocate*, there are other respected tasters whose judgments can be read in the professional wine journals. For *en primeur* buyers these judgments are important.

The Rise of Cult Wines

The last ten years have nevertheless shown that top wines from other regions also have speculative potential if they fill at least three criteria: they must enjoy a great reputation, they must be rare, and they must be long-lived. With wines that mature quickly, there is no chance to make a profit. Anyone who looks closely recognizes that these criteria are met by only a tiny percentage of the wines produced worldwide, namely the so-called cult wines. The majority of these come from New World countries. In California and Australia, especially, wines are now being produced that are in no way inferior to the great vintages of Europe, and they are sought after accordingly. But to make money on them requires more than a sensitive tongue. You need current information about the wine market and the possibility of getting your hands on the given vintage. In Europe, too, new cult wines appear all the time: the great red wines of Tuscany and the Piedmont, for example, as well as a few prestigious Spaniards. And even in Bordeaux there are unclassified wines that people clamor for even more than the classified ones (see box).

Buying and Selling

The most important salesrooms for high-priced wines—whether classics or cult wines—are auction houses. Roughly 90 percent of the trading in long-lived top wines is accomplished in the wine auction houses of Christie's and Sotheby's in London and their branches in America, Asia, and Australia. There are also smaller auction houses, such as Butterfields (San Francisco), Wermuth (Zurich), or Koppe & Partner (Bremen). Originally established to offer mature wines to connoisseurs, these firms now hammer down more and more young wines that are being disposed of by investors eager to take a profit. Investors need to recognize, of course, that auction houses charge a 10 percent premium (at some houses, 15 percent) above the hammer price—not to mention the (modest) lot fee, the sales tax, freight costs, and transportation insurance. At the sale there is also a delivery fee ranging between 10 and 15 percent. All of these extras can reduce your profit considerably. This is why only wines with high speculative potential make sense as investment. Chances of a sale are better with larger bottles and unopened wooden cases. Damaged labels are bound to drag down the price.

The World's 50 Most Sought-After Cult Wines

France
La Tâche/Dom.Rom.-Conti
Montrachet/Dom.Rom.-Conti
La Mondotte/Comtes Neipperg
Valandraud/Jean-Luc Thunevin
La Gomerie/G. et D. Bécot
California
Cab. S./Screaming Eagle
Cab. S./Bryant Family
Cab. S. Eisele Vyd/Araujo
Cab. S. Herb Lamb Vyd/Colgin
Cab. S. Volcanic Hill/Diamond Creek
Maya/Dalla Valle
Harlan Estate
Cab. S./Grace Family
Cab. S. Hillside Select/Shafer
Cab. S. Howell Mountain/Dunn
Cab. S. Spec. Selection/Caymus
Cab. S. Montebello/Ridge
Pinot Noir/Marcassin
Australia
Astralis Shiraz/Clarendon Hills
Balmoral Shiraz/Rosemount
Cab. S. BIN 707/Penfolds
Cab. S./Greenock Creek
Cab. S. Merlot/Cullen
Mount Edelstone/Henschke
Odyssey Shiraz/Katnook Estate
Run Rig Shiraz/Torbreck
Shiraz Hanish/Veritas
Shiraz Reserve/Fox Creek
Shiraz Reserve/Noon
Shiraz/Turkey Flat
Spartacus Shiraz/Punter's Corner
Terra Rossa First Growth/Parker
South Africa
Cab. S. Peter /Barlow/Rustenberg
Cab. S./Thelema Mountain
Merlot/Veenwouden
Shiraz/Boekenhoutskloof
Vergelegen
Chile
Almaviva
Montes Alpha M/Montes
Seña
Italy
Barbera d'Asti Quorum/Hastae
Masseto/Ornellaia
Merlot Vigna l'Apparita/Ama
Montiano/Falesco
Paleo/Le Macchiole
Redigaffi/Tua Rita
Rubino/Palazzola
Tenuta di Trinoro
Vigna Larigi/Elio Altare
Villa Fidelia/Sportoletti
Spain
L'Ermità/Alvaro Palacios
Pingus/Dominio de Pingus

Legislating Quality

Quality wines supposedly represent the apex of the quality pyramid, but with many of them, this is in fact not the case.

cum of comparability with respect to types and qualities, each wine region has set more or less precise restrictions on its production. Table wines represent the lower level of wine production. Only the most minimal requirements are made of their origin and production standards. A large amount of table wine is never bottled but instead sold by the barrel. Later it may be marketed by the cask, in wicker-covered demijohns, in cartons, or in wineskins.

Quality Wines

Quality wines are always tied to a given wine region. The grapes have to originate in a clearly defined district. For this reason, many labels bear the code VQPRD, *vin de qualité produit dans les régions déterminées,* that is, quality wine of specified areas of origin. Within the EU, certain general rules apply to quality wines:

- As a rule, the minimum alcohol content of wines must be at least 8.5 percent.
- In most wine regions, the maximum level of chaptalization is set at 2.5 percent.
- Deacidification is permitted as well as acidification, though not simultaneously with chaptalization.
- Wine additives (e.g., sulfur, bentonite) are regulated.
- Volatile acids present in a wine may not exceed 1.2 grams per liter.
- Quality wines may not be blended with wines from outside the European Union.

Over and above these general rules, regulations are promulgated by each region for the production of its own wines. Some of the subjects covered by these local regulations include:

- Admitted grape varieties
- Maximum grape yields per hectare
- Minimum alcohol levels
- Minimum acidity levels
- Minimum maturation periods
- Earliest permitted marketing times

The purpose of wine laws is to give the buyer some assurances concerning the provenance of the wine as well as a minimal quality guarantee. In fact, wine laws are confusing, at least in Europe. Their logic is clear only to administrators and statisticians.

The countries of the European Union have agreed to categorize wines into two major groups: table wines and quality wines. Only wines from outstanding growing areas within each country should be included in the quality wine class. So as to guarantee some modi-

Italy and Spain have subdivided their quality wines into categories subject to further controls and qualifications. France and other wine nations have not created any subcategories.

Further Distinctions

In Germany and Austria, quality wines are further subdivided into quality wines from designated regions and wines with a *Prädikat*, or "distinction." This basic distinction is based purely on must weight (see page 42). The law also disallows increasing the alcohol content of *Prädikat* wines by chaptalization.

In France and Italy, the range of quality wines has been extended in a downward direction by the creation of a new category. In France it is called VDQS *(vin délimitée de qualité supérieur).* In Italy the same intermediate class is designated IGT *(indicazione geografica tipica).* There is no guarantee that wines in this category are either of higher quality than table and country wines, or lower than quality wines.

Table Wines

In the wine hierarchy of the EU, table wines are on the lowest rung and subject to the least stringent requirements. They either come from the mass-production areas of France, Italy, and Spain, are grown in those areas of Germany and Austria less well suited to viticulture, or actually come from vineyards outside any formal wine region. The following regulations apply to table wines:

- They can originate from any of the wine regions of the EU.
- Grape yield in the vineyard is completely unrestricted.
- Minimum must weight is set at 50° Oechsle.
- Minimum acidity is set at 4.5 grams per liter.
- Chaptalization is permitted.
- Any of the grape varieties within the EU are permitted.
- Blending of wines from any EU countries is permitted.
- Neither vintage nor grape varieties need be mentioned on the label.

Country Wines

About 65 percent of all the wine produced within the EU is designated table wine. A large portion of it cannot be sold; annually about one quarter of total production is taken off the market to be distilled into industrial alcohol.

In order to offer more marketable table wines, in 1973 the EU created an intermediate class, the country wines. These were intended to be the elite table wines. They come from large designated wine regions, countries, or *départements.* Their grape varieties are clearly defined, they must contain at least .5 percent more alcohol than table wines, and they have to be finished dry. They are intended to be delicious, tasty, reasonable everyday wines. France's country wine production now represents 20 percent of the total, but in other countries the concept has not caught on.

The Newer Wine Countries

Outside of Europe, fewer regulations govern wine production. Although since 1983 the United States has defined over a hundred regions of origin called American Viticultural Areas (AVA), there are no legal regulations about production within these regions. For example, there are no restrictions on the yield per acre of vineyard. The only categories that exist are table wines (up to 15.9 percent alcohol), dessert wines (from 16 percent up), and sparkling wines. There are some regulations concerning labeling: 85 percent of the wine must be of the variety given on the label. The same level is required in Australia, while in South Africa and Chile only 75 percent has to be of the stated variety. There is no restriction on the quantity of grapes harvested. Chaptalization is forbidden in all of these countries except New Zealand, but acidification is allowed.

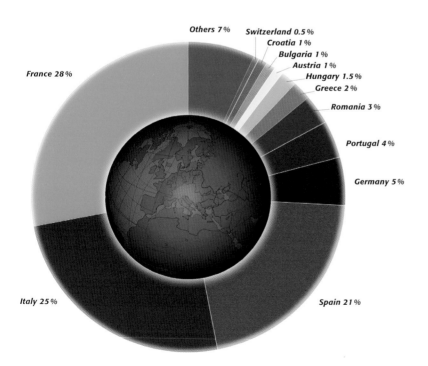

Each wine-producing country's proportion of Europe's total output

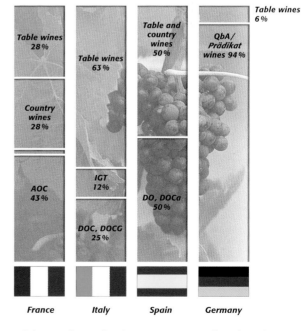

Italy has very few quality wines, Germany practically nothing else.

How Much Wine Can a Person Take?

Wine, a traditional foodstuff.

Wine—A Matter of How Much

The amount of wine we can drink without worrying varies from person to person. Physical constitution, weight, gender, and the training of a person's organs all play a part in setting our limits.

On the average, the male liver can process 30 percent more alcohol than the female. However, this general statistic is qualified by the age and health of a wine drinker. The American medical establishment speaks cautiously of one or two glasses of wine per day as being certain to promote health in an average male of medium weight. In this discussion, a glass contains .1 liter of wine.

One or Two Glasses per Day?

The recommendations of the British Medical Association are also very conservative. They speak of weekly rations: 21 units for men, 14 units for women, where a unit corresponds to 8 grams of alcohol (a .75-liter bottle of wine with an alcoholic strength of 12 percent contains about 70 grams of alcohol). This means that men can drink 2.5 bottles and women 1.5 bottles of wine over a week without worrying; this amount will in fact promote better health. The daily amount recommended in Britain then is one and a half glasses (of .1 liter) for women and two and a half glasses of the same size for men. Doctors everywhere agree that during pregnancy women should abstain from alcohol.

Wine consists of about 85 percent water and 12 percent alcohol. It is mostly its alcohol content that has given wine a questionable reputation. Yet for the most part the medical establishment agrees that moderate wine consumption is healthier than abstinence. This is not in little measure due to the remaining 3 percent of the ingredients in wine.

For centuries, wine was considered a foodstuff, and in many parts of the world it continues to be regarded as daily fare. It is easily forgotten in all the talk about potential alcoholism that wine has a contribution to make to both our nourishment and to our health. On the one hand, wine contributes a lot of calories to a meal. On the other hand, glycerin and acids, the two qualitatively most significant components of wine beside water and alcohol, invigorate the metabolism and the immune system. Wine also contains vitamins and minerals, though in amounts so small as to represent a minimal percentage of our daily requirements. Other positive effects on our health can only be guessed at, among these the preventative powers of wine with respect to rheumatism and osteoporosis. The most important scientific discovery of the last few years is the positive connection between wine consumption and a lower risk of heart failure. This led to the concept of the "French Paradox."

The French Paradox

On November 17, 1991, CBS dedicated its regular news program *60 Minutes* to an unexpected subject: red wine. The moderator, Morley Safer, raised a glass filled with red wine and declared that in its content may lie the explanation for the low rate of coronary infarctions that France enjoys. Then he went on to explain what he called the French Paradox, namely that the French, despite eating a lot of such dangerous things as butter, cheese, fois gras, and cream sauces, had a statistically lower rate of heart infarctions than the United States or any other western nation. His explanation: the daily glass of red wine, which every French person enjoyed. The hour-long program profoundly affected North American attitudes toward drinking alcohol, a substance that had previously been regarded by many people as an unmitigated evil, to be approached with great caution. The media explored the theme in the months following, and the consumption of red wine went up by 39 percent in 1992, whereas it had been falling by almost 5 percent a year.

Red Wine against Cholesterol

In the intervening years, scientific studies in England, the United States, France, and Denmark did establish a connection between red wine consumption and a

lessened risk of coronary decease. It seems that the group of phenols present in red wine is chiefly responsible. Included in this group, among about one hundred other substances, is tannin. Just as in wine, phenolics have an antioxidant effect in the blood, preventing the oxidation of the "malign" LDL lipoproteins, also known as cholesterine. A high cholesterine level in the blood can lead to a slow narrowing of the arteries near the heart; this can in turn lead to arteriosclerosis and a heart attack. Laboratory tests have shown that red wine, more even than alcohol, has a tendency to thin the blood. This is another way in which it aids health, that is, by reducing the risk of blood clots.

Red wine has more phenols than white wine or rosé.

Negative Effects of Drinking Wine

Whether drinking wine will have a positive or negative effect depends entirely on the amounts consumed. Drinking a lot of wine in a short time will certainly damage the body. Even with moderate but regular consumption of wine it is necessary to have regular checkups, in order to monitor the liver, the nervous system, the digestive system, and other organs. Among the negative side effects of drinking wine are:

Drunkenness: One bottle of wine with a 12 percent alcohol level contains 70 grams of pure alcohol (ethyl alcohol). The human liver, which bears 90 percent of the responsibility for processing alcohol, can handle a maximum of 10 grams per hour. Until the liver is able to process it, any remaining, excess alcohol circulates in the bloodstream as acetaldehyde, an intermediary product in the decomposition of alcohol. The result is an impaired capacity to react and concomitant damage to the nervous system. Sparkling wines speed up the process of alcohol absorption.

Enlargement of the liver: If the liver and other tissues—such as muscles—are unable to process all the alcohol, the intermediary products—acetaldehyde and acetate—are converted to fat. The person

Migraines: Headaches with nausea can occur with some people even after only moderate wine intake, especially of red wines. The reason is the reaction of some people's nerve cells to the phenols, of which there are more in red wine.

Allergies: Wine can in a few cases cause itchy skin and breathing difficulties. Usually the cause is a reaction to the sulfurous acids that are present to a small extent in all wines as preservatives. Histamines, protein components that occur in some but not all red wines, can aggravate allergies. Although they occur in minute amounts, people who react to them must switch to other wines.

Happy France: Lots of butter, cream, animal fats—and yet protection against heart damage with the daily glass of red wine.

develops a so-called fatty liver. In the advanced stage of this enlargement, the functioning of the liver and of the entire metabolism is seriously impaired.

Headaches: These are usually the result of excessive alcohol intake. It is not so much the pure alcohol but the less pure alcohols, that is the methyl alcohols (fusels), which are a part of all wines, that cause the headaches and the circulation problems known as a hangover. The proportion of methyl alcohol in wine is less than 1 percent. It is higher in red than in white wines.

Stomach problems: People with a sensitive stomach may find that wine irritates their stomach lining. This would be especially true of white wines, which tend to have a higher acid content than red wines. Excess stomach acids lead to a feeling of fullness, loss of appetite, and heartburn.

Excessive calorie intake: A bottle of wine (12 percent alcohol) contains almost 500 calories. With each gram of residual sugar, 12 calories are added. Wine is thus very nourishing. What with its ability to stimulate the appetite, it can certainly induce wine drinkers to consume more calories than intended.

How Lipoproteins Work

The level of fat in the blood is largely a matter of the genetic makeup of each person, but cholesterol levels are also affected by diet. The more fat we take in, the fattier our blood will become. High-fat diets increase the production of LDL in the blood. LDL, or low-density lipoprotein, builds a permanent, waxy layer along the inside walls of the arteries, narrowing the passage of the blood. Even worse is LDL's tendency to combine with oxygen. It takes the oxygen out of the blood, possibly reducing the oxygen supply to the heart muscle. This process increases the risk of heart attack. Until recently, vitamin E and beta-carotene were considered the best protection against the activities of LDL because of their antioxidant properties. Yet there are three phenols—all three occurring in red wine, more abundantly in tannin-rich red wines—that are more effective than vitamin E and beta-carotene:

• Quercetin (also present in onions and apples)

• Catechin (present in all wine grapes in very large amounts)

• Resveratrol (formed in grapes that are attacked by fungi).

These three phenols prevent the oxidation of LDL. More important still, they promote very effectively the formation of the useful HDL (high-density lipoprotein). A high HDL level is the best protection against fatty blood; at least, this is the conclusion to be drawn from a study done in 1990 in France. Of three experimental groups, the first received only diluted, pure alcohol, the second only white wine, and the third only red wine. The red-wine group showed the highest rise in HDL and the greatest drop in LDL.

Aftertaste: The taste of a wine after it is swallowed. Also called the finish.

Alcoholic: A wine that tastes of alcohol; hot, heavy.

Allier oak: A fine-pored oak from the French *département* of the same name. It is a preferred oak for building *barriques*, and because of its sweet flavor it is often used for maturing chardonnay wines.

Ampelography: The science of the grapevine.

Annata: Italian for "vintage." Also: a young wine that is released after a few months.

AOC or *appellation d'origine contrôllée:* The highest quality classification for French wines.

Assemblage: A French term for the blending of wines from different lots or barrels or of wines with the same origin but from different grape varieties.

Assorted batch: A wine in which several grape varieties are included at the fermentation stage.

Astringent: Referring to taste, a rasping, dry quality, a puckering of the tongue, common in young, tannin-rich red wines.

Ausbruch: A wine from Rust, on the Neusiedlersee in Austria, made of overripe or botrytized selected harvest grapes. The required must weight is at least 138° Oechsle.

Auslese: Selected harvest, a high German designation *(Prädikat).* It is usually applied to sweet or nobly sweet wines, but may be used for high-grade dry wines. Required must weight: 90° to 100° Oechsle.

Barrique: A wooden barrel of 225-liter capacity, once used only for bordeaux wines but now popular all over the world.

Bâtonnage: Stirring up the yeast in the barrel with a pole or baton. This method, originated in Burgundy, intensifies flavors in wines that are barrel-fermented.

Blanc de blancs: A sparkling wine fermented from only white grapes.

Blanc de noirs: A sparkling wine fermented from only red grapes.

Blending: Mixing of different lots of wines, i.e., from different varieties or from different regions, into a new wine.

Botrytis cinerea: Noble rot, a desirable mold for sauternes and select harvest and dry select harvest wines.

"Bottling sickness": A term that might be applied to a recently bottled wine that still suffers from a disturbance of its aroma due to the bottling process.

Brick red: A red wine with an orange-red color, which indicates that it has reached its highest point of perfection, or may even have passed it.

Cabbagey: The obtrusive aroma given off by immature cabernet franc, cabernet sauvignon, and merlot wines.

Cantina: Italian for cellar or winery.

Cava: A Spanish sparkling wine from the Penedès region.

Cave: French for cellar and also for winery.

Chai: A Bordeaux term for a barrel cellar at ground level.

Champagne method: Bottle fermentation used in Champagne.

Chaptalization: *See* Enrichment.

Character: A wine with character stands on its own and does not follow fashions.

Charmat method: A method of making sparkling wines without using bottle fermentation. Instead, the second fermentation of the wine takes place in large, pressurized stainless steel tanks.

Claret: A term used in England for bordeaux wines in general.

Clone: Derived from the Greek word for *branch,* the term refers to a grapevine that was propagated by rooting a shoot from a selected plant.

Clos: A good-quality, enclosed vineyard. A term used in Burgundy, where *clos* are often surrounded by walls.

Closed: A young wine, whose greatness is still undeveloped.

Complete fermentation: Dry as dust, without any residual sugar at all.

Cooler: A light wine. This is a North American term.

Crémant: A sparkling wine from some region in France other than Champagne, e.g., Alsace, Loire, Burgundy. The amount of carbon dioxide is lower than in Champagne by two or three atmospheres.

Cru: An especially great vineyard location.

Cuvée: 1. A high-value must from the first pressing in Champagne. 2. The *assemblage* of various Champagne base wines before bottle fermentation.

Cuvier: French for a fermentation cellar.

Decanting: Transferring the wine from bottle to carafe by slow pouring.

Designation of origin: All European quality wines are legally defined by origin.

Diabetic wines: A dry wine with at most 4 grams residual sugar per liter.

Domaine: A French wine estate.

Early frost: A frost at the end of October or the beginning of November may be desirable for the chance it offers of pressing ice wine.

Edelzwicker: An Alsatian name for wines fermented from various different grape varieties.

Enrichment: Adding sugar to the grape must to achieve a higher alcohol content in the wine. Also called chaptalization.

Estate bottled: A wine that was bottled on the wine estate where the grapes were grown and fermented.

Euro-dry: Residual sugar in a Euro-dry wine can be anywhere up to 9 grams, according the EU formula of "acidity plus two." Thus a wine with 6 grams of acidity may be designated dry if it contains 8 grams of residual sugar.

Extract sweetness: Wines rich in extracts are often experienced as sweet even if they are completely fermented, that is, bone dry. The cause for this is their high glycerin content. Glycerin is an alcohol compound and an important part of extract.

Fattoria: Italian for wine estate.

Finesse: French for delicacy.

Fortified wines: Dessert wines with an alcoholic strength of at least 15 percent.

Free-flow must: The most valuable part of the grape must, which flows freely from the press after the first, gentle pressing of the grapes.

Full-bodied: A heavy wine, rich in alcohol and in extracts.

Fumé Blanc: A California sauvignon blanc wine, aged in wood.

Grain Nobles: High-quality Alsatian wines made of select-harvest and dry-select harvest grapes. Their Oechsle levels are at least 110°, and they can only be made of Riesling, muscat, Gewürztraminer, and pinot gris grapes.

Grape juice: One kilo of grapes yields about 0.7 liters of juice, also called must.

Green: A term applied to wines with unripe acids.

Hard: A term applied to wines with unripe tannins.

Heuriger: 1. In Austria: a wine pub attached to a wine estate. 2. Wine of the most recent vintage.

IGT: *Indicazione geografica tipica,* a newish wine term in Italy corresponding to the French VDQS wines. Many of the high-class wines formerly classified as *vini da tavola* are now included in this category.

Integrated Pest Management or **IPM:** A combination of pest control and restorative viticulture, which involves striking a balance between severity of the damage, prevailing atmospheric conditions, and the interaction between various pests, in terms of the health of the grapevines. It is supposed to be a way of reducing the uses of pesticides.

International grape varieties: A common collective term for cabernet sauvignon, merlot, pinot noir, sauvignon blanc, and chardonnay.

Johannisberger Riesling: North American name for the Riesling grape variety.

Lese: German for grape harvest.

Liebfraumilch: A term used outside Germany for the simplest and loveliest German wines usually made of Müller-Thurgau grapes, but also of Riesling, Kerner, and Silvaner.

Light: A wine with low alcoholic strength and low in extracts.

Long: A wine that has a long-lasting aftertaste.

Maderization: In Madeira, a deliberate oxidation by warming wine; in other wines, a fault caused by high storage temperatures. *See also* Oxidation.

Malo: A short form of malolactic fermentation; also known as biological acid reduction, or secondary fermentation.

Méthode champénoise: Bottle fermentation method used in Champagne. Legally, other EU sparkling wines made by that method must be labeled *méthode traditionelle* or *méthode classique*.

Millésime: French for vintage.

Mineral: Descriptive term for the aroma of certain white wines, e.g., a few German and Alsatian Rieslings, as well as Pouilly-Fumé.

Must: The juice of pressed grapes.

Must clarification: The use of various methods to clear the must before it is fermented.

Nachgärung: An undesirable continuation of fermentation of the wine after it is bottled.

Negative selection: Picking out rotten grapes before the harvest.

Nervous: Quality of a delicate, acidic wine.

Nobly sweet: A term used to describe wines made of grapes affected by noble rot, shriveled, or frozen, in any case, very high in fructose.

Nose: Bouquet.

Oenology: The science of viticulture and vinification.

Oxidization: Spoiled by long exposure to air. When a wine's extracts have been oxidized, it contains many aldehydes and smells tired, lacks freshness, and tastes of poor sherry. Wines very rich in alcohol, like sherry, Madeira, port, and Vin Santo, even marsala, are given a deliberately oxidized finish. *See also* Maderization.

Passito: Wines made of dried grapes, for example, Sfursat (Valtellina), Amarone (Valpolicella), Vin Santo (Tuscany).

Peppery: A typical aroma of Grüner Veltliner.

Perlage: The bubbles of carbon dioxide as they escape up the glass filled with sparkling wine.

pH value: A measure of total wine acidity.

Normal values are between 2.8 (tart) and 3.5 (mild).

Pomace: The grape skins and pits after pressing. Pomace is processed as fuel, as organic fertilizer, or to make pomace brandy (grappa).

Positive selection: The selection, after the harvest, of healthy or botrytized grapes for immediate vinification.

Prädikat wines: The highest grade for quality wines in Germany and Austria. Wines qualify according to their must weight, and qualified wines may not be enriched. In Austria all nobly sweet wines are classed as *Prädikat*.

Pre-phylloxera: Before the grape louse catastrophe hit European vineyards in 1870.

Pure-toned: A wine with a clean aroma and taste, both typical of the grape variety of which it is made.

Quality wines: This is the highest level of wines, according to the wine laws of the European Union. In France, 40 percent of all wines fall into this category (VDQS, AOC); in Italy, 15 percent (DOC, DOCG); in Spain, 25 percent (DO); and in Germany, 95 percent (QbA, QmP).

Quinta: A wine estate in the port wine region of Portugal.

Rectified grape concentrate: Concentrate of grape sugar in water, made of grape must and used for enrichment of wines. *See also* Enrichment.

Reductive: A wine that is fragrant and slightly fizzy, having been vinified largely in the absence of oxygen.

Remuage: In the *méthode champenoise*, the process of repeatedly turning bottles of Champagne (often by hand). The bottles, placed head first in a stand, are gradually tilted so that the yeast settles in their necks.

Secondary fermentation: Malolactic fermentation.

Semidry: An EU term for wines with up to 18 grams of residual sugar per liter; for sparkling wines (extra sec), up to 20 grams per liter.

Short: A wine without much aftertaste in the mouth.

Sommelier: A wine waiter.

Sparkling wines: A generic term for Champagne, crémant, Sekt, cava, spumante, and other wines with carbon dioxide.

Spritzig: German term, now used internationally, for a wine with residual carbon dioxide.

Staves: The bent boards that form the walls of a barrel.

Still wines: Wines without carbon dioxide, as opposed to sparkling wines.

Succinic acid: A fresh, dry fruit acid, which is found in small amounts in all wines, in addition to tartaric and malic acids.

Sur lie: French for resting on the lees, a method for making white wines more intensely flavored and fresher.

Sweet reserve: Preserved grape juice held for sweetening wines.

Taille: A French term used in Champagne to refer to pressed grape must, as against the free-flow must, which is more valuable. The most valuable free-flow is called cuvée. The press must itself is then classified into the first and second *tailles*.

Tanning agents: Tannins. Red wines contain high levels of tannins, while white wines have much lower levels.

Tartaric acid: A natural fruit acid that occurs in grapes, and increases with ripeness.

Tartrate: A potassium salt that is precipitated by tartaric acid in the bottle as small white crystals, or argols. These do not effect the wine's taste.

Terroir: A French concept in winemaking: a complex interplay of the soil and climate.

Tronçais oak: A very desirable oak from the forests around the city of Nevers. It is fine-pored and has soft, sweet tannins.

Varietal: A wine made of a single grape variety.

VDQS, or **vin délimité de qualité supérieure:** A French wine category for quality wines of the second rank.

Vendange tardive: French for late harvest; a name for semidry or nobly sweet wines.

Vieilles vignes: French for old grapevines.

Vigna: Italian for vineyard.

Vigneto: Italian for vineyard.

Vin de table: French for table wine.

Vinification: The process of making wine, specifically, pressing the grapes and fermenting the must.

Vino da tavola: Italian for table wine. Until 1996, many of Italy's best wines were deliberately and provocatively declassified as table wines by their makers in order to protest the inappropriate requirements for quality wines then in force.

Vintage: The harvest of any one year.

Vollmundig: A full-bodied wine with an attractive alcoholic strength.

Vosges oak: A fine-pored, relatively neutral barrel oak from the Vosges mountain range.

VQPRD, vin de qualité produit dans une région déterminée: French wine category, corresponds to German quality wines of defined origin.

Weissherbst: The German name for rosé wines.

Wurzelecht: Old, ungrafted grapevines.

PICTURE CREDITS

ARTOTHEK 16, Joachim Blauel; © Günter Beer/Der Feinschmecker 85 top; Jan Bendermacher 76; © Bildarchiv Preussischer Kulturbesitz, Berlin, 1997, 17 background, Alfredo Dagli Orti, 1993; 17 Amphora, Antikensammlung Berlin; 143; Bildarchiv BILDER PUR/K. Wanecek 91 background; /Beate Brömse 244–45 large picture; CHAMBRAIR/Hamburg 243 bottom; Christie's Images 244; Walter Cimbal 230, 231 left, top right, and bottom, 240 top; Comité Interprofessionnel du Vin de Champagne in Epernay 110 right, 111 bottom right, 111 top right, 112 right; /John Hodder 122 large; Deutsches Fernerkundungsdatenzentrum der DLR, Oberpfaffenhofen 120, 142, 158, 168 left, 176 top, 182 top; Dieth & Schröder Fotografie, Robert Dieth 35 top right, 35 bottom right, 38 top left, 40 bottom, 43 bottom (photo), 45 center, 46 left, 46 right, 47 bottom left, 51 top right, 51 bottom, 58, 60 background, 61 1st from right, 61 2nd from right, 62, 63 2nd from left, 63 1st from right, 65 2nd from left, 65 1st from right, 68 large, 86, 97 left, 104–5 background; Frank Duffek 107 bottom; Eurocave 225 bottom; FoodPhotography Eising jacket front, spine bottom, 7 1st from top, 7 3rd from top, 7 4th from top, 22, 23 left, 23 right, 210–11, 228–29, 231 center, right 2nd and 3rd from top, 232, 234–35, 237, 242 left-hand column, 243 right-hand column, all wine bottles, Armin Faber 4 3rd from top, 52–53; Faber & Partner 169, 174, 175 right, 201; Carlo Gehring 181; Kartographie Huber 136, 137 top, 144 left, 145, 148, 178–79, 180, 198, 207, 208; INTERFOTO 71 right; Enno Kleinert 21, 26 bottom left, 26 bottom right, 27 bottom left, 27 bottom right, 32–33, 72, 80–82, 84, 85 bottom (left, center, right), 87; Herbert Lehmann 63 1st from left, 177 top, 177 bottom, 179 bottom; Martin Ley 218 (photo), 219 top (photo); Herb Lingl Photography/San Francisco 190–91 top, 192–93 top; Luftbildverlag Bertram/Gorkenant, Photos 126–27, 128–29 top, 132 top, 132–33 bottom, 134–35 top right, 152 top, 153 bottom, 170–71, 172–73 bottom, Manfred Mahn 242 right; Siri Mills 218, 219 top; Moët Hennessy Deutschland 112 left; © Enrico Necade 57 1st from right, 57 2nd from right; Kai-Uwe Nielsen 106, 238, 239 left; Root Stock/Patrick Eager 199; Root

Stock/Hendrik Holler front cover, front and back endpapers, 5 2nd from top, 24 (photo), 27 top right, 43 top, 49 bottom, 55 1st from left, 55 2nd from left, 55 2nd from right, 56 background, 57 1st from left, 57 2nd from left, 58 background, 59 1st from right, 59 2nd from right, 61 1st from left, 61 2nd from left, 63 2nd from right, 65 2nd from right, 66–67, 69 bottom, 74 top, 75 bottom, 75 top, 79 right center, 88, 94, 95 bottom, 98, 102–3 background, 124 bottom, 197, 200, 205 top, 205 bottom, 209; Klaus Rummel 126–27, 128–29 top, 132 top, 132–33 bottom, 134–35 top right, 152 top, 153 bottom, 170–71, 172–73 bottom, 190–91 top, 192–93 top; Satellite Imagemap © 1997 Planetary Visions Limited 18–19 (picture), 188, 196, 202 top, 206 top; Schloss Johannisberger Weingüterverwaltung 47 top right; Carl von Schubert 50 top; Christian Schulz 7 2nd from top, 108–9, 213, 216–17; Scope/Jean-Luc Barde 4 2nd from top, 5 3rd from top, 6 2nd from top, 8–9, 12–13, 38 center, 40 center, 68 small, 73 bottom center, 77 top, 79 top left, 79 top right, 103 left, 105 center, 107 top, 125 background, 125, 138, 140–41, 152 bottom right, 160 top, 161 background, 162, 163, 236 top, 248 right, Scope/Bernard Galeron 146 top, 146 bottom, 147 background; Scope/Michel Gotin 151, 153 top; Scope/Philip Gould 31 top left; Scope/Jacques Guillard 4 4th from top, 6 3rd from top, 14–15, 20, 34 center, 34 bottom left, 41 top, 49 center left, 54 background, 69 top, 99, 104 bottom, 104 center, 104 top, 105 top, 114 left, 114 right, 115 center, 117 top, 122 small, 124 top, 126 top, 156–57, 159; Scope/Michel Guillard spine top, 4 1st from top, 6 1st from top, 10–11, 26 top left, 35 top left, 35 bottom left, 37 top left, 38 top right, 38 bottom left, 39 center, 39 top left, 39 top right, 39 bottom right, 40–41 background, 41 center, 45 bottom, 48, 49 right center, 70, 73 bottom left, 78–83, 79 bottom right, 79 center left, 100 left, 105 bottom, 118–119, 121, 131 top, 133 top, 134 top left, 134 bottom, 215 bottom, 236 bottom, 242–243, 243 left, 243 center, 247 bottom right (photo); Scope/Frederic Hadengue 31 bottom left, 41 bottom; Scope/Sara Matthews 49 top center, 147 bottom right, 154 background; Scope/Michel Plassart 123; Scope/Eric Quentin 215 top;

Scope/Nick Servian 95 top, Sherry Informationsbüro 116 top; Spectre 18–19, 19 bottom, 24, 25, 26–27, 37 bottom, 38 right, 39 bottom left, 43, 45 top, 45 bottom, 47 top left, 71 left (bottom, center, top), 73 top, 91 small picture, 97 right, 111 left, 116 bottom left, 212, 214 bottom, 219 bottom, 247 left, 247 right; StockFood/CEPHAS/Auberson 183 bottom left; StockFood/CEPHAS/Nigel Blythe 38 right, 39 bottom left (photo), 175 left; StockFood/CEPHAS/Andy Christodolo 6–7 background, 74 center, 202 bottom, 203 top; StockFood/Eising 239 right; StockFood/S. & P. Eising 232; StockFood/Bernard Gilly 186; StockFood CEPHAS/Kevin Judd 203 bottom; StockFood/Joerg Lehmann 137 bottom left; StockFood/J.J. Magis 249; StockFood/Martina Meuth 240 left; StockFood/Lars-Olof Nilsson 187; StockFood/CEPHAS/Alain Proust 5 4th from top, 92–93; StockFood/CEPHAS/Mick Rock 4–5 background, 5 1st from top, 6 4th from top, 26 top right, 27 top left, 28–29, 30 right, 32–33 background, 36 top, 36 bottom, 44, 47 top left (photo), 47 bottom right, 49 top left, 49 center center, 51 top left, 62 background, 64, 64 background, 65 1st from left, 73 top (photo), 73 bottom right, 74 bottom, 75 center, 77 right, 79 bottom left, 90, 101 left, 101 right, 102 left, 111 center right, 113 top, 116 bottom right, 130 background, 130, 131 bottom, 139 top, 139 bottom, 144 right, 149 top, 149 bottom, 150, 154 small picture, 155 left, 155 right, 164, 165 left, 166–67, 172 top, 183 background, 184, 185, 190 bottom, 194 right, 195 background, 195 left, 195 right, 214, 242, 248 left; StockFood/Bodo A. Schieren 246; StockFood/CEPHAS/Roy Stedall 117 bottom, StockFood/CEPHAS/ Ted Stefanski 40 top, 189, 191 bottom, 193 bottom, 194 left; StockFood/CEPHAS/Wine Magazin 115 left; Olaf Tamm 19 bottom (photo), 54, 56, 59 1st from left, 60; Gerhard Theato 17 bottom left, 55 1st from right, 59 2nd from left; Verband Schweizer Weinexporteure/SWEA/Berlin 182 bottom; Veuve Clicquot Import GmbH 110 left; Visum/Günter Beer 89, 102 right, 103 right; Visum/Christoph Engel 96; Zero 30 left, 31 top left, 31 bottom left; ZS Verlag 34 top, 37 bottom (photo), 42, 45 top (photo), 49 top right, 113 bottom, 244.